The Empirical and
the Transcendental

Photograph of J. N. Mohanty

The Empirical and the Transcendental

A Fusion of Horizons

EDITED BY
BINA GUPTA

ROWMAN & LITTLEFIELD PUBLISHERS, INC.
Lanham • Boulder • New York • Oxford

ROWMAN & LITTLEFIELD PUBLISHERS, INC.

Published in the United States of America
by Rowman & Littlefield Publishers, Inc.
4720 Boston Way, Lanham, Maryland 20706
http://www.rowmanlittlefield.com

12 Hid's Copse Road
Cumnor Hill, Oxford OX2 9JJ, England

British Library Cataloguing in Publication Information Available

Library of Congress Cataloging-in-Publication Data

The empirical and the transcendental : a fusion of horizons / edited by Bina Gupta.
    p.   cm.
   Includes bibliographical references and index.
   ISBN 0-7425-0819-6 (hardcover : alk. paper)—ISBN 0-7425-0820-X
(pbk. : alk. paper)
   1. Mohanty, Jitendranath, 1928– 2. Phenomenology. I. Gupta, Bina, 1947–
B5134.M644 E67 2000
181'.4—dc21   00-038740

Printed in the United States of America

♾️™ The paper used in this publication meets the minimum requirements of American
National Standard for Information Sciences—Permanence of Paper for Printed Library
Materials, ANSI/NISO Z39.48–1992.

Contents

Preface

On rare occasions, it is not only the work of a philosopher that makes him or her so intriguing, perhaps even important to us, but also the personality of that individual. Professor J. N. Mohanty has served as teacher, mentor, and collaborator to a vast number of philosophical scholars; his influence is often personal, direct, individual—and indelible. When I began to ask some of Mohanty's former students and his younger contemporaries whether they would be interested in honoring him on the occasion of his seventieth birthday, even I was overwhelmed by the enthusiasm of their response.

The birthday celebration began at the Society for Asian and Comparative Philosophy (SACP) international research conference held at Utkal University in Bhubaneswar, Orissa, India, January 4th-7th, 1999. Part of the planned program for this conference included a special recognition of J. N. Mohanty for a lifetime of distinguished scholarship and teaching in the field of philosophy. Following a banquet and a panel on his philosophy, he was presented with a volume containing a collection of letters from his students and peers offering their own personal accolades for, and insights into, this extraordinary man. Contributors were invited to express themselves as they felt natural doing on this occasion. Hence, some of these letters were open epistles; others were more personal missives, directed to Mohanty himself. All shared a common respect and high praise for one of the most accomplished scholars of our age, not only for his intellectual and professional achievements, but for the kind of person that he is. It is fair to say that Mohanty is not only admired among his students and colleagues, but that he is loved by them, as well. He is held in a high level of esteem by those whose lives he touches. A cursory review of these letters themselves makes it indubitable how well-deserved that esteem is.

I felt that this recognition would be incomplete without a collection of essays to mark the occasion. I discussed the idea with a few potential contributors; the prompt and enthusiastic response which I received left no doubt whatsoever in my mind that I should go ahead with this volume.

"Why a book on the philosophy of J. N. Mohanty?" is a question answered in the introduction of the volume you now hold in your hands. "Why have these people decided to contribute to it?" is a question not often asked of such collections which I will answer here. The fact that the essays included herein are, indeed, *critical* examinations of Mohanty's ideas brings us to the realization that we are dealing with someone quite extraordinary, someone who does not engender a neutral or uninterested reaction. I hope, Reader, that you will discover through this volume your own reaction, and be prompted—if you have not done so before—to delve into the vast wealth of Mohanty's work for yourself.

It is a pleasure to express my sincere thanks to those friends and scholars who have contributed to this work in numerous ways. I also thank my husband, Madan, and daughter, Swati, for believing in me, and supporting me.

Introduction

Bina Gupta

This volume is a collection of critical studies of Professor J. N. Mohanty's work on phenomenology and Indian philosophy. The essays included herein are written especially for this collection. Philosophers from India, Europe, the United States, and Australia discuss and offer constructive but critical analysis of his philosophical ideas. Professor Mohanty was supplied a copy of these essays and given an opportunity to respond to the critics. The concluding chapter of this volume contains his assessment of his own philosophical position and his response to the critics.

These essays provide insights into both philosophy and Mohanty—philosophy *via* Mohanty and Mohanty *via* and beyond philosophy. They make the multifaceted character of Mohanty's writings obvious. The diversity of the topics on which he has written attests to the multidimensional character and fecundity of his work. He qualifies for the highest marks in the insightfulness, depth, and breadth of his work. I hope that these essays facilitate the sort of "comparative philosophy" which Mohanty himself has pursued so vigorously, and provide the impetus for further research into directions which his work brings—and continues to assist in bringing—to full brilliance.

This introduction proceeds in three parts: the first provides the biographical sketch and some insights into the man, J. N. Mohanty; the second deals directly with the essays included in this volume; and the third contains my general reflections regarding the theme—*the empirical and the transcendental*—along which the essays in this volume have been structured. It is my hope that these reflections will provide the reader with a frame of reference for all the essays included in this collection.

1

Rather than describe the number of books he has written and the many articles he has published (which I am sure most of the readers of this volume can easily access), I am going to limit my remarks to two facets of Mohanty's work which are often overlooked. I am going to discuss how he did what he has done and provide some personal observations about him.

No philosophy or philosopher originates and develops in a vacuum. All human activity, philosophical or otherwise, takes its distinctive shape within a cultural setting. No philosophy or philosopher develops bereft of an under-girding context. We always have a contextual interpretation and reinterpretation. We have a culture, a tradition, in reference. In order to accurately understand Mohanty's approach to philosophy, one must take into account the philosophical climate of his time, the teachers and the tensions which shaped his views.

J. N. Mohanty was born in 1928 in Cuttack, Orissa, India. After completing his schooling there, he went to Calcutta in 1945 to pursue his bachelor's degree which he completed in 1947 at the Presidency College. He received his M.A. from Calcutta University in 1949. During these years he studied Advaita Vedānta, initially with Nalini Kanta Brahma and subsequently with the late Mm. Yogendranāth Tarkavedāntatirtha. In 1949, he was introduced to another great teacher in Indian philosophy, the Naiyāyika, the late Pandit Ananta Kumar Tarkatīrtha, who not only taught him Navya-Nyāya, but impressed upon him the *logical* foundation of all Indian philosophies. He spent ten years studying with this Nyāya Pandit, except for the period from 1952 to 1954 which he spent in Germany earning his doctorate in philosophy.

A glance at the above chronology makes it obvious that the young Mohanty spent his teen years feeling the influence of India's Freedom Movement. These were very volatile years for India as the nation struggled to gain its independence from British rule. This period of intense political upheaval culminated in the independence and partition of India in 1947, and the attendant communal killings in Calcutta and other cities in India. Therefore, it should come as no surprise to the reader that political events and ideas—especially the political philosophy of Gandhi—were a powerful influence on Mohanty's way of thinking. He himself has conceded this at various places. For example, writing in response to his critics in *The Philosophy of J. N. Mohanty*, he notes that "When I started studying philosophy, there were two problems that had gotten hold of me. The problems were still understood in terms of persons, as though one had to choose between contending masters. They were 'Śaṃkara vs. Sri Aurobindo' and 'Marx vs. Gandhi.' They were deep problems, but the depth (of any philosophical problem) is, for you, only so much as you can measure."[1]

The struggle, however, was not simply political; it was also valuational. An examination of Indian cultural values and traditions was needed to determine whether the country deserved independence by virtue of its antiquity, history, and culture. The tension between the historical forces through which the Indian tradition had grown and the new forces of modernity had increased. Hindu intellectuals found themselves in an ambiguous situation; there was at once both an awareness of a sense of cultural responsibility and a sense of distance from that culture. Educated Hindus, including Mohanty, studied, absorbed, and understood Western social and political concepts. This led to an examination of their own culture in light of new experience. Western dynamism, realism, and secularism provided a much-needed corrective to Indian thought. These Hindu thinkers seized the opportunity before them to demonstrate that Indian philosophy is as great as any other, without need of its reduction to some amorphous spiritual claims.

Mohanty recalls in his memorial essay on Matilal that young philosophers in Calcutta at that time were searching for some satisfactory way of doing Indian philosophy.[2] They had already been disappointed with the way Indian philosophers before them had thought—that is, they were disappointed with the way absolute oppositions were asserted between Indian and Western thought. Some such contrasts were the spiritual nature of Indian philosophy vs. the materialism of the West, the use of intuition in Indian thought vs. the discursive and intellectual character of Western philosophy, and the practical intention of Indian thought vs. the purely theoretical thinking of the West. It hardly needs to be argued that such contrasts were false, possibly even insincere and dishonest. It was clear to these young philosophers that Indian thinking had reached a great intellectual and discursive height, just as Western philosophy had given rise to great spiritual systems. So they determined this way of comparing East and West to be utterly useless, misleading, and possibly politically motivated. Younger generations of philosophers were seeking a sense of direction; in that quest, young Mohanty went to meet Radhakrishnan, who was a powerful figure in those days. Mohanty has recalled meeting Radhakrishnan as a young graduate student; he went away from the encounter with the impression of a man who had a deeply committed and profound mind, but who was not doing the kind of philosophizing that younger philosophers were looking for. Perhaps two persons in Calcutta at that time showed them some possibilities of further work: one was Ras Vihari Das, with his skeptical questionings and insatiable scholarship; the other was Kalidas Bhattacharyya, who as Mohanty often says, "taught us how to think." Among the students and research scholars, Sibjiban Bhattacharyya, and several years later Bimal Matilal, were doing Indian philosophy in new ways.

Given that the practical nature of Indian philosophy was never in dispute, the points at issue became its theoretical, discursive, and intellectual content. Thus it is not surprising that in Indian philosophy, Mohanty's work has focused primarily on the theories of knowledge, the nature of cognition, form vs. content, idealism and realism, the phenomenology of consciousness, and truth. His essay, "A Fragment of the Indian Philosophical Tradition,"[3] very succinctly brings into relief the epistemological framework (the *pramāṇa* theory) within which the *darśana*-s (philosophical systems) work, and points to some of the distinctive features of the *pramāṇa* theory in comparison with Western epistemological ideas. In many respects, this essay is a short summary of Mohanty's more extensive treatment of this subject in *Reason and Tradition in Indian*

Thought,[4] it focuses on theoretical rationality, namely, upon how cognitive claims are to be criticized, examined, and justified. It provides an overview of the *pramāṇa*-s with an emphasis on *śabda* (word), which is a very distinctive part of Indian rationality. *Śabdapramāṇa* (word as a means of true cognition) not only justifies beliefs, but also actions—it is a kind of link between justifications of certain kinds of beliefs, and those of certain kinds of actions. Three essays on Indian philosophy included in this volume focus on issues relating to Mohanty's interpretation of epistemology.

Some of his important works in the area of Indian philosophy include: *Gaṇgeśa Theory of Truth* (1966), *Reason and Tradition in Indian Thought* (1992), *Essays on Indian Philosophy: Traditional and Modern* (1993), and *Classical Indian Philosophy* (2000). Mohanty's analysis of Indian philosophy dispels its characterization as merely spiritualistic. Indian philosophy is not simply a search for the spirit; it is also a critical analysis (*ānvīkṣikī*) of the data provided by experience. For those who have been told, time and again, that Indian philosophy is not different from religion, his writings are a breath of fresh air.

In 1949, during one of his visits to the home of his teacher, Ras Vihari Das, young Mohanty picked up a copy of Husserl's *Ideas*. Although Mohanty continued to study Navya-Nyāya and Vedānta, his main philosophical concern became Kant and German phenomenology, especially that of Husserl. It is not an exaggeration to say that J. N. Mohanty is the leading and most influential expositor of Husserlian phenomenology of our times. I know of no one who has done more than Mohanty to make Husserl accessible to both the philosophical and intellectual world. Some of his important works on this subject include: *Edmund Husserl's Theory of Meaning* (1966), *Phenomenology and Ontology* (1970), *The Concept of Intentionality* (1972), *Husserl and Frege* (1985), *The Possibility of Transcendental Philosophy* (1985), *Transcendental Phenomenology: An Analytical Account* (1989), and *Phenomenology between Essentialism and Transcendentalism* (1997).

Most of the essays in this volume provide insights into Mohanty's vision of phenomenology in general and Husserl's ideas in particular. They not only provide a preliminary orientation to Husserlian phenomenology but also insights into hermeneutics, post-structuralism, and deconstructionism in the context of the philosophical views of Heidegger, Sartre, and Merleau-Ponty. The editors of *Phenomenology: East and West* begin their introduction with the following words:

> To know the work of Jitendra Nath Mohanty even slightly is to commence to appreciate it immensely. Lucidity and sagacity have been its armor; originality and ingenuity have been its strength. . . . It has fulfilled the most welcomed promise of striking the chords of both imagination and reason by exposing Husserlian phenomenology to the concerns of both the so-called "analytical" and "continental" traditions and

by exposing the philosophical tradition of Indian thought to
the intricacies of Husserl.[5]

I agree with this assessment; the clarity, lucidity, and comprehensiveness of
Mohanty's thought is phenomenal. Irrespective of whether the language he uses
is German, Sanskrit, or English, this clarity shines through. The essays
collected here should not only be of immense help to scholars in phenomenology, but also make evident Mohanty's complex philosophical agenda.

Mohanty has devoted his entire life to understanding and interpreting
Husserl. He himself concedes that he is a "Husserlian of a sort"[6] and acknowledges the impact of Husserl on his way of thinking: "[I]t is often surprising for
me how in these more than three decades of concern with various powerful
philosophical schools, Husserl fares so well. If one test of a great philosopher is
that he lets us be free to pursue our own interests, Husserl certainly satisfies this
test. He taught us how to think with a sensitivity to phenomena and with a self-
critical attitude."[7] Mohanty argues that one can truly understand another only
when the other is seen not as an extension of oneself, but rather when one
respects the other *qua* other. Based on this principle, Mohanty describes
various fruitful ways in which the East and the West can educate each other. He
himself concedes that Husserlian thinking has helped him to understand and
interpret the Indian philosophical tradition:

> Almost forty years of preoccupation with Husserl has—as I
> look back, I find—set me free to relate to other traditions and
> other schools of philosophy. Being a "Husserlian" of a sort, I
> have not found my access to other philosophies blocked. On
> the contrary, what is distinctive about the Husserlian path—
> this being: an openness to phenomena, to the given qua given,
> to the intended meanings precisely as they are intended
> challenges you to face up to the task of understanding the
> other, the other culture, the other philosophical school, the
> other person. While it has been a long and arduous process
> trying to understand and appropriate the Husserlian opus, the
> more I have succeeded in it, the freer I have felt to relate
> myself to the thoughts of the others.[8]

Much of his intellectual work has focused on how best to understand and
interpret these two traditions from within, always hoping that in the long run
they would come together. He has done us an immeasurable service by bringing
the philosophical traditions of East and West closer to each other in a way that
does not violate the spirit of either. All of us know that there are various excellent scholars who have been working on Kant, Husserl, Śaṃkara, and Aurobindo, but it is Mohanty who has made both Indian and Western thought accessible to the modern philosophical world. Let us see how he has accomplished
this.

In response to his critics in *The Philosophy of J. N. Mohanty*, he notes: "One may prefer to pursue philosophical interests within both traditions wherever they may lead with the secret hope that in the long run they will throw light upon each other. This is indeed what I did—looking back, that is at least how it appears I did—as I pursued my interest in phenomenology and Indian philosophy from within each tradition."[9]

His goal was not to make comparisons between the traditions, but rather to examine issues from within each tradition to see how they might enlighten and enhance each other; in so doing, he placed living philosophical questions into their full context for the purpose of approaching truth. Mohanty tackles issues and questions by invoking whoever or whatever seems relevant and useful to the task. In other words, he does not place philosophical problems into watertight compartments, considering them from only one perspective—rather, his work reflects the cumulative influence of the many traditions he has studied and the great teachers he has studied with. Such an approach puts an awesome responsibility on those who, like Mohanty, have pursued Western philosophical ideas from within the Western tradition, and who after decades of being immersed within it have emerged prepared and willing to do their thinking from within any tradition. (This means that there must come a time in the life of a philosopher when he can openly declare "I am simply doing philosophy.") In this regard, the example of Raghunātha Śiromaṇi, the great Naiyāyika, is always cited by Mohanty. When Raghunātha proposed a complete revision of the categories of the system of Nyāya-Vaiśeṣika, and as a result was challenged by the orthodox Naiyāyikas, he replied: "It does not matter whether the Vaiśeṣikas or the Naiyāyikas agree with me; it is I, Raghunātha, who says this."

His writings show that East and West are not two disparate horizons after all; it is simplistic to claim that "East is East, and West is West, and never the twain shall meet." That "East is East, and West is West" is not true in Mohanty's work. In his writing one finds that the philosophies of East and West meet in what Hans Gadamer refers to as a "fusion of horizons." This explains why the Humboldt Foundation chose to award Mohanty the Humboldt prize in philosophy for his distinguished lifetime career in philosophy. Thus, it comes as no surprise that he is one of the leading philosophers of not only the Indian subcontinent, but the American and the European continents as well.

As a collaborator, Mohanty is challenging, but he lets you be yourself. As a person, he is modest, kind, and helpful. He likes to meet and talk with people whom he previously has not met, especially young scholars. He will take them out for a meal in order to explore their individual potential as philosophers, to glean what the younger generation is thinking, and to present them opportunities to help themselves. This is utterly characteristic of the man whom I have come to know in the last several years.

Thus Mohanty is an extraordinary individual; people like him are rare indeed. It is not surprising that Richard Schusterman (Chair of the Philosophy

Department at Temple University, where Mohanty teaches), has said that he wishes that he could clone him, so that Mohanty would never have to retire.[10] Or that Eliot Deutsch (Chair of the Philosophy Department at the University of Hawaii), asserted in his letter of tribute to Mohanty that "I was told once in India that sages are expected to live to be 120. It seems, then, that many others will have the benefit of our person and wisdom for another 50 years."[11]

Although Mohanty has largely been away from India for almost three decades, he remains Indian at heart and finds his sense of self in being an Indian. During the course of a conversation with me several months ago during the American Academy of Religion meetings in Orlando, Mohanty said in no uncertain terms that the "biggest mistake of his life" was leaving India. In the author's prologue to his *Essays on Indian Philosophy,* he notes "after a lifetime of research on phenomenology and relating it to modern analytic philosophy, it is a cleansing experience, elevating emotionally and challenging intellectually to return to one's roots. As one advances in age, that return is almost a spiritual need." Again, Indian philosophy "is exhilarating. . . . We have in this tradition a moving spirit which, once you open yourself to it, sweeps you away and overwhelms you."[12]

Today, young Indian philosophers are trying to emulate Mohanty and translate their thoughts into the language of modern Western epistemology and logic; their work is primarily interpretive. A growth of interest in *śabdapramā-ṇa* can be traced back to Mohanty's "Presidential Address to the Indian Philosophical Congress" in 1986, in which he outlined a reconstructed theory of *śabdapramāṇa.* His work inspired Bimal Matilal and P. K. Sen to further examine the issue in an important paper in *Mind.*[13] The discussion culminated in Matilal and Chakrabarti's edited epistemological work entitled *Knowing from Words.*[14] Some of these philosophers also think that using formal logic is the way of doing Indian philosophy; Matilal's *The Navya-Nyāya Doctrine of Negation*[15] and Sibajiban's *Gadhādhara's Theory of Objectivity*[16] provide two excellent examples of this sort of endeavor. Employing a method that combines philology and philosophy, both attempt to render the Navya-Nyāya logic into the extensional language of modern Western logic.

Before concluding this section, I would like to bring to the attention of the reader another issue, that is, how Mohanty's training in Indian logic and Vedānta has impacted his decision to work on Husserlian phenomenology, rather than, say, on Descartes. In other words, did his study of Vedānta in any way predispose him towards Husserl or influence his understanding of Husserl? I have tried to press this point with Mohanty several times; however, no answer was forthcoming until as luck would have it, an audience member at the 1999 American Philosophical Association Pacific Division meeting in Berkeley, California, asked him about the possible influence of Indian philosophy on his reading of Husserl. (This question followed Mohanty's lecture on "The Other Husserl.") He again avoided a direct thematic answer.

A review of the biographical details of his life reveals that long before

Mohanty ever picked up a copy of Husserl's *Ideas* at the home of his teacher Rash Vihari Das, he was trying to come to grips with issues such as the intentionality of consciousness, reflexivity of consciousness, and the locus of consciousness in the context of Advaita Vedānta. Thus it is not surprising that a person already steeped in Vedāntic learning could be fascinated by Husserl's concern with consciousness, his distinction between transcendental and empirical consciousness, and the thesis that all objects owe their constitution to consciousness. We also know that though Vedānta was his first love, Mohanty realized very early on that a proper development of Vedānta cannot take place without the study of Navya-Nyāya. When he came to study Nyāya with Pandit Ananta Kumar, his teacher was researching and writing on Buddhism—resulting in his famous book in Bengali *Vaibhāṣkadarśana*. Mohanty appropriated all three *darśana*-s—Nyāya, Vedānta, and Buddhism—and his writings on Indian philosophy bear testimony to this fact. I would venture to say that his study of Śaṃkara's *Brahmasūtrabhāṣya* with Pandit Ananta Kumar played a decisive role in his captivation with Husserlian phenomenology. One could even go a step further and argue that his training in Indian philosophy, especially Vedānta and Buddhism, has played an important role in shaping his interpretation of Husserlian phenomenology. For example, in his "Intentions of Intentionality: 20 Theses,"[17] Mohanty gives a schematic representation of the implications and significance of the idea of intentionality. These theses capture Mohanty's own position, carefully considered through such Husserlian pieces as "The Problem of Relativism in Husserl's Late Manuscripts" and "The Relevance of Husserl Today," by taking into account the various critical discussions that have been going on for nearly half a century. It is important to note that in his final thesis (number 20), Mohanty asserts that the empirical *is* the transcendental, which only *seems* to be a surprising twist to the meaning of transcendental phenomenology. For more on this, I would refer the reader to Mohanty's *The Possibility of Transcendental Philosophy*. One wonders if in the formulation "the empirical *is* the transcendental," Mohanty is not influenced by Nāgārjuna's thesis that *saṃsāra* and *nirvāṇa* are identical.

If philosophy is to be an endeavor by which we seek—and hopefully find—the truth, we need more philosophers like Mohanty to show us how to converse between traditions and establish a dialogue that will lead to a better understanding of the philosophical issues that have preoccupied Mohanty and us for a long time. In my view, Mohanty is neither a Naiyāyika, nor a Vedāntin, nor a Buddhist, nor a Husserlian, but rather a "Mohantian" in whom one finds an excellent fusion of all four of these. He is a consummate philosopher; he is, in the language of the Upaniṣads, *ekam eva ādvitīyam*, "one without a second."

With this in mind, I will now analyze the specific issues raised by the authors of the essays collected in this volume.

2

In the concluding paragraph of the first chapter of *Phenomenology: Between Essentialism and Transcendental Phenomenology*,[18] Mohanty notes:

> This last distinction [between transcendental and empirical subjectivities] is no doubt "enigmatic." In distinguishing between them, and in using the epoché to move from the one to the other, Husserl asserts a difference. He also affirms their identity: the empirical *is* the transcendental, only when stripped of the naturalizing interpretations. More famously, he affirms a parallelism between the two: each numerically selfsame intentional experience of an empirical ego is also a transcendental experience of the "corresponding" transcendental ego. To think these aspects of the relation—identity, difference, and parallelism—together would appear to be baffling. And yet, we do not understand transcendental phenomenology if we do not understand this enigma.[19]

The majority of the papers included in this volume examine the above distinction, as well as Mohanty's interpretation and defense of it in an attempt to unpack and resolve the ramifications of this baffling enigma.

Since Kant, it has been common for philosophers who considered themselves practitioners of transcendental philosophy of one sort or another to draw a distinction between the empirical and the transcendental. More specifically, the distinction is about two forms or levels of consciousness; however, one may also speak of two kinds of truth: the empirical and the transcendental. As is well known, Kant often reiterated that the epistemological theory that he developed in the *Critique of Pure Reason* is not an empirical theory. An empirical theory of knowledge in Kant's view is a psychological theory, which he attributes to Locke; Kant himself, however, had a different agenda. To say that empirical consciousness is psychological implies that it really consists of the mental states which fall in the domain of psychology. Such a consciousness is individual; it belongs to the order of nature, being subject to the principle of causality which rules in that order and is causally intertwined with the human body. Kant was concerned rather with the *a priori* condition of the possibility, not only of empirical cognition, but also of synthetic *a priori* knowledge—such as the knowledge of mathematics and physics. Transcendental consciousness, on the other hand, is neither psychological nor individual, nor does it belong to the causal order of nature. It is discovered by reflection on the possibility of all knowledge, and is universal in the sense that it is common to all rational thinkers. Husserl, who also considered himself to be a transcendental philosopher, further developed this distinction with the help of the method of reduction or *epoché*. He held that consciousness, once freed from the naturalistic presuppositions of the context in which it is interpreted, becomes transcendental. In Husserl's writings, the basic contrast is between the constituting and the constituted: whatever is constituted is not transcendental, thus material objects, essences, and numbers belong to the constituted domain.

In his various works on phenomenology, Mohanty has interpreted and defended some version of the distinction between the empirical and transcendental. The essays in the first two sections of this volume deal directly with this distinction. Whereas the authors of the essays in the first section of this collection reject the distinction between the empirical and the transcendental, the authors in the second section propose to revise this distinction. I will elaborate on these points with the help of the essays included in the first two sections of this collection.

Joseph Margolis's paper is a critical reflection not only on the empirical-transcendental distinction but also on Mohanty's ongoing attempt to understand that distinction. In his essay, Margolis provides his readers with a very complex argument which on the one hand claims to preserve the substance of Mohanty's point of view, while at the same time argues that the distinction between the empirical and the transcendental must be abandoned. Margolis emphasizes the influence of the Advaita Vedānta theory of the relation between the *jīva* (empirical individual) and the *ātman* (pure consciousness) on Mohanty's understanding of the relation between the empirical and the transcendental, and shows a preference for what he takes to be the Vedāntic identification of the two. Focusing on Mohanty's rejection of the two-world theory, Margolis arrives at the conclusion that the distinction between the empirical and the transcendental is spurious. He notes that "the distinction between 'empirical' and 'transcendental' is a logical or conceptual distinction, a distinction of 'philosophical grammar,' *not* a distinction within any actual hierarchy of cognitive powers"[20]—a conclusion which he takes to be consistent with that of Mohanty. However, I should point out that if Margolis prefers the Advaita Vedānta thesis of identity, better yet, the non-difference between the empirical and the transcendental, then what remains need not be the empirical; it may well be the transcendental which under a certain interpretation appears to be the empirical. I would imagine that on Margolis's view it is the empirical which under a certain construal appears to be the transcendental; however, he does not show that the other possibility is invalid, namely, that it is the transcendental which on a certain construal appears to be the empirical.

Be that as it may, Margolis's rejection of the empirical/transcendental distinction is in consonance with his often expressed view that transcendental phenomenology is of a piece with naturalism. He also argues that there are not different levels of knowledge (as with Kant, who makes a distinction between two levels of knowledge: empirical knowledge and reflective philosophical knowledge), but rather that the same cognitive capacity operates in two different contexts. From this it follows that phenomenological reflection cannot be completely independent of our empirical involvement with the world, which in turn implies that complete phenomenological reduction is not possible.

Tom Rockmore arrives at the same conclusion by traversing a somewhat different route. He questions the tenability of Husserl's and Mohanty's essentialism and argues that because the cognitive subject is a finite human person involved in history, any presumed essence must be historically conditioned. As he puts it: "It is a deep mistake to think that claims to know are ever unrelated to the context in which they emerge and through which they are justified."[21] In other words, the context of discovery and the context of justification can never be separated; so while there may be invariances which look like the essences, they are in reality local and cannot be absolutely invariant. Rockmore wishes to replace the role of essences in cognition with the role of concepts, which are historically constituted and thus may become historically obsolete. It seems to me that Rockmore would replace Husserl with Hegel and would regard Husserl's later attempt to take history into account to be consistent with the rest of his views.

The third essay is by Amedeo Giorgi, a professional psychologist who engages in scientific psychology while still following Husserl's methodological constraints. Giorgi has found Mohanty's reconstruction of the phenomenological method helpful for his own research as a scientific psychologist, and the goal of his essay is to preserve both essentialism and the descriptive method. A psychologist continually struggles with the question of how to describe the experiences of another person, and several of Giorgi's suggestions in this regard are valuable. Besides imaginative self-transposal and cooperative encounter, he emphasizes the way that *noematic* clues are given to a researcher's consciousness. The essences which a psychologist may try to identify through imaginative variation need not be essences in any absolute philosophical sense, but rather in a modest psychological sense. Thus in a curious way, Giorgi agrees with Rockmore's critique of strict essentialism and favors Mohanty's earlier construal of essences as meanings. He also argues for the convergence of the two methods of description and hermeneutic interpretation, although his own inclination is to emphasize the descriptive method. Giorgi asserts that a suitably construed phenomenological method need not be totally cut off from empirical research—as a psychologist, he does not need a conception of the transcendental that is separate from the empirical. It should be noted that Giorgi is not willing to pass any judgment on the philosophical viability of the concept of the transcendental; he is only concerned with phenomenology as a method for scientific psychology. Giorgi's paper reminds us that Husserl's well-known critique of psychologism must not be understood as an opposition to psychology. I am sure Mohanty would concur with Giorgi on this point. Indeed, in his essay "Phenomenology and Psychology,"[22] Mohanty demonstrates to what extent Husserl's phenomenology can be used today to understand and interpret both cognitive psychology and psychoanalysis. In other words, both Giorgi and Mohanty would agree that phenomenological psychology in itself is a thriving discipline.

In the next essay, Donn Welton challenges the temptation of classical transcendental philosophy to regard consciousness as transparent, disembodied, rule-prescribing (in the manner of Kant), self-enclosed, and individual. As Merleau-Ponty had already shown, the lived body refuses to be classified either as being-for-itself or being-in-itself. It is reflexive without being transparent, has a solidity without being simply a lump of matter, and has intentionality which simply does not prescribe *noemata* to sensory impressions. Yet the body is both constituted and constituting, and Welton develops this thesis further. The putative transparency of consciousness is challenged on the ground of its temporality and consequently ineliminability of traces in the heart of a living impression. Nor is consciousness permanently centered around a unity, but is rather dispersed in the world through the lived body. All constitution is not through *noemata*; genetic constitution leads to social and impersonal dimensions. All these phenomena disrupt Husserl's program of "static constitution" and the role of constituting transcendental ego. In all this it is not quite clear if Welton rejects transcendental phenomenology in general, or only certain versions of it. I would venture to say that he does the latter.

As Welton reiterates, it is well known that Mohanty had clearly located corporeality, linguisticality, and historicity within the heart of the transcendental subjectivity, but did not quite suspect that this recognition would upset the apple cart. Adequate givenness is not possible, Husserl conceded famously in the *Cartesian Meditations,* even in the case of the Cartesian *cogito,* but he did not question apodicticity. One may point out that all those phenomena which Welton so aptly brings to light are "disclosed," "brought to givenness," even if inadequately, their concreteness certainly allows for an eidetic insight, for example, to the way or ways hands function. We are inadvertently extending the scope of Husserl's project, not undermining it.

The last essay in the first section is by Günther Patzig. The title of the essay might create the misleading impression that it stands by itself among the others, the concerns of which are the empirical and the transcendental, but nothing could be further from the truth. One of the world's leading Aristotelian scholars, Patzig has been a close friend of Mohanty for nearly half a century; they have shared common friends and teachers at Göttingen University in Germany; among these, physicist-cum-philosopher Carl F. Von Weizsäcker is worth noting. This piece by Patzig is part of a still-unpublished Howison Memorial lecture delivered at Berkeley in 1971. The central concern of this essay is the relation between logic and reality, but its immediate context is a proposal by von Weizsäcker that the results of quantum physics require that the classical two-valued logic be abandoned in favor of a multi-valued logic. Von Weizsäcker's suggestion is based on the idea that logic must be closely related to our understanding of the general structure of reality, and that logical laws must be the laws of being and not merely the laws of the human mind. If quantum physics shows that there are propositions for which the disjunction, either true or false, does not hold, then the principle of excluded middle is no longer valid in the domain of elementary particle physics. The result is that logic needs to be revised in light of the advances of physics. Patzig argues that Von Weizsäcker is mistaken in drawing this conclusion—that he has asked logic for "services" it cannot supply, and makes a powerful case for separating logic from reality. Such an operation, however, is not very far from essentialism, that posits invariants that would be unaffected by the progress of empirical knowledge and against which Margolis and Rockmore have so vehemently argued in this volume. Although Patzig does not deal with the notions of the empirical and the transcendental, he explicitly deals with the relation of formal logic to the empirical knowledge of reality—and we know that formal logic, at least in the thinking of Kant, is closely related to the transcendental.

Authors belonging to the second group do not reject the empirical/transcendental distinction as such but proceed to revise it; in so doing, they provide a new formulation of transcendental philosophy. Christina Schües provides her readers an alternative way of conceiving the relation between the empirical and the transcendental; Gereon Kopf, following certain suggestions of Mohanty, proposes a transcendental relativism which he finds in Buddhist non-dualism; David Carr rejects as misleading Heidegger's very influential interpretation of transcendental philosophy; Rudy Makkreel offers a new understanding of Kantian philosophy; David Smith proposes a new account of transcendental phenomenology; and Lester Embree tries to provide a response to the following question: Are there intentional experiences which are not temporal, that is, not experienced to be in time?

I will begin with Schües. She starts with the enigma of the distinction between the empirical and the transcendental subjectivity and provides an alternative way of conceiving the relation between the empirical and the transcendental. After giving an account of Husserl's transcendental phenomenology, especially in regard to his theory of the transcendental ego, Schües focuses on two fundamental concepts with which a phenomenologist must come to grips. She argues that classical transcendental phenomenology is not equipped to deal with the phenomena of birth and death. While mortality has been thematized by thinkers such as Heidegger, birth, or what Hannah Arendt calls "natality,"[23] resists a phenomenological treatment. Here Schües makes use of ideas from Husserl's late manuscripts, generally known as "generative phenomenology,"[24] which describe how generations are linked together by birth and death that take one outside the limits of transcendental phenomenology.

Classically, the transcendental ego has been supposed to be without birth or death. Husserl, in many of his manuscripts, articulates the phenomenon of birth as a kind of waking up from a deep sleep and death as passing into such a sleep. Schües takes birth as "the first primal appearance of an essence, a singular unrepeatable, gendered, and bodily reality for and with other human beings."[25] It leads one to a fundamental plurality of transcendental egos. Everyone is an

absolutely new beginning, and with every birth there is a new ethical responsibility, as well as a tension between the beginning and its continuation. Schües
does not deny the empirical and the transcendental distinction, but emphasizes
the need for reformulating this distinction in view of the phenomenon of
natality. Although she claims that the enigma on which Mohanty has often
remarked—viz., the enigma of the relation between the empirical and the
transcendental—can be resolved with the help of the concept of natality, she
does not substantiate her claim. She does not demonstrate exactly *how* the
enigma of the empirical-transcendental relation can be so resolved.

As his point of departure, Kopf takes Mohanty's remarks about the baffling
puzzle concerning the relationship between the empirical ego and the
transcendental ego, as well as his suggestions for an Advaitic solution of this
puzzle. He proceeds to give an account of what he calls "transcendental
relativism," building upon the ideas of Dōgen and Nishida. Following what
Kopf calls "Buddhist non-dualism" (I am not sure which traditional Buddhist
school he has in mind), he not only rejects the reification of the empirical and
transcendental into different realms, but also argues for a non-dualism of
identity and difference. Fundamental to this idea is a distinction among three
conceptions of selfhood: the *cogito* or the empirical ego; the transcendental
ego, which Kopf, following Dōgen and Merleau Ponty, takes to be the lived
body; and the transcendental non-ego, following Nishida and Sartre. The third
conception of self, viz., the transcendental non-ego, arises out of the conflict
between the first two. The Buddhists refer to it as *anātman* and Mohanty refers
to it when he says that "the transcendental ego is anti-monistic, (in that) it
respects pluralism and is tolerant of diversities."[26] The ground of all things then
is the non-ego. This is not to deny transcendental phenomenology, but to
suggest that a new conception of the transcendental is called for which is anti-
monistic, respects pluralism, and tolerates diversities. Whereas Husserl's notion
of the transcendental ego seems to be closely tied to his essentialism, and so is
rejected by all anti-essentialists (such as Margolis and Rockmore in this
volume), Kopf's transcendental non-ego (along with Dōgen's and Nishida's) is
compatible with anti-essentialism and relativism.

In his essay, David Carr reflects on the idea of transcendental philosophy,
articulating the differences between Kant and Husserl, in an effort to flesh out
underlying themes which make transcendental philosophy, as he puts it, "a
unified project." He forcefully argues that Heidegger's "caricature" of
transcendental philosophy "overlooks what is distinctive about it." The goal of
his paper is to demonstrate where Heidegger, one of the most severe critics of
transcendental philosophy, went wrong. Carr takes up four theses which,
according to him, constitute Husserl's understanding of transcendental philosophy, and all of which he argues are based on Heidegger's deep misunderstanding of the Kantian-Husserlian project. First of all, Carr argues *contra*
Heidegger that transcendental philosophy is not simply a variety of meta-

physics. It is rather in both cases (Kant and Husserl) based on a critique of metaphysics. Secondly, Heidegger, according to Carr, is also mistaken in thinking that transcendental philosophy remains a philosophy of representation (*Vorstellung*). Both Kant and Husserl, insofar as they emphasize the intentionality of consciousness, reject the primacy of representation. Thirdly, Heidegger is said not to be justified in understanding transcendental philosophy as a straightforward kind of idealism. This is worth noting in light of the claim that the goal of both Kant and Husserl was to transcend the familiar opposition between realism and idealism. Finally, transcendental philosophy cannot be regarded as a theory of method which, according to Heidegger, is based on metaphysical presuppositions. Carr, on the other hand, argues for the neutrality of a method that involves an unending process of critical self-reflection. He does not question the empirical/transcendental distinction in this essay, although in some of his earlier writings he has done so. Here, however, he shows that one of the more familiar critiques of transcendental philosophy by Heidegger is based upon a profound misunderstanding of the Husserlian project.

Rudy Makkreel, drawing from various Kantian texts, shows in his essay that while the formal and *a priori* nature of the Kantian transcendental as formulated in the *Critique of Pure Reason* is well known, these stereotypical conceptions of the transcendental and the *a priori* need to be revised. If Makkreel is right, then a certain familiar understanding of Kantian transcendental philosophy and its difference from Husserlian phenomenology must be seriously flawed.

Transcendental principles, for Kant, are not to be understood as truths preceding experience, but as inseparable from objective experiences. In other words, they must always be understood in conjunction with possible experience, but once apperceived, they are independent of all subsequent experience. Thus Makkreel's thesis amounts to saying that the Kantian *a priori* should not be completely separated from the empirical, which brings his position into the vicinity of Margolis and Rockmore, while quite coinciding with theirs. The concreteness of transcendental subjectivity even in Kantian thinking comes out most clearly in the *Critique of Judgment*. Though *a priori*, it is inseparable from the sense of the community of persons. Aesthetic judgments do not have the necessity of mathematical judgments; rather, they remain presumptive. Makkreel suggests that given this Kantian "loosening" of the *a priori*, the similarity between Kant and Husserl becomes clearer. He situates Dilthey at this point of transition between Kantian and Husserlian philosophy. Makkreel's paper raises many questions about interpreting Kant that I cannot go into here; however, he has made a good case for questioning the standard stereotype of Kant and in so doing shifts the focus from the first to the third *Critique*.

David Smith argues in his paper for the interdependence of phenomenology and ontology. In his lecture at the World Congress of Philosophy in August 1998, he labeled his account of phenomenology "ontological phenomenology."

In the essay included in this volume, he uses this ontological perspective to reformulate a transcendental philosophy. Besides formal categories, Husserl writes about three material categories, viz., nature, culture, and consciousness. These three define the highest regions in the world. Beginning with Husserl's conception of formal ontology, Smith develops a special *three-phase* ontology.

Smith holds that every entity in this world has three *phases:* a form, an appearance, and a substrate (the stuff out of which it is made). He argues that in this ontology, intentionality exists and has its own specific form. Consider any entity in the world, such as the coffee cup present before me. It can be described in the context of its role in intentionality (this is what phenomenology does), or by its position in the total scheme of things (ontology), or with respect to its material substrate (the domain of natural and cultural sciences). This three-phase structure leads him to formulate his transcendental philosophy. A philosophical theory of the mind and the world taken together may either begin by considering the basic structures of the world, or by characterizing our basic experience of the world. However, in both cases we would be moving from consciousness to the world, or back from the world to consciousness. For Smith, this back and forth movement, this two-way traffic between consciousness and the world, is called transcendental philosophy. Intentionality, in his account, forms the fundamental structure for phenomenology; it is the edifice on which the structure of phenomenology is erected.

With this conception of transcendental phenomenology, Smith hopes to be able to integrate phenomenology, ontology, and natural science, which he thinks would be an advance over the currently anti-ontological and anti-scientific temper of phenomenology. Smith has provided various sketches of such a theory of transcendental phenomenology. The chief merits of his account, besides its claim to integrate ontology and natural science, lie in its avoidance of reductionism: reducing consciousness to the world or the world to consciousness, and in construing intentionality as the consciousness-world-consciousness structure to be a fundamental concept. In so arguing, his position is in accord with Mohanty's "20 Theses" in which he argues that, when taken together, the two theses, viz., consciousness constitutes the world and the world constitutes the consciousness, entail that consciousness and the world cannot be separated, thereby implying that both idealism and naturalism are one-sided.

Another paper which seems to stand apart from all the foregoing is a short piece by Lester Embree. In this essay, Embree recalls a question he put to Mohanty while on a flight from New Delhi to New York after the conference on Phenomenology and Indian Philosophy in 1988: Can a person be conscious of something without any awareness of time? Embree takes a few short steps toward suggesting an answer. I think Embree's solution seems to be that if one cultivates an utterly unreflective attitude toward ideal objects, as numbers for example, one may have no accompanying awareness of time. I find it an interesting suggestion, though Embree does not develop it further. Additionally, if such a suggestion were to be true, then it would have important consequences for phenomenology. It is often taken for granted that all consciousness is consciousness of time. If Embree is right, then all reflective consciousness is temporal; one may even suggest that all consciousness of objects that endure in time, such as a musical performance, unfold in time. Phenomenologists cannot simply disregard Embree's suggestion that a purely unreflective consciousness of such a non-temporal object as a number need not be accompanied by an internal time-consciousness; this must be taken seriously. Should we then revise Husserl's fundamental thesis? Is it possible that there is always a layer of consciousness which is not temporal underlying the temporal? If that were so, Advaita Vedānta would have a lot to teach a phenomenologist.

This brings me to the third group of essays in this volume, all of which concern Mohanty's work on Indian philosophy. These three essays include Arindam Chakrabarti's questioning of the distinction between "knowing" and "understanding," Purushottama Bilimoria's remarks on Mohanty's work on śabdapramāṇa (word as a means of true cognition), and Mark Siderits's examination of Mohanty's defense of the Nyāya realism.

We know that as a young student Mohanty spent a great deal of time studying and analyzing Navya-Nyāya texts with his mentor Pandit Ananta Kumar Tarkatīrtha, which eventually led him to investigate the issues relating to the Indian semantical theories of meaning and reference. Mohanty uses the conceptual apparatus of Western philosophy and insights gained from Western phenomenology to explicate Indian philosophies on these issues. He raises and discusses the question whether there is a theory of *sense* as different from *reference* in Indian philosophy; using the Fregean distinction, Mohanty tries to come to grips with some of the central epistemological issues in Indian thought.

Mohanty argues that since Indian philosophers do not for the most part make a distinction between sense and reference, the meaning of a word is indistinguishable from its referent (for example, for the Mīmāṃsaka it is universal property; for the Naiyāyikas it is a particular characterized by that universal). In the Indian account, there is no place for grasping the meaning of a sentence that is not also a knowing that something is the case; a purely referential theory does not leave any room for the possibility of understanding false sentences. Mohanty also holds that only the Buddhists made a distinction between sense (as *apoha* or exclusion) and reference. So the idea of Fregean sense is available to some extent in the Buddhistic *apoha* theory. It is not possible for me to discuss in detail the Buddhist theory of *apoha* here, but suffice it to say that this theory of meaning is a corollary of the Buddhist metaphysical tenet that reality is an instantaneous, unique particular that is not characterized by any property, and that such a particular is what it is by virtue of its differences from other particulars. Accordingly, the term "horse" means "not non-horse." Mohanty further shows that some kind of sense expressed apart from reference is also found in the Grammarians' theory of meaning and in the *Yogasūtra* idea of *pratyaya* (a cognitive state that is expressed by a word) as well as in the idea of *vikalpa* (a mental representation having no ontological reference). For a detailed analysis of this issue, readers might wish to consult Siderits's article.[27] Siderits, it seems to me, has provided what may be the most convincing response to Mohanty's question as to whether Indian philosophy anywhere makes a distinction between sense and reference. Siderits was successful in pointing to places where this distinction is found in the Indian context.

Both Chakrabarti and Bilimoria are concerned with one of Mohanty's favorite themes in Indian epistemology, viz., *śabda* or word as a means of knowing. In the 1970s, Mohanty questioned the theory of *śabdapramāṇa* on the basis of the distinction between *understanding the meaning* of a sentence "p" and *knowing* that p. He initially argued that the Indian theory of *śabdapramāṇa*—which holds that simply on the basis of understanding the meaning of a sentence that one hears one can know the fact that is stated by that sentence—failed to take into account the distinction between understanding and knowing. The problem becomes more pertinent when we come to false sentences. A false sentence can be understood but cannot give rise to knowledge because there is no fact to be known. Mohanty's interpretation of *śabdapramāṇa* brings several issues to the forefront. For example: Is linguistic understanding (*śābdabodha*) also true knowledge (*pramā*)? Or does linguistic understanding amount to true knowledge only when certain conditions are satisfied?

In his essay, Chakrabarti again takes a stab at Mohanty's interpretation of the theory of *śabdapramāṇa*, but he seems to have modified his initial response to Mohanty's position. In his earlier paper, "Understanding Falsehoods: A Note on the Nyāya Concept of *Yogyatā*,"[28] Chakrabarti argued that although semantic fitness (*yogyatā*) prevents sentences such as "honesty is green" from generating *śābdabodha* (linguistic understanding), it does not rule out sentences such as "there is an elephant in my yard" (when in fact there is no elephant in my yard). In an attempt to rule out contingently false sentences, Chakrabarti further argues that a sentence such as "a is F" is characterized by fitness only if "a *is* F," thereby making fitness and truth indistinguishable. Only true sentences are fit to generate *śābdabodha*, false sentences do not and cannot.

Chakrabarti seems now to have abandoned the claim that false sentences do not generate *śābdabodha*. He argues that we *do* have "knowledge" upon hearing and understanding a false sentence, and elaborates upon the kind of knowledge to which understanding amounts, and whether such an understanding can be taught and transmitted. He seems to follow Dummett's suggestion that knowing the meaning of a sentence is a unique kind of knowing, which differs from knowing an object or from grasping a thought. It is rather more akin to an intuitive grasp of how to follow a rule, which is partly the result of training, and partly acquired from personal contact with a teacher.

Whatever may be the value of this suggestion, I would like to return to

Chakrabarti's response to Mohanty's position. Mohanty takes it as "uncontroversial that 1) *we do* understand false sentences, but 2) do not have *knowledge* upon hearing and understanding such a sentence"[29] (emphasis supplied). Chakrabarti, on the other hand, argues as follows:

> When I understand, even believe someone's statement that Indira Gandhi was Mahatma Gandhi's niece (which is a falsehood) I do understand and to the extent have knowledge* in so far as I have correctly interpreted the speaker's utterance, though it is not a piece of knowledge** about Indira Gandhi. I have gathered knowledge about the meaning of an utterance and also its falsity can be detected only in the back-drop of a whole lot of true beliefs. I know correctly who Indira Gandhi was and who Mahatma Gandhi was and what it is for someone to be someone else's niece, etc. And thus although my resulting belief turns out to be false, like all cognitive contents, the content of that false belief is made out of bits of correctly cognized or *known* objects and properties and relations. So in a sense, we could say that a falsehood too can be known, albeit in its bits and, after all, what is beliefless understanding except knowing the bits correctly and also knowing how they were to be connected had the entire content been believed? What is known when we cognize erroneously are bits of the same reality, which would have been known, *in the right order*, if we had been cognizing veridically.[30] (* supplied).

But this sort of knowledge is nothing but the knowledge of the meaning of a sentence; it is not the kind of knowledge that Mohanty argues we do not get from understanding a false sentence. Indeed the sentence "Indira Gandhi was Mahatma Gandhi's niece" generates a mental state consisting of the referents of the component words, for example, "Indira Gandhi," "Mahatma Gandhi," "niece"; however, they do not and cannot generate a relational cognition, because *ex hypothesi* no such relational entity exists. On Mohanty's position, a correct interpretation of a sentence heard does not amount to true knowledge (*pramā*); it is simply *śābdabodha*. Accordingly, if what linguistic understanding generates is knowledge,* it has to be sharply distinguished from knowledge** in the true sense of the term "knowledge." It is the latter which, on Mohanty's thesis, is different from linguistic understanding.

Śābdabodha may mean either "understanding the meaning of a sentence" or "knowing on the basis of such understanding." Many authors use this ambiguity to their advantage. The distinction becomes crucial when it is asked: What do you grasp when you hear the false sentence "Indira Gandhi was Mahatma Gandhi's niece"? Can one be said to know, when indeed there is no fact to be known (since the uttered sentence is a false sentence)? Since the sentence uttered is false and there is no fact to be known, one cannot be said to know.

Most Indian theories in this context do not leave any room for grasping the meaning of a sentence separate from knowing that something is the case. It seems to me that the use of the term "knowledge" by Chakrabarti is ambiguous; knowledge* refers to "understanding the meaning of a sentence," not to *pramā*, whereas knowledge** does. In so arguing, Chakrabarti collapses the distinction between understanding the meaning of a sentence and knowledge as *pramā*. On Chakrabarti's interpretation, any understanding of the meaning of words, even when there is no relational cognition generated, would constitute knowledge. Even assuming for the sake of argument that Chakrabarti's interpretation is plausible, it further seems to me that his thesis that understanding a false sentence does amount to a kind of knowledge stops short of being his final answer. I think he must return to the question whether in Indian epistemologies there is any concept of sense or thought or proposition, specifically in the context of the Nyāya school with its Russellian theory of meaning. Is there any satisfactory way of making room for a mere understanding the meaning of "p" which is *not yet* knowing that p?

Bilimoria also takes up the issue of *śabdapramāṇa* as discussed by Mohanty and proceeds to distinguish between several components of Mohanty's continuing concern with this problem. He shows that Mohanty's critique is not only concerned with the absence of the distinction between sense and reference, understanding and knowing, in Indian epistemologies, but also (as Mohanty shows in his later writings on these themes) with the contrast between fact and value, the *is* and the *ought* and—in the long run—between knowledge and morality. In this sense Bilimoria's account of Mohanty's position is more comprehensive than Chakrabarti's.

Mohanty, in his various writings, agonizes over the issue of reconciling *śabda* with *pramāṇa* as a theory of rationality. Discussion of *śabdapramāṇa* in the context of the authority of the Vedas as *śrutiprāmāṇyam* and its authorlessnesss (*apauruṣeyatva*) not only does not help much, but further compounds the problem, thereby making any reconciliation all the more problematic. Earlier (in an as-yet-unpublished 1986 presidential address delivered at the Indian Philosophical Congress), Mohanty criticized the claim that *śabda* is an irreducible source of cognition. It is important to remember that although Mohanty began with what seems to be a rejection of the thesis of *śabdapramāṇa*, he gradually came to rehabilitate it. In the essay, "Is There an Irreducible Mode of Word-Generated Knowledge?"[31] Mohanty rejects much of his own earlier criticism, and argues that while knowledge about matters of fact acquired through *śabda* may be shown to be inferential, knowledge of moral rules, of what one ought to do, is uniquely derived from *śabda*. Again, in *Reason and Tradition*, he reiterates that *śabda* as one of the means of true cognition needs to be reexamined :

[*Ś*]*abdapramāṇa* cannot any longer provide the theoretical basis for a satisfactory philosophy. But that is not to reject language (*śabda*) altogether as a means of true cognition (*pramāṇa*). What is necessary is to re-examine the priorities and relative strengths and weaknesses. . . . But one also needs to recall the distinction between understanding a sentence p and knowing that p, the different ways in which language is central to cognitive enterprise and to normal and religious life, and the problems connected with the notions of a text and its interpretations. The methodological insights would, I believe, rehabilitate the tradition's self-understanding, without returning to the naive use of *śabdapramāṇa* to which a return is just impossible.[32]

Mohanty concedes that although *śabda* is not an autonomous source of knowing empirical facts, it *is* an autonomous source of knowing about supersensible moral rules. Finally, Mohanty proceedes to give a novel construal to the claim that *śruti* is *apauruṣeya*, meaning thereby that the texts of the *śruti*, as contrasted with the texts that describe empirical reality, have inexhaustible possibilities of interpretation quite independent of the question of authorial intention.

Mohanty's critiques and interpretations of Indian epistemologies presuppose certain binary oppositions which he almost takes for granted. Once these oppositions are called into question, as they are in post-modern thinking, his criticisms would yield place to a more positive and possibly valuable interpretation of the role of *śabda* in Indian epistemology. Bilimoria recognizes that Mohanty's writings on these epistemological topics have opened up all sorts of new doors for philosophers engaged in Indian epistemology. They brought to the forefront and forced philosophers to think afresh questions that previously had not been reflected upon. Therefore, while Mohanty's work remains valuable, it is time we get beyond them and question the binary oppositions on which his criticisms and interpretations are based. I think the more fundamental question to be considered is as follows: Can we today confine our attempts to understand and interpret the Indian epistemologies to the narrowly formulated logical and semantical questions that have been raised by Mohanty and Matilal? Or, now that the works of Mohanty and Matilal have had their influence, is it now time for us to go beyond them without falling back into the speculative and metaphysical morass in which Indian philosophers found themselves in the middle of this century? I will let my readers decide how best to answer these questions.

Siderits, on the other hand, in his paper remains methodologically faithful to the logical and semantical questions raised by Mohanty (and Matilal). He takes up the issue between Nyāya realism and Mādhyamika anti-realism (Siderits's interpretation of the Mādhyamika thesis of emptiness). To be specific, his essay is a response to Mohanty's defense of Nyāya realism. That the Nyāya position is a realism was never doubted until Daya Krishna, in his article "Is Nyāya Realism or Idealism?" raised a question that was meant to elicit responses.[33] Daya wondered whether it is appropriate to call the Naiyāyikas realists, given their doctrine that all existents are cognizable, that is, that they are both knowable and nameable. He argued that if "to be real" is "to be knowable," then following the Berkeleyan dictum "to be is to be perceived" (*esse est percipii*), the Nyāya view would unwittingly coincide with Berkeley's idealism. Mohanty,[34] like many others, responded to Daya Krishna's very interesting and pertinent question and made several points to preserve the integrity of Nyāya realism. He did so by showing how the Naiyāyika's position differs from Berkeley's idealism. Some of the points that Mohanty made are as follows:

1. We are reminded that on the Nyāya view, "to be real" is not necessarily "to be knowable." In other words, the correlation between being real and being knowable is extensional, and it is not conceptually necessary in Nyāya as distinguished from Berkeley's dictum.

2. In Berkeley, perception points to a kind of direct, unmediated apprehension of the immediately presented object. For the Nyāya, cognition is much broader; it does not refer simply to perception but may also be purely inferential or word-generated.

3. According to the Nyāya, veridical knowledge is *caused* by an object testifying to its independence from the knowledge, which is not found in the Berkeley's dictum. So the Nyāya can preserve its realism even while maintaining that all that is real is knowable.

Leaving aside these points, Siderits discusses another of Mohanty's claims that he has made in many of his writings—viz., that realism is preserved and strengthened by the Nyāya position that cognition is formless (*nirākāra*) but not self-manifesting (*svaprakāśa*),[35] while Yogācāra idealism takes cognitions to be both formed (*sākāra*) and self-manifesting.

Siderits brings out two important arguments to show why Mohanty's defense of Nyāya realism still fails. In the first place, he considers it possible that there is a variety of Yogācāra which regards cognition as formless and may also, as Mohanty himself recognizes, subscribe to a causal theory of knowledge. In that case, it would seem that Nyāya realism would not follow from those two theses. Secondly, Siderits moves on to consider the Mādhyamika critique of causation, taking it to imply that construing reliable knowledge to be causally produced does not succeed in escaping the charge of circularity that the Mādhyamika brings against the *pramāṇa* theory.

Siderits does not discuss another important point of Mohanty's response, namely, the role of ignorance or not-knowing in both Nyāya realism and Advaita Vedānta's empirical realism. It seems to me that the role that the notion of witness-consciousness plays in Advaita Vedānta's empirical realism, as contrasted with its absence in the Nyāya realism, is central to the issue under consideration; however, Siderits disregards it completely. Before proceeding further, I will elaborate on this point.

To argue that everything is a possible object of consciousness does not go against realism, provided that "everything" is taken to imply all objects and that "existence" is taken to be a real predicate. The Vivaraṇa school of Advaita Vedānta argues along these lines, when it states that all things are objects of witness-consciousness either as known or as unknown (*sarvam vastu jñātatayā ajñātatayā va sākṣicaitanyasya viṣya eva*).[36] The point that the Advaitins were making is as follows: knowing an object is accompanied by knowing its previous unknownness. Without knowing the earlier non-cognition, it is not possible to apprehend an object as being now known (*pūrvānavagatim avijñā-ya idānīmeva avagatam ityavadhāraṇāyogāt*).[37] In other words, prior to my apprehending an object as known, the witness-consciousness apprehends the object as unknown. When the object is directly known, as in "this is a chair," the knowledge of the object (the chair) is immediate. The witness-consciousness reveals the object as having been unknown prior to the perceptual experience of the chair. Thus, as long as I am perceiving the chair, the witness-consciousness in me reveals the chair *as known*. However, prior to the occurrence of the perceptual cognitive act, that is, prior to my apprehending the chair, the chair exists *as unknown*. So, at any particular time t_1, the witness-consciousness knows a particular object or a set of objects as known, and all remaining objects as unknown. Therefore, everything known or unknown is an object of the witness-consciousness. In other words, the witness-consciousness reveals everything either as known or as unknown.[38] The Advaitins argue that every-thing in the world falls into two classes: the known and the unknown. This thesis not only encapsulates Advaita idealism, but it also succeeds in preserving the integrity of Advaitin's empirical realism. The Nyāya does not have the notion of witness-consciousness at its disposal, so it does not have any other option beyond realism.

Siderits constantly reminds us that the Nyāya theory is consistently externalist, while Western epistemology is in large measure internalist. Never-theless, the dispute between the Nyāya and Buddhism with regard to "realism vs. anti-realism" still needs to be continued and reexamined—a dispute that has yet to reach closure.

This brings me to the essays in the fourth and concluding section of this collection. It contains two essays, the first one by Stephen Phillips and the second by Eliot Deutsch. These essays do not fit into any of the three sections outlined above because they are concerned neither with Western phenomenol-ogy exclusively, nor with Indian philosophy solely. Given that these two essays are concerned with philosophy in a global sense, they situate themselves in the middle group of this collection, encompassing within their fold issues which concern all philosophers, irrespective of whether they are speaking from the Eastern or Western persuasion.

The essay by Phillips begins by undertaking a general overall evaluation of Mohanty's work in the area of Indian philosophy and provides a special evaluation of the advance of Indian philosophy in Mohanty's various works. I think he brings out several aspects of Mohanty's works, not all of which go well together. For example, one component is the "dream" (as he calls it) of Mohanty and others to realize the ideal of global philosophy, where Western philosophers would refer to thinkers such as Bhartṛhari, Gaṅgeśa, and Raghunāth, while specialists in Indian philosophy would reference Quine, Husserl, and Davidson. The latter part of the dream has been partly realized in the works of Matilal, Mohanty, and others—but the former has yet to occur. Thus the dream remains just that, which might suggest that it is flawed. The other component of Mohanty's work is to advance Indian philosophy by emphasizing problems, issues, and concerns rather than systems, thereby making possible new combinations of ideas, and perhaps, new systems. This would mean that we discuss questions and offer answers by their purely conceptual nature and sheer philosophical interest, without worrying about their proper attribution to systems and or philosophers. This is illustrated in many of Mohanty's writings.[39]

These two components are compatible in that the second would feed the first. However, what comes in conflict with the dream is a third component that has surfaced in Mohanty's writings in the last decade or so, viz., a growing emphasis on the role of tradition, the foundational nature of *śruti,* and the spiritual and moral cognitions that *śruti* makes possible. While Phillips views the *pramāṇa* theory and many epistemological and semantical theories of Indian philosophy as contributing to a global philosophy, he has serious reservations whether the ethical and spiritual components of the Indian tradition can play a similar role. Are they are so intimately bound up with the Indian life-world that they cannot be detached from it and dealt with in the same way as one deals with the *pramāṇa* theory? It perhaps might be said in Mohanty's defense that in his discussions of tradition, *śabdapramāṇa,* and ethical cognitions, he has tried to convey to his readers that irrespective of the traditions of East or West— Indian or Chinese, Greek or European—ethical knowledge is derived from a tradition that is established, nurtured, and continuously interpreted through moral discourse. In the Indian context it is grounded in the texts known as *śruti,* but other traditions have different literary sources, such as sacred texts. Thus the claim of universality attaches to the *pramāṇa* theory, that is to say, to a theory about the origin of ethical cognitions. The same universality, however, does not attach to all the ethical beliefs and rules within a tradition. Let me elaborate on this point further.

The question is: What are the sources of our knowledge of what we ought to do? To the extent that ethical rules may be subject to epistemological questionings—assuming the form "what are the sources of our knowledge of moral rules?" one could universalize them. Such rules cannot be derived from perception, inference, etc; they can only be derived from *śabda,* which in the Indian tradition is *śruti* and in the Western tradition may very well be, for example, the word of the Bible. This in turn implies that only verbal transmission remains as the means of teaching morality and deriving moral cognitions. I suspect Mohanty was not claiming that the Indian *śabda* is the source of all our moral cognitions, but rather that in any culture knowledge of ethical rules is derived from tradition and its own *śabda*. However, only the Indian philosophy developed, in a sophisticated way, an epistemology of *śabda,* and therein lies one of its greatest achievements.

The volume concludes with an essay by Eliot Deutsch that does not deal with any specific tradition, but rather raises questions about how different cognitive, ethical, and artistic traditions may understand each other. It discusses fundamental questions about the possibility of intercultural philosophy. Deutsch avoids both a pernicious relativism and ethno-centricism, as well as an equally misguided absolutism. As a matter of fact, the two extremes feed upon each other. Deutsch argues for the possibility of creatively engaging oneself with the other tradition, for a willingness to revise and modify one's own presuppositions if necessary. But most of all he invites his readers to accept a plurality of traditions, of modes of life and practices, not merely as given but also as something to be celebrated rather than rejected.

Much of the details of Deutsch's essay rest on a distinction between what he calls "exclusionary principles" and "positive principles" of a tradition. He allows for some measure of universality with regard to exclusionary principles, especially if they are foundational. For example, no tradition can afford to admit as rational what violates the principle of contradiction. However, many exclusionary principles within a tradition are not fundamental; they are rather what Deutsch calls "operational," that is, they can be changed, even abandoned. I think the real crux of pluralism concerns the positive principles and here the best one can hope for is some measure of creative understanding, ethical imagination, and self-critical attitude toward one's own tradition. Whereas Mohanty reiterates in his writings that a common world is in the process of being constituted through conversation leading to a mutual understanding (in Husserlian jargon, through a common *noematic* content emerging out of overlapping *noemata*), Deutsch finds no need for such a common world and celebrates the fact that there is a plurality of traditions and life-worlds.

3

In order to understand the nature of the terrain covered in these essays, it is necessary to say a few words about how Indian philosophy relates to the tradition of transcendental phenomenology. We have seen that in this tradition, the contrast between the empirical and the transcendental occupies a central place. For a phenomenologist the transcendental is not that which transcends the empirical; it is rather that which makes the empirical possible. The transcendental is recovered by a methodological process known as *epoché* or reduction. Besides the empirical and the transcendental, there is the *a priori*, which in itself is neither empirical nor transcendental. Husserl called his phenomenology "transcendental phenomenology," and his use of the term "transcendental" has Kantian overtones. For Husserl, "transcendental" means that everything in the world, the world itself, derives its meaning from consciousness and its intentionality. Consciousness is transcendental insofar as all things are constituted in consciousness. Consciousness, however, is not only intentional; it is also temporal. Accordingly, the process of constitution is a temporal process, giving rise to the historicity of the transcendental consciousness and the world which it constitutes. Thus we must confront the question of how I, as a transcendental ego, come to share a common world with other co-constituting transcendental egos.

It is important to remember in this context that all that is *a priori* is not transcendental; for example, mathematical truths may be *a priori*, but they are not transcendental. Some of the transcendental may be, as the essay by Makkreel suggests, closer to the empirical; for example, the *a priori* and the *sensus communis* of the *Critique of Judgment*. Again, the transcendental, strictly speaking, may not be *a priori;* for example, Husserl's internal time-consciousness, though transcendental, is empirically verifiable.

Although Western philosophy has had a strong empiricist strand, it has been opposed by an equally strong rationalistic viewpoint. In an interesting way, Indian philosophy has been empirical. Almost all schools of Indian philosophy regard sense perception as a means of true knowledge. Other means of knowing, for example, inference, word, have been taken to be dependent on sense perception. Even the pure existence of Advaita Vedānta and the bare particular (*svalakṣaṇa*) of Buddhism are taken to be cognized in a nonconceptual and non-linguistic (*nirvikalpaka*) mode of sensory perception. The Nyāya, perhaps the most outspoken empiricists among the schools of Indian philosophy, hold that in sense perception one not only apprehends a physical object and its qualities, but also the universals that are instantiated in them, and relations between objects that instantiate these universals. Consequently, the Platonic need for positing a higher faculty of cognition such as reason, which apprehends the Platonic universals, is not needed in the Nyāya school. Thus Western philosophy's perennial question: "Do our cognitions arise from experience or reason or both?" has not been raised, indeed such a question cannot even be formulated in the language of Indian philosophy. It seems to me that in this regard Indian thinkers are closer to Aristotle than to Plato. The cognition of the universal, as well as universal truths, arises from sense perception. All knowledge begins with experience. It reminds us of Kant, who at the outset of the *Critique of Pure Reason* informs us that although "all our knowledge begins with experience, it does not follow that it all arises out of experience."[40] Although it is difficult to answer whether the second half of Kant's dictum is true in Indian thought, there is no doubt that the first half characterizes

Indian philosophy. Indian epistemologists do not contend with a purely rational faculty of cognition. It is important to note in this context that there seems to be no fitting synonym in Sanskrit for the Western term "reason."

It may be argued that while Indian philosophers seem to be committed to a kind of overall empiricism, what is called transcendental philosophy should be regarded exclusively as a Western phenomena. While popular authors ascribe a certain "transcendentalism" to Indian philosophy, they do not realize that what is called transcendental philosophy arose with Kant and reached its maturity in Husserl. It arose out of the tension between empiricism and rationalism, and out of a peculiar kind of questioning regarding the possibility of cognition. The question may be formulated: "how" can consciousness escape its immanence (its own domain) and reach out to the world? This peculiar "*how*" question— "How is it possible that?"—is not raised by Indian philosophers. That consciousness apprehends by reaching out to its objects in the world has seemed to them to be an undeniable fact. It is worth noting that among the Indian schools of philosophy, the Nyāya-Vaiśeṣika took consciousness to be intrinsically intentional; Yogācāra Buddhism, though denying the existence of external objects, argued for a subject/object distinction within consciousness (which roughly approximates *noesis-noema* structure); the Advaita Vedānta has denied intentionality and taken consciousness to be definable as self-shining or self-manifesting, attributing its objective directedness to ignorance (*avidyā*). The one philosopher who has sought to combine both the self-shining nature of consciousness and its object directedness is Rāmānuja, who has taken these two features to be mutually dependent. Consciousness, he held, reveals itself to its locus (owner or ego) only when manifesting its object.[41] The Indian schools of philosophy, irrespective of whether we are talking about the extreme realists (for example, Nyāya, Vaiśeṣika, and Mīmāṃsā) or the extreme idealists (for example, Yogācāra), did not arrive at their respective positions by way of answering the "how" question. So one could say that transcendental thinking of the Western kind has not arisen in the Indian context.

Since in these essays the question of the relation between the empirical and transcendental is raised, discussed, rejected, and brought into the vicinity of the typically Advaita Vedānta problem of the relation between *jīva* and *ātman,* and since solutions are offered by appeal to ideas in Buddhism (see the essay by Kopf), it must then be true that although Indian philosophers did not engage in the Western kind of transcendental philosophy, they must have done *some* kind of transcendental philosophy. If that is the case, the question arises: What is the nature of this transcendental philosophy? I will shed some light on this question by primarily by focusing on Kant and Husserl from Western philosophy and the Advaita Vedānta tradition from Indian philosophy.

Before proceeding to answer this question, let me briefly review at the risk of what might appear to be a digression, the distinction between Kantian thinking and Husserlian thinking, in order to assess whether this distinction provides any clues for our inquiry. Kantian thinking is concerned with the con-

ditions of the possibility of experience, while Husserlian thinking is concerned
with describing exactly what is given in experience and in what precise manner.
So one could say that Kantian transcendental thinking is regressive: it posits
entities, processes, and functions that are not directly amenable to introspective
evidence, (for example, all Kantian synthesis). In contrast, Husserlian transcendental phenomenology is descriptive, and through a series of methodological steps brings to explicit givenness aspects of experience that otherwise
would remain covered up by extraneous factors.

In Advaita Vedānta, the ultimate presupposition of all cognition is *sākṣin*
or the witness-consciousness. Etymologically, "*sākṣin*" means direct and immediate perception, or that which directly or immediately perceives; it refers to
the agent of such perception. Consequently, the term "*sākṣin*" also signifies a
witness, both in the context of a court of law, and in the context of epistemology, the context that concerns me here. It is a witness in the sense of the
phenomenologically pure spectator, who observes without bringing anything to
the observation; its interests are not involved in what occurs. It signifies the self,
which though not itself involved in the cognitive process, functions as a disinterested, uninvolved onlooker or witness-consciousness. The witness-consciousness in Advaita, though indifferent or detached, is intelligent, and its
disengagement is really its refusal to acknowledge the illusory distinctions of
names and forms that fragment reality. It is a form of apprehension that is direct,
nonrelational, non-propositional, and non-evaluative in both cognitive and
practical affairs. It is the basis of all knowledge.

The concept of the *sākṣin* in Advaita is the single most important postulate
of the principle of revelation operative in experience—cognitive and noncog-
nitive alike. A phenomenological exploration leads to the recovery of this
principle as a necessary ingredient in any epistemological process. In simple
terms, it represents an attempt to understand experience and its implications.
Ignorance is one of the objects of the witness-consciousness, which is
expressed in the judgment "I am ignorant." However, the function of the
witness-consciousness is not limited to simply making us aware of ignorance; it
goes beyond that. It helps us answer such questions as: "How do I know an
object?" and "How do I know that I know an object?" The object to be known
is covered by ignorance and there must be something or someone responsible
for removing the ignorance covering the object that is to be known. The mental
mode performs this function. It makes the object known by removing ignorance. However, although the object is manifested by the mental mode, the
mental mode cannot perform the function of manifesting the object without the
witness-consciousness, insofar as the mental mode must itself be manifested by
the witness-consciousness. Thus, we can say that the witness-consciousness is
involved directly in manifesting the mental mode and indirectly in making the
object known or manifest. It is important to remember in this context that the
focus of attention in Advaita is not the object as such. Rather, the focus of

attention, vis-à-vis the object, is consciousness, which functions as the medium of manifestation of the object.

Kant, unlike the Advaitins, does not have a conception of positive ignorance; in fact, *the concept of ignorance does not play any part in his theory of knowledge.* Thus, unlike the Advaita Vedānta philosophers, he does not hold that to know an object is to remove the ignorance that has been covering it. The question for Kant is not how ignorance is removed, but rather how an object is known.

In Kant, as in many Western philosophers, we find the peculiarly Western notion that there is a kind of knowledge of an object which is *a priori.* The contents of our knowledge are derived from experience, argues Kant, but the mind arranges them according to certain *a priori* categories of the understanding. He argues that the mind can know an object *a priori* only if and to the extent that the mind is responsible for the formal structure of the object. Sensations only furnish the content of experience; they must be placed in relation to other sensations in the context of space and time. The mind is responsible both for organizing sensations according to the forms of space and time, and for providing a set of concepts by which the sensory impressions are synthesized in the form of representations of an object.

This latter notion, that is, the notion of synthesis of sensations into the form of representations of an object, leads to Kant's theory of the transcendental unity of self-consciousness, which presupposes an identity of the self in time—a self that is able to organize, synthesize, and conceptualize the material that the mind receives. Thus, the activity of the self is responsible for the possibility of knowledge of the object. Kant further maintains that although we do not know the self as an object, all our experiences presuppose a unitary self-consciousness that accounts for whatever we know.

Thus, both the witness-consciousness and the Kantian unity of self-consciousness serve to make possible the knowledge of the object, as well as the knowledge of such knowledge. For Kant, the unity of apperception is also the unity of self-consciousness. Likewise, the witness-consciousness is not only the awareness of our knowing ("knowing" taken in the sense of an inner mental process, a mental mode in Advaita epistemology), but it also makes knowledge of the object possible. The witness-consciousness, however, is not an active principle that constitutes an object. All constitution of the object is ascribed to the principle of ignorance, and therein lies the important and decisive difference between the Kantian and the Advaitin positions.

The Kantian unity of apperception is a necessary condition for the possibility of the representation of the object; there could be no knowledge of the object otherwise. Kant is both an empirical realist and a transcendental idealist. He holds that there are unknown things—that things exist independently of our knowledge of them. But our knowledge of the object is made possible by functions exercised by the transcendental unity of apperception. So, the unity of apperception is an activity that shapes our representations of the object; it is responsible for the possibility of knowing the object. The witness-consciousness does not have any such function. It is a passive principle of manifestation in the sense that it only receives impressions from without, rather than an active principle that either creates or shapes the object via the imposition of categories. It is an absolutely impartial spectator, it does not identify itself with a particular position, it has no Archimedean point from which to orient itself in any relational mode of cognition. In other words, the witness-consciousness is totally receptive; it is not creative. The only way an object is made possible by the witness-consciousness is that the witness-consciousness may be construed as the substratum on which the object is superimposed. Insofar as the super-imposed object is made possible by the substratum, all objects of knowledge presuppose the witness-consciousness. It, however, does not give shape to them; it does not give form to them, manufacture them, or construct them in any way. What makes objects possible in Advaita metaphysics is not the activity of the self but rather ignorance.

To sum up: the witness-consciousness is not posited in the same spirit as Kantian acts of synthesis because these acts are posited, not lived through experiences (*Erlebnises*). The witness-consciousness, on the other hand, is a component of every experience, itself experiencing and experienced, standing in the midst of stream of consciousness, perpetually testified by such introspective judgments as "I am sad," "I am happy," "I know," "I am ignorant," and so on. The Western phenomenological tradition from Husserl through Heidegger, Merleau-Ponty, and even Derrida has looked at this notion of a disinterested witness with varying degrees of suspicion. Husserl seems to have found some place for it in his transcendental phenomenology, but with Heidegger begins a criticism of this notion which persists throughout European thought. Husserl in *Cartesian Meditations* argues:

> If the Ego, as naturally immersed in the world, experiencingly and otherwise, is called "*interested*" *in the world,* then the phenomenologically altered—and, as so altered, continually maintained—attitude consists in a *splitting of the Ego:* in that the phenomenological Ego establishes himself as "*disinterested on-looker,*" above the naively interested Ego. That this takes place is then itself accessible by means of a new reflection, which as transcendental, likewise demands the very same attitude of looking on "disinterestedly"—the Ego's sole remaining interest being to see and to describe adequately what he sees, purely as seen, as what is seen and seen in such and such a manner.[42]

Keeping in mind that the notion of the "disinterested on-looker" in Husserl very closely captures the concept of the witness-consciousness, as well as the differences between Kantian and Husserlian transcendental thought, it might be argued that the Indian kind of transcendental philosophy to be found in Vedānta, and for that matter, in Buddhism, is closer to Husserlian phenomenology. If this is so, where does this affinity lie? For a volume of essays, such as the volume under consideration—which not only is concerned with Husserlian transcendental phenomenology but also Indian philosophy, and is further devoted to a thinker like Mohanty who has been deeply concerned with both traditions—it is imperative that we assess the affinities and differences between Husserlian transcendental phenomenology and Indian philosophy.

I will begin with some preliminary remarks for the sake of clarity. With the exception of the realist theory of universals found in the Nyāya and the Mīmāṃsā schools of Indian philosophy, there is nothing in Indian philosophy—certainly not in Vedānta and Buddhism, the two schools that primarily concern me here—which may be construed as essentialism. I need not argue for this claim so far as Buddhism is concerned, for anybody mildly familiar with the Buddhist philosophy is very well aware of their opposition to any universality or anything invariant. In fact, this anti-essentialism reaches its high point in the Mādhyamika rejection of *svabhāva* (one's own nature) of anything. The famous doctrine of *śūnyatā* or emptiness of things, whatever else it may mean, certainly means *nisvabhāvatā* (essencelessness). Even Advaita Vedānta replaces real universals of Nyāya and Mīmāṃsā with concepts, and accepts *brahman-ātman* as the only invariant, the only essence. However, we must note in this context that though Advaita Vedānta recognizes *brahman-ātman* as the *only* invariant, it is the same in all things, empty of all determinations and yet compatible with all possible theories about the empirical world. Many critics of essentialism, some represented in this volume, turn to a historicism or a theory of flux. The Buddhist may have some sympathy with the idea of "flux"; the Advaitin, however, does not. The denial of essence still leaves us with an empirical world of things and persons having relatively stable structures. The only other alternative cannot be a turn to history. So in our search for an affinity to Husserlian phenomenology, let us remember that we need not look for Husserlian essentialism in Indian philosophy.

The pure consciousness of Advaita Vedānta is not something one posits to account for the empirical world or empirical cognition; it is that which is concretely experiencable once erroneous interpretations are set aside. In this context, we must keep in mind that, unlike Husserl's transcendental subjectivity, the Advaitin's pure consciousness is neither intentional nor temporal, and so it cannot also be said to be constitutive of the meanings embedded in the world and in our cognitions. Intentional reference to the world would then be degraded ontologically to the status of a false mis-representation of the nature of consciousness, thereby establishing a wide gap between the Husserlian thinking and the Advaitin, a gap that is impossible to bridge. One has to look into other systems of Vedānta, for example, Rāmānuja's Viśiṣṭādvaita or the Kāshmir Śaivism, for a doctrine of intentionality so central to modern phenomenology. If transcendental subjectivity is taken to be the constituting subjectivity, and the empirical as that which is constituted, then the distinction between the empirical and the transcendental *in this sense* is not available either in Advaita Vedānta or Buddhism.

Finally, the notion of the "disinterested on-looker" is only an approximation of the notion of the witness-consciousness. It is an "approximation" because Husserl's concept of the "splitting of the ego" does not, and for that matter, cannot appear in the Advaita theory. This on-looker, argues Husserl, is revealed in reflection, but its existence is not a necessary condition for the occurrence of any cognition. The Advaitins, on the other hand, maintain that without this on-looker, no cognition at all would be possible. The Vedānta finds the witness-consciousness at the heart of every experience, every cognition, and every action. It is not the constituting transcendental ego of Husserl, but it is that without which no knowledge, experience, or even admission of one's ignorance, (that is, not-knowing), would be possible.

Thus whereas in the Husserlian tradition consciousness is transcendental in the sense that it constitutes the world, in the Indian tradition, especially in Advaita Vedānta, consciousness is transcendental insofar as it detaches or dissociates itself from the world and enjoys its freedom within itself. It is worth noting that only in the Sāṃkhya schools is the empirical world taken to be a product of *prakṛti* and *puruṣa,* giving rise to the philosophical problem: if each *puruṣa* has its world, how could there be one common world? Finally, I would point out that it does seem as if it is only in one system of philosophy, that is, the Kāśhmir Śaivism of Abhinavagupta (a form of Advaita Vedānta), that the pure consciousness itself is taken to have a temporal dimension, or better yet, as time itself.

However, we find in the Indian context something of which Western phenomenology has had glimpses, though never thematized clearly. I am referring here to the concept of *avidyā* or ignorance as the constitutive source of the world. As beginningless, it may be regarded as the only *a priori* in the strict sense of the term in Indian thought. It reminds us that a phenomenologist's attempt to trace the origin of the world in consciousness must be an endless process, an endless quest for clarity never to be realized, and perpetually being postponed (as Derrida often says with regard to Husserl's thinking). So while a phenomenologist claims to make clear the origin of the world in consciousness, that program remains perpetually unfulfilled. Merleau-Ponty points out that every constitution has to be forgotten. This forgetting is a condition of the world's appearing to be already there. One only needs to ask: How is this forgetting possible? How is this forgetting related to the Advaitic and the Buddhist concepts of ignorance? These are deep and difficult questions, the answers to which would bring the Indian tradition in close proximity to the Derridian deconstruction of Husserl.

In the end, the problem of Vedānta phenomenology, if we can speak about it, would center around the question of whether phenomenology can free itself from the constraints imposed on it by the thesis of intentionality, with which its beginning in modern times are entangled. One may ask, in other words, whether a non-intentional consciousness may be regarded as a phenomenon and so a proper theme of phenomenology. I leave aside for the present the phenomenology of waking and dream consciousness that we find in the Upaniṣadic and the Vedāntic texts. These are still intentional. The question is: Can there be a phenomenology of deep sleep as well as of the fourth state, *turīya,* that is to say, of pure, unobjective, non-individualized consciousness? I think this is where Advaita would part company from Husserlian phenomenology, though not entirely. We know that Husserlian phenomenology began by placing intentionality at the center, yet as it developed, especially in Husserl's work on time-consciousness, it succeeded in unravelling depths of consciousness that are not intentional but that make intentionality possible. This is the case with what Husserl calls "the absolute flow of consciousness." It is important to remember that what he calls the absolute flow of consciousness is described as a flux only metaphorically. Husserl finds it difficult to conceptualize and at one place calls it both simultaneously standing and streaming.[43] It is not *of* anything in Brentano's sense; it does not have the correlative *noema,* but in it are constituted all levels of intentional consciousness. In the last analysis it is also described as the living present from which all temporal dimensions flow, the original source-point of conscious life. With this notion, we again begin to see the affinity with Advaita that we seemed to have lost track of a little while ago.

The above remarks are made in the hope that they help the reader not only to appreciate the contribution of Mohanty's essays to understanding and interpreting Husserlian phenomenology, but also to appreciate their relevance for understanding Indian thought (though the latter is not the explicit goal of these essays).

Several authors in this volume have noted with interest Mohanty's introduction of the theme of Advaita Vedānta into phenomenological discourse. A detailed analysis of these hints is not possible in this introduction. We have already seen that Advaitic themes emerge within Husserlian phenomenology, as Husserlian themes emerge within Advaitic phenomenology; however, when the dust settles, the two discourses again part company and go their separate ways. But in such situations, following Gadamer's suggestions and Deutsch's reconstruction of them, we can say that what we need is a creative understanding that would respect differences while allowing a fusion of horizons to take place.

Notes

1.   Daya Krishna and K. L. Sharma (eds.), *The Philosophy of J. N.*

Mohanty (New Delhi: Indian Council of Philosophical Research, 1991), 199.

2.   P. Bilimoria and J. N. Mohanty (eds.), *Relativism, Suffering, and Beyond: Essays in Memory of Bimal K. Matilal,* (New Delhi: Oxford University Press, 1997), 3.

3.   Bina Gupta (ed.), *Explorations in Indian Philosophy* (Oxford: Oxford University Press), forthcoming.

4.   J. N. Mohanty, *Reason and Tradition in Indian Thought* (Oxford: Oxford University Press, 1992). Henceforth, this book will be cited as RTIT.

5.   Frank M. Kirkland and D. P. Chattopadhyaya (eds.), *Phenomenology: East and West* (Dordrecht: Kluwer, 1993), xi.

6.   "Phenomenology and Indian Philosophy: The Concept of Rationality," *Journal of the British Society for Phenomenology* 19, no. 3 (October 1988), 269.

7.   Kirkland and Chattopadhyaya, *Phenomenology: East and West,* 292.

8.   Mohanty, "Phenomenology and Indian Philosophy: The Concept of Rationality,"269.

9.   Krishna and Sharma, *The Philosophy of J. N. Mohanty,* 201.

10. Taken from the collection of letters presented to him on his seventieth birthday.

11. Ibid.

12. Purushottama Bilimoria (ed.), *J. N. Mohanty: Essays on Indian Philosophy* (New Delhi: Oxford University Press, 1993), xxxvi.

13. Bimal K. Matilal and P. K. Sen, "The Context Principle and Some Indian Theories of Meaning," *Mind,* Jan. 1988, 73-97.

14. Bimal K. Matilal and A. Chakrabarti, *Knowing from Words* (Dordrecht: Kluwer, 1994).

15. Bimal K. Matilal, *The Navya-Nyāya Doctrine of Negation* (Cambridge, Mass.: Harvard University Press, 1968).

16. S. Bhattacharyya, *Gadādhara's Theory of Objectivity* (New Delhi: Indian Council of Philosophical Research, 1990).

17. Bina Gupta (ed.), *Explorations in Western Philosophy* (Oxford: Oxford University Press), forthcoming. I think the most novel thesis that Mohanty proposes is expressed in 14 through 16; 15 *seems to* reverse 14, primarily because the sense of "constitution" has been reversed so that even for transcendental phenomenology it makes sense to say that the world and consciousness are inseparable.

18. J. N. Mohanty, *Phenomenology: Between Essentialism and Transcendental Phenomenology* (Evanston, Ill.: Northwestern University Press, 1997).

19. Ibid., 13.

20. See section 1 of Margolis's paper (in this volume).

21. See the section entitled "Some Consequences of Contextualism."

22. The essay was an invited lecture given at the annual meeting of the American Psychological Association in 1996 and is being published for the first time in *Explorations in Western Philosophy,* forthcoming.

23. We also know that Hannah Arendt has emphasized the importance of the concept of natality and mortality for political theory. See her book *The Human Condition* (Chicago/London: University of Chicago Press, 1958).

24. There has been a spate of writings in the last few years on generative phenomenology. See Anthony Steinbock's, *Home and Beyond: Generative*

Phenomenology after Husserl (Evanston, Ill.: Northwestern University Press, 1995).

25. See section entitled "Characteristics of Generative Problems."

26. J. N. Mohanty, *Transcendental Phenomenology: An Analytical Account* (Oxford, UK: Basil Blackwell, 1989), 143.

27. Mark Siderits, "The Sense-Reference Distinction in Indian Philosophy of Language," *Synthese* 69 (1986), 81-106.

28. "A Note on the Nyāya Concept of *Yogyatā,*" *The Journal of Asiatic Society* 28 (1986), 10-20.

29. RTIT, 254.

30. See this volume, p. 187. See also RTIT, 249-59.

31. Matilal and A. Chakrabarti, *Knowing from Words*, 29-49.

32. RTIT, 22-3.

33. Daya Krishna, "Is Nyāya Realist or Idealist?" *Journal of Indian Council of Philosophical Research* 12, no.1 (1994), 161-3.

34. J. N. Mohanty, "Is Nyāya Realism or Idealism?" *Journal of Indian Council of Philosophical Research* 13, no.1 (1995), 167-9.

35. Ibid.

36. Prakāśātman's *Pañcapādikāvivaraṇam,* eds., Srirama Sastri and S. R. Krishnamurthi Sastri (Madras: Madras Government Manuscripts Library, 1958), 110.

37. Ibid., 95.

38. Ibid., 262.

39. See Mohanty's *Classical Indian Philosophy* (Lanham, Md.: Rowman & Littlefield, 2000). Also see, RTIT.

40. Immanuel Kant, *Critique of Pure Reason,* trans. Norman Kemp Smith (London: Macmillan, 1973), B-1.

41. See my "Phenomenological Analysis in Husserl and Rāmānuja: A Comparative Study," in *International Studies in Philosophy,* 15, no.1 (1983), 19-32.

42. Edmund Husserl *Cartesian Meditations: An Introduction to Phenomenology,* trans. Dorian Cairns (The Hague: Martinus Nijhoff, 1973), "Second Meditation," 35.

43. Husserl, *On the Phenomenology of the Consciousness of Internal Time,* trans. J. Bough (The Hague: Kluwer, 1991), 371.

PART 1

Is the Empirical versus Transcendental Distinction Spurious?

Chapter 1

Some Difficulties
for Husserlian Phenomenology

Joseph Margolis

1

At the heart of Husserl's work there is a nest of puzzles of considerable strategic importance and difficulty that Jitendra N. Mohanty has addressed with his usual mix of matter-of-fact explication and completely unguarded candor. Mohanty always searches for a formulation that satisfies both a scruple for textual accuracy and a willingness to replace infelicities of any kind in whatever of Husserl's doctrines he does not abandon. For me, the charm of the argument lies not merely in confirming Husserl's profundity (which seems to me absolutely genuine) but also in confirming again and again that, by altogether different dialectical routes, I find Mohanty and me at more or less the same conundrum; and I, a beneficiary for having found Mohanty already there waiting for me. On the essential puzzle, it seems to me—I had suspected it before but lacked the evidence—that Mohanty's analysis of Husserl draws on his command of Indian philosophy and, possibly, that his grasp of the latter is informed by his reading of Husserl.

The great puzzle I have in mind is obliquely (but certainly not inessentially) approached by Mohanty's having raised the question of the relationship between the empirical and the transcendental ego in Husserl's philosophy. This he does quite pointedly in the very last remark of his book, *Phenomenology: Between Essentialism and Transcendental Philosophy,* which one cannot help sup-posing was meant to serve as a deliberate clue to a deeper connection that we can expect to learn more of in the offing. There, acknowledging the contested standing of the distinction and necessary linkage between the two concepts, which recalls the vexed issues Eugen Fink had posed in what is known as the "Sixth Meditation,"[1] and which may well "Kantianize" Husserl (perhaps with Husserl's acquiescing), Mohanty appeals to the analogy (at least) between *jīva* and *āman*. He notes that the characterization of the "empirical" "would serve no purpose" except in terms of the contrasted concept, and that the same is true of the "transcendental"; further, that in providing the contrast, "it is also necessary to get rid of the connection of 'transcendental' to the 'transcendent.' The Platonic two-world theory dies hard, [he adds] and once the two are separated, any attempt to put them together is destined to fail."[2]

I have always believed this dictum ought never to be set aside or diminished, though I apply it with an emphasis of my own in reading Husserl and Kant and—if I may say so—in analyzing Descartes' problematic realism, which I believe seriously infects both Kant and Husserl. In any case, I am happy to agree with Mohanty (and if possible, through him, with Vedantic views) in urging that, whether metaphysically, epistemologically, semantically, conceptually, psychologically, or phenomenologically, the resources of the one cannot be disjoined from the resources (and influence) of the other. I am not entirely sure, however, whether Mohanty would agree with me, if I also insist that to segregate the conceptual and cognitive resources of the one and the other *is, effectively, to reinstate "the Platonic two-world theory."*

To put my own conviction in a word, which Husserl would never allow and which I am uncertain Mohanty would countenance, the distinction between "empirical" and "transcendental" is a logical or conceptual distinction, a distinction of "philosophical grammar," *not* a distinction within any actual hierarchy of cognitive powers—freed, somehow, in the ascending direction at least, from operative constraints thought to be housed in the "lower" (empirical) competence. That cannot be true, I say, without violating the injunction against the two-world thesis.

The ulterior puzzle concerns what we should understand by "exists" or "existence" (as opposed to what is "real" but does not "exist"). As I see matters, whatever is real but does not exist is completely confined to predicative matters or, benignly, to what is nominalized from what is validly predicable: for example, the "objects" of a *noema* (in Husserl's sense)—or, better, *noemata* themselves—are, can be, no more than abstracted "parts" of real predicative distinctions (or nominalizations over such predicables).[3] If you agree, you must admit (you may wish to concur in any case) that the "empirical" and the "transcendental" are grammatical distinctions within the inclusive cognizing competence of human beings. I say "cognizing competence," in order to emphasize that the distinction between the "natural" and the "phenomenological," or between the "empirical" and the "transcendental" (which are hardly the same), is primarily an epistemological distinction, not a metaphysical one; although I am prepared to insist as well that the epistemological and the metaphysical cannot, in the final analysis, be conceptually disjoined. That is in fact precisely what I mean by intruding Descartes' paradoxes regarding realism into our critical reading of Kant and Husserl.

On Mohanty's reading, Husserl avoids both Platonism and idealism (in the technical sense now favored since Kant), and replaces the phenomenological analysis of "essences" by the analysis of "meanings" (*noemata*)—which disputatiously would have had to be the supervening "correlates" of would-be essences if the latter were thought to "constitute" the empirically intelligible world *ontically* (that is, the existent world). However, if I am right in this, then the analysis of "meaning" or *noema* (*not* to be identified with Frege's *Sinn*, as Mohanty warns) still permits us to speak of "essences" though now restricted to the epistemological or conceptual side of our encounter with the world. Husserl's maneuver would *never* be strong enough to raise the separate question of the existence *überhaupt* of *noemata* as distinct ideal or abstract individuals of any sort.

If this be granted, then I am prepared to argue that there may be (I think there is) a fatal difficulty in Husserl's program: in the precise sense that it would still be impossible for there to be a phenomenological analysis of the "essences" (or *noemata*) of existent things *that was not, qua phenomenological, already empirically encumbered through and through—and*, because of that, inoperative at the point of discerning the haecceity of each individual thing. Put another way, on the argument, there can be no disjunction between the empirical and the transcendental (or the natural and the phenomenological)—in either direction: they cannot be more than paired aspects of the same cognizing competence that admits that first-order, truth-bearing distinctions and second-order, legitimating distinctions are inseparable from one another (*pace* postmodernists like Rorty and Lyotard). And, if that were granted, we should be forced to admit the need for culturally contingent practices to provide tolerable but not confirmable grounds for fixing numerical identity. Failing that, we should have to rely on similar practices to ensure predicative success. I believe Husserl cannot escape these difficulties without abandoning one or another crucial thesis of his own, and I am frankly uncertain what Mohanty would offer from his side. The beauty of these puzzles is that they are among the most ancient puzzles of Western philosophy and have bedeviled contemporary analytic philosophy every bit as much as Husserl, though for very different reasons.

2

Mohanty offers two observations in explaining phenomenological "constitution" and its yielding, transcendentally, the "essences" of particular existent things. First, paraphrasing Husserl, he affirms, without qualification, that "all constitution is constitution of sense, not of thing. Creation, on the other hand, is creation of things."[4] We are to understand by this that Husserl escapes idealism precisely by distinguishing our positing (by eidetic experiment) the *noematic* sense (by which the actual experienced world is originally experienced) from the preposterous notion that the world is somehow created by such thoughts. Constituting is said to be "passive," speaking of the perceived world; that is, it is already implicated in what is experienced in everyday life, *and only then* recovered by being "reflectively isolated and fixed" phenomenologically—that is, by bracketing "existence."[5] In any case, the *noematic* is primarily occupied with predicated distinctions. I shall come back to that: it's the pressure point of the puzzle I have in mind. Second, Mohanty marks as an unavoidable philosophical "task"—not merely a phenomenological task, though it is that at least, and was that for Husserl—the need "to combine essentialism with change, history and open-endedness, and [to] set aside that meaningless picture of radical contingency, according to which just everything is possible next instant."[6]

I trust I may risk agreeing with Mohanty at this point (though it may surprise him), *if* I take what he says in the spirit in which he acknowledges that, "amongst philosophers of contingency, Merleau-Ponty recognizes the role of essences, even if that role is provisional" and that, "amongst historicist philosophers, Marx and Marxists (such as Adorno) have recognized that without essences in a purely nominalistic ontology, history would have no structure." It may be the same sense in which Mohanty holds that "in the heart of temporality, and of the flux-character of consciousness, Husserl discovered an abiding character: the forms of the living present."[7] At any rate, that is what I mean to test: I see a troublesome equivocation there.

Mohanty provides a pretty taxonomy of alternative views of essences, which assists my cause. First of all, he says, there is "the Platonic essence," which both Husserl and Mohanty reject—rightly I believe, not merely because of the two-world difficulty but because no one has ever satisfactorily explained how we may board the Platonic Forms epistemically. Second, there is the would-be essence of natural objects, "the Kripkean essence" (Mohanty says), as in holding that the essence of water is H_2O. It is clear from Mohanty's remarks that would-be natural essences are not demonstrably necessary *de re* or *de cogitatione*: we must always wait to see, he notes, whether "the theory holds up." I agree. The third and last option is that of "the phenomenological essence, the entire or part of the *what* of the real individual, as abstracted from its instantiations or embodiments in real existence, and as determined to be invariant amidst imaginative variations."[8] Thus, the question nags: Does Mohanty mean "invariant" in the sense that accommodates Merleau-Ponty and Marx (and, accordingly, Husserl) or does he mean that Merleau-Ponty, Marx, and Husserl themselves mean "invariant"—within flux and historicity—in some very strong modal sense?

I offer a dilemma for both Husserl and Mohanty: if it is the first, then Husserl's project fails, though not a phenomenology that admits the cognitive inseparability of the empirical and the transcendental; if it is the second, then Husserl fails again, because there can be no modal necessity recoverable by phenomenological reflections that already admit the reciprocal penetration of the empirical and the eidetic. Any third strategy requires the two-world thesis, because, of course, the three views of essences depend on the same predicative competence.

Here I note an important equivocation on the idea of "radical contingency." Mohanty uses the expression in a pejorative sense, as in speaking of "the meaningless picture of radical contingency, according to which just everything is possible next instant." I make out two senses of "radical contingency"—the same is true for "flux" and "historicity": one signifies an original "chaos," which Mohanty rejects (with my blessing, if I may say so); the other signifies no more than the denial of all *de re* and *de cogitatione* necessities. I know no one who seriously supports the first option, unless in something like the spirit of the *Timaeus* or Heraclitus's insertion of the *logos* in the flux or certain interpretations of God's Creation reported in Biblical texts. But the second option could not possibly support *any* modal invariance regarding the "constitution" of sense (in the sense supplied) and could not possibly disqualify our confining ourselves to experienced structures that *were not* modally necessary in any way. Why not? Where is the argument that shows that if the "world" is not a chaos, it must harbor, by the constitution of sense, modally invariant structures—or eidetic approximations to such invariances? I cannot find the argument, and I note with interest that Mohanty finds Foucault's "constitution" of "man" congenial to his own account of Husserl. Yet, he nowhere recovers invariance in Foucault.[9]

I am afraid I read Foucault's texts quite differently, though they are coherent enough. They suggest that we encounter new conceptual constellations from time to time in our historically changing experience—"passively," if you please—but *never* in a way that confirms *more* than an experiential "invariance" or salience, that is, a regularity for a time that, for all we know (and that history recommends we believe), may well be otherwise—and probably will appear to be otherwise in due course. Foucault acknowledges no more than the "historical *a priori*" (which has affinities with Husserl's own idiom), but now means no more than a working regularity within the continually reconstituted conceptual regime (discontinuous in that sense and in that sense alone).[10]

I call this a "philosophical bet," *not* a modally necessary universal or invariant structure that flux reveals. If Foucault meant the latter, then of course he would have spoken in a transparently self-defeating way. But even if he *had*, *we* can surely reconcile the doctrine of the flux with coherent thought and discourse. What has to be shown otherwise, whether in Husserl, Kant, or Aristotle, is that the denial of modal invariance must be paradoxical or self-defeating or simply self-contradictory. Aristotle fails to make the case in *Metaphysics* Gamma; Kant fails to demonstrate that his own synthetic *a priori* propositions must stand; and, as far as I can see, Husserl makes an explicit positive claim about invariance, *not* a *faute de mieux* disclaimer that cannot stand *if* the second reading of "radical contingency" proves coherent with respect to our discursive needs. I cannot see how it has been shown, or even could be shown, that Husserl's claim is inviolably true.

I am very close to formulating my principal objection to Husserl's theory. But before I venture it, I must mention Mohanty's characterization of those who support the doctrine of the flux, that is, the denial of necessary invariance, the denial of the necessity of admitting necessary invariance *de re* and/or *de cogitatione*. (I admit I am one of that company.) I must report in all candor that I do not find Mohanty's line of reasoning compelling here. In fact, it provides a clue to the essential weakness of Husserl's program—which, on the argument I have promised, marks a potential incoherence in Husserl's theory.

Mohanty chides the fluxists with holding, in effect, that the world is necessarily in flux (or with holding some weaker approximation to same). Of course, if they admitted that, they would be transparently inconsistent. The heart of the matter is that they *need not* hold that: they may favor no more than what I'm calling a "philosophical bet," namely, that no one will ever convincingly demonstrate that Husserlian (or Kantian or Aristotelian) or similar invariances *are* conceptually necessary.[11] Mohanty himself affirms the following: "temporality . . . has an abiding structure, and experience bears witness to both change and permanence of forms, structures, types, and patterns, even of the simplest qualia."[12] But that is to deny the option of the "bet," the possible sufficiency of experienced or salient regularities that are *not* yet shown to be, or to approximate, modal inflexibilities of any sort *and* that cannot be directly cognized as such. But where is the argument?

3

The key to understanding Husserl, Mohanty indicates, requires our grasping "that Husserl conceived of transcendental phenomenology as a science of essences as distinguished from sciences of facts: a science which aims exclusively at establishing 'knowledge of essences' and absolutely no 'facts', that is, 'a science of essential Being' (as 'eidetic' Science)."[13] I doubt that there is a bolder and more forthright reading of Husserl's intention than Mohanty's rendering of "phenomenological reduction." But I cannot see how there can be a science of essences separated from a science of facts. Mohanty is quite willing—in laying out the distinction between "*eidetic* reduction" and "phenomenological reduction," that is, differences in the depth and scope with which we "bracket" or "abstract from" experience, existence, belief, real and ideal entities, real individuals, and ideal essences—to declare that "with the bracketing, and consequent suspension—not denial—of belief in the world, the ego, identically the same ego [the natural or empirical or psychological ego], becomes a transcendental ego who seeks to uncover within his own reflective and prereflective experiencings the constitution of the sense of the world and of the things in the world."[14]

Certainly one of the most puzzling features of Husserl's undertaking concerns how to *reverse* (or to appear to reverse or to "recover") the apparently natural order of proceeding *from* empirical experience (or from putatively primordial or original experience) *to* a *noetic* grasp of its intentional structure, *within* psychological experience, *through* an ascending grasp of "essences," *through* deeper and deeper bracketings—which ultimately yields, *at* the "pure" phenomenological level, essences that constitute the "sense" of the essential or invariant experienced world.

Husserl anticipates, in *Ideas I* (on which Mohanty draws), that it will soon seem commonplace that "phenomenology (or eidetic psychology) is, methodologically, the basic science for empirical psychology." "The old ontological doctrine," he advises, namely, *"that the knowledge of possibilities must precede that of actualities* (*Wirtlichkeiten*) is, in my opinion, in so far as it is rightly understood and properly utilized, a really great truth."[15]

It is hard to see how this could possibly escape invoking something akin to the Platonic two-world theory that Mohanty rightly dismisses. Yet, if I understand him rightly, Mohanty refuses to allow any difference in number between the empirical and transcendental egos, only a difference in functional activity. On the argument I have suggested, that would disallow a hierarchy of disjoint cognitive powers assignable to one or the other "ego," and *that* would signify that phenomenological reflection could never convincingly be detached from the contingent encumbrances of the empirical and natural world. This is indeed the generic form of the puzzle I wish to press. Many, I think, have preceded me in sensing the puzzle.

Most readers of Husserl will have found Husserl's reduction of the real ego to the transcendental ego, as in the Fifth Meditation, decidedly problematic.[16] For, *if* following Mohanty, the empirical ego (the ego that manifests itself empirically) "becomes a transcendental ego," then the ultimate bracketing that yields pure phenomenology (the bracketing of the existent ego) cannot possibly go through; and if the transcendental ego's function completely displaces the empirical ego's function, then we surely must admit two different egos, and that would return us to the Platonic theory.

The point is this: without the required *epistemic* reduction, Husserl's conception of "the Cartesian ideal of a philosophy as an all-embracing science grounded on an absolute foundation" utterly founders. I freely concede that Husserl's idea of such a science is coherent enough—in a formal or conceptual sense—for, on Husserl's view, what we abstract from experience is already implicated in experience, in its constituting role.[17] Nevertheless we do begin empirically and, in Husserl's own words, finally justify positing what is "a necessary and indubitable beginning and an equally necessary and always employable method—whereby, at the same time, a systematic order of all senseful problems is predilineated."[18] I confess I cannot see how that can be achieved or even responsibly affirmed or approximated. For example, I cannot see how Husserl hopes to escape a condition akin to what Foucault sketches as the "historical *a priori.*"

Let me close this brief harangue by offering a few last words on what I think is the ultimate and specific weakness of Husserl's project, namely, the import of the relationship between *existence* and *essence.* You remember, of course, that Husserl presents phenomenology as a science of essences completely bracketed from facts, that is, from what concerns would-be truths about what actually exists. If what I have said before provides the generic argument against Husserl, what I now have in mind may be dubbed the specific argument. It makes itself felt if you concede two very powerful theorems familiar to those who have reflected on the ancient problems of denotation and predication, or of number and nature, or of individuation and being of a kind. The first affirms that nothing can be individuated by purely predicative means; and the second affirms that, paradigmatically, predication presupposes individuated *denotata.* The relevance of these considerations is entirely straightforward. If we suppose that, in the real world, what is individuatable must at least feature (even if it cannot be restricted to) what exists, then there is no epistemically accessible predicative competence that is not functionally tethered to the recognition of what exists. But if, according to Husserl (rightly enough), such predication belongs to the world of natural science, then phenomenology, as a science of essences, *cannot* have application to the real world except parasitically, that is, with respect to whatever can be individuated and reidentified as what exists. But if that is true, then, functionally, the realm of possibilities cannot be accorded priority over actuality, except on actuality's say-so. QED.

It has been known ever since Plato's *Philebus* and the medieval disputes involving Thomas Aquinas and Duns Scotus that there are serious (possibly insurmountable) difficulties in claiming to *know* individual entities *as* the unique entities they are. The only promising line of inquiry that provides for such knowledge (or at least for a tolerably workable practice that makes no pretense of specific knowledge) requires no more than a grasp of the operative conditions under which a society of individual selves identify themselves and the things of their world in at least a "story-relative" way (as Strawson says) within their effective practices. I won't attempt to pursue these complications here, but they obviously entrench the contingencies of actual historical life. The theme belongs to the tradition that links Hegel and Foucault.

On this same matter, Mohanty reports Husserl as holding the following two doctrines, which (he says) serve to distinguish Husserl's concept of essences from "the classical Platonic theories in at least two respects": "first, in its recognition of eidetic singularities; second, in recognizing that an individual has its own essence which is not the essence of another individual."[19]

Now, on the argument I have just offered, there is no known way, predicatively, by means of "essences" (or "meanings") of any familiar kind (whether Platonic or eidetic), to capture the unique individuality of any particular thing.

As far as I can see, Husserl must have realized that he would have to have a suitable substitute at the eidetic level (leading to a full phenomenological reduction of eidetic essences) if he were ever to free himself in the way he required from an obvious epistemic dependence on the empirical and natural order of things *at every point in the phenomenological ascent.* That now seems impossible to escape. The conditions stipulated knock out both of Husserl's doctrines. For, although eidetic essences are "embodied," not instantiated, in individuals, allowing that hardly clarifies the actual cognizing of any "nature" or "general nature" or "essence" or "general predicable." Predicative similarity calls for discerning a "unity" among "differences" and, avoiding Platonism, is known to be as difficult a puzzle as that of numerical identity. Both require the viable practices of a society of existing selves and preclude direct cognition. Admitting that, Husserl's doctrine seems a purely formal possibility; or, if thought to be more robust in epistemic terms, it cannot be more than a deviant form of Platonism. I cannot see any way to escape these difficulties.

Notes

1. See Eugen Fink, *Sixth Cartesian Meditation: The Idea of a Transcendental Theory of Method,* trans. Ronald Bruzina (Bloomington: Indiana University Press, 1988).
2. Mohanty, *Phenomenology,* 92-93.
3. Compare Mohanty, *Phenomenology,* chs. 1, 5.
4. Mohanty, *Phenomenology,* 91.
5. Mohanty, *Phenomenology,* 90.
6. Mohanty, *Phenomenology,* 90.
7. Mohanty, *Phenomenology,* 90.
8. Mohanty, *Phenomenology,* 90.
9. See, Mohanty, *Phenomenology,* 91; also, ch. 8.
10. See Michel Foucault, *The Order of Things: An Archaeology of the Human Sciences* (New York: Vintage, 1970), ch. 10.
11. See, further, Joseph Margolis, *Historied Thought, Constructed World: A Conceptual Primer for the Turn of the Millennium* (Berkeley: University of California Press, 1995).
12. Mohanty, *Phenomenology,* 89.
13. Mohanty, *Phenomenology,* 3. See Edmund Husserl, *Ideas: General Introduction to Pure Phenomenology,* trans. W. B. Boyce Gibson (New York: Collier Books, 1962), introduction, 40. I have taken the liberty of adding Husserl's phrasing just before the line Mohanty cites.
14. Mohanty, *Phenomenology,* 10.
15. Husserl, *Ideas,* §79 (213).
16. See *Cartesian Meditations,* Fifth Meditation, notably §44.
17. Husserl, *Cartesian Meditations,* Fifth Meditation, 96.
18. Husserl, *Cartesian Meditations,* Fifth Meditation, 152.
19. Mohanty, *Phenomenology,* 5-6.

Chapter 2

Essentialism, Phenomenology, and Historical Cognition

Tom Rockmore

The best way to honor the distinguished phenomenologist J. N. Mohanty is to address a central theme in his conception of phenomenology. The essentialist strategy for knowledge, which originates in ancient Greece and is central to some recent forms of philosophy, including phenomenology, is based on the idea that an appeal to essences is necessary to make out objective claims to know. This idea has recently been raised again in phenomenological terms by the distinguished phenomenologist J. N. Mohanty. In what follows, I will talk less about people than problems, in favor of turning away from a well-known, widely favored atemporal approach toward a historical approach to cognition. I will further argue that although the latter is inconsistent (on my interpretation) with the major varieties of essentialism, phenomenology cannot understand itself as historical if it continues to insist on essentialism.

Mohanty on Phenomenology and Essentialism

In a recent book (*Phenomenology: Between Essentialism and Transcendental Philosophy*), J. N. Mohanty calls attention to the problem of how to combine phenomenology—understood as essentialism—with change, history, and open-endedness without falling into radical contingency.[1] I think this is a general problem not only for phenomenology, some forms of which I favor, but for all forms of theory of knowledge, which need (as Mohanty suggests about phenomenology) to address the question of their relation to history, while maintaining a plausible view of cognitive objectivity.

Claims to know depend on the nature of the knower. It seems obvious that all knowledge is human knowledge and that human beings are finite, historical beings. If the knower is in all cases a real person, then claims to know can never surpass the capacities of human beings. If people are intrinsically historical, then it needs to be shown that claims to know are other than or more than historical, that is, beyond time and change.

The term "phenomenology," which is far from univocal, covers a vast multitude of sins. For obvious reasons, Husserlians prefer to include only Husserl and his followers as genuine members of the clan. Yet what Spiegelberg calls "The Phenomenological Movement," by which he ostensibly means the train of thought initiated by Husserl, is fraught with internal strains so great as to threaten the claim that this great family adheres to any single recognizable doctrine or set of doctrines.[2]

Husserl's conception of phenomenology is "officially" essentialist. In the programmatic text *Philosophy as Rigorous Science*, he typically identifies essences and essential relations with objective validity as the basis of empirical cognition and all cognition whatsoever.[3] At a minimum, this means that Husserl and, for this reason, Husserlian phenomenologists, are committed to essentialism. Yet all those committed to essentialism, even all phenomenologists committed to essentialism, are not Husserlians.

Is there an identifiable essence of essentialist phenomenology? Heidegger, his most famous student, is firmly opposed to his views in nearly every conceivable way. If Heidegger were right, Husserl would be wrong about a great many things, starting with the conception of the transcendental subject.[4] Through *Dasein*, Heidegger replaces this basic cornerstone of transcendental phenomenology with a rough conception of the subject as immanent.

In arguing against essentialism, I take myself not to be opposing but rather to be agreeing with Mohanty. I suspect that the main difference in our views lies in the fact that Mohanty is still, for many good reasons, more attached to Husserlian phenomenology than I ever was, and so is somewhat conflicted about how to deal with Husserlian essentialism. As someone appreciative of Husserl but not committed to any of his specific claims, I am not knowingly committed to anything resembling essentialism, hence perhaps more willing, maybe even too willing, to argue straightforwardly that essentialism is incompatible with the historical turn in phenomenology that is older than Husserl.

In his most recent book on the subject, Mohanty works out a phenomenological version of essentialism that may not correspond to his own position.[5] Elsewhere he develops a transition from essences to meanings understood, not as historically invariant but rather as dependent on what we take the thing to be about, something about which, as he concedes, we may simply be mistaken.[6] It may be, as Mohanty suggests, that essentialism, in at least some of its forms, cannot be reconciled with Husserl's position. One reason for this inference is, as he points out, that to adopt essentialism precludes making good on the concept of phenomenology as a presuppositionless science. Another is because historically variable meaning is the sense of Husserl's conception of *noema*. Yet if one gives up essentialism I see no way to make out a claim for apodicticity. I also detect no way to preserve the claim for phenomenology as the foundational discipline, which is, in Husserl's words, "the secret longing of the whole philosophy of modern times."[7] To adopt a revised view of the phenomenological method as clarifying meanings, which is eminently defensible, makes it equally difficult to understand essences, hence phenomenology, as Husserl does.[8]

What Is Phenomenology?

It sometimes seems as if there were as many views of "phenomenology" as there are phenomenologists. Even to discuss phenomenology in general, we will need to settle on an "average" view of it that is plausible across the board, so to speak.[9] Although such a conception will slight some approaches while favoring others, and perhaps be fully adequate to none, it is the only one which holds any promise of even raising the issue in general fashion.

We can start by noting that in phenomenology, as elsewhere in the philosophical discussion, interpretive charity is unfortunately not a widespread philosophical virtue. Normative views tend to correspond to their author's vision while retiring all other conceptions; if strictly followed, the normative view of phenomenology as basically Husserlian, eliminates several figures including: Heidegger, Husserl's most persistent critic; Sartre, whose realism is intended to contradict Husserlian idealism; Merleau-Ponty, for whom the reduction cannot be more than regulative; and my own favorite phenomenologist, Hegel. Interestingly, in France, at least until recently, not only were Hegel, Husserl, and Heidegger all thought to be phenomenologists, but Hegel and Husserl were even notoriously thought to have the same method. Yet whether Hegel can have anything so grand as a specifiable method in light of his criticism of Kant's distinction between the process of knowledge and the general conditions of knowledge is a controversial interpretive issue.

What does "phenomenology" mean? Is there a common essence to the term? One idea, apparently common to all forms of phenomenology, originates in the Cartesian conviction that claims to know must arise from the perspective of the subject. The suggestion that phenomenological claims to know must be first person claims does not help us much and creates new problems. This hint allows us to group together such phenomenologists as Hegel, Husserl, and Heidegger, but it also suggests that we include under this rubric many others, such as Descartes and Kant, who are not usually regarded as phenomenologists, or the British empiricists, who normally fall outside of even the widest, most charitable construal of "phenomenology."

My own approach to phenomenology derives from my understanding of knowledge as deriving from the first person experience of the cognitive subject. By "subject" I have in mind one or more finite human beings. Since I reject the idea of knowledge as such in favor of human knowledge, I favor an epistemological approach centered on the cognitive subject. I hold that claims to know can never surpass what we can reasonably attribute to humans beings singly or in groups. Now as I understand it, essentialism precisely violates this criterion in making absolute claims to know that go beyond anything people can do more than dream about, as in the famous series of Cartesian dreams of perfect knowledge that continue to bewitch the modern philosophical discussion. This same alluring, but implausible, dream peaks in Kant, recurs in Husserl, and still attracts numerous contemporary analytic writers raised on the epistemological hopes of Frege, the early Wittgenstein, and Moore.

What Is Essentialism?

As for phenomenology, so for essentialism there is no alternative to adopting an "average" conception in order to discuss it in general. In different ways, essentialism goes back in the tradition at least to Plato. He often says that we must know the definition (*eidos*), for instance, the definition of virtue,[10] in order to pick out the thing. In more Fregean language, this amounts to a semantic claim that sense determines reference.

Essentialism has had a checkered career ever since Plato. Aristotle is generally regarded as giving a strong boost to essentialism in his question about what it is to be a thing (*to ti en einai*) and in his distinction between predication *kat'auto* and *kata symbebekos*. For Aristotle, who restricts definition to universals, there are no individual essences. He maintains that some universals are essential to what an object is and some are inessential, or merely contingent. Leibniz is usually understood as insisting that each individual has an essence peculiar to it. Recent discussions of essentialism in the context of the problem of semantic reference, focussing on *de re* modality, or necessary truth in all possible worlds, is very different from the Aristotelian and post-Aristotelian focus on what something is and how it is.

In Mohanty's account, truths about contingent particulars presuppose necessary truths about essences, described as the "apodictic foundational framework that is presupposed by all empirical cognition."[11] Apparently, he believes, or at least believes that the argument for essentialism requires him to affirm, that fallible empirical cognition is grounded in an infallible cognitive framework. What that means is not at all clear. My puzzlement can be captured in a series of questions about the relation between empirical cognition, which is fallible, and the cognitive framework, which on Mohanty's view is infallible: Why must fallible cognition require an infallible framework? What would such a framework look like? How could it be identified? If cognition is human cognition, how can it be infallible? Is there any reason to think that anything human beings know or can know meets this criterion?

Mohanty, who is aware of the problems, distinguishes three kinds of essentialism according to whether the essence is posited as unknowable within experience (Plato), or as a theoretical entity within a scientific theory (Kripke), or finally as experiencable and experienced (Husserl). He reminds us that for Husserl, the so-called phenomenal essences are given unreflectively in everyday experience, used even by those who deny them,[12] and isolated reflectively through the technique of imaginative variation.

These three kinds of essentialism are dissimilar. Plato is usually understood to hold that the epistemological knowledge of particulars depends on an onto-logical relation of participation (*methexis*). He is routinely taken as suggesting that ideas are the condition of knowledge of what he calls appearances, although on grounds of nature and nurture some among us can in principle directly grasp reality as the necessary condition of knowledge. Kripke, who is concerned with definite reference, which he calls rigid designation, addresses essentialism as the intuitive belief in modality *de re,* that is, as a claim that necessarily holds in all possible worlds. Husserl maintains that we can and do pick out particulars in virtue of a prior grasp of universals.

Is there a common thread in these three forms of essentialism? Perhaps it is the idea that it is only on the basis of *a prior* universal that we can identify a particular as one, or in current jargon, as a token of a type. The alternative is not feasible since, according to Mohanty, anti-essentialism is only a species of psychological reductionism starting with "bare particulars which [do] not exem-plify or embody types,"[13] something which sounds very much like, even indis-tinguishable from, nominalism. If I understand him correctly, Mohanty is suggesting that the choice is one between the alternatives of essentialism and nominalism which, taken together, exhaust the universe of discourse.

Phenomenology and Essentialism

There is no point in attempting to defend, or even to discuss, nominalism as a theory of knowledge.[14] The suggestion, familiar in Kant and later writers, that a denial of essentialism amounts to psychologism, or psychological reduction-ism, is significant if and only if a firm distinction can be drawn between the logical and psychological conditions of knowledge. This distinction is more often invoked than grasped. Certainly Kant was notoriously unsuccessful in isolating what we in fact do from the general conditions of knowledge, which the critical philosophy continually conflates. Perhaps, as I believe, such a distinction cannot be drawn in practice, since all logical conditions must be met by human knowers and there are no other cognitive subjects.

If we bracket this problem to concentrate on essentialism, it is not clear what it contributes to a theory of knowledge. Why do we even need to appeal to it? If a firm distinction cannot be drawn between the logical and the psychological conditions of knowledge, the answer cannot be to avoid psychol-ogical reductionism. Other than nominalists such as Goodman, few writers are likely to reject general concepts, although many more would balk at universals or essences. It is indeed difficult to talk without using concepts since, as Hegel reminds us, language is composed of words that have at least general intent. But to admit that we appeal to concepts does not necessarily tell us anything useful about either concepts or knowledge.

What role do concepts play in knowledge? A Husserlian claim that the empirical is preserved in the transcendental is problematic. If one takes the reduction as putting existence out of bounds, it is unclear how to preserve (or perhaps to reacquire) a link to the empirical world. On the contrary, if existence remains after the reduction, then the latter is at best incomplete.

There is an obvious difference between essences, or universals—for present purposes I am using "universal" and "essence" as synonymously— which I reject, and generals, or general ideas, which I favor. I understand the former as the type of objects identified in Plato's theory of forms, for instance as stated in his *Parmenides*.[15] This amounts to the view that we require universals that are beyond time and place in order to identify particulars. By "generals" I have in mind ideas, or concepts, which are not beyond time and place but that derive their cognitive utility from their temporary acceptance at a given time and place; for instance in a club, a town, a nation, a profession, among partisans of a particular approach, and so on. Essences, or universals, are in time but not of time—indestructible, unchangeable, fixed, inalterable, they neither come into being nor pass away. General ideas, or general concepts, are in time and of time—mutable, impermanent, malleable, alterable—they come into being and pass away.

Arguments for essentialism see it as offering the only plausible way to make out claims for objective knowledge. A powerful reason to invoke essences, either in the form of Platonic ideas, Aristotelian universals, or Kantian *a priori* categories, is to be able to know something unchangeable, hence beyond time and place and for that reason immune to the flux. Since Aristotle, the Platonic concept of a universal has been criticized as being vulnerable to the so-called third man argument. Let us, however, for present purposes, suppose that the idea of a universal or essence can be successfully stated.

Plato and later essentialists of all kinds share a concern to bring a given object under a universal in order to identify it. The argument against the essentialist view of cognitive objectivity in its Platonic form can be made by showing that objective claims to know need not invoke essences. In my view, the kind of essentialism which arises in Plato and many, perhaps all, later essentialists is not descriptive of anything that occurs in experience, but rather a (transcendental) deduction intended to describe what must be the case.

For Plato, the problem is simple. We identify, say, a hammer as one in virtue of its exemplification of an ideal, essence, or concept. Plato's claim seems to rest on two points unrelated to the attack on psychologism which develops in Kant's wake.[16] On the one hand, independently existing ideas offer both the ontological condition of appearance as well as the epistemological condition of their identification. On the other hand, there is, or in principle can be, direct knowledge of independent reality underlying appearances.

Both these claims seem false. There seems to be no good reason to invoke an independent realm of reality to explain either the existence or knowledge of appearances; in a word, no reason to invoke anything more than what is itself given in experience. It follows there is no reason to appeal to such universals as fixed essences to understand knowledge. In my view, the most economical explanation is that our mutable ideas emerge from, and remain relative to, the sociohistorical context. Since we do not need unchanging Platonic universals to identify particulars, we do not require a priori concepts to function in daily life. At most, we require ideas that are relatively stable against the changing background in which they arise and against which we apply them.

This has not always been understood, particularly by phenomenologists in our century. Phenomenologically, anything like the Platonic claim that we know particulars in terms of a fixed a priori essence presupposes a false description of what in fact occurs.

Writing more than two millennia after Plato, Heidegger is less than clear about his response, as illustrated by his famous discussion of the hammer in *Being and Time*.[17] Anyone who reads his discussion carefully will be aware that Heidegger is of two minds, so to speak. He is never able to decide whether we identify the hammer as a hammer in terms of a property it uniquely possesses, such as being able to deliver blows to nails, as in realism, or whether we in some way construct the capacity we attribute to a given object we then call a hammer, as in idealism.

I would like to suggest that for a phenomenologist the latter is the proper response. With the important exception of Kant, most empirical realists simply ignore the way we perceive what we ourselves in a sense "construct" against the background of the prevailing context. It seems obvious that we do not identify particulars independent of perspective, facts or apart from context. There is no fact of the matter, as Quine famously says. To take only a single, but familiar example, a chair is only identifiable for someone who has lived in, or is at least familiar with, societies in which such objects exist. It is on the basis of such experience that one is able to pick out a chair as a chair. Otherwise, it is simply an unfamiliar, unrecognizable object.

Some Consequences of Contextualism

I believe it is a deep mistake to think that claims to know are ever unrelated to the context in which they emerge and through which they are justified. If that is true, then three consequences follow. First, both the objects and the concepts that designate them are contextual in a sense to be specified. Neither the concept chair nor the object that exemplifies it is an invariable universal or an equally invariable essence. Both are at most locally stable but historically variable, since they change over time. We understand the idea corresponding to the word "chair" differently in different times and places, and we do not require a further universal chair to which the various contextualized concepts refer on either epistemological or ontological grounds. Meanings are constituted and change within a historical context. As concerns meanings and, *a fortiori,* concepts, there is at best, as Wittgenstein suggests, a family resemblance, although sometimes the differences are so great as to make it difficult to see what links together the different instances.

Second, we do not need, or ever actually utilize, essences in the specifically Husserlian or other main senses of the term since in practice we employ general ideas that are meaningful against the background of a particular social context. General ideas do all the work we need to permit us to identify particulars, to the extent that they can be identified at all. As even Kripke realizes, identification is mainly informal but not formal; identification is often linguistic in character. Yet if Hegel is correct, it never suffices to identify particulars in any formal manner because language is general. Further, a theory of concepts needs to account for mistakes, which cannot be done if claims to know are apodictic in any usual meaning of this term. There is always the possibility of misidentification, of outright mistakes, through misconstruing a concept, misperceiving an object, and so on.

Third, it seems obvious that what is contextual is also historical, hence historically variable. Wittgenstein's suggestion in *On Certainty* that claims are true or false relative to a context falls short of recognizing that contexts are themselves subject to change. One way to put the point is that first-order constative claims are always indexed to time and place, in a word, relative to the historical moment. The claim that, say, Euclidean geometry describes real space was only true, if it was ever true, before the discovery of non-Euclidean geometry.[18]

Essentialism and Phenomenology

Essentialism has been hotly debated in this century. Despite the obvious difficulties, phenomenologists have often appealed to various conceptions of essence as if the concept itself were unproblematic, and the only difficulty lay in choosing the right interpretation, in order to justify claims to objective knowledge. I believe that the results of the essentialist approach in phenomenology have often been meager and that the very practice, far from justifying the legitimacy of claims to know, is open to profound abuses.

It is difficult to justify so much of what passes for phenomenological seeing as opposed to the endless discussion about it. Few phenomenologists seem to be very good at this practice. Whereas Sartre's brilliant discussions of looking through a keyhole are genuinely enlightening, I believe that Husserl's rare efforts, such as his attempt to understand Galileo's mathematization of nature, are not. At the risk of heresy, I submit that more can be learned by reading Galileo or numerous philosophers of science than by reading Husserl on this theme. Heidegger's efforts to identify existentialia range from genuinely enlightening to the phenomenologically indefensible, most notably in his politically "opportunistic" but philosophically debatable revision of the concept of silence, when his own silence in the face of the Holocaust became an issue, as the only authentic mode of speech.[19]

To say that an essence cannot be reduced to mere existence only raises the question of how to differentiate an essence, any essence, from a mere appearance (as Hegel remarked about Kant's view of morality, from one's personal inclinations) unless one resorts to empirical considerations. Heidegger provides an interesting, albeit contentious, example. One could argue that his decision to rally to Nazism and his continued adherence, even after he had withdrawn from real Nazism, to what we can call ideal Nazism, results from a dismal failure to perceive the nature, an essentialist would say the essence, of National Socialism. This point motivates the suggestion of a recent defender, Julian Young, who is concerned with defending Heidegger at all cost, to contend that Nazism has no essence.[20] Young's aim is obviously to free Heidegger from the reproach based on his manifest inability to grasp what he himself, in an infamous affirmation of Nazi faith in *An Introduction to Metaphysics,* euphemistically calls the movement (*die Bewegung*).[21] The problem of distinguishing between an essence and a mere appearance is only compounded by Miguel de Beistegui's sober account of Heidegger's three efforts to think the political, which progressively loses contact with anything resembling politics as we know it.[22] We are left with the intractable difficulty of separating what a given person, in this case Heidegger, in fact thought was essential at different periods, from what is essential. But, then, perhaps there is no difference, in which case the very concept of an invariant essence becomes difficult to maintain.

General Ideas, History, and Cognitive Objectivity

As concerns essence, I have so far made two suggestions: First, we do not need essences to make out claims to know since general ideas indexed to the historical background are sufficient; second, we in fact operate with such ideas and not with essences. If we rely on general ideas instead of universals, we need to ask ourselves what remains of objective cognition, a feature obviously required by any theory of knowledge.

Recently, the claim that to know is to know in an absolute sense, or absolutely, has been frequently voiced: in Thomas Nagel's view from nowhere;

in Bernard Williams' absolute conception; in Robert Nozick's idea of invariance under transformation. According to Nagel, a view becomes more objective as subjectivity, that is, the individual, is (somehow)—it is never made clear how— subtracted from it to reveal reality independent of the self.[23] According to Williams, we must seek to depict independent reality, and science in fact succeeds in doing so.[24] According to Nozick, objective knowledge claims are invariant through any transformation.[25] In my view, each of these claims reveals an unworkable commitment to a theoretical standard, a form of Platonism, which cannot be (fully) realized in practice.

The venerable idea that to know is to know independent reality as it is underlies Platonism, echoes through the later discussion, for example, in Kant's famous letter to Herz, where he describes his task as understanding the relation of the representation to the (independent) object.[26] Yet there is no way to know reality as it is, either by somehow "subtracting" subjectivity to reveal objectivity, or showing rather than simply asserting that science reveals the way the world is, or even by identifying objects or laws invariant on all levels.

Failing the capacity to know reality, we must fall back on the application of whatever procedures we have available in the different disciplines, such as poetry, philosophy, or physics, to identify our claims to know against the background of the ongoing discussion in a particular discipline. Pierce clearly saw that claims to know are always relative to what those working in the discipline think at a given point in that dialogue.[27] Cognitive objectivity does not disappear when we give up essentialism, although it is reworked as relative to claims that are never fixed but always in flux.

A Husserlian Response and a Rejoinder

This paper has been examining a generally Platonic view of essentialism. I have so far argued that we get along fine without essences while suggesting a different notion of cognitive objectivity located within rather than outside history. My overall point is that the problem is not how to go from essentialism, or the basis of objective claims to know, to history, but how to go from history to objective claims to know.

My overall claim is that Platonic, or strong, essentialism fails and that, properly understood, historicism can provide an adequate replacement view for it. I am willing, however, to acknowledge, but not yet to concede, Mohanty's interesting remark that the replacement doctrine is perhaps fairly described as weak essentialism.[28] It is unclear whether my criticism applies to Husserl, in part because it is unclear what his mature view is. I have been assuming that Husserl's presuppositionless form of foundationalist essentialism is basically Platonic.

One could counter this criticism by maintaining that Husserl finally breaks with Platonism as concerns the nature of the essence. In anticipating the criticism I have been making, Husserl rejects any conflation of object and empirical object, or reality and empirical reality in favor, ultimately, of the principle of all principles as mandating acceptance of what is given in intuition.[29] His response clearly presupposes the correctness of his own position, more precisely his elaboration of the Kantian form of anti-psychologism on which he insists as early as the *Logical Investigations*. Yet this possible response will not suffice because it rests on a distinction between what a phenomenological subject must do in order to make out Husserlian phenomenology and what finite human beings are known to be capable of doing. Although I cannot make the argument here, suffice it to say that I see no way to bring together what finite human beings are capable of and the "pure" philosophical subject, for instance as a Cartesian *cogito*, as the subject of transcendental phenomenology, or as Kant's transcendental unity of apperception.

Conclusion: Essentialism, Phenomenology, and History

I have argued that essentialism is beset with intractable difficulties and unnecessary, and that we should give up universals for general ideas. We began by considering Mohanty's concern to combine essentialism with history. If knowledge is historical knowledge, then it cannot be essentialist. If, as Mohanty suggests, and I concur, phenomenology needs to turn toward history, then to understand phenomenology as intrinsically historical we must abandon essentialism, at least as it has usually been understood.

Notes

1. Mohanty, *Phenomenology*, 90.
2. See Herbert Spiegelberg, *The Phenomenological Movement: A Historical Introduction* (The Hague: Martinus Nijhoff, 1982).
3. See Edmund Husserl, *Philosophy as Rigorous Science*, in *Phenomenology and the Crisis of Philosophy*, trans. Quentin Lauer (New York: Harper and Row, 1965), 116.
4. See *Cartesian Meditations*, Fourth Meditation, 65-88, especially §§ 33-34, 67-72.
5. He usefully points out that Husserl defends a view of essence as equivalent to meaning in the first edition of *Logical Investigations* and a view of essence as distinct from essence in the second edition. See Mohanty, *Phenomenology*, 46.
6. See Mohanty, *Transcendental Phenomenology*.
7. Husserl, *Ideas*, §62, 166.
8. See *Transcendental Phenomenology*, 36.
9. Janicaud has recently raised the question from the perspective of

identifying an appropriate minimalist program for phenomenology. See Dominique Janicaud, *La Phénoménologie écatée* (Paris: Editions de l'Eclat, 1998).

10. See for example, *Meno,* 70A-71A, in *Five Dialogues of Plato,* trans. G. M. A. Grube (Indianapolis: Hackett, 1981), 59-60.

11. Mohanty, *Phenomenology,* 88.

12. See Husserl, *Ideas,* § 22, 80-82.

13. Mohanty, *Phenomenology,* 90.

14. See for example, Nelson Goodman, *Ways of Worldmaking* (Indianapolis: Hackett, 1978).

15. See Parmenides 130 E-133 B, in *Plato and Parmenides: Parmenides' Way of Truth and Plato's Parmenides,* trans. F. M. Cornford (Indianapolis: Library of Liberal Arts, no date), 84-95.

16. See Martin Kusch, *Psychologism: A Case Study in the Sociology of Philosophical Knowledge* (London: Routledge, 1995).

17. See Martin Heidegger, *Being and Time,* trans. John Macquarrie and Edward Robinson (New York: Harper and Row, 1962), § 15, 95-102.

18. Reichenbach, for instance, suggests it was never true; pure geometry is exact but not descriptive of real space, whereas applied geometry is inexact but describes real space. See Hans Reichenbach, *The Philosophy of Space and Time,* trans. Maria Reichenbach and John Freund (New York: Dover, 1958).

19. See Martin Heidegger, *Beiträge zur Philosophie* (Vom Ereignis), ed. Friedrich-Wilhelm von Hermann (Freiburg i. B.: Vittorio Klostermann, 1989), 510.

20. See Julian Young, *Heidegger, Philosophy, Nazism* (New York: Cambridge University Press, 1997).

21. See Martin Heidegger, *An Introduction to Metaphysics,* trans. Ralph Manheim (New Haven: Yale University Press, 1977, 199).

22. See Miguel de Beistegui, *Heidegger and the Political: Dystopias* (London: Routledge, 1998).

23. See Thomas Nagel, *The View from Nowhere* (New York: Oxford University Press, 1986).

24. See Bernard Williams, *Ethics and the Limits of Philosophy* (Cambridge, Mass: University Press, 1985).

25. See Robert Nozick, "Invariance and Objectivity," in *Proceedings and Addresses of the American Philosophical Association,*72, no. 2, November 1998, 21-48.

26. See Letter to Herz, in *Immanuel Kant, Philosophical Letters,* 1759-99, trans. Arnulf Zweig (Chicago: University of Chicago Press), 70-76.

27. "The Fixation of Belief," in *The Essential Peirce,* (eds.), Nathan Houser and Christian Kloesel (Bloomington: Indiana University Press, 1992), 109-123.

28. See Mohanty, *Phenomenology,* 89.

29. See, for example, Husserl, *Ideas,* § 22, 80-2, § 61, 163-5.

Chapter 3

The Similarities and Differences between Descriptive and Interpretative Methods in Scientific Phenomenological Psychology

Amedeo Giorgi

Introduction

Husserl[1] ultimately envisioned phenomenology as a transcendental and descriptive enterprise. Both dimensions have been criticized by followers and opponents alike, which has led to interpretive positions that often coalesce into a movement know as hermeneutic or interpretive phenomenology. This latter movement has been almost universally adopted by social or human scientists who wish to ground their concrete work in phenomenological philosophy. On the surface there seems to be a certain worldliness and modesty about hermeneutic phenomenology that is attractive to the mentality of present day social scientists, perhaps highly influenced by the temper of present-day postmodern views. The language and position of Husserl, on the other hand, seems off-putting and dogmatic since much of his writing is influenced by a quest for certitude.

J. N. Mohanty, however, is a philosopher who has situated himself within the context of the descriptive-transcendental Husserlian project and has argued cogently for the viability of the approach. To be sure, he has modified some of Husserl's specific ideas and even turned over some others because of the force of the criticisms put forward (for example, essences as *de dicto* instead of *de re*), but he has not given up on the approach itself. The modifications and changes he has added to the Husserlian corpus were all made to be consistent with the descriptive-transcendental perspective.

Now when I speak of scientific phenomenology, I refer to a field of study in which scientists want to situate themselves within phenomenological philosophy but who nevertheless want to conduct analyses that would be appropriate for scientific disciplines. One way of appreciating what I am trying to do is to consider the following questions: Can phenomenological philosophy be the basis for a scientific outlook and praxis? Or, is empirical philosophy the only philosophy that can found a science even if it is, practically speaking, the only one that has done so thus far, historically speaking? If other philosophies can also found sciences, what are the steps that they must go through? Can phenomenological philosophy allow those steps to be implemented? There is really no precedent for this effort. All the questions and answers have to be posed almost simultaneously, and the parameters constraining and guiding the scientific activities have to be established since one often practices in the breach.

Since I am a psychologist, I want to use phenomenological thought to help me ground the discipline of psychology which, since it broke away from nineteenth-century philosophy, has been trying to operate as a natural science. While it has had partial success and that approach has enabled it to become institutionalized within academia, many psychological critics over the past century have been dubious about its ultimate success under such self-interpretation. However, I try to avoid the term "phenomenological psychology" because Husserl[2] used that term for his 1925 summer lectures and it means something different for him. Basically, Husserl substituted the term for a branch of philosophy that used to be called "rational psychology." One could also call Husserl's lectures, as Scanlon[3] does, reflections on philosophy of mind or essays in phenomenological philosophy. However, if I were to use the term "phenomenological psychology" I would mean a type of scientific psychology that draws all of its fundamental principles from phenomenological philosophy and practices both research and other applied activities strictly on the basis of phenomenological philosophical principles and guidelines. Thus, it would be a scientific psychology whose concepts and practices would be based entirely upon phenomenological philosophical principles and ideas. However, this would not be a direct application of philosophical phenomenology to psychology. The effort would be mediated by the criteria of science and certain modifications would have to be introduced.

The issue then becomes, which interpretation of phenomenological philosophy best lends itself to this task? As I said earlier, most social scientists seem to favor the interpretive phenomenological approach for this task, but for many reasons, I would rather operate within the descriptive-transcendental tradition because I believe that the highest standards of science can be achieved within that perspective. Too often qualitative research, an approach that I believe is necessitated by phenomenological principles (although I don't believe that quantification is excluded in principle) is seen as "soft science" or a poorer version of science. For me, the descriptive-transcendental perspective offers strong, logically coherent arguments for reinventing and redescribing science along strictly descriptive lines. A philosophy like descriptive-transcendental phenomenology would be necessary to establish the human or social sciences as coequal to the sciences of nature.

The Phenomenological Method Designed for Scientific Psychological Analysis

Husserl's phenomenological method can be said to be carried out in three steps: First, one assumes the attitude of the *phenomenological reduction*, which means that one takes whatever is given to be present such as it is without claiming that it exists the way it is presented, and it implies that no arbitrary presuppositions concerning the given are entertained. Second, with the help of free imaginative variation, one determines the *essence* of the given, and third, one *describes* the essences within the constraints of the given evidence.

In order to meet the three phenomenological criteria of phenomenological reduction, essential determination and description and at the same time meet general scientific criteria, I have modified the method in the following way. I shall try to be brief, since I have described this method elsewhere and it is not the main point of this essay.[4]

The first step requires that a person describes a concrete experience from the perspective of the natural attitude. Obviously, this means that the phenomenological psychologist has to analyze the experience of the other as described, and it seems to violate the dictum that requires everything that is to be analyzed be given directly to the phenomenologist's experience. Nevertheless, I do believe that this step can be phenomenologically justified.

First of all, it should be noted that the reason that descriptions of experiences from others is required is to meet a criterion of contemporary science. While the philosophical tradition is more tolerant of self-produced descriptions, the scientific tradition would not allow one to get beyond the first step. The unanswerable question to the phenomenological researcher would be: How do I know that your description is not unconsciously in the service of your theory? While phenomenologists could satisfactorily answer that question, it is almost impossible for researchers to do so and still maintain standard empirical criteria for doing science. However, there were additional benefits to not taking the strict phenomenological path and attempting to justify it. For one thing, I have to confess that I received descriptions of learning that I could not have imagined and, for another, my learning examples could be extended to other languages and other cultures. A phenomenologist, of course, maintains that the point of departure can be either empirical or imaginary examples.[5] A case can be made that the phenomenological approach has been extended by legitimating the analyses of the experience of others.

The one philosopher who has seen this problem most clearly is Spiegelberg.[6] Spiegelberg was impressed by the achievements of certain psychiatrists (for example, Jaspers, Straus) with respect to mental patients and who tended to credit phenomenology for their achievements. However, Spiegelberg knew that these men were not themselves "schizophrenic" or "paranoid" and so he wondered how the phenomenological method, which, as stated before, required that the phenomenon be given directly to one's own experience, could have helped researchers gain such insights. Spiegelberg, obviously, was aware that Husserl tried to legitimate access to intersubjectivity via his theory of appresentation as well as his notion of empathy. Spiegelberg found these attempts at legitimating "direct access" to the experiences of others difficult and limiting, but Spiegelberg basically affirms the effort.

The coverage of all of the aspects of this issue could be an article in itself, so I do not want to dwell on it too much, but I would like to bring closure to the issue by briefly noting Spiegelberg's and my own solution to the problem. Spiegelberg offers two solutions: imaginative self-transposal and cooperative encounter. For Spiegelberg, imaginative self-transposal is: "A peculiar style of occupying the place of the other by our transformed self, not a complete fusion for good, but one which allows us to shuttle back and forth between our own understanding self and that of the other who is to be understood. At the same time we shall have to mobilize our critical faculties in order to avoid the pitfalls of imaginative license."[7] The second strategy that Spiegelberg suggests is cooperative encounter or cooperative exploration. What this implies is that the researcher enters into a "specific cooperative relationship" with the person who experiences the phenomenon and they "embark on a joint exploration of phenomena" which only the subject experiences directly, while the researcher "can do so only through the subject."[8] It is interesting to note that this problem announces itself within a scientific context and that both of Spiegelberg's solutions are borrowed from therapeutic practices.

Elements of Spiegelberg's solution are present in my solution as well, but I add the idea of *noematic* clues. The "imaginative self-transposal" is part of the attitude that the researcher adopts when analyzing the description. The "cooperative encounter" part is the research interview wherein the researcher attempts to get as full and concrete a description of the phenomenon of interest as possible. What I also add is the fact that descriptions also reveal aspects of the situation as phenomenal *noematic* clues that can be correlated with acts that constituted them. Moreover, these *noematic* clues appear directly to the researcher's consciousness as phenomenal givens and it is precisely the phenomenon (not the objective situation nor an abstract mental process) that is revealed to the researcher. With the help of free imaginative variation, what is essential about the concrete experience can be discovered. In other words, the description of the experience contains expressions that release concrete meanings directly accessible to the consciousness of the researcher, and these form the basis of the imaginative variations whereby the essential structure of the experience appears to the consciousness of the researcher. For example, a person describing learning how to drive a car stated that the car seemed "huge" to him and it did not seem to "be steady and go straight," etc. After having learned, the car seemed normal and holding the steering wheel in the usual way was sufficient to produce straightness. But one knows that physical things do not expand and shrink and that holding a car wheel firmly will guide it straightly. Thus, a researcher does not have to be a direct experiencer of that situation to understand that for a beginning driver there can be *noematic* meanings that distort the givens of a situation because of anxiety or fearfulness. What is involved here is not the projection of the researcher's personal experience into that situation, but rather a sensitivity to the demand characteristics of such a situation and how one, in general, might respond to it. The researcher's sensitivities as a scientist also has implications for the idea of presuppositionlessness, but we cannot go into that thorny problem here.

Even if all of these attempts at justification are faulty or flawed, the implication for me would be to make better efforts to legitimate the analysis of the experiences of others rather than deny the effort, because otherwise a rich source of data will be lost to phenomenology. Spiegelberg concluded one of his articles on this problem by saying:

> What is more, I have come to see that this [phenomenological analysis of the experiences of others] is also an opening for an enlarged phenomenology which need not be a diluted phenomenology. There is every reason not to embark on it rashly and to keep up one's guard. But there is also no good reason for being a phenomenological purist and for barring the road to a genuine phenomenology with a wider and richer scope.[9]

In any case, in that step, the descriptive criterion is met in two senses: not only is the research participant descriptive, but the researcher also provides findings that are completely descriptive in nature.

It was mentioned in passing that the researcher adopted the viewpoint of the phenomenological reduction. However, this is not the transcendental reduction, but the psychological phenomenological reduction. In this, only the objects of the experience are reduced, not the acts. Thus, it is really a partial reduction. The objects or worldly aspects of the situation are considered as intentional objects, but the acts are considered to be correlated with an existing, worldly subjectivity. This is how the criterion of the phenomenological reduction is met.

Finally, the goal of essential intuition is still maintained, but also in modified form. Because the operation here takes place at the level of scientific phenomenology, the priority is first given to the disciplinary perspective, in this case psychology, and then the phenomenological criteria are brought into play. Consequently, in seeking essential intuition it is the psychological essence that is being sought and not the more absolute philosophical one. The method of free imaginative variation is still employed, but it is constrained by the disciplinary perspective. To appreciate this, the reader can imagine trying to obtain the psychological, sociological, and anthropological essence of learning. One can sense that there would be significant differences, and behind them, of course, a more universal essence of learning would be presupposed.

I maintain that the above method meets the Husserlian criteria of description, reduction, and essential intuition and so phenomenological claims can be made for it. The modifications introduced were done in order to meet scientific criteria and the claim is also made that "this is achieved" with this method, but the demonstration of that point is not required for this essay.

Objections to The Descriptive Method

In a previous article,[10] I argued that the above method was a legitimate alternative to interpretive methods, although the latter also had their legitimacy. Based upon Mohanty's[11] writings on philosophical description and his defense of transcendental philosophical approaches, I defended the scientific descriptive phenomenological method against criticisms that tried to state that the very application of the method was not possible. It is one thing to express a preference for a method; quite another to claim that a method is invalid. Mohanty[12] covered philosophical objections to the descriptive approach and I took the ones most relevant for scientific practice and showed how they were used to defend the necessity of interpretations.[13] In summary, these arguments were (1) that meanings were polysemic and not universal; (2) that in order to go beyond given data one had to interpret; (3) that interpretations were necessary because of the unconscious; (4) that interpretations were necessary because humans are self-interpreting creatures; and (5) all meanings intrinsically are interpretations. Based on Mohanty,[14] the response of those who would argue for a descriptive approach to each objection, briefly, would be:

1. Meanings do not have to be univocal, and multiple or complex meanings can be described.

2. It is true one would have to interpret in order to go beyond any given set of data, but since one is not compelled to go beyond the data it is also possible to choose to stay within such limits.

3. One can also describe those aspects of a situation which motivate the introduction of the unconscious. The appeal to the unconscious is based upon something that is given and those givens can be described.

4. Humans are self-interpreting beings and those interpretations can be described.

5. To say that all meanings are interpretations is one theory of meaning, not a description of a state of affairs. The Husserlian understanding of meaning as a determinate relationship between an act of consciousness and its object does not necessitate such a theory.

The above counter-arguments maintain the viability of the descriptive approach against the (surprisingly) universalist claims of the interpretive methodologists. The descriptive methodologist allows that interpretative methods can be practiced and such a theorist ties the choice of method to conditions or explicit bias. In order to appreciate the distinction better, let's clarify the terms. Description can be said to be the use of language to articulate the intentional objects of consciousness or experience within the constraints of the presenting evidence. Or as Mohanty[15] expresses it, "a sentence is truly descriptive if the meaning intention expressed in it is fulfilled in appropriate intuition, where the intention and fulfilling experience coincide." In other words, with description, a certain index of certitude goes along with the claim. Obviously, one can be wrong, but a claim of certitude accompanies the description, and critical evaluation of the statement would obviously be called for as well.

My understanding of interpretation would be the articulation of the intentional objects of experience in a situation of doubt, incertitude, ignorance, or unclarity. The doubt leads to three possible responses, each of which would be interpretive. The first would be to articulate the intentional objects of experience in the light of a supporting non-given factor, such as an assumption, theory, hypothesis, or whatever. Thus the doubt can be overcome or the closure can be obtained with the help of the non-given factor, but, of course, since the helpful factor is non-given, the result can only be tentative. The second response is that several alternatives for articulating the intentional objects present themselves, but the choice among the alternatives is not decisive, so one alternative is chosen as the articulatory expression. However, one is aware that competing alternatives have not been eliminated and so the results are equally tentative. Finally, one alternative may stand out clearly above competitors, but is still less than conclusive, and even though one may choose to go along with it anyway because of its superior status, it would still be tentative because of the lack of fulfillment. For each of those three conditions, however, the descriptive approach would describe precisely what was found: the list of alternatives, the fact that one is stronger than others but not conclusively so, and the nature of the lack of fulfillment.

If the above is true, then it becomes easier to relate the strategies to conditions. When conditions do not spontaneously allow closure, then interpretive strategies are called for. If the conditions do allow closure, then it is better to follow descriptive guidelines. Within psychology, the former are usually applied situations and the latter are usually basic research situations. For example, if a clinician is working at a hospital and the police bring in a person who attempted suicide, the clinical psychologist may interview the person, give him a battery of tests, and after several hours may decide that the results are ambiguous. However, the staff are waiting for a "yes-no" decision. Does one keep the person in the hospital or let him go? The psychologist would have to make a decision based on the best possible interpretation; he cannot simply say the results are ambiguous. However, if as a research psychologist I undertook a ten-year project whose purpose it was to try to understand suicide attempts better, and after three years someone were to ask me what I found, I could describe the results as being ambiguous. There is no pressure on me to make a decision on the basis of inadequate or conflicting data, and if the data never reaches genuine closure, I could describe them exactly as they are.

In my earlier article comparing descriptive and interpretive methods I was simply arguing for the viability of the descriptive alternative. It seemed as though the whole world of qualitative researchers in the social sciences were only interested in some version of the hermeneutic method. However, further reflection leads me to the realization that although the two methods are closer than I had thought, they are not quite identical. The critical difference is whether to stay only with evidence, whatever it may be like, or to try to "improve" upon the evidence, with the introduction of a non-given factor. Before returning to this crucial difference, allow me to demonstrate the affinity of the two methods. I shall first indicate the steps of the hermeneutic method as applied to scientific issues.

Description of Procedures for Hermeneutic and Descriptive Methods

Hermeneutic or Interpretive Method: It is not easy to find consistency in the application of the hermeneutic method by social scientists. In fact, it is more often talked about than exemplified. The best I could find is the discussion provided by Radnitzky.[16] For him, utilizing a hermeneutic method would involve the following basic steps:

1. Enter the hermeneutic circle with preunderstanding. The preunderstanding gets modified and deepened with the process.

2. One then tacks between the parts and the whole, implying a dialogal procedure.

3. The process of tacking helps uncover hidden assumptions that are guiding the event as described.

4. One then searches for the interpretation that is maximally good.

5. The resulting description of the findings are guided by the anticipated explanation.

Descriptive Phenomenological Method: In this method, one must first obtain a concrete description of a specific experience from a person in the natural attitude. The researcher then assumes the attitude of the phenomenological psychological reduction and a psychological perspective and then engages in the following steps:

1. The researcher reads the entire description in order to get the sense of the whole. Nothing else is required here, but the phenomenological approach adopts a holistic perspective and analytic steps cannot be taken without some sense of what the entire description is about.

2. The next step is the constitution of parts within the description. Since phenomenology ultimately seeks meanings, these parts are called meaning units and they are constituted as follows: The researcher goes back to the beginning and rereads the description, and every time he or she experiences a transition in meaning within the description, a mark is placed on the paper. The result of this step is a series of meaning units. There is always an element of arbitrariness in the constitution of these units, but it is basically a practical step since no one can retain the whole description in one's head while performing subsequent steps of the method.

3. The third step requires the researcher to transform the subject's everyday, commonsense language into phenomenological psychological expressions. The researcher employs the method of free imaginative variation extensively in this phase in order to come up with the most apt *eidetic* expression that captures what was empirically expressed. This step may require several attempts in order to get the most essential expression for each part. However, it is not a strict one-to-one analysis because the context of the description contributes to the meaning of the linguistic units.

4. Finally, the researcher examines each of the transformed meaning units and, once again, with the help of free imaginative variation, the constituents that are truly invariant or essential are selected out and are used as the basis for a description of the structure of the experience. In other words, the researcher provides a second order, psychologically sensitive description of a life-world experience provided by the research subject.

In steps 3 and 4 of the above method, I claim that one encounters eidetic presentations, but whether they are genuine essences or clarified meanings, I am not yet sure. I sometimes describe the structure obtained as "the most invariant meaning for a given context." Mohanty seems to vacillate on this point. Earlier, he[17] spoke about essences as "meaning clarifications" because of the circularity critique, but later he[18] suggested putting aside the interpretations of essences as meaning clarifications and discussed them again as independent entities. Certainly, subjects' descriptions in the natural attitude give the researcher access to *noemata,* and the analysis raises the givens to higher levels and more invariant eidetic givens. In a sense, the deeper question of whether they are essences or meaning clarifications does not prevent the analysis from happening and being useful. However, ultimate clarification of this issue would be necessary for the full legitimation of the method.

Relationship Between the Two Methods

I will now detail the hermeneutic method again and show how the descriptive method meets its criteria.

1. Enter the hermeneutic circle with preunderstanding: Undoubtedly, if one is doing descriptive phenomenological work, one clearly has some life-world preunderstanding of the phenomenon to be researched. One is never completely in the dark about such phenomena. However, the change in perspective from the life-world expressions and understandings to the more rigorous psychological understandings provides an opportunity to see the phenomenon differently, and perhaps freshly. Consequently, some genuine discoveries are made, but still the process is such that the sense of what is new about the phenomenon under scrutiny seems to come with a sense of belonging to the phenomenon itself. In other words, there is clarification, but it is new with respect to what is implicitly understood. In a sense then, the discovery of the invariant dimensions of a concrete experience is like the clarification of something preunderstood. One could compare the process to the hermeneutic circle. This point was brought up by Levin[19] and recently, as indicated, Mohanty[20] has conceded that this critique of Husserl's position seems undeniable. I would only add that the issue is not necessarily closed for me, but it would take more space than is available here to discuss it thoroughly. I would say that more clarification of the process itself is called for here; we have too few words carrying the burden of a complicated process that requires a far more nuanced description. Perhaps what is prior is not so much preknowledge or preunderstanding as a sheer presence that calls for a development that is accompanied by new insights rather than being determined *a priori* by a preknowing. In any case, as the matter now stands, a process similar to the hermeneutic circle is lived out in the course of the descriptive analysis.

A more analogical example of the hermeneutic circle would be the way that the context of the description announces itself as highly relevant for the third step of the analysis. The transformation of parts of the description call for the clarification of the relationship of the part being considered with other parts and the context. Consequently, the context serves as a type of co-understanding that helps clarify the parts.

2. Tacking between parts and whole: Since the descriptive method calls for the constitution of parts, parts are determined and a certain kind of tacking among parts and between parts and the whole takes place. Without this tacking, clarification would not be so sharp.

3. Uncovering of hidden assumptions: A key factor in the process of transforming meaning units is the transformation of implicit meanings into explicit ones. Thus, a good part of the uncovering of hiddenness takes place with meanings rather than assumptions, although in the natural attitude descriptions there are hidden assumptions also that get revealed. Strictly speaking, then, the descriptive method does this step as well. The uncovering of something hidden is usually associated with hermeneutics, but Mohanty[21] has pointed out how such a process is not in conflict with a descriptive approach.

4. Maximally good interpretation: One of the criticisms against the descriptive approach is that it is impossible, or too difficult, to obtain an accurate description. However, it seems to me that if one is not content to simply list possible interpretations, but to try to pick the one best interpretation, or the interpretation that is maximally good, then that problem is no easier than attempting to get a precise description. Basically, it is the same problem. Either one is trying to eliminate alternative plausible interpretations to legitimate the better one, or one is trying to improve the description by supplanting poorer words with better ones. The only difference, really, is the final designation of the outcome.

5. Descriptions guided by anticipated explanations: I don't know if this would be true of the philosophical level, but there is at least an analogous step with scientific phenomenology. Since within the framework of scientific phenomenological practice a disciplinary perspective has to be assumed (for example, psychology), then the ultimate essential description has to meet the demands of the psychological perspective. That is why the linguistic transformations that are guided by the psychological intuitions that occur to the researcher's consciousness take place in the third step of the method. It's the psychological relevancy of the subject's everyday statements that matter. One could also describe this step by saying that the descriptions are guided by the anticipated psychological relevancy. In a large sense, one could say that the researcher arrives at a psychological interpretation of a life-world event by means of a descriptive method.

Thus, even though the principles of the hermeneutic method are not explicitly posited as guidelines for the descriptive method, in actual practice they are respected. Conversely, the hermeneutic method also respects descriptive guidelines without explicitly saying so. I think that this can be demonstrated more briefly. Again, the steps of the descriptive method are as follows:

1. Sense of the whole: The first step of the descriptive method was to read the entire description so that a sense of the whole can be obtained. While the hermeneutic method does not specify this, it obviously has to be done. Otherwise, tacking between the whole and the parts could not take place. The sense of the whole that is gained serves in the role of the preunderstanding within the hermeneutic circle.

2. Constitution of meaning units: The purpose of this step in the descriptive method is to establish parts. Again, there could be no tacking between parts and wholes if parts were not at least implicitly established, and since the interpretive method has as its goal the clarification of meanings, the meaning of the parts would have to be considered.

3. Transformation of data into disciplinary language: Since the interpretive theorists admit that the results are guided by the "anticipated explanation," it indicates that some kind of transformation of the original data takes place. Moreover, the interpretive framework, more than anything else, means that whatever is given can be taken up by another perspective and be expressed differently. In other words, transformation of any given into something else is precisely the heart of the interpretive method.

4. Essential structure: In the strict sense, the descriptive method would try to describe the essence that is intuited by the researcher, and in the larger sense, would try to describe the network of invariant meanings that emerged from the data. The interpretive researcher tries to come up with the maximally good interpretation, that is, the meaning that best comprehends all of the data. While the interpretive researcher would not call it an essence, it serves the same function for him or her in the research context.

One sees, therefore, that despite the different labeling of the two methods, a fuller analysis and description of the procedures actually employed shows a great similarity between the two allegedly different methods. How is this possible? Probably because the two strategies are dependent upon two different philosophical outlooks with different emphases and so the same procedures receive different names. Each method seems to make explicit what the other leaves implicit. Could one not argue that there is one descriptive-interpretivemethod?

There seems to be at least one stumbling block to that idea and that is the key difference between interpretation and description that was described above. Practically, the matter comes down to this: is it permissible to allow non-given factors into the description of research findings? If so, at what times and under what conditions would such introductions be permissible?

The use of non-givens, that is, theories, hypotheses, suppositions, conjectures, etc. is almost axiomatic in science. A tradition that simply follows close upon the data also exists, but it has fewer adherents. Consequently, it would not be reasonable to expect most scientists to give up centuries-long practices that have proved useful. Perhaps that's why most social scientists turn toward the interpretive method when they are influenced by phenomenological philosophy. However, one important scenario has to be noted. In following the descriptive method scientifically, one has to realize that the researcher is quite active in constituting the data themselves. Since the task of the researcher is to discover the invariant eidetic "meanings or essences" that are based upon the discriminated *noemata* within the descriptions, then it behooves the researcher to stay close to the given. In other words, when it comes to the process of data constitution itself, the refusal to introduce non-given factors would seem to be the preferred strategy. Theory-laden data offers a far more complicated picture and would lead to a different sort of evaluation. Once the data are constituted, theoretical elaboration could follow, but a descriptive methodologist would simply stay with a description of the given and point out the gaps that would have to be filled with further data acquisition.

A second key difference is the use of the reduction with the descriptive method. The interpretive method does not use it and relies instead upon the detection and rendering explicit of presuppositions when they are encountered. Obviously, the interpretive method stays with existential claims as well.

Implications for Other Issues

If the above analyses are accurate, certain implications about the relationship between philosophy and science follow, as well as implications about hermeneutic and descriptive strategies. Unfortunately, these issues cannot be pursued in this essay, but I would like to mention at least one of them, viz., the issue surrounding the nature of the human sciences. Must the human sciences be hermeneutic? Mohanty[22] seems to accept that the human sciences are hermeneutic and he strongly asserts that transcendental phenomenology is not a *Geisteswissenschaft*. I would agree that philosophy is not science and that transcendental phenomenology is not a scientific method. The question is, can the philosophy known as transcendental phenomenology be the grounds for or the basis of a scientific method that is descriptive and not hermeneutic? I believe it can. According to Spiegelberg,[23] Husserl expressed the same opinion in a letter to Bühler. The major problem thus far is that no one has shown how that could be done. My own efforts are in this direction.

With respect to the first point mentioned above, I do not believe that the human sciences necessarily have to be hermeneutic. The argument is usually made that in the human sciences there are no "brute" data, that the human scientist works with meanings already constituted by others. Of course, it depends upon what "brute" means. If one recalls that in phenomenological research one is dealing with phenomena, that is, the relationships lived through by acts of consciousness with respect to objects of the world, then one cannot get more primary than such a relationship. So, if "brute" means getting to the primary level, the descriptive method described above does that. To split the act from the object violates the very meaning of "phenomenon" and it seems arbitrary to carry over from the natural science tradition the idea of "brute" as the relationship between consciousness and a nonconscious object. "Brute" should be understood in terms of primary rather than as a special type of object. Finally, the invariant "meanings or essences" that the researcher "constitutes or discovers" are truly primary for him or her, and would simply not be known in the world if they did not present themselves to the researcher, and if he or she did not articulate them.

Notes

1. Edmund Husserl, *The Crisis of European Sciences and Transcendental Phenomenology* (Evanston, Ill.: Northwestern University Press, 1954 /1970).
2. Edmund Husserl, *Phenomenological Psychology*, trans. J. Scanlon (The Hague: Nijhoff, 1977).
3. Edmund Husserl, *Phenomenological Psychology*, trans. J. Scanlon, (The Hague: Nijhoff, 1977), ix-xv.
4. See the following: Amedeo Giorgi (ed.) *Phenomenology and Psychological Research* (Pittsburgh, Pa: Duquesne University Press, 1985); Amedeo Giorgi, "One Type of Descriptive Data: Procedures involved in following a Scientific Phenomenological Method," *Methods* I, no. 3 (1989), 39-61; Amedeo Giorgi, "Some Theoretical and Practical Issues Regarding the Psychological Phenomenological Method," *Saybrook Review* 7, no. 2 (1989), 71-85; Amedeo Giorgi, "A Phenomenological Perspective on Certain Qualitative Research," *Journal of Phenomenological Psychology*, 25 (1994), 190-220; and Amedeo Giorgi, "The Theory, Practice, and Evaluation of the Phenomenological Method as a Qualitative Research Procedure," the *Journal of Phenomenological Psychology*, 28, no. 2 (1997), 235-60.
5. Maurice Merleau-Ponty, "Phenomenology and the Sciences of Man," in J. Edie, *The Primacy of Perception* (Evanston, Ill: Northwestern University Press, 1964), 43-95.
6. Herbert Spiegelberg, "Phenomenology through Vicarious Experience," in H. Spiegelberg, *Doing Phenomenology* (The Hague: Nijhoff. 1975); Herbert Spiegelberg, "Putting Ourselves into the Place of Others: Towards a Phenomenology of Imaginary Self-transposal," in H. Spiegelberg *Stepping-stones Toward an Ethics for Fellow Existers* (Dordrecht: Kluwer, 1986), 99-104.
7. See Spiegelberg, *Doing Phenomenology*, 49-50.
8. See Spiegelberg, *Doing Phenomenology*, 50-51.
9. See Spiegelberg, *Doing Phenomenology*, 53.
10. Amedeo Giorgi, "Description versus Interpretation: Competing Alternative Strategies for Qualitative Research," *Journal of Phenomenological Psychology* 23, no. 2 (1992), 119-135.
11. J. N. Mohanty, "Philosophical Description and Descriptive Philosophy," in J. Sallis (ed.) *Phenomenology: Descriptive or Hermeneutic* (Pittsburgh, Pa: Duquesne University Press, 1987), 39-62; and J. N. Mohanty, *Transcendental Phenomenology: An Analytic Account* (Oxford, U.K.: Blackwell, 1989), 1-66; Mohanty, *Phenomenology*, ch. 6.
12. See Mohanty, *Phenomenology: Descriptive or Hermeneutic*, 58-60; Mohanty, *Transcendental Phenomenology*, 21-24.
13. See Giorgi, "Description Versus Interpretation," 121-31.
14. See Mohanty, *Phenomenology, 58-60; Descriptive or Hermeneutic,* 55-58; Mohanty, *Transcendental Phenomenology*, 19-21.

15. See Mohanty, *Transcendental Phenomenology,* 19.

16. Gerard Radnitzky, *Contemporary Schools of Metascience* (Göteborg, Sweden: Scandinavian University Books, 1970).

17. See Mohanty, *Transcendental Phenomenology,* 33.

18. See Mohanty, *Phenomenology,* 8-9.

19. David Levin, *Reason and Evidence in Husserl's Phenomenology* (Evanston, Ill.: Northwestern University Press, 1970), 183-90.

20. See Mohanty, *Transcendental Phenomenology,* 33.

21. See Mohanty, *Transcendental Phenomenology,* 59-60.

22. See Mohanty, *Transcendental Phenomenology,* 24.

23. Herbert Spiegelberg, *Phenomenology in Psychology and Psychiatry* (Evanston, Ill.: Northwestern University Press, 1972), 9.

Chapter 4

Hands

Donn Welton

1

When one sees men and women in procession—be it down an aisle leading to a wedding altar or on cobblestone leading to a graveyard—our attention is fixed on faces. Faces lead the march with bodies, dressed in the white of a new day or in the black of a lost night, trailing behind. We, the spectators, search for the eyes of the bride or the widower, for we know that only in their gaze do these moments of radiant anticipation, veiled in hope, or of broken recollections, veiled in despair, dwell in their fullness. As our gaze inhabits theirs, we too are suffused with joy or sorrow.

In such ceremonies, which suspend the rhythms of everyday life, the hands are often gloved or hidden behind a bouquet of flowers. They are not at work. Hands contribute nothing to processions such as these, and so they recede from view. It is only at those moments when the ritual marks a future state and a return to the everyday that they are allowed to appear. The couple exchange rings, which both binds the hand and identifies it as belonging to the other. The widower slowly spades moist earth on the coffin and begins the long process of leaving behind what is eternally lost. Even here, however, the hands are hesitant, for they await the return of the plow or the sword, or, for those blessed with leisure, the return of the pen or the paintbrush.

Once they are ungloved and allowed to go free, however, the hands are what carry our existence. They are connected to the body in a way that the hollow of the eyes is not. There is no dividing line between the hand and the arm, with the quality of one melding into that of the other. The broad, rounded hand of the longshoreman or the farm woman is continuous with his or her large, muscular forearm. The movements and rhythms of a strong or even delicate arm with its hand are palpable modulations of his or her very existence and then essence. George Eliot, the English novelist, captures this as she describes the arm of a woman as the presence of her beauty: "Who has not felt the beauty of a woman's arm?—the unspeakable suggestions of tenderness that lie in the dimpled elbow, and all the varied gently-lessening curves, down to the delicate wrist, with its tiniest, almost imperceptible nicks in the firm softness."[1] The extension of the arm into a smooth, white hand, unsoiled and manicured, would only expand such beauty, making it all the move captivating—at least for Indian nobility or British gentry living in earlier days.

But for those who labor, hands display skill and power. To take a tool in hand is to commit oneself to transforming the materials at hand. The style of the action exhibits the skill of the hands, and the effectiveness of the action their power. Hands are hands-on. Hands also come as a pair and they work together. Both in terms of each other and in terms of the world, they bespeak involvement and participation. We not only have hands but we have a hand-in. What we construct with hands-on and hands-in is usually done for the sake of others. What is built is done so that it might be handed-over. Vision never gives; hands do.

Had philosophers begun with the hand as lived, we might not have been tempted to posit a chasm between external reality and us. Perhaps it is because we have thought of the ego as dwelling in the head and not in the hands that we came to believe that there is a gap in need of bridging between the subject and the world. Hands literally cease to exist as hands and become mere appendages if there is nothing to take to hand, if a tool invites not their grip or unharvested wheat beckons not their labor. And through that transference of significance so characteristic of the body in action, what is touched or gripped can itself be described as a hand, as when we—feeling its fineness, texture, and durability—speak of the "hand" of a fabric or a carpet.

There is an objectivism that would reject this characterization of hands, that would argue that the hand is simply like any other measurable object, and that we must look to the empirical sciences to discover its intrinsic properties. The hand, it is said, is the terminal part of the human arm located below the forearm consisting of the wrist, palm, four fingers, and an opposable thumb. Furthermore, the firing of certain neurons and the contractions of various muscles can explain the function of the hand. But notice that this type of description would apply equally well to corpses. In fact, it was only as the corpse became the site of revelation for the medical disciplines and the science of the body that it gained ascendancy. They assume that there is only one region of reality, the physical, and that to describe hands is to explain them with concepts that translate into operations of measurement. The reduction of reality that attends a scientific point of view, however, always fails to approach the meaning or significance of hands and always finds itself on the other side of the way hands fit into the circuit of our existence. Over against objectivism, phenomenology is concerned with the latter, that is, with the *essence* of hands.

The way in which we experience our hands-in-action prethematically or precognitively serves not as a foundation but certainly as a background to the various ways in which hands are elaborated thematically. To lend a hand is to lift another's burden or help pull a wagon across a ford. Hands speak of possession or ownership, as when the jewels are in my hands or the task has been give over to my hands. But they also bespeak authority, as when a person has been given into our hands, or responsibility, as when the evening meal is in your hands. And they solidify our contact with others, when we in lighter moments greet each other with a shaking or slapping of hands. Follow the elaborate hand-clasping routine of black kids; they rarely look each other in the eyes as part of the greeting, as though the look would spoil the touch. Even vows and promises are sealed with a grip of hands. By contrast there are hands that have been taken over by others. With the introduction of slave labor, sailing ships, and then factory work, there was a reduction of a person to "a hand" and a reduction of a hand to its sheer labor power. At the most extreme, there is the deeper shame associated with hands nailed to wooden planks.

A phenomenological approach thinks of these thematic elaborations and metaphorical extensions as dependent upon an experience of hands that is at work in our basic involvement with environments and situations. It does not begin with texts nor does it start with a truth functional analysis of the semantics of the term "hand." Rather, the appeal is to what would give metaphors their background or field of intelligibility. In turning to experience before it becomes encumbered, the task is to account for hands at the level of their active engagement. But how is this to proceed?

2

Husserl argued that an essential analysis of experience, be it of the body or perception, involves a moment of suspension. In order to reflect philosophically we must not only set aside our inherited conceptions and theories of reality, we must also pull back from our everyday absorption in the world in order to discover the interplay between the way phenomena are given and the way they are intended or taken. At the same, time phenomenology is no chronicle of facts: the reflection always involves eidetic analysis or what the later Husserl calls eidetic variation. We pass from facts to recurring and invariant structures. Still, these movements of reflection and eidetic analysis are not peculiar to phenomenology. Most philosophy has at least this much.

If the analysis of essences is to be genuinely phenomenological, phenomena and then essences must be understood in terms of their constitution. For Husserl, this means that reflection is a form of self-reflection in two senses: first, essences are conceptualized through an achievement of a knowing subject; essences, in prescribing ontic conditions for the being of different types of phenomena, also give epistemic conditions for their apprehension. They specify structural conditions for subjects engaged in a world. The genius of Husserl's phenomenology was to think of essences in terms of meanings and meanings in terms of our active involvement with things. Because of the way in which phenomena and then essences are tethered to schemes of constitution, "essences are destined to bring back all the living relationships of experience," as Merleau-Ponty puts it so well.[2] To understand hands essentially is to conceptualize the meaning of hands, to grasp the manner in which they modulate our existence.

There is one side of Husserl that understands this all too well. When he is not looking over his shoulder at Descartes and at the epistemological requirements he thought necessary to support his rigorous transcendental program, when he is given over to tracking the ebb and flow of experience, he conceptualizes an irreducible element of contingency built into essences. In both *Ideas I* and in the 1913 preface to the second edition of the *Logical Investigations,* Husserl expressly argues that all empirical essences are "morphological" in contrast to "exact." This would entail that there is no algorithm or rule that can exhaustively specify all the features of a region of objects. When is an object too short to be taken as a table or a text too narrative to count as a poem? In the final analysis, regional essences, or what Merleau-Ponty calls the structures of the various orders, can never be severed from their constitution and their constitution from the concrete presence of those phenomena that exhibit such structures. Indeed, as Mohanty points out, phenomenology as a foundational discipline is itself morphological.[3] This side of Husserl's account was augmented by his discovery during the 1920s of several "paths" into transcendental analysis different from the Cartesian way. Both the way through regional ontologies and the way through the life-world entail that whatever direct, intuitive insight we have into the nature of consciousness must be supplemented with a reconstructive account that articulates its structure according to the various ways in which it is deployed. The correlation of *noesis* and *noema,* which Husserl uses to define the basic structure of intentionality, is *a priori* in the sense that without it we cannot account for the unity and diversity across various fields of constitution. With the enlargement of the notion of reduction by the recognition of different paths into the transcendental, the notion of intuition gives way to the notion of critique.

But the other side of Husserl is preoccupied with the strong notion of evidence he thinks necessary to secure his transcendental account of consciousness as certain and indubitable. As part of this program, Husserl contrasts the "inadequate" givenness that attends "outer perception," making its evidence subject to correction and improvement, to the "adequate" givenness and absolute evidence that accompanies our reflections upon consciousness.[4] As was true of Leibnitz and Fichte, two of his favorite philosophers, Husserl believes that adequate intuitive evidence is required if we are to secure the existence and the structure of transcendental subjectivity.

The relentless effort to apply this strong notion of evidence to the apprehension of consciousness, however, led Husserl to restrict the scope of adequacy in important ways.[5] A further clarification of the relationship between inadequate and adequate evidence will enable us to see this.

There are different kinds of evidence, but in general the nature of the evidence attending our apprehension of essences depends upon the manner in which their underlying phenomena are given. In the case of real objects, the play of profiles (the sides directly given) and object (the whole co-given), as well as the causal nexus in which all material objects are located, means that they are always given perspectively. And because there are profiles that are not immediately but only mediately present and because of the open, "presumptive" nature of all perceptual experience, real objects are given only inadequately. Not only are there manifold determinations that become manifest only in the course of further perceptual experience, but it is also the case that with the next turn of the object something new and surprising can appear and the entire experience becomes transformed. When what we saw as a raccoon turns out to be the neighborhood cat, the phenomena itself is retrogressively reorganized. This entails that the evidence of external perception is always open and "impure." Husserl puts it this way: "In principle something that is [physically] real, a being that has this sense, can appear in limited fashion and thus only "inadequately." Essentially tied up with this is the fact that no rational claim [*Vernunftsetzung*] based on such an inadequately given appearance can be "final" and "incapable of being overturned."[6] At best, adequate givenness in the case of real objects is recovered only at the level of a projected ideal of what that type of object would be like if we did have an exhaustive experience of it. He envisions regional ontologies that articulate the "rules," which Husserl characterizes as ideas in the Kantian sense, that prescribe the course of ongoing experience for different types of objects and thereby hypothetical ideals of their essential determinations.[7] However, what belongs to that rule, itself adequately given as an *eidos,* is the stipulation that any actual, real object be given inadequately. What is real, then, is perspectively given and thus arrested in horizons. Any claim based on the real, as a consequence, is provisional and open to correction. Only what is ideal and involves eidetic insight has evidence marked as adequate.

But what happens when, in reflection, the "object" being apprehended is consciousness itself? This is where we find a decisive tension in Husserl's theory. Initially he argued in *Ideas I* that mental processes are adequately given in our reflections upon them. Unlike external objects of perception, mental processes or events lack sides or profiles. They are given all at once and thus fully.

> Let us develop the specific contrast between thing and mental process [*Erlebnis*] from the other side. The mental process does not present itself, we said, [through adumbrations or profiles]. That means that the perception of a mental process is a simple viewing of something *that is perceptually given as absolute* and not given as something identical through

> modes of appearance, each of which is an adumbration. . . . A
> mental process of feeling is not adumbrated. If I look at it, I
> have something absolute; it does not have sides that present
> [the mental process] sometimes in one mode, sometimes in
> another.[8]

Because it lacks different modes of appearance or profiles, the mental process is
given "absolutely." Adequate evidence is "in principle incapable of being
'strengthened' or 'diminished,' thus without graduations of weight."[9] With his
strong view of evidence in play Husserl summarizes his position in this way:

> We therefore hold fast to the following: whereas it is essential
> to givenness by appearances [that is, profiles] that no one of
> them presents the matter as "absolute" instead of in a one-
> sided presentation, it is essential to the givenness of some-
> thing immanent to give precisely something absolute that
> cannot ever be presented in sides and be adumbrated.[10]

Eidetic insight, as a consequence, could claim to read not the structure that consciousness would have were it given completely, but the structure that it actually
does have because it is given without remainder. The *a priori* structure of consciousness is not a hypothetical construct and this is the main reason Husserl
thinks he has escaped the Kantian and neo-Kantian "mythic" construction of the
transcendental ego. The fact that it is "given" in transcendental reflection meant
that we have secure, "actual," not presumptive, "hypothetical" evidence for it.

> Obviously, the necessity attached to the being of the actual
> mental process currently present is not a pure essential
> necessity, that is, not a purely *eidetic* particularization sub-
> sumed under an *eidetic* law. [Rathe]r it is the necessity of a
> fact [*Faktum*], so called because an *eidetic* law is involved
> in the fact and, indeed, in the existence of the fact as fact.[11]

Because the evidence of consciousness is about an absolute "fact," intentionality
as its *eidos,* as correlational *a priori*, can be read directly from it and secured
as a foundational structure.

But in these paragraphs Husserl probes deeper and then hesitates. He
realizes:

> It is also the case that a mental process is never perceived
> completely, that it cannot be adequately seized upon in its full
> unity. . . . Only in the form of retention do we have a
> consciousness of the phase that has just flowed away, or else
> in the form of a retrospective recollection. And my whole
> stream of mental processes is, finally, a unity of mental
> processes which, of essential necessity, cannot be seized

upon completely in a perceiving that "swims along with it."[12]

One of the passages cited above is also reworked in Husserl's personal copies. His insertions (underlined) further specify the difficulty he finds with his initial position:

> The mental process does not present itself *as perceptually present according to its whole present content (and thus in each moment)*. That means that the perception of a mental process is a simple viewing of something that *in its present, at every point in its Now* is perceptually given as absolute and not given as something identical through modes of appearance, each of which is a *one-sided* adumbration. . . . A mental process of feeling is not adumbrated. If I look at it, I have *with respect to each point of its continuous present* something absolute; it does not have sides that present [the mental process] sometimes in one mode, sometimes in another.[13]

At best, only the momentary Now, only the swell of the Now and not the entire mental process with its phases is adequately given. But this means that in both (a) the presentation of whole spatial objects in and through profiles, and (b) the presentation of whole temporal mental events in and through retained and then recollected past phases, we have profiles or phases that are not immediately present. One cannot escape the implication of this for the theory of evidence: any apprehension of consciousness must be necessarily inadequate.[14] Yet it is only on the basis of a grasp of consciousness as a whole, not on the basis of a momentary phase given in the Now, that we can make inferences about the structure of consciousness. Since that is not adequately given, the justification for the foundational status of transcendental consciousness is threatened.

3

From the tensions we just discovered, I want to argue that Husserl's strong theory of evidence used to secure his transcendental notion of consciousness is untenable, as is the way that theory, Cartesian in nature, affects or directs his characterization of consciousness. Husserl's Cartesian requirement that consciousness as phenomena be "adequately given" entails both the idea that our reflective experience of consciousness itself have the form of a direct and complete apprehension (in the sense of an act free from any dependence upon co-functioning, implicit indirect acts), and the idea that what is so apprehended be itself transparent, given without hidden features or aspects. For it to be adequately given, as we have just seen, it would have to be present without profiles. To use Husserl's terms, this means that it must not only be manifest in a sheer act of presentation (*Gegenwärtigung*) without the co-functioning of presentification or re-presentation (*Vergegenwärtigung*), but that it must also be given within presentation in a direct presentation (*Präsentation*) without the interplay of co- or appresentation (*Appräsentation*). It must be given transparently, that is, with all of its aspects fully manifest. The first is a *noetic* requirement, the second a *noematic* one. But neither is the case.

At best, what is directly given as we reflect upon consciousness, according to Husserl's own admissions, is the impressional Now or, to draw from his later theory, the living Now. But even if we treat the impressional Now as directly given, this does not mean that it is adequately given. Husserl confused these two in *Ideas I* but later realized that they are different.

There are indeed significant distinctions between (a) objects and profiles as they are given in normal perception, and (b) conscious events given in phenomenological reflection. I am not claiming that mental events are given in profiles, as are perceptual objects. All objects of external perception are necessarily spatial; I can walk around them. This is not true of mental events. Try as I will, I cannot catch them from behind. But this does not mean that mental events lack "contours" that involve an interlacing of impressional and trace elements, of impressional (*in-* + *premere*) and re-pressional (*re-* + *premere*) materials. Husserl acknowledges this but initially preserves the thesis of adequacy by treating all re-pressional materials held in retention and eventually recollection as strictly derivative, coming from im-pressional materials as they fade from view. This implies, though, that the impressional phase could be given in an act or a phase of an act that is independent of appresentation. But this is highly questionable. Studies in perception show that what is optimally Now is dependent upon a field. Impressions arising in presentification are not free of appresentational materials. If trace or re-pressional material is not merely a re-presentation of what was originally presented but also functions as the field or background within which all im-pressional materials have their determinacy and their significance, then all presentation is inescapably linked to and even dependent upon re-presentation. Appresentation supplies not an "objective background" but a background belonging to the "conscious quality of the experiential moment" to borrow a phrase from Husserl's Göttingen lecture course from 1906-07.[15] He even wagered to call such background material "prephenomenal."[16] If what is not directly given but retained is necessary to what is directly given in the mental event apprehended in reflection, and if appresentation is involved in the functioning of that background, then any mental event "directly" given in a Now will not be a mental event "adequately" given. The event will always be a phase of a whole and never phenomenally present in isolation. There is always this "surplus" over and above what is directly present, not itself directly manifest yet constitutive of what is present. Ironically, one could even claim that this is not only a consequence of but even the deeper insight of Husserl's own theory of the consciousness of time.

There is a second difficulty. To isolate what is directly manifest in presentation always involves an abstractive procedure and thus the results count as phenomena only in an attenuated sense. But even if we could do this, even if we could isolate a mental event or phase from what is held in retention, we still would not have something adequately given. With rare exceptions, there are always other features not in focus that could be explored. Anger, for example, seems to involve a mixture of pain, shock, perception, and perhaps hate. The third note of a melody (taken only as an experienced unit) can have various intensities, pitches, and even be the result of several instruments that can be identified by those with a trained ear. In Husserl's terms, there is an "inner horizon" at work and this means determinations hidden in what is directly manifest.

Since any mental act that would be directly manifest has itself elements that are concealed, the claim of transparency is thereby undercut. And since any conscious event directly manifest actually involves an intertwining of impressional and re-pressional materials and thus an interplay of presentation and appresentation, what is presented is necessarily inadequate. From the perspective of his later thought, adequate givenness is a requirement superimposed upon mental phenomena, coming from Husserl's Cartesian view of evidence. By contrast, direct yet inadequate givenness interlaced with protentions and retentions is closer to what his own phenomenology actually discovered for mental acts.[17] This is why his earlier emphasis upon adequacy gives way in his later thought to an originary evidence for consciousness in which the feature of self-awareness and not full givenness becomes the decisive criterion.

4

Hands touch. What we take in hand is sensed as smooth, rough, warm, cold, etc. Touching, however, has the peculiar feature that in perceiving the tactile properties of the object, the hand is also offered to itself. In sensing the rough wood I also sense the fingers as they cross the surface of the board. The sensing fingers are themselves sensed *reflexively*. Were there a gap between fingers and object, neither the fingers as sensing nor the roughness sensed would exist. Perhaps we can say that the action of reaching for the wood finds a double "fulfillment": in the process of giving what is touched to the hand, the hand touching is also presented.

Touch stands in striking contrast to sight and this has implications for the nature of evidence. The dyadic play of profile and object given in vision does not co-give the act of seeing itself. Nor does what is seen provoke a reflexive awareness of the *noetic* state of seeing or of the organs of sight (except in unusual cases). The experience of seeing is itself grasped only in a subsequent reflection that distances itself from the seen in order to turn back upon and intuit the mental event and then articulate its structure. But in the case of touch, before the onset of any reflection, there is already a reflexive awareness that keeps the touched, always inadequately given, tied to touching, and then touching to the body or part of the body performing the touching. "All sensations thus produced have their *localization*, that is, they are distinguished by means of their place on the appearing corporeality [*Leiblichkeit*] and they belong phenomenally to it."[18] The experience itself involves an awareness of both the action of touching (and thereby the body) and the material object touched.[19] Since this is built into the nature of the experience reflexively, and since the reflection cannot alter but only represent the experience, it follows that the reflection upon tactile experience cannot transform these ties to the body into constituted appearances and free the presence of the mental experience from them. Unlike sight, the intentional bond is such that we cannot call into question either the existence of the body or the world, as Husserl's procedure of bracketing requires, without changing the nature of the experience. In fact, this might be true of all sentient actions. Because it is first given at a reflexive level, any suspension of our belief in the existence of the world or the body would cause the experience itself to collapse. Yet without this severance, consciousness itself cannot be set in opposition to the world and isolated as the distinct field of transcendental analysis, as Husserl's Cartesian way proposes. The reduction, as a consequence, can never be completed.

The most interesting feature of touching, however, comes when the object touched is the body itself. This also occurs at a prereflective yet reflexive level and induces an auto-constitution of the body. When the left hand grasps the right hand, a circuit of exchanges is established in which the left hand touching is not only reflexively aware of itself as the organ touching but as the organ being touched by the right hand. In the dynamic interplay of touching-touched-touching, subject and object pass over into one another and thereby the body becomes *Leib*, lived-body. Here are Husserl's own word describing this in *Ideas II*:

> Let us choose the special case where the spatially experienced body perceived by means of the lived-body is itself the physical lived-body [*Leibkörper*] . . . . Touching the left hand I have tactile appearances, that is, I not only sense [*empfinde*] but I perceive and have appearances of a soft, smooth hand formed in a certain way. The indicating sensations of movement and the representing tactile sensations, which are objectivated as features in the thing "left hand," belong to the right hand. But also in the left hand being touched I find a series of tactile sensations; they are "*localized*" in it but do not constitute properties (such as roughness and smoothness of the hand, of this physical thing). If I speak of the *physical* thing "left hand," I abstract from these sensations "in the left hand" (a bullet does not have these sensations, nor does any "mere" physical thing that is not my lived-body). But if I

include these sensations it is not that the physical thing becomes enlarged; rather it becomes lived-body, it senses [*es empfindet*]. The tactile sensations belong to each appearing objective spatial position on the touched hand as it is touched precisely at that particular place. In like manner the touching hand, which for its part appears as thing, has its tactile sensations on the spatial surface where it touches (or is touched by the other).[20]

This places a strain on the very terms organizing the theory of intentionality. As touched the hand is object. But as the object touched is also touching, it is subject. In this shift, the body is known as ours and thus as *Leib*. Yet this also has the consequence of decentering consciousness by deploying it in and through the lived-body. In place of synthesis, in place of unity, we have constant reversal, unbridgeable juxtaposition, and irremediable reversal. With this doubling of touch there is a doubling and then a distributing of consciousness in and through our actions. It is no longer one. And at the level of our reflection upon it, it can never be grasped as the "self-contained complex of being, a complex of absolute being"[21] required by Husserl's Cartesian analysis.

There is one remarkable passage where Husserl suddenly realizes the implication of his analysis of touch for the way in which the body is given. The efforts to visually perceive one's own body and thereby constitute it as an object meet with frustration. Not only are there parts that I cannot see but the very process of objectifying the body rids it of those sensings [*Empfindnisse*][22] so essential to the way it is experienced. Including sensings, however, means that "the same lived-body which serves me as means for all my perception obstructs me in the perception of it itself and is a remarkably imperfectly [or incompletely, *unvollkommen*] constituted thing."[23] To the extent that tactile experience is itself distributed across the body, we can say that consciousness is also "a remarkably imperfectly constituted thing." If it is the case, as Mohanty suggests, that "in the very structure of the transcendental subjectivity, as constituting both my body and nature [as *noematic* sense-structures], there is involved a stratum of corporeality,"[24] then that corporeality completely disrupts that elements of Kant's purely formal theory of consciousness that linger in Husserl's analysis.

5

Whatever I take in hand takes me in hand. When the hand touching our hand is not ours but that of another, when our hand is itself taken in hand, the circuit of exchanges encompasses others and becomes intercorporeal.[25] In certain contexts this is the basic form of interrelationship and is deeper and more intimate than the face-to-face.

But those of us who live in North America have created a culture in which our technologies constantly impose a distance that keeps others at bay. By reducing the object of our touch to a keyboard, a remote control, or a disc player, hands are insulated from the touch of others. We flee being touched. The more we transform intimate subjects that could touch into airbrushed images or reels of celluloid, the more touch becomes lost in self-reference. The screen and then the mirror become the primary form of sociality. The only warmth we find is our own.

In touching another I am immediately at one with the person touched but only in his/her difference, only as "an imperfectly constituted" other, only as one that also escapes me. The internal disseverance already found within the reflexive experience of touching myself is thrown outside one's own body and opens upon, at the limits, two possible forms. This disseverance can be redoubled if the other person is either master or slave, to use Hegel's categories, and if touch is caught up in a circuit of control of one over the other. Or the opposition can be attenuated as in a relationship of mutual care, for under these circumstances the difference between touching and touched enhances the desire and then the pleasure of each, in the case of lovers, or it carries the affection and then undertaking of one on behalf of another, in the case of caregivers and friends.

Once we see the link between hands, the dynamics of touch, and the reversibility of the conscious states, then we have a key to the internal connection between the structure of conscious life and the lived-body. Consciousness ceases to be one and, at the level of sentience, is deployed in and through the lived-body. And once we have integrated this into our theory, we will no longer be tempted to treat consciousness as transparent and as a self-enclosed or irreducible sphere of being.

Notes

1. George Eliot, *The Mill on the Floss,* bk. 6, ch. 10 (1860).
2. M. Merleau-Ponty, *Phenomenology of Perception*, trans. Colin Smith (New York: Humanities Press, 1962), xv.
3. J. N. Mohanty, "Husserl's Transcendental Phenomenology and Essentialism," in *The Possibility of Transcendental Philosophy* (Dordrecht: Nijhoff, 1985), 195.
4. This paper will not sort out this matter further in terms of the difference between a (phenomenological) psychological and a transcendental phenomenological account of consciousness, a complication that would take us too far afield.
5. In this essay I will restrict my account to *Ideas I* (1913) and will not trace the development of this concept that occurs between the *Logical Investigations* (1900-01) and *Ideas I.* Edmund Husserl, *Logische Untersuchungen*, 2nd rev. ed., 2 Bände. (Halle, a.d.s.: Max Niemeyer, 1913 and 1921). All page

references to the *Logische Untersuchungen* are to this edition. The English translation is *Logical Investigations,* by J. N. Findlay, 2 vols. (New York: Humanities Press, 1970). Edmund Husserl, *Ideen zu einer reinen Phänomenologie und Phänomenologischen Philosophie,* Vol. 1: *Allgemeine Einührung in die reine Phänomenologie,* in *Jahrbuch für Philosophie und Phänomenologische Forschung,* Band 1 (Halle, a.d.s.: Max Niemeyer, 1913), 1-323. Since there are two different Husserliana editions of *Ideen I,* all page references to *Ideen I* are to this edition. The English translation is *Ideas Pertaining to a Pure Phenomenology and to a Phenomenological Philosophy,* Book 1: *General Introduction to a Pure Phenomenology,* trans. F. Kersten, *Collected Works,* Vol. 2 (The Hague: Martinus Nijhoff, 1983). Husserl in the *Investigations* was convinced that one's own experiences are adequately perceived and he seems to mean by this the whole stream of these experiences. See *Logische Untersuchungen,* II/2, 240; Eng. trans., II, 866. Unless otherwise noted, all translations are mine.

6. Husserl, *Ideen I,* 286-87; Eng. trans., 331. Italic removed and somewhat freely translated.

7. See Husserl, *Ideen I,* 297-98; Eng. trans., 342-43 on this point.

8. Husserl, *Ideen I,* 81; Eng. trans., 95-6.

9. Husserl, *Ideen I,* 288; Eng. trans., 333. Italics removed.

10. Husserl, *Ideen I,* 82; modified Eng. trans., 96-7.

11. Husserl, *Ideen I,* 86; modified Eng. trans., 103.

12. Husserl, *Ideen I,* 82; modified Eng. trans., 97. Italics mine.

13. Husserl, *Ideen I,* 81; Eng. trans., 95-6. Italics removed. Insertions according to Eng. trans.

14. There are other dimensions of why we cannot adequately grasp mental events as singular that we cannot go into here. For one of the most interesting see Edmund Husserl, *Einleitung in die Logik und Erkenntnistheorie: Vorlesungen 1906-1907,* ed. by Ulrich Melle, *Husserliana,* Vol. 24 (The Hague: Martinus Nijhoff, 1984), 220-24.

15. Husserl, *Einleitung in die Logik,* 243.

16. Husserl, *Einleitung in die Logik,* 245.

17. It will not do to attempt to recover adequacy at the level of the essence. If Husserl claims that it is the idea of consciousness or consciousness as a "rule in the Kantian sense" that is foundational, then he is back in the lap of neo-Kantianism. Even worse we also run afoul of Wittgenstein's deep insight that there is no rule for the application of rules. Whatever essence consciousness has it cannot be put in the form of a hypothetical rule that prescribes what it would be if it were adequately given.

18. Edmund Husserl, *Ideen zu einer reinen Phänomenologie und Phänomenologischen Philosophie,* Band 2: *Phänomenologische Untersuchungen zur Konstitution,* ed. by Marly Biemel, *Husserliana,* Vol. 4 (The Hague: Martinus Nijhoff, 1952), 145; *Ideas Pertaining to a Pure Phenomenology and to a Phenomenological Philosophy,* Book 2: *Studies in the Phenomenology of Constitution,* trans. Richard Rojcewicz and Andre Schuwer, *Collected Works,* Vol. 3 (Dordrecht: Kluwer, 1989), 153.

19. This is why the experience of touching does not fit well into what Husserl thinks of under the heading of *Erlebnis.*

20. Husserl, *Ideen II,* 144-45; Eng. trans., 152-53. For a fuller analysis of Husserl's theory of the body see my "Soft, Smooth Hands: Husserl's Phenom-

enology of the Lived-Body," in *The Body: Classic and Contemporary Readings* (Oxford: Blackwell Publishers, 1999), 38-56.

21. Husserl, *Ideen I*, 93; after Eng. trans., 112.

22. Husserl, *Ideen II*, 146; Eng. trans., 153. I am following the Rojcewicz and Schuwer translation of *Empfindnisse* as "sensings." It might also be rendered "sensorial event."

23. Husserl, *Ideen II*, 159; slightly modified Eng. trans., 167.

24. J. N. Mohanty, "Transcendental Philosophy and the Hermeneutic Critique of Consciousness," in *Possibility of Transcendental Philosophy*, 242. Also see in the same volume his "Intentionality and the Mind/Body Problem," where he argues for "the *intrinsicality of corporeality* to the life of consciousness," 128.

25. From the point of view of a structural reconstruction, using what Husserl called static method, we began with the isolated individual. But using what he called genetic method, the social dimensions of touch are primary for it is rooted in the relationship between caregiver and infant before there is an experiential difference between subject and object. From a genetic perspective, our beginning structural analysis can be understood as applicable to adult experience.

Chapter 5

Logic and Quantum Physics: Some Simple Reflections*

Günther Patzig

In my first lecture I took the following, conservative position in the old discussion on the sea-battle tomorrow: If there will be a sea-battle tomorrow, then the sentence, "Tomorrow will be a sea-battle," uttered today, is true.

We must accept the fact that we have no methods at our disposal to find out today if the sentence in question is true or not. Tomorrow evening we will know, however, if the sentence, as uttered today, was true. Some people may think that it does not make sense to use the predicates "true" and "false" for such sentences which at a given time cannot be verified or falsified in principle.

I find this difficulty real, but less objectionable than the idea that sentences or propositions *acquire* a truth value at the time they become verifiable. A prediction is correct or incorrect, and therefore true or false, even before it is evident whether the event that has been correctly or incorrectly predicted has occurred or not. We have seen that fear of determinism brought Aristotle to admit a truth-value gap for statements concerning contingent events in the future tense. Lukasiewicz introduced a third truth-value, the "Neutral," to fill in these gaps; he thought that even for past events that have left no causal traces in the present the same restrictions must hold.

No doubt the study of many-valued logic, as a formal theory, is of great scientific interest. It would add, of course, to its scientific importance, if we could find applications for the system in other fields of knowledge. In the case of *contingentia futura,* the application does not seem necessary or even profitable. There is no need to introduce a third truth-value besides "true" and "false" to cover the logic of these statements. If, however, we would insert "demonstrably true" or "demonstrably false," or "known to be true" or "known to be false" instead of the truth values "true" and "false," we might then define a third value like "uncertain" or "undecidable." But this would not give us the right to say we had introduced a third truth-value, since all three values would then be dependent on the *state of our knowledge*.

This interpretation of many-valued logic in terms of knowledge or certainty has attracted the interest of those philosophers of science who have been confronted with the logical and philosophical difficulties occurring in the field of modern physics. There we find propositions the truth of which can only be ascertained if we accept the fact that by the very operation of verification of this proposition other propositions will become unverifiable. It is common knowledge that this situation, among other features, distinguishes classical physics from modern quantum physics. Classical mechanics allows us to attribute a position and a momentum to a macro-physical body simultaneously. Optical observation of the position of a macro-physical body does not increase the momentum of this body in any significant way. The result of a later measurement of momentum may, therefore, be safely dated back to the time of measurement of position. On the other hand, the short-wave radiation necessary for determining the position of an electron will add to the momentum of the electron. If later we measure the momentum, we cannot transfer the result of our experiment back to the time of fixing the position without making due allowance for the increase in momentum due to the operation of position-measurement. But there is no known procedure to determine this effect. Therefore, we cannot attribute meaningfully both momentum and position to a given electron at a given time. It is natural to express this fundamental fact by saying that the question whether a certain electron has at a given time a certain momentum or not is, for suitable cases, without any meaning. A proposition which nevertheless attributes a certain momentum to the electron in question would be neither true nor false. This has led some experts to assert that the *tertium non datur* is not applicable in modern physics. Accordingly, we find many people asserting that the results of modern physics show the inadequacy not only of classical physics but also of traditional logic.

That quantum theory might need a special logic had been suggested by John Von Neumann in 1932; G. Birkhoff and Von Neumann developed a formalism of quantum mechanics that could be called a logic in 1936. H. Reichenbach (1944) and P. Destouches-Février (1951) introduced different models for quantum logic. The critical statements of the type we mentioned are counted as "indeterminate" (Reichenbach) or "absolutely false" (Destouches-Février).[1]

I want to discuss some of the philosophical implications of these developments by examining some arguments taken from the writings of Carl Friedrich Von Weizsäcker, who in Germany has been the most influential author in this field. Since his works have also been translated into English, you may have heard about his ideas or in case of interest will not find it difficult to get acquainted with them. It is clear that the ideas of physicists on these topics are connected with the development of physics. What physicists say about the subject can be evaluated only by fellow physicists. But the question of whether or not quantum physics calls for a revision of traditional logic is a philosophical one of some importance. Therefore, philosophers must decide whether or not the arguments taken from physics for a change of logic are conclusive. I shall concentrate on some arguments presented by Von Weizsäcker in his book *Zum Weltbild der Physik*. I quote from the ninth edition (1962). The passages are taken from the two studies contained in this volume called "The Importance of Logic for Natural Science" (1954) and "Complementarity and Logic" (1955), the latter being Von Weizsäcker's contribution on the occasion of Niels Bohr's seventieth birthday.

Von Weizsäcker starts with the remark that it is no real inconsistency if we describe and design our instruments and experimental apparatus according to the laws of Euclidean geometry and show, by using these very instruments, that physical space is non-Euclidean.

Correspondingly, according to Von Weizsäcker, a physicist may use two-valued classical logic in order to show that the phenomena of quantum physics are subject to a logic that must be regarded as non-classical. The hypothesis that many-valued logic is related to classical logic as non-Euclidean geometry is related to Euclidean geometry must be particularly attractive. It occurs in the works of the Russian mathematician Vasiliew, who was one of the pioneers in the field of many-valued logic, and we find it in Lukasiewicz just as we encounter it in Von Weizsäcker's works. I think it is very improbable that any of these writers took over the idea from one of the others. Classical logic is regarded to be an "especially simple case of general many-valued logic," rather like Euclidean geometry may be characterized as a special simple case of non-Euclidean geometry. This analogy, however, is endangered by two objections: First, two-valued logic is indispensable as a meta-theory for all non-standard logics. Whatever truth-values we may introduce, the attribution of one of the truth-values to a given sentence will be a matter of "yes" or "no." A sentence has to take the value "neutral" or has it not—it cannot remain "neutral" again whether the sentence is "neutral" in truth-value or has another value. In this way, many-valued logic seems to be founded on two-valued logic, while there is no corresponding relation between non-Euclidean geometry and Euclidean geometry. Second, Euclidean geometry is a limiting case of non-Euclidean geometry, since it can be used instead of non-Euclidean geometry for describing special relations in spaces of slight curvature, in small dimensions, and for dealing with bodies of relatively small mass and relatively negligible relative acceleration. The possibility of demonstrating the non-Euclidean structure of physical space with the help of instruments that are built on Euclidean principles rests precisely on just this fact: that in such small dimensions, Euclidean principles give a sufficiently close approximation to what would be the true, if more complicated, description. But the situation has no counterpart, again, in logic. We cannot meaningfully say that the divergence of classical logic from the true non-classical logic will be so small in some given field as to be practically negligible. Shall we say that in a short deduction the precision of classical logic is reliable enough to guarantee the truth of the conclusion, given the truth of the premises, while a longer chain of deduction may be invalidated by the divergence between classical logic and the true non-classical logic? And what could be the unit by which we could measure the magnitude of error between our classical logic and the other logic that would correspond to the space-curvature of non-Euclidean geometry?

Von Weizsäcker, while introducing the analogy between non-Euclidean geometry and many-valued logic, is aware of the disapproval of those who, as he says, "have grown up with the conventional ideas of the nature of logic." What we need in this situation is an analysis of the nature of logic. Only after such an investigation may we be in a position to answer the question of whether or not empirical science, like quantum mechanics, may cause changes in logic. Well, in some measure this is a point of view even Quine has expressed sympathy with, e.g., in his book *Philosophy of Logic.*[2]

If leading physicists and one of the best logicians tend to entertain a certain idea, it is worthwhile to look more closely into it. Von Weizsäcker suggests we should examine the hypothesis that logic is tied more closely to reality than general opinion among logicians would allow. If our logic would reflect some very general structures of reality, new insight into the most fundamental structures of reality, which quantum mechanics promises, may prompt us to revise and improve our logic. This, as I said, sounds not unfamiliar to a reader of Quine. Bertrand Russell also, in some of his works, played with similar ideas.[3] But Von Weizsäcker is more hard-line here than Quine and Russell: He quotes with agreement sentences from Georg Picht's essay "Bildung und Natur-wissenschaft": "The general form of proposition is not based in the nature of our human intellect, but is a feature of reality, made visible. . . . Logical laws are laws of being, recognised as such."[4]

This thesis is obviously based on the acceptance of a disjunction: Logic must be either the science of laws of thought or of general laws of reality. Since obviously logic cannot be defined as a branch of the psychology of thinking, we seem to have to accept the remaining possibility, namely, that it is concerned with structures of reality. But of course, there is no justification for accepting the disjunction in the first place: Logic may represent a type of science concerned with laws that may be different from psychological laws on the one hand and structural principles of nature on the other.

A favorite idea of Von Weizsäcker refers to the fact that the notion of truth has a wider application than is recognized by formal logic. For instance, the truth we find in poetry, which we might call "poetical truth," is attributable to sentences which are, from the logical point of view, not true. Now, just as logical truth does not cover the whole of truth, since there are fields of truth outside the problems of logic, so may we have reality outside the scope of formal logic, which is not dreamt of in our pseudo-philosophy, suggested to us by being raised in the conventional ideas on formal logic. Since physics may present us with entirely new knowledge concerning such fields of reality, it may also lead to an expansion and revision of logic.

Now I think this argument is not successful. Poetical truth is not different so much from *logical* truth but from truth in the *theoretical* sense. Logic is concerned with theoretical truth, of which logical truth is a special case. And poetical truth and theoretical truth are not different branches of truth, but different *meanings* of the expression "truth." A form of words may be "true" in both senses, or "false" in one and "true" in the other. That we may talk about a "truth" that is not subject to the canons of logic is no more surprising than the fact that we cannot determine in centigrade the warmth of a smile. Let us put on record for future references three main ideas we found in Von Weizsäcker's study on the "importance of logic for the natural sciences": (a) the analogy between non-Euclidean geometries and non-Aristotelian logic; (b) the notion that logic is a science of very general structures of reality, which would open the way to reforms of logic on the basis of discoveries in physics; and (c) an extension of the concept of truth such that theoretical truth appears to be a particular kind of truth to which other kinds may be added.

We now turn to Von Weizsäcker's study on "Complementarity and Logic" which he published one year later, in 1955. Von Weizsäcker argues that Birkhoff and Von Neumann have shown that the well-known mathematical foundations of quantum mechanics may be formally regarded as an extension of the calculus of propositions which is part of classical logic. Now we ask: "In what sense and with what justification may we describe this extended calculus as a kind of logic?" "Complementarity" is a fundamental feature in all discussions of quantum theory: We have complementarity of concepts like position and momentum; we have complementarity of sentences and complementarity of theories (like the wave picture and the particle picture). Therefore, a logic of quantum mechanics would have to take account of the particular relation between complementary concepts, sentences and theories. Von Weizsäcker would call a logic which satisfies these requirements a "Komplementaritäts- logik," and he suggests that this logic of complementarity would be related to classical logic in the same way as quantum physics is related to classical physics. Under this interpretation, the logic of complementarity would be the *true* logic, containing classical logic as a limiting case which would, in its simplicity, cover many cases that can be described without reference to complementarity.

Von Weizsäcker refers to this hypothesis as the main idea of his study. It is undoubtedly an interesting notion and, if true, would show us a new way out of the logical difficulties of quantum physics. We must, however, consider it more closely. Some difficulties are immediately visible: It is certainly very difficult to state exactly the relation of classical physics to quantum mechanics, and physicists have not yet reached agreement on this question. But at least we can say what is meant by the concept of "approximation" of predictions made on the basis of the classical theory to the predictions according to computation on the basis of quantum mechanics. Again we may ask: What is the counterpart of this concept of "approximation" in the relation of quantum logic and classical logic? How should we measure the possible error involved and who is to decide, when this error becomes grave enough, that we must change logics? How lightly, for instance, is the computing error in the case of an alternation as "The sun is shining or the sun is not shining" treated according to the methods of classical logic? Is this divergence from the true logic of complementarity influenced by the degree of vagueness of the concepts involved?

Von Weizsäcker does not attempt to answer such questions. As the strongest argument for the hypothesis that classical logic needs revision in the light of quantum logic, he introduces some consequences drawn from Young's interference experiment which has, as Von Weizsäcker tells us, often been discussed by Niels Bohr and his pupils. Young's interference experiment may be described like this: From a source Q electrons may travel towards a screen S that has two small openings, S_1 and S_2. Both holes may be closed or opened independently from one another. Most electrons actually reaching S will be absorbed by it. Those electrons, however, which pass through one of the openings S_1 or S_2 will leave a trace on a photographic plate P which is fixed behind the screen S.

If we reduce the intensity of the radiation from source Q sufficiently so that only one electron at a time will make its passage through the apparatus, we have, for every electron that has passed through S, one black spot on the photographic plate. Now if electrons are truly particles and behave as such, the passage of an electron through S_1 would exclude the passage of the same electron through S_2 and vice versa. The probability of the passage of an electron through S_1 and leaving a trace in the point x of P would also be independent of the fact that S_2 is opened or closed. This independence would hold in the other direction too. From these premises it is natural to derive the following conclusion:

If the probability that an electron will hit point x of P is W_1 (x) in case only S_1 is open, and the probability is W_2 (x) in case only S_2 is open, the probability of an electron hiting point x, in the case of both S_1 and S_2 being opened, would be equal to the sum of W_1 and W_2. Now the study of Young's interference experiment has amply shown that just this simple hypothesis is not verified by the experiment. In order to formulate the actual results of this experiment we must introduce complex numbers as probability amplitudes. For the probability of an electron hitting x of P provided S_1 and S_2 are simultaneously opened, we have a more complicated formula:

$$W_1 = \varphi_1 2; W_2 = \varphi_2 2 \ W_{12} = \varphi_{12} 2; \text{ where } \varphi_{12} = \varphi_1 + \varphi_2$$

Von Weizsäcker naturally asks what may be the mistake in the "classical" interpretation. According to logic, he says, the proposition "This particle has passed through S_1" will be true or false, even if we do not know which is the case. And according to the physics which we have presupposed, this sentence is true if the sentence "This electron has passed through S_2" is false and vice versa. From this presupposition and the accepted laws of the calculus of probabilities the formula follows, which was proved to be misleading. Therefore, we must ask: "Is the logical presupposition, namely, the validity of the *tertium non datur* mistaken, or is it the calculus of probabilities, or the physics of the particle picture?"

Every physicist, Von Weizsäcker says, faced with such a dilemma would naturally be inclined to sacrifice first the particle picture theory. This picture leads to the assumption that an electron which has reached point x of plate P must have passed through S_2 if it has not passed through S_1. It is a physical presupposition that an electron, if it has passed S_1, cannot also have passed through S_2 simultaneously. Here we must be careful to draw the boundaries between logic and physics correctly. Logic in its classical form lays down that, for all propositions, either the proposition or its negation (that is the proposition with a sign of negation added) is true. A certain electron either has passed through S_1 or has not passed through S_1, and the same, of course, holds for S_2. But logic cannot say anything about the assumption: A particle that has not passed through S_1 must have passed through S_2 if it reaches plate P. As far as classical logic is concerned, electrons may travel through two holes simultaneously, or they may even cease to exist somewhere between the source and the screen, and return somehow to existence somewhere between the screen and the plate later. Logic cannot justify or be made responsible for our assumption that from "The particle has not passed through S_1" the sentence "The particle has passed through S_2" follows for all particles that reach plate P.

Surprisingly, Von Weizsäcker sums up his considerations by saying: "We adopt the hypothesis: it is logic and only logic that stands in need of revision." Besides the traditional truth-values 1 and 0 (standing for "true" and "false") we must, therefore, introduce additional values, represented by complex numbers, to be interpreted as degrees of probability.

I think it is rather obvious that Von Weizsäcker has asked logic for services logic cannot supply and that therefore he wanted to introduce a new logic that might give him what he wanted. He postulated that the *tertium non datur* should guarantee the truth of a proposition that has the form "a v b", not just propositions of the form "a v a." Since logic could not guarantee the truth of propositions like "The electron has passed through S_1 or has passed through S_2," he looked for a logic that might be strong enough to do so. But a theory that does justice to these requirements could not be regarded as a logic. Any theory that tells us something about the behavior of things will be a part of physics—in a wide sense. We must be careful not to let our everyday convictions blur this difference. If we know that a person has been in a room with doors A and B but no windows and I later meet this person outside the room, it is natural to say that we conclude by mere logic that he must have left through door A or through door B and only through one of them. Granted our knowledge about normal behavior of human bodies, we can use parts of this knowledge as suppressed premises in our deduction. Our inference will then be logically safe. But logic alone would not justify us in deducting our conclusion from the explicitly given premises. Logic cannot exclude the possibility that human beings may split in two, go through walls, or vanish inside a room to resume existence outside it later on, etc. It is *physics* that makes us think such behavior so improbable as to be practically impossible.

The dissatisfaction with classical logic in the case of Von Weizsäcker is, I think, also motivated by the following idea: Classical logic has grown out of Aristotelian ontology. One important feature of this ontology is the division of all objects into substances and properties. Macrophysical bodies have properties that we attribute to them just as we do to substances. These exhibit the structure "S is P," which is the fundamental propositional structure of Aristotelian or classical logic. But the relation of elementary particles to some of their "properties" is not of this kind. Particles are not strictly identifiable as individuals, and not everything that we may truly say about them concerns properties that apply to them, taken as substances. Often we can only attribute to them the probability of some results of measurement. If, in this way, the ontological basis of classical logic is proven to be inapplicable to quantum mechanics, how can classical logic, being its superstructure, fare any better?

But to say that for such sentential variables as a, b, c or p, q, r in the calculus of propositional logic we may only introduce sentences that are either the Aristotelian standard form "S is P" or reducible to it is clearly mistaken. Nothing keeps us from introducing, for p or q, a sentence like "the particle x is correlated to the probability amplitude *eidetic*" or something of that type. Our logic is not at all affected by such replacements.

We must, however, take seriously the proposal, made by many experts, that we should take account, even in our logic, of the fundamental fact that in many fields we cannot determine the truth-value of relevant propositions with any certitude. This applies to decisions of human beings; it applies equally to mathematical propositions if we talk about numbers that are not effectively computable, or for propositions such as Goldbach's theorem. It applies also to quantum physics and especially to the type of sentences that attribute position and momentum to a given particle. We might be tempted to introduce a new logic with more values than just the two truth-values. But then we should not forget that these values cannot be accepted as *truth-values in the normal sense*. They will be values of certainty of knowledge, concerning known truth, known falsity, and the impossibility of decision. To say that this kind of formalism would define a new ontology would just mean that we should let shrink our ontology to a description of things known or knowable. In this way, we could make human knowledge all-inclusive by definition, because we just exclude the possibility that there are many things we do not know and shall, possibly, never know.

It would also be a grave loss in simplicity to admit intermediate stages between "true" and "false." Meaninglessness of sentences is something we always have to reckon with, but these sentences should be placed outside the alternative of "true" and "false." We also saw that the notion according to which physical discoveries could teach us which logic is the "true" one, rests on confusion. How could one justify the relevant discovery as knowledge, and the deduction of new logical principles from these informations, if not by using the very canons of logic which are supposedly shown "invalid"? After dismissing the alleged parallel between Euclidean geometry and classical logic, we will find that such an enterprise cannot succeed.

The question as to which formalism is most convenient for the formulation of the results of physical research in the field of quantum physics is, of course, something for the physicists to decide, in possible cooperation with mathematicians and logicians in their capacity as specialists of formal systems. We may also leave it to the decision of physicists if they want to call such a formalism a "logic." But it would be overstating the case if a physicist would argue for the thesis that the formalism adopted by physicists for quantum mechanics should be also supposed to be the true general logic, simply because the physical phenomena he studies are, in some sense, fundamental to all reality. If the physicist advises a reform of logic, his proposal must be evaluated on the basis of logical and philosophical considerations. Our examination of the proposals Von Weizsäcker has put forward has shown, I think, that this attempt to solve the difficulties of understanding quantum physics by a revision of logic has not much to recommend it. The problem of the relation obtaining between the new logic and the classical logic, and especially the question in what sense classical logic may be valid in special limiting cases, are more difficult to answer than the initial question of how we might describe the relation of quantum physics to classical physical theory. This latter question is a genuine problem that may be cleared up by patient investigation and discussion among physicists. The first problem, however, that of the relation of the new quantum logic to classical logic, has the ring of a pseudo-problem.

Notes

*This is the text of the second of my "Howison Memorial Lectures," given 1971 in Berkeley, California, which has never been printed up to now. But since it deals with discussions held at Göttingen while J. N. Mohanty was present, he might like this souvenir, and since the question of the relevance of logic for science—and vice versa—is still debated today, it may be of interest to other readers as well.

1.   J. Von Neumann, *Mathematical Foundation of Quantum Mechanics* (Princeton: Princeton University Press, 1957); G. Birkhoff und J. Von Neumann, "The Logic of Quantum Mechanics," *Annals of Mathematics* 37, (1936), 823-43; and H. Reichenbach, *Philosophical Foundations of Quantum Mechanics* (California: University of California Press, 1944).

2.   W. V. Quine, *Philosophy of Logic* (Engelwood Cliffs, N. J.: Prentice Hall, 1970), chs. 6 and 7.

3.   B. Russell, *Introduction to Mathematical Philosophy* (London: George Allen & Unwin, 1948), 273.

4.   C. Münster and G. Picht, *Naturwissenschaft und Bildung* (Würzburg: I. M. Werkbund, 1953), 33-116.

PART 2

Transcendental Phenomenology Revisited

Chapter 6

Empirical and Transcendental Subjectivity: An Enigmatic Relation?

Christina Schües

> —*Mein Leben ist das Zögern vor der Geburt.* Kafka, Tagebuch 24. January 1922.

> —*Geburt als transzendentales Rätsel.* Husserl, Ms. AV 20.

Is the relation between empirical and transcendental subjectivity enigmatic? An enigma is a riddle or something baffling. What could be enigmatic or baffling about the relation between empirical and transcendental subjectivity? Why might this relation be an enigma? Mohanty writes that this is so because the relation includes an identity, difference, and parallelism. "To think these aspects of the relation—identity, difference, and parallelism—together would appear to be baffling."[1] In what follows, I will investigate these questions and offer an alternative way of thinking about the relation between the empirical and the transcendental.

The question of the relation is only relevant for a phenomenologist; it would not be relevant either for the empiricist or for the strict rationalist. Phenomenologists, such as Husserl or Merleau-Ponty, criticize and reformulate the alternatives of empiricism and rationalism which, despite their differences, are both held to be victims of the prejudice of the same natural objective attitude. In other words, they would argue that the empiricists and the rationalists are both rationalizing the same *doxa:* the former sees in his unreflected natural experience the human being in its bodily thinghood and behavior which, as such, lacks interiority; the latter envisages an all-encompassing consciousness. To be sure, the human sciences and our ordinary human understanding already presuppose the philosophical knowledge of the world and its principles, therefore, so the phenomenologist argues, we need to question the relation between the empirical subjectivity and philosophical principles underlying beliefs and reasons brought to light by way of the phenomenological reduction. With a view to examining the relation between empirical and transcendental subjectivity, I will begin by presenting the phenomenological project of transcendental subjectivity with reference to descriptive and constitutive phenomenology. Then, I will turn to Husserl's later work in which he addresses the topic of generative phenomenology in the context of a phenomenology of the lifeworld. Finally, I will bring into the discussion the most fundamental problems of phenomenology, birth and beginning, and I will look at things from the standpoint of natality in the hope that this might serve to ground the relation between the empirical and transcendental subjectivity in a different way.

The Phenomenological Project of the Period around *Ideas I*[2] and the *Analysen zur passiven Synthese:* Descriptive and Constitutive phenomenology

Phenomenology is the science of those "phenomena" that present themselves in consciousness. The notion of the "phenomenon" has been used in a wide variety of ways by different philosophers: For Kant the whole world is a phenomenon for the subject, dependent upon how the thing-in-itself affects us in sensation, and upon the way the mind looks at it. The notion of the phenomenon implies there must be something corresponding to it that is not a phenomenon. For this reason, Kant postulates a thing-in-itself independent of our sensible constitution, a noumenon which transcends the phenomenon. Hegel rejects the distinction between phenomenon and noumenon. For him the real is the path of spirit. The phenomenon is the reality itself as it appears to consciousness. There are no essences behind or beyond phenomena, essences appear in and through existence. "Essence does not exist outside, or apart from or behind, or beyond its existential appearance."[3]

Husserl's notion of the "phenomenon" differs from both the Kantian and the Hegelian. He upholds the objectivity of the phenomenon, but gives it a meaning that accords with his form of transcendental phenomenology. Transcendental phenomenology is not a factual science like psychology, but is a science of essences and the essential structures of consciousness. Therefore, the phenomena of transcendental phenomenology will be characterized as non-real but certainly not as ideal in a platonic metaphysical sense. Phenomenology is a theory of essential being, dealing not with real, but with transcendentally reduced phenomena.[4] To take the appearance of the world as phenomena means to consider the world as "meaning." In other words, objects are thematized according to their modes of presentation for consciousness. The phenomenon is an object as it appears, together with its mode of givenness for consciousness. Consciousness constitutes the meaning of the world, that is, the phenomenon "world." Thus, phenomenology is a descriptive science of experience that does not concern itself with either the subject or the object alone but with the field of appearing appearances in which an object or a human being is perceived as such and such, that is, as meaningful. Along these lines, Mohanty also draws the following conclusion regarding the phenomenon that had been thought to surpass the strictly transcendental-phenomenological domain: Every feature of the empirical—corporeality, historicity, linguisticality—are preserved in the transcendental, only, as Husserl would say, "within quotation marks."[5] The meaning of the quotation marks will be considered by describing how we gain access to the domain of transcendental subjectivity.

The Phenomenological Method

Phenomenology discloses consciousness as a uniquely privileged realm, prior to every other domain, including that of the objective world. This disclosure of a privileged realm of consciousness proves necessary in order to avoid a vicious circle that becomes most conspicuous when problematizing experiences. For as long as the phenomenological reduction has not been applied, consciousness is just another domain of the real world. And, therefore, experiences are interpreted as causally dependent upon real things, that is, upon physical and psychological events that are both external and internal to the organism of the experiencing subject. In other words, a duality is assumed to prevail between the real world and consciousness, and, as a result, countless questions, such as those concerning the problem of "reference" continue to haunt the philosopher who theorizes about experience from the standpoint of the natural attitude, that is, from the standpoint of a concept of objectivity, which is the prevailing concern of the positive sciences. The interpretation of these different ways of apprehension of an experience leads to the demand that every reference to physical or psychological processes is excluded from any phenomenological description. Radical philosophizing demands that the existence of Cartesian, worldly subjectivity be justified as stringently as the existence of the objective world. Therefore, in order to investigate the sense, or meaning, of experiencing and understanding human beings as agents whose actions are manifest in particular customs and practices, as persons who hold opinions, as perceivers who perceive something as something, we must take ourselves to be transcendental subjectivities.

Taking ourselves as transcendental subjectivities requires a self-reflection on the structures of our own consciousness, and this in order to open up the field of transcendental subjectivity, a field within which one can then go on to study the sense-constituting structures of intentionality. Thus, phenomenological reflection is motivated by a mundane interest in directing one's attention toward a theme one wants to determine more specifically. The theme under investigation is taken as the guideline for the phenomenological method.

Phenomenology can be understood as a method; however, one should not understand "method" as a neutral instrument. Rather, it furnishes the phenomenologist with a way of approaching a theme in question. Hence, the way of approaching a theme, that is, the thematization, and the theme itself are methodically intermingled in the concept of "phenomenon."

Basically, one can distinguish two reductions in order to explain the project of transcendental phenomenology: the eidetic and the transcendental reduction. The eidetic reduction[6] is used in both descriptive and transcendental phenomenology. It searches for the invariant and regulative structure of a phenomenon by means of imaginative variation, so that the invariant feature is abstracted from the contingent and individual particularities of the phenomenon in question. The transcendental reduction not only thematizes that "as which" something appears, but also the appearing of this "something as something." The belief in the existence of what is posited as existent is bracketed, inhibited, and then thematized by way of an intentional analysis. In order to understand the function of inhibiting a belief and the resulting phenomenological turn of attitude, we have to study the transcendental reduction in its executive power.

The Husserlian radicalization of Cartesian skepticism and empiricist introspection, and the move from the natural (personalistic) attitude to a transcendental attitude (*epoché*) is only fully achieved with the transcendental reduction. This further step is needed in order to justify the claim to universality and the foundational character of phenomenology. The transcendental reduction turns consciousness back on itself, explicitly and methodically, in order to clarify how consciousness constitutes objectivity and how one's belief in the world takes place. By way of transcendental reflection, I not only suspend my belief in the world, that is, neutralize my relation to the world, at the same time, the "object" is thereby put in "quotation marks" and named the "intentional object." The simple denial of "existence" or a skeptical approach towards existence would then feature as a modalization rather than a suspension of belief.[7] Thus, any phenomenological reflection radicalizes Cartesian skepticism not by doubting but by inhibiting, that is, by suspending the "existential belief"; it puts it out of action and turns one into a "disinterested observer," or better still, into a "non-participating observer," one who remains detached from the execution of the belief in existence. It also opens up the transcendental sphere of subjectivity by focusing on operative acts in the sphere of subjective consciousness. Thus, we can investigate what was still covered over in introspection: doxic-thetical acts (acts of believing and positing) and their modifications, the correlative intentional objects with their characters of reality, doubtfulness, etc., vis-à-vis an intended object and myself.

Transcendental Subjectivity-Mundane, Empirical Subjectivity

The transcendental reduction does not change the world; the world is not different in the transcendental attitude. It is the same world but it appears different—as emergent, accessible or inaccessible, appearing, nascent. Transcendental subjectivity "stands for that field of experience in which all interpretations have their source . . . the life of an ego is a developing process—psychologically as well as historically: this indeed is a consequence of the thesis of parallelism between the empirical and the transcendental."[8]

Every transcendence of my natural consciousness (and even the world as a whole) is reduced to the transcendental immanence of my pure consciousness. Thus, by means of transcendental reflection, I approach the field of transcendental subjectivity, which is purified, or liberated, from all beliefs in being or modes, and in which I can thematize the field of my cogitations in terms of the life of my streaming acts of consciousness with their intentional correlates. Thus, the transcendental attitude is not just an act of distancing myself from the being of the world; it is also the elucidation of this act in order to have access to the experience of being. The intentional "relation" to the object as it emerges becomes the focus of transcendental reflection, not the "object" itself. The intentional correlation establishes a "relation" between an actual lived activity and the intended objects. Thus, intentional analysis reveals the real (*reel*) components of the act of consciousness, under the name of *noesis* and *hyle*, together with their intentional correlate, called the *noema*.

In focusing on the immanent acts of intentionality in terms of their *noetic-noematic* components, (that is, their meaning and meaning bestowing function), the "world" is regarded as a correlate of transcendental subjectivity. Hence, phenomenological reflection radicalizes the reflective "inner experience" of the tradition of British empiricism, from Locke to Hume, and transforms it into a study of the anonymous transcendental structures of consciousness.

The phenomenologist can disclose or elucidate the anonymity of the structures of consciousness both in static analysis and in *genetic analyses*.[9] Static analysis describes experiences as they are already constituted in terms of the *noema-noesis* correlation. By abstracting from considerations of the temporal structure and constitution, static analysis is concerned with the description of how things are experienced.

Questions concerning how things come to acquire the sense that they have for experiences belong to a genetic analysis. The concept of constitution (that is, the emergence, appearing, or disclosure, of sense and the full functioning of intentionality) can only be brought out through a genetic analysis that works in a way that is complementary to the transcendental reduction. The advantage of transcendental phenomenology is that it provides a *method* enabling the phenomenologist to reach back to the foundational field of knowledge;[10] it opens up the field of transcendental subjectivity as the founding dimension for all intentional acts in their correlation with intentional contents, (that is, *noematic* senses). Thus, transcendental subjectivity is constitutive of all mundane objectivities. It seeks, by using the method of transcendental reflection, to arrive at an understanding of the categorical features and structures of our experiences and of our world in terms of the meaning-structures of human subjectivity.

Human subjectivity is taken as the ultimate regulating principle and as the basis of all structurings and orderings, meanings and interpretations.[11] At this point it seems as if the question between empirical subjectivity and transcendental subjectivity has been shifted to the concept of correlation. Husserl does indeed carry through and investigate the correlation between *cogito* and *cogitatum,* that is, an examination of the relation between the act modality and its object. However, this form of correlation, which is particularly relevant in descriptive phenomenology, becomes problematic in constitutive phenomenology because we then ask for the fundamental principle relating constitutive transcendental subjectivity to constituted empirical subjectivity. And this relation might not be as clear a correlation as it appears in descriptive phenomenology.

Transcendental Ego-Mundane, Empirical Ego

When I have access to the domain of transcendental subjectivity, I am using the reflective stance of the transcendental ego. However, this does not mean that the transcendental ego is some sort of super-ego that reaches over all empirical, mundane egos. The transcendental ego stands for the field of experiences in which all interpretations have their source.[12] The enigmatic relation between the transcendental ego and the mundane ego can now be considered, but only from the transcendental stance: They are identical in so far as, and here I refer to Mohanty, "the empirical ego and the transcendental ego are . . . one and the same—the same entity considered from two different standpoints . . . in so far as I am the (reflective) source of all those interpretations with which I understand myself and my world, I, this very same ego that was identified as an empirical ego, is a transcendental ego."[13] One evidence for this is to be found in the self-experience. However, to simply identify the two would mean to fall in the trap of a metaphysical error of ascribing a constituting function to the empirical, such as, for instance, psychologism does.[14] The difference between the two attitudes is well established by means of the phenomenological reduction that allows us to move in between the two—whereas it still has to be determined how we "move back" to the empirical.

A parallelism appears when we realize that:

> the very same experiences which, construed as belonging to nature, are empirical events subject to the causal or other laws of nature, are understood in their essential structure, intentional acts which, by virtue of their intentional contents, confer sense on their objects and so are transcendental. This is the sense of that "wonderful parallelism" between the empirical and transcendental to which Husserl often referred.[15]

In other words, each "numerically selfsame intentional experience of an empirical ego is also a transcendental experience of the 'corresponding' transcendental ego."[16] These aspects of the relation—identity, difference, and parallelism—can only be considered from a transcendental stance because only then the experiences as "empirical" make sense; that is, every feature of the "empirical" is preserved (only in quotation marks) in the transcendental.[17]

Now we can come back to the question of considering why this relation is baffling. Certainly, to think together identity, difference, and a parallelism is rather baffling, but it seems to me that this is not the whole story. It is somewhat enigmatic only because the simple reference to the quotation marks undermines an unbridgeable difference, a deep gap between the mundane and the transcendental ego that cannot be accounted for by the transcendental attitude.

The difference between the empirical and the transcendental is already implied by suggesting that, from the transcendental standpoint, the phenomenologist becomes a disinterested observer. And from here the question of how to "move back" to being an interested participant in-the-world becomes pertinent.

Husserl's Later Works: Critical and Ethical Concerns[18]

In his later work, Husserl questioned the rigid distinction between the transcendental and the empirical, mundane attitude, he introduced the idea of a mundanization (*Verweltlichung*) of the "transcendental" itself. This means that the transcendental flows back (*einströmen*) into the mundane world. Mohanty concludes from the idea of mundanization that the transcendental actually needs the empirical mundane: "Without such mundanizing self-interpretation, the transcendental would not apperceive itself as transcendental."[19] This thesis can be interpreted in two ways: one interpretation could be followed up with Merleau-Ponty, who argued that transcendental reflection can never be based upon a fully complete reduction.[20] His point is that we cannot even get to the transcendental right away, even from the beginning of life, because our bodily anchorage keeps us in the world. The other way would be to press the question as to how this mundanization could take place, and to ask whether perhaps the empirical-transcendental relation should be founded on another dimension. With a view to answering this latter question I will take another look at the difference between the two.

There is an even deeper issue that makes the difference enigmatic, or even unbridgeable: the transcendental ego, considered in genetic analysis, has never been born and will never die;[21] therefore, birth and beginning cannot be thematized from genetic analysis. Genetic analysis thematizes the constitution of sense and self-temporalization only within the life of an individual consciousness, that is, between the limits of birth and death. It also treats the temporalization of individual subjectivities and their experiences of others, worlds, and communities on the basis of an egology.[22] In this analysis, birth and death of an ego can only be treated as "phenomena of a limit" (*Grenzphänomene*).[23]   In genetic analysis, Husserl cannot thematize birth, death, and generativity as moments of the entire relational context (*Gesamtzusammenhang*) of human life. From the transcendental stance, birth, death, and generativity are "transcendental enigma,"[24] which means at this point that, so far from having solved one enigma, we have rather simply acquired a second.

Generative Phenomenology

In his later works, Husserl refers to notions such as generativity, birth, death, historicity. He also seem to see the phenomenological task as describing "phenomena" and as adopting a critical approach even to the point of demanding the participation of the phenomenologist in the procedure of sense constitution within the world.[25]

I would like to defend the thesis that the perspective of natality serves to ground a generative phenomenology that turns phenomenology into an investigative and critical enterprise. The perspective of natality not only sheds light on the enigmatic relation between the empirical and the transcendental subjectivity, but also on the idea of birth and death being a "transcendental riddle."

In the *Cartesian Meditations,* Husserl refers to generative problems that are highly concrete and that need to be worked out in order to ground genetic transcendental phenomenology.

> The fundamental level is . . . the one pertaining to "my" ego in respect of his primordial own-essentialness. Constitution on the part of the consciousness of internal time and the whole phenomenological theory of association belong here; and what my primordial ego finds in original intuitive self-explication applies to every other ego forthwith, and for essential reasons. But with that . . . genetic problems of birth and death and the generative nexus of psycho-physical being have not yet been touched manifestly they belong to a higher dimension and presuppose such a tremendous labor of explication pertaining to the lower spheres that it will be a long time before they can become problems to work on.[26]

Moreover, Husserl chooses, for instance, the title "*Generativität-Geburt und Tod als Wesensvorkommnisse für die Weltkonstitution*"[27] in order to express that birth, death, and generativity belong to the essential structure of human beings and function as constitutive of the world. The question concerning the work sphere of a generative phenomenology leads, on the one hand, to the question concerning the characteristic of generative problems and, on the other hand, to the question of the generative phenomenological method itself. I will begin with generative phenomenology.

Characteristics of Generative Problems

Transcendental phenomenology has its starting point either in individual subjectivity itself or in a synchronic field of contemporary subjects, or else it takes its start in an intersubjectivity founded on an egology. Generative phenomenology, as could be understood with Husserl, treats phenomena that are intersubjective, historical, cultural, and generative. On the one hand, "generativity" or "generative" means, for Husserl, a process of becoming that is generative in the sense of constituting of meanings (in the genetic sense) and, on the other hand, a historical and social development reaching over generations—a spiritual generativity that stands along with natural generativity in a bodily intertwinement (*leibliche Durchdringungsverhältnis*). "Generativity signifies then, that I do not only come and am with others in the world, but also I come from others and continue living in others."[28]

All of the phenomena in generative phenomenology concern borders, thresholds, and transitions that are most fundamental for the understanding not only of birth, death, and beginning, but also of language, personal relations, gender relations, and history. All of these phenomena are thresholds in an asymmetrical sense because the "before" and the "after" are not reversible locations.[29]

Generative phenomena are not given in experiences, as are, for instance, perceptual objects. They never concern only one individual; therefore, their constitution does not even make sense without some reference to the generative dimension. Even the relation between universal, transcendental subjectivity and concrete, mundane, individual subjectivity must be referred to the more fundamental dimension of generativity.

In order to address the question of the relation between the transcendental and the empirical, or the transcendental ego of the phenomenologist and the mundane ego of individual subjectivity, the perspective of natality, that is, the perspective of the individual beginning in-the-world, is quite fundamental, even in comparison to the other generative problems.[30] The reference to the fact of being-born and the principle of natality have consequences for our thinking of temporality and generativity, the relation between universality and concreteness, transcendentality and mundaneity. They both are based on one absolutely certain truth: the fact of being born, which itself lies in the past but opens up the future, that is, the possibility of personal and historical beginnings. Hence, human beings are born to live and not born in order to die.[31] My birth is apodictic *qua* my existence but also presumptive because I know about it only by way of others and not as a memorable *cogitatum*. The fact of my birth gives me the insight that others must be mundanely primary.

A few remarks on the structure of birth shall shed light on the reason for assuming that the perspective from our own birth, that is, the perspective of natality, is the most essential for the phenomenologist's "personal change . . . the most existential change"[32] to the transcendental attitude and the investigation of world constitution.

Birth

The notion of birth concerns basically three aspects: giving birth, the process of birth, and being-born. From our point of view, it is this third aspect which is relevant. Being-born concerns a threshold of beginning for an ego in its concrete complexity that differs from the Husserlian investigation concerning the self-presentation of the transcendental ego. Being-born does not mean a "waking up" of a sleeping ego, as Husserl, at times, seems to imply.

When we reflect upon the fact of being-born, we are, at the same time, obliged to come to terms with the fact of being-born-from-somebody, the mother.[33] With the reference to the delivering mother, birth should be taken to mean generative birth. Birth, in the sense of the physiological process, already presumes an abstraction. The fact that there was some other who has been delivering somebody "new" and who guarantees the constitutive aspect of being existent in the world means that existence should be primarily defined as relation. The "ex," the from-the-mother who is the threshold of an exit from, as well as being the entrance to, the world, together with the newcomer, who is defined as existence, asserts the necessity of the relation, that is, a "cum" (a with). "In the beginning stands for the existent, the relation. Or better, the relation is the beginning: a concrete, final relation to another existent. A contingent, but at the same time unreplaceable, relation."[34]

With the reference to the primal occurrence of the existence of the existent we undermine a philosophical tradition that speaks of THE HUMAN in general. Birth is the first primal appearance of an essence, a singular, unrepeatable, gendered, and bodily reality for and with other human beings. This occurrence is the manifestation of a fundamental difference and relation between human beings. Human beings are trivially equal insofar as they are human beings, yet each human being is different from another human being "who ever lived, lives, or will live."[35]

Being-born means that from the time of being-in-the-world this social and material world can be intentionally explored.[36] Intentionality, we learned generally from phenomenology, is the basic structure of being-in-the-world, it is perceptually being directed toward objects or persons; it implies, in speaking and acting, being directed towards meanings, relations with other human beings, being directed towards tasks and events. Intentionality implies directionality but also a striving for . . . something or somebody—for meanings. Provided one does not reduce this striving-for to some notion of instinctual drive, it may be regarded as opening up a sphere of possibilities and freedom in which initiative is anchored.[37]

Initiative, the capacity for beginning, finds its origin in the turn, or "*Grund-Satz*,"[38] from prenatal existence to natal existence.[39] "*Satz*" means, on the one hand, a leap from one mode of being to another whose essential trait is intentionality. Hence, this leap is fundamental to intentionality, which is always in the world and constitutive of the world. And intentionality is the constituent of being-there, therefore, being-there is natal (*gebürtlich*). That is, the sense-constitution of having-begun-being-there (*angefangenes Dasein*) finds its entrance into the world as beginning-being-there (*anfängliches Dasein*). On the other hand, "*Satz*" also means a transmission (or meditation) of sense between such meaning regions of the before and the after. This transmission refers only secondarily to the physiological sense of the intra- and extra-uterine life; more primarily, it refers to the transmission of this constitution of being-there and to a transmission between the generations—concretely speaking, the parent and the child. The general transmission of sense between generations and the constitution of history finds its exit at this point. Even if the transmission of sense between generations can be reciprocal, there remains the asymmetry we also find on the threshold of being-born. During birth there is a pull to being-there, to the future, towards-the-world without the possibility of return. With the interpretation of being-there as beginning (*anfängliches*), we assume that the threshold to the end of beginning is never fully achieved. Being-there means that we have passed the threshold between prenatal and natal existence but, at the same time, birth leaves its traces in our being-there and depicts it as having-begun-beginning-being (*angefangenes anfänglich-sein*).[40]

To summarize briefly the last thoughts concerning birth: Birth marks a basic plurality between human beings; it stands for the fact that relation is the beginning and that beings-born means to have the capacity to begin.

Generative Method from the Perspective of Natality

For Husserl, the phenomenological method is intertwined with the topic of investigation. Since neither a mundane reflection, which tries to grasp the beginning in-the-world *qua* memory, nor the transcendental reflection, which tries to gain access to such threshold phenomena (*Schwellenphänomene*) by way of a genetic analysis, were successful in describing them, we must consider a more fundamental phenomenological method, one that might be capable of coping with this demand. A generative reflection can be applied to the different phenomena that concern generativity. But in connection with our concern with the enigmatic relation between the mundane ego and the transcendental ego, we need to take up the perspective of natality. This means that the phenomenologist has to think the relation between I and other from the standpoint of its very first beginning and not from the standpoint of an isolated ego. In other words, the perspective of natality requires a thinking that does not so much lead up to a unity as it includes a crosswise duality, of which one axis is the relation between past and future by way of the being-born-from-somebody, and the other is the relation with (*Verbindung*) and the release from (*Entbindung*) the other and towards the world. The threshold of birth marks this dual aspect of the generative reflective stance, which is constitutive for the relation with oneself and others, and which binds the concrete and the universal.

The perspective of natality, that is, the thinking from one's own birth, means that the phenomenologist completes the twofold intertwinement of method and issue (*Sachverhalt*) with the third component of the "investigating self." Therefore, I understand phenomenology as philosophy of interrogation because the self of the phenomenologist is also located in a generative context and, therefore, s/he participates at the development and constitution of sense in an intersubjective and historical structure. As a constituting subjectivity, I am co-constituting and co-constituted as being born into, and dying out of, an historically and normatively significant world.[41] In other words, phenomenology is done from within generativity and "the phenomenologist and even phenomenology itself takes its stand within this historicity."[42] This means that if the phenomenologist takes the process of ongoing sense constitution into account, then s/he will realize that the activities of the transcendental ego are constantly flowing back into the world. From here the phenomenologist can either go the way of pure transcendental phenomenology and be faced with borderline phenomena s/he cannot have access to, or s/he takes the generative framework into account and so takes up the perspective of natality—which means philosophizing out of responsibility in the light of both being-born and being-born for the renewal of humanity.[43] Thus, doing generative phenomenology means becoming self-responsible for one's own being-there and its capacities for beginning, as well as for one's own generation and the constitution of the world.

The idea of taking on responsibility was first addressed by Husserl in the early twenties, and later in the *Krisis*, where Husserl saw the task of phenomenology as not simply one of furnishing description out of some pre-socratic wonder but rather out of an ethical concern for the course of humanity. However, when he mentioned generativity, Husserl seems to have had in mind the platonic motive of the "turn of the whole human being,"[44] which even leads to a "radical turn of the whole of humanity."[45] With this change of attitude the philosopher becomes an "absolute beginner"[46] because, at least in the Husserlian transcendental project, he gets access to the transcendental subjectivity and in this perspective he can question the theme of life-world. Being a "beginner" was already the theme in reference to birth, and we have already noticed that beginning is one of the phenomena that the transcendental phenomenologist cannot address, either in and from himself or even in reference to the transcendental ego. In generative phenomenology, the phenomenologist is considered to be a beginner; however s/he is not an absolute beginner because, first, a beginning is never absolute but always relative to that which was before; second, beginning means, as we saw in the context of the description of birth, a relation with somebody. From the perspective of natality, responsibility takes place principally with respect to the relation between human beings, to the relation between past and future, and to the sense constitution of the world. Hence, the possibility of beginning, being new, and making renewals requires a critical stance towards the past and towards the future.

By pointing towards the critical stance adopted by the generative reflection we can now readdress the enigmatic relation between the mundane and the transcendental. By following the line of thought presented above, it turns out that the perspective of one's own natality can ground this relation between two different attitudes concerning the world. When the transcendental phenomenologist turns upon him or herself, then s/he is already isolated and s/he has already begun. If one grounds the vertical relation between the concrete, mundane and the universal, transcendental ego on a generative dimension, then it no longer seems at all enigmatic. The complexity between identity, difference, and parallelism seems understandable and less baffling if one respects the natal perspective, which opens up a horizontal relation between ego and other in a generative complexity. Thus, generative phenomenology is grounded in a field of *tension* between beginning and continuation, existence and appearance, the ego and the others, the world and plurality. "The end of the common world has come when it is seen only under one aspect and is permitted to present itself in only one perspective."[47] This understanding of the constitution of the world depends upon the understanding of human relations and differences, for it is based upon the most fundamental perspective of all: the perspective of natality.

Notes

1. Mohanty, *Phenomenology,* 13.
2. Edmund Husserl, *Ideas Pertaining to a Pure Phenomenology and to a Phenomenological Philosophy, First Book: General Introduction to a Pure Phenomenology,* trans. F. Kersten (The Hague, Boston, Lancaster: Martinus Nijhoff, 1976). Henceforth, this book will be cited as *Ideas I.* Also see, Edmund Husserl, *Analysen zur passiven Synthese,* M. Fleischer (ed.), Husserliana X (The Hague: Martinus Nijhoff, 1966).
3. G. W. F. Hegel, *Encyclopedia of Philosophy,* trans. G. E. Mueller (New York: Philosophical Library, 1959), § 82.
4. See *Ideas I,* § 44.
5. Mohanty, *Phenomenology,* 93.
6. Intertwined with the transcendental reduction is the eidetic reduction. It is necessary (even though rarely discussed by Husserl himself) since it transforms transcendentally reduced phenomena into *exempla* characterized by an essential generality. (See *Ideas I,* § 47).
7. See, for example, *Ideas I,* § 31, 32 and Husserl, *Cartesian Meditations,* § 9-11.
8. Mohanty, *Transcendental Phenomenology,* 157.
9. See Husserl's works after *Ideas I,* for instance, CM, *Formale und transzendentale Logik: Versuch einer Kritik der Logischen Vernunft,* P. Janssen (ed.), Husserliana XVII (The Hague: Martinus Nijhoff, 1974).
10. See Edmund Husserl, *Die Krisis der Europäischen Wissenschaften und die Transzendentale Phänomenologie: Eine Einleitung in die Phänomenologische Philosophie,* W. Biemel (ed.) Husserliana VI (The Hague: Martinus

Nijhoff, 1962), § 26. Henceforth, this book will be cited as *Krisis*.

11. Transcendental philosophy does not concern itself exclusively with transcendental arguments, they can be only part of a larger philosophic strategy. Compare Mohanty, *The Possibility of Transcendental Philosophy*, xvii.

12. See Mohanty, *The Possibility of Transcendental Philosophy*, 156.

13. Mohanty, *The Possibility of Transcendental Philosophy*, 153.

14. Mohanty, *Phenomenology*, 93.

15. Mohanty, *Transcendental Phenomenology*, 153.

16. Mohanty, *Phenomenology*, 13.

17. Mohanty, *Phenomenology*, 93.

18. Husserl, *Krisis* and *Vorträge und Aufsätze* (1922-1937), T. Nenon and H. R. Sepp (eds.), Husserlina XXVII (The Hague: Martinus Nihoff, 1993). Henceforth, this book will be cited as Hua XXVII.

19. Mohanty, *Phenomenology*, 93.

20. Maurice Merleau-Ponty, *Phenomenology of Perception*, trans. C. Smith (London: Routledge & Kegan, 1962), introduction.

21. For a discussion, see my article: "Generative Probleme als transzendentale Leitfaden," in E. W. Orth, K. H. Lembeck (eds.), *Phänomenologische Forschungen*, Neue Folge 2 (Frankfurt/München: Alber, 1997), 206 - 22.

22. For instance in the *Cartesian Meditations*.

23. Edmund Husserl, Unpublished Manuscript, Ms. C8, 2ff. The notion of limit implicates an egological reduction, which is a steady impoverishment of the egological life up to a limit. Husserl speaks in this context also of the analogy to an ego which falls asleep and awakes.

24. Edmund Husserl, Unpublished manuscript, AV20/15a: "Aber die Transzendentalität der Rückfrage von der seienden Welt führt . . . nicht zum Ziel-sie führt nur zum Tod und zur Geburt als transzendentales Rätsel."

25. See for this issue Husserl's lectures on "the renewal" (*Die Erneuerung*) which at first were printed in the Japanese journal *The Kaizo*, Hua XXVII.

26. Husserl, *Cartesian Meditations*, § 61.

27. Edmund Husserl, *Zur Phänomenologie: der Intersubjektivität. Text aus dem Nachlaß*, I. Kern (ed.), Husserliana XV, (The Hague: Martinus Nijhoff, 1973), 171. Henceforth, this book will be cited as Hua XV.

28. Bernhard Waldenfels, *Das Zwischenreich des Dialogs. Sozialphilosophische Untersuchungen in Anschluss an Edmund Husserl* (The Hague: Martinus Nijhoff, 1971), 346. My translation.

29. See Bernhard Waldenfels, *Ordnung im Zwielicht* (Frankfurt a. M.: Suhrkamp, 1987), 29f.

30. At this point I would distinguish my account of generative phenomenology from the interpretation by Anthony Steinbock, "Generativity and Generative Phenomenology," in *Human Studies*, 12 (Dordrecht: Kluwer, 1995), 55-79.

31. Hannah Arendt, *The Human Condition* (Chicago/London: University of Chicago Press, 1958), 246.

32. *Krisis*, § 35.

33. See Adriana Cavaero, "Schauplätze der Einzigartigkeit," in S. Stoller, H. Vetter (eds.) *Phänomenologie und Geschlechterdifferenz* (Wien: Universitätsverlag, 1997), 211ff.

34. Caverero, "*Schaupläze der Einzigartigkeit*," 212 (my emphasis).

35. Hannah Arendt, *The Human Condition*, 8.

36. See my exposition of the birth as a fundamental condition of intentionality: "The Birth of Difference," in: *Human Studies* 20 (The Hague: Kluwer, 1997), 243-52.

37. See Hans Saner, *Geburt und Phantasie* (Basel: Lenos 1987), 26.

38. Schües, "The Birth of Difference," 246.

39. Birth means also a biological development from one state to the next. But this is not my concern here.

40. Hannah Arendt characterizes birth as the condition of the possibility and capacity of beginning, as the "beginning of the beginning," as a being-natal, that is, being a beginning. If birth is the condition of the possibility of beginning, then natality is the essential structure of each human being-born through with s/he can be initiative. She writes: "Because [men] are *initium*, newcomers and beginners by virtue of birth, men take initiative, are prompted into action. "g" Hannah Arendt, *The Human Condition*,177.

41. See Hua XV, 139.

42. "Aber der Phänomenologe und die Phänomenologie stehen selbst in dieser Geschichtlichkeit," Hua XV, 393.

43. Compare Antony Steinbock, "Spirit and generativity," in N. Depraz, D. Zahavi (eds.) *Alterity and Facticity: New Perspectives on Husserl* (Dordrecht: Kluwer, 1998), 163-204.

44. Martin Heidegger, *"Platons Lehre von der Wahrheit" Wegmarken* (Frankfurt: Klostermann, 1978), 25. My translation: "Umwendung des ganzen Menschen."

45. "Radikale Änderung des gesamten Menschentums," *Krisis*, 154.

46. *Krisis*, 136.

47. Hannah Arendt, *The Human Condition*, 58.

I thank Professor R. Bernet, Director of the Husserl-Archiv Leuven, for his kind permission to quote from unpublished Husserl manuscripts.

Chapter 7

Toward Transcendental Relativism: Reading Buddhist Non-Dualism as Phenomenology[1]

Gereon Kopf

In his book *Phenomenology: Between Essentialism and Transcendental Philosophy,* Professor J. N. Mohanty locates phenomenology between transcendental constitution theory and essentialism. A similar discussion, albeit with a different focus, can be found in the perennial controversy between existential and transcendental phenomenology. While the former debate focuses on the status of essences and the latter on the viability and nature of the transcendental ego, ultimately, both explore the feasibility of reliable if not indubitable knowledge and, unable to come to an agreement, split along the lines of relativism and foundationalism. The former position, which includes a transcendental constitution theory and an existential phenomenology, à la Jean Paul Sartre, posits a relativity of constituting subjectivity and constructed objectivity (in Sartre's case the relativity of the projecting consciousness and its own ever-elusive existence) and subsequently implies an inherent perspectivalism and an impossibility to grasp things-(or essences)-as-they-are. The latter, essentialism and transcendental phenomenology, on the contrary, postulate essences and/or a transcendental ego respectively and, subsequently, a transcendental foundation of human experience. Relativism, thus defined, bases its main argument on the intentional nature of consciousness, which posits the object of knowledge vis-à-vis the *noetic* act of knowing. Subsequently, the knower is not only stuck in a circle of subjectivity but, moreover, is separated from the thing-in-itself and also from the objective meaning *qua noema,* as Jacques Derrida has argued, by an infinite abyss of difference and by an "endless postponement, deferral."[2] At the same time, however, as Mohanty argues, relativism is inherently self-defeating: What is the foundation that justifies the universalist claim of relativism and individualism? If experience is open-ended, how can the definite assertion concerning the open-endedness of experience be made? The very notion of perspectivalism necessitates the transcendental ego before which "all possible standpoints are arraigned."[3] In this paper, I will propose a third position, which I term transcendental relativism and which derives from Buddhist non-dualism. It is my belief that such a transcendental relativism theorizes a transcendental realm without committing to absolutism and accepts the perspectival and relative predicament of human experience without having to concede the self-defeat inherent in radical relativism and perspectivalism. For practical reasons, I will limit the present discussion to the transcendental ego or the lack thereof, which (or better, the Buddhist version of which) plays a central role within Buddhist non-dualism. I will hint at the status of essences within a non-dualistic phenomenology whenever prudent; however, the topic will have to be discussed in a separate study in more detail.

Preliminary Reflections

At the onset of this essay, three basic considerations are necessary. First, in order to enable a comparative study between thinkers belonging to the phenomenological movement[4] on the one side, and Buddhist philosophers on the other, I would like to distinguish between the phenomenological movement in particular and the phenomenological project in general, which is not bound to a specific philosophical tradition but rather to a particular philosophical method. In using the label "phenomenology," it is not my intention to either assume or argue that phenomenology is monolithic or to negotiate the differences between different phenomenologies. Rather, it will designate the phenomenological project as the particular philosophical methodology and enterprise, which rejects metaphysical speculations in favor of a return *zu den Sachen selbst* (to the things themselves), as Edmund Husserl puts it, or, in Zen terminology, to reality-as-it-is, in order to unravel what the members of the phenomenological movement call essences and Buddhists call suchness (*tathatā*). By the same token, I will use the term "phenomenologist," if not indicated otherwise, to designate a philosopher dedicated to the phenomenological project in general rather than to a member of the phenomenological movement and his/her phenomenology in particular.

Second, I would like to outline three fundamental characteristics of the phenomenological project: adoption of the *cogito* as the starting point of the phenomenological project, the Kantian legacy, and the return to the given "facts." This list is not designed to underprivilege issues such as the suspension of "all 'theory'" and the status of essences, but is rather motivated by the scope of the present essay. Phenomenologists of varying persuasion locate the beginning of philosophy in the self-conscious and self-reflective "I." After all, it is the experiential "I" which reflects about what-it-is, regardless of whether it is an individual "I" constructing his/her own self-identity or whether it is a philosophical "I" reflecting about philosophical issues in general; in either case, the experiential "I" functions as the author of its theory of this thought. Contrary to René Descartes' assertion, however, the self-conscious "I" encounters a world of objects, which does not comprise the things-in-themselves but the realm of the Kantian phenomena. In contrast to Cartesian philosophy, the phenomenological project is modified by the Kantian or Yogācāran legacy, which emphasize the predicament that what is given in experience does not comprise the things themselves but rather "the world existing for and accepted by me in such a conscious cogito,"[5] or in Yogācāra terminology, *vijñaptimātra*, "representation-only." It is this existential relationship between the self-conscious *cogito* and the world of objects given to the *cogito* in everyday awareness (and neither the Cartesian *cogito* nor the empirical sense-data by themselves) that comprises the evidence on which the phenomenological project is built. This binary structure of everyday awareness has been alternatively identified as: the polarity of *cogito* and *cogitatum* by Husserl; the "facticity" of self and world or the correlativity of the sentient and the sensible given in perception by Maurice Merleau-Ponty; the correlativity between the grasper (Skrt.: *grāhaka*) and grasped (Skrt.: *grāhya*)[6] by Vasubandhu; the juxtaposition of self (Jap.: *jiko*) and the world *qua* "all dharmas" (Jap.: *manbō)* by the Japanese Zen master Dōgen Kigen. This correlativity of *cogito* and *cogitatum* constitutes the starting point for the phenomenological quest for the transcendental ego or its rejection.

However, and this is the third point to be considered, the relationship between the phenomenal and the transcendental provide the phenomenologist with what Mohanty terms a "baffling enigma."[7] In his *Phenomenology: Between Essentialism and Transcendental Philosophy,* Mohanty rejects a dualism between the transcendental and the phenomenal. While the transcendental realm escapes the phenomenal field in which it does not appear as an object, it also grounds and permeates the very realm it transcends; this existential predicament of the transcendental creates a paradox in that the phenomenal and the transcendental are both identical and different as well as, to use Merleau-Ponty's terminology, "infinitely distant" and "absolutely proximal." This paradoxical predicament of the transcendental is best illustrated in the relationship between the *cogito,* which Mohanty refers to as the empirical ego, and the transcendental ego. Leaving aside the issue of whether the transcendental realm takes on personal characteristics (as does Husserl's transcendental ego), or impersonal ones (in analogy to Sartre's "transcendental field, purified of all egological structure"[8]), the empirical ego *qua cogito* and the transcendental ego—or transcendental non-ego, for that matter—are simultaneously identical and different. (While Sartre does not have to worry about the relationship between the transcendental ego and the *cogito,* he cannot avoid having to clarify the relationship between *non-positional* awareness and *positional* consciousness;

I believe that both problems constitute similar dilemmas.) At any rate, in order to explore the relationship between the phenomenal and the transcendental realm, I would like to briefly define the two main players, namely the *cogito* and the transcendental ego. The *cogito* comprises the experiential "I" that encounters the world, perceives sense-data as well as mental images, and possesses one particular standpoint; the transcendental ego, on the other side, constitutes meaning, comprises "the identical pole of subjective processes,"[9] and possesses "no standpoint: All standpoints (and subsequently, empirical egos) are arraigned before his look."[10] However, while the *cogito* and the transcendental ego exhibit diametrically opposed and incompatible qualities nevertheless, they display an inherent identity; Mohanty argues that they are "the same entity considered from two different standpoints."[11]

So how can we resolve this dilemma? This question is especially important since a discussion of the relationship between the empirical and the transcendental will, ultimately, determine which interpretation of phenomenology (relativism, foundationalism, or transcendental relativism) constitutes the most feasible position. In the final chapter of his *Phenomenology: Between Essentialism and Transcendental Philosophy*, Mohanty offers three suggestions on how to resolve this enigma. First, he rejects the dualism inherent in the Platonic two-world theory. By the same token, he rejected a monistic interpretation of the transcendental ego in his *Transcendental Phenomenology*. Second, he points out the metaphysical fallacy of reifying the empirical and transcendental into the realms of immanence and transcendence respectively. Third, and finally, he suggests receiving some clues from Advaita Vedānta that may help to describe and theorize the relationship between the empirical and the transcendental ego without having to settle for either the dualistic or the monistic position. Buddhist non-dualism not only agrees with Mohanty's former two observations concerning the reification of the phenomenal and the transcendental, but also suggests, not unlike Mohanty, that a non-dualism of identity and difference may shed some new light on the "baffling enigma" of the relationship between the *cogito* and the transcendental ego.

A Non-Dualistic Phenomenology

Introduction

Having outlined the fundamental features of the phenomenological project, I would like to return to my original project, a Buddhist non-dualistic phenomenology, which does not side with either relativism or foundationalism, but rather proposes a transcendental relativism as intermediate position. Starting with the Gautama Siddhartha's assertion that suffering (*dukkha*) is caused by ignorance (*avidyā*), that is, by attachment to the I-factor, Buddhist non-dualism has traditionally focused on the exploration of the self. This centrality of the quest for self-awareness was summarized by Dōgen, who argued that "to study the buddha-way is to study the self."[12] Early Buddhism rejected any meta-physical reification of the self and defined the self *qua* no-self (Skrt.: *anātman,* Jap.: *muga*), avoiding both dualistic and monistic terminology, as either the middle path between eternalism and annihilationism or, during the foundational period of Mahāyāna Buddhism, as suchness, which entails both the transcendental realm *qua nirvāṇa* and the phenomenal realm *qua saṃsāra.*[13] In particular, the Mahāyāna Buddhist account of *nirvāṇa* as at once identical with and different from *saṃsāra* and as ultimately empty, defies metaphysical reification and bifurcation. In the thirteenth century, C. E. Dōgen, influenced by the non-dualistic models of the awakening of faith and of the Tʻien Tʻai thinker Chih-i, formulated a threefold conception of the non-dual self *qua* self (Jap.: *jiko*), no-self—literally "forgetting the self" (Jap.: *jiko o wasureru*), and the "actualization of myriad *dharmas.*"[14]

Dōgen's threefold model of the non-dual self is reflected in his non-dualistic phenomenology, which can be found in the opening paragraph of his "Shōbōgenzō Genjōkōan." Dōgen observes:

> When all *dharmas* become the buddha-dharma, there is illu-sion and enlightenment, there is practice, there is birth and death, there are buddhas and sentient beings. When all *dharmas* and the self are without a self, there is neither illu-sion nor enlightenment, neither buddhas nor sentient beings, neither birth nor death. Because the buddha-way originally transcends abundance and deficiencies, there are generation and extinction, illusion and enlightenment, beings and buddhas.[15]

Dōgen's non-dualistic phenomenology displays two basic characteristics: First, it discloses a three-step process that comprises a sequence of metaphysical claims expressing an affirmation ("there are buddhas and sentient beings"), a negation ("there are neither buddhas nor sentient beings"), and what appears to be a return to affirmation ("there are . . . beings and buddhas"). I believe that the third layer can be understood, in contradistinction to the first one, as dialectical affirmation or, as Tamaki Kōshirō translates/interprets in his translation of the *Shōbōgenzō Genjōkōan* into contemporary Japanese, as "that which surpasses the world of being-and-non-being."[16] Nishitani Keiji describes the third layer as the "standpoint which transcends being and non-being," as "being-and-non-being-mutually-identical" (Jap.: *umusōsoku*),[17] and evokes the paradoxical language of the *Heart Sūtra,* as "being-*qua*-non-being" (Jap.: *usokumu*).[18] The final layer seems to suggest the non-duality of not only identity and difference, but also of the preceding layers, expressing being and non-being respectively. Second, each of these metaphysical statements seems to be anticipated and contextualized by an introductory phrase that explicates its con-dition and phenomenological context. I take this to mean that Dōgen is not interested in a hierarchy of metaphysics, à la the Chinese Buddhist *p'an chiao* systems, but rather in describing, albeit in symbolic language, three layers of experience and selfhood, which he identifies by means of these quasi-metaphysical statements. For the present purpose it is important to note that Dōgen proposes three phenomenological realms: The first is characterized by affirmation and, as I will argue later, duality; the second, by negation and oneness; and the third by a dialectical affirmation expressed as "being-*qua*-non-being."

In order to conceive of a non-dualistic phenomenology, I would like to apply both existing phenomenological interpretations of Dōgen and insights of the philosophy of Nishida Kitarō to Dōgen's threefold schema. Even though predominantly driven by epistemological rather than soteriological concerns, Nishida's threefold system of universals (Jap.: *ippansha)* and/or worlds (Jap.: *sekai)*, which Nishida develops to investigate and clarify the structure of human knowledge, clearly reflects Dōgen's threefold model of affirmation, negation, and dialectical affirmation discussed above.[19] As Robert J. J. Wargo, Yuasa Yasuo, and Nagatoma Shigenori have shown, this theory of universals suggests three layers of the human experience that culminate in the mature expression of Nishida's conception of self-awareness *qua,* in his terms, *contradictory self-identity* (Jap.: *mujunteki jikodōitsu),* and can be interpreted epistemologically and psychologically. I believe that a discussion of these three worlds will shed light on Buddhist non-dualism, the paradoxical predicament of the transcendental, and the standpoint of transcendental relativism. Inspired by Merleau-Ponty's and Nishida's terminologies, I refer to these three phenomenological layers as *phenomenal world, lived world,* and *actual world* respectively.

The Phenomenal World

Buddhist non-dualism identifies as characteristic of everyday awareness a first realm of experience characterized by a binary structure and an affirming, if not naive, world view that takes appearances at face value. The first line of Dōgen's phenomenological schema "there is illusion and enlightenment, there is practice, there is birth and death, there are buddhas and sentient beings," describes the world view of an unenlightened being, which is Dōgen's synonym for everyday awareness. Dōgen characterizes the standpoint of everyday awareness as overly simplistic and concretistic: everyday awareness believes that things are what they appear to be. To everyday awareness, the words "illusion," "enlightenment," "practice," "buddhas," "sentient beings," "birth," and "death," designate identifiable, individual, real objects. This description of everyday awareness is reminiscent of Chih-i's contention that the beginner interprets even the symbolic language of *sūtras* literally and strives to identify, for example, the "marks" and "apparitions" of Buddha in the world of *saṃsāra*.[20] By the same token, everyday awareness tends to reify and substantialize the phenomena and facts of experience, self, others, and objects as-they-appear. This reification gives rise to a positivistic metaphysics, which overlooks the most salient feature of this world, namely, the interdependence of these seemingly independent and individual substances. Influenced by the Mahāyāna Buddhist tradition (and G. W. F. Hegel's dialectic), Nishida argues that the particulars that make up the world of objects are in-relation-to and opposed-by (Jap.: *ni tairitsu*) each other and, subsequently, disclose a *mutual relationship* (Jap.: *sōgō kankei*) and *mutual determination* (Jap.: *sōgō gentei*), juxtaposing particular and particular, particular and universal, and affirmation *qua* what-a-thing-is and negation *qua* what-it-is-not.

While Nishida develops this logic for the *abstract world* of ideas, his *world of judgment* (Jap.: *handan no sekai*), which is constructed by the dis-embodied *knowing self* (Jap.: *chiteki jiko*), he applies it to the juxtaposition of the *desiring self* (Jap.: *hossuru jiko*) and its environment (Jap.: *kankyō*).[21] Similarly, Dōgen locates the self (Jap.: *jiko*) in an *existential ambiguity* between self and other (Jap.: *tako*) and self and myriad *dharmas* (Jap.: *mambō*), which Tamaki takes as "environment" (Jap.: *kankyō*). This world, where *cogito qua* embodied-yet-alienated *cogito* reminiscent of Sartre's *being-for-itself* opposes the environment in a relationship of *mutual opposition,* I call the *phenomenal world.* This is the world where the empirical ego *qua* embodied-yet-alienated *cogito* encounters an external world, separated from itself by an infinite abyss, vis-à-vis which it defines itself as an individual self-conscious self. Dōgen explicates this existential isolation of the self in a passage from the "Shōbōgenzō Sansuikyō," in which he contrasts the *cogito* symbolized as "people outside the mountains" and, as I will discuss later, the *lived world qua* "people inside the mountains." "People outside of the mountains" are characterized by an existential isolation and alienation from their environment and, ultimately, from themselves. Dōgen utilizes phrases such as "not experiencing and not knowing" (Jap.: *fushin fuchi*) and "not seeing and not hearing" (Jap.: *fugen fubun*)[22] to express the self's existential alienation from the world. Here, Dōgen recognizes a lack of connection between the "person" and the "mountains." He attributes this existential alienation to the separation between epistemological subject and object. It is because subject and object are separate that "awareness," "understanding," "seeing," and "hearing" cannot occur. Given the individual nature of both subject and object, a coming-together of both is impossible; as a consequence, mountains (symbolizing the world) cannot be understood. In addition to this existential alienation of the self from its environment, the self experiences an existential alienation from itself, in Dōgen's words "if you doubt that mountains walk, you also doubt that you walk."[23] Dōgen maintains that "the person outside the mountains," incapable of understanding the mountains, is also incapable of knowing her/himself; alienation from the world is accompanied by self-alienation. In this quote, the term "doubting," literally, "the arising of doubt" (Jap.: *gichaku*), symbolizes the existential alienation the self experiences from the world it lives in as well as from itself. This alienation of the isolated *cogito* from itself is reminiscent of Sartre's *being-for-itself*, which is not able to comprehend its own existence *qua being-in-itself*.

However, neither Nishida nor Dōgen define the *cogito* in mere opposition to its environment but attribute to the *cogito*, in addition to its independent-yet-isolated existence vis-à-vis the world of objects, the character of a momentary awareness event (rather than a substance) and, more importantly, intentionality. Nishida's *desiring self* and Dōgen's self, subsequently, not only encounter but construct the world consisting of individual, seemingly real objects *qua object-for-itself*. The world of objects which appears in the *phenomenal world* is not an objective world but an object-world. By the same token, however, the *positional cogito* posits itself as an object and is thus incapable of knowing itself. Given the *positional* character of everyday awareness, Dōgen argues, the self *qua cogito* is inherently unable to understand either its own existence (Sartre's *being-in-itself*) or the world-as-it-is. Dōgen reinforces this contention in his fascicle "Shōbōgenzō Genjōkōan," where he observes that "it is delusion to practice-actualize myriad *dharmas* by applying ourselves to the *dharmas*;[24] it is enlightenment to practice-actualize the self when *dharmas* approach (the self)."[25] Here, the fundamental problem lies in the epistemic attitude of the *cogito* in separating itself from the world and positing the world *qua* object. The self that is being known is, as Immanuel Kant observed in his "Paralogisms," the self-*qua*-object. The object of the self's knowledge comprises, at best, an image of the self, which is not necessarily identical to the self-*qua*-subject, that is, to the self that does the studying. However, in the case that self-*qua*-subject and self-*qua*-object do not coincide, it is impossible for the self to "study" or know itself. The problem of self-consciousness constitutes a dilemma of far-reaching consequences, pronouncing the ineffability of the self-*qua*-subject and, concomitantly, the inherently subjective and evasive dimension of human existence. Dōgen's terminology of "the mind that cannot be grasped in a phrase" (Jap.: *shinfukatoku*) refers to the ever-evasive character of the self. The conception of "the mind that cannot be grasped in a phrase" echoes in some sense the elusiveness of Sartre's *being-for-itself*, which permanently escapes the grasp of its own *positional* awareness. Elsewhere, Dōgen argues that self awareness *qua* "to study the self" necessitates an existential and "epistemological re-orientation."[26]

However, while the subjectivity of the embodied-yet-alienated *cogito* necessitates the constructed world *qua cogitatum* in one sense, this opposition lacks true mutuality. To the contrary, given the unilateral nature of the *cogito's* intentionality, which extends from the *cogito qua noesis* to the *cogitatum qua noema*, it is possible to say, as Nishida often says, that the "*noesis* envelops the *noema*"[27] and that the "*noema* sinks into the middle of the *noesis*."[28] Thus defined, a unilateral intentionality that is directed and extends from the *cogito* to the world results in a solipsism if not monism of subjectivity where particular objects, as well as the world of intersubjectivity are posited *for-me*. This monism of subjectivity is diametrically opposed to the binary structure of the *phenomenal world* and, in some sense, negates this very binary structure and, subsequently, the *phenomenal world* itself. However, as I will argue later, these considerations do not abolish the *phenomenal world* or render obsolete the postulate of the *existential ambiguity* of *noesis* and *noema*, but rather supplements the duality of the *phenomenal world* with the monism of the *lived world*.

The Lived World

Buddhist non-dualism contrasts the standpoint of everyday awareness, which juxtaposes the *cogito* and the world of objects, with the *Weltanschauung* of the practitioner, who recognizes the emptiness and non-existence of all *phenomena*, symbolized by Dōgen as birth and death, as well as the absence of any form of duality. Nishida applies the epistemic structure of the practitioner's mind to the activity of what he calls the *willing self* (Jap.: *ishiteki jiko*) and argues that the *phenomenal world* is "enveloped" in the *lived world*, his *world of self-awareness* (Jap.: *jikakuteki sekai*), insofar as the *willing self* posits the *phenomenal world* as its own object.[29] While it is relatively simple to explain the monism of the *lived world*,[30] it is more difficult to account for its negative character. In his essay "The World of Intelligibility" (*Eichiteki Sekai*), Nishida argues that the *willing self* as well as the "standpoint of the acting self" (Jap.: *kōiteki jiko no tachiba*) unites *noesis* and *noema* in order to overcome self-alienation and to achieve self-awareness at the price of a solipsism of subjectivity. While self-awareness constitutes the self's knowledge of itself and, subsequently, the coincidence of the self-*qua*-subject and the self-*qua*-object, activity unites and engages the self with its environment. Therefore, self-awareness and activity, which Nishida defines alternatively as *acting-intuition* (Jap.: *kōiteki chokkan*), comprising the activity of acting directed toward the world and the passivity of experiencing, and as *unifying activity* (Jap.: *tōitsu sayō*), necessitates the "unity of acting and seeing"[31] as well as a subject-object-unity (Jap.: *shukyakuteki tōitsu*). At the same time, this very unity of *acting-intuition*, where self and world intermingle negates the static dichotomy between *cogito* and *cogitatum* characteristic of the *phenomenal world*; subsequently, the *lived world* negates the *phenomenal world in toto*. By the same token, the static dichotomy of the *phenomenal world* negates the *unifying activity* characteristic of the *lived* world and, subsequently, the *lived world* itself insofar as a static dichotomy, as Nāgārjuna has demonstrated, cannot be reconciled with the activity of the *lived* world. Nishida defines the world of subjective will and self-awareness, his *world of self-awareness*, as antithesis to the *phenomenal world* insofar as it discloses a monistic and negative structure, as if to say that the practice of meditation as well as any kind of activity transcends the dualism between self and world. At the same time, however, this *lived world* does not exist in a vacuum but posits and dialectically opposes the phenomenal world in toto as its *noematic* content. In short, the *lived world qua* unity of self and world posits the static opposition between its *noetic* and *noematic* aspect as its objective content.

However, Nishida and Dōgen do not conceive of the *lived world* as an abstract unity but rather as the *lived body*. Like Sartre, Dōgen and Nishida hold that the human body discloses the key to the world of otherness, the world that transcends individuality and opens an entrance to interpersonality; unlike Sartre, however, Dōgen and Nishida do not conceive of the human body as the mere object of objectification and alienation by the other and myself, that is, as something which clumsily stands between me and my freedom, but, on the contrary, as the gateway which discloses the "intercorporeal world"[32] where the self encounters the other and the individual encounters the world. If conceived of as an embodied-yet-alienated self, the "I" of everyday awareness statically opposes the world of phenomenal objects. Constituted vis-à-vis the world of phenomenal objects, the experiential "I" conceives of its somaticity as its existence (Sartre's *being-in-itself*) which is given to the *cogito* as its past; the body, thus conceived, becomes, at its best, an object "ready-to-hand" (Ger.: *Zuhandensein*), as Martin Heidegger would say, a tool in the service of the *being-for-itself* and, in the worst case scenario, dispossessed as a mere object for-the-other, whether it be individual or collective. However, when the self steps out of the confines of its static and solipsistic isolation vis-à-vis the world of objects, it existentially encounters, as both Nishida and Merleau-Ponty argue, the multifarious world of otherness in the place of their common somaticity. Through habitualization and sedimentation[33] of its engagement with the world, the self slowly assimilates and incorporates what appears to be external. Nagatoma identifies as "detensionality" this process in which the "tensionality" between *cogito* and environment is transformed, "whereby attending unself-consciously becomes an essential characterization of the person."[34]

The practice of any skill, such as playing the piano or riding a bicycle, illustrates how in the process of self-cultivation what-appears-to-be-external reluctantly enters my lived world, which it inhabits after being incorporated into my activity. Prior to the commencement of my practice, I experience the bicycle as a foreign object, which limits my freedom and, consequently, my self-projection. While practicing, I get used to the bicycle, which becomes a "part of my body" to the degree that I can unthinkingly control the bicycle as I control my body. In the process of self-cultivation *qua* "attunement,"[35] Heidegger's *ready-to-hand* loses its tool-character and becomes an extension of the *lived body*. Learning to ride a bicycle, the practitioner, at first, comprehends the *modus operandi* of riding a bicycle with her/his mind, that is, the practitioner attains the theoretical knowledge, *theoria*, of biking. In a second step, the body follows the instructions, first awkwardly, then, attempting to keep balance and to attune self and bicycle over and over again, gaining familiarity, until praxis and theory coincide in the very act of biking, when the practitioner rides his/her bicycle, to cite Kasulis's translation of Dōgen's "*hishiryō*," "without thinking." An examination of any instance of somatic learning, that is, any kind of learning which involves the psycho-physical complex, discloses a similar process, regardless of whether one engages in sport disciplines, martial arts, playing a musical instrument, or acquiring a simple everyday function such as walking to the grocery store.

Even though the *lived world* encompasses the *phenomenal world* as its *noematic* content, Nishida argues that the "juxtaposition" and "balance" between *noesis* and *noema* remains. In order to be rescued from its solipsism of subjectivity, the *willing self* has to encounter external objectivity. Furthermore, the very conception of the *noesis qua* the *lived world* necessitates its opposite and, subsequently, a *mutual opposition* of *noesis* and *noema.* While the *lived world* is characterized by the precedence of the *noesis* over the *noema,* Nishida postulates a third world, his *world of intelligiblity* (Jap.: *eichiteki sekai*), which incorporates the dialectic of *noesis* and *noema.* This world follows neither binary logic nor "sinks into the *noesis*"; on the contrary, the *world of intelligibility* discloses the existential correlativity of *noesis* and *noema* or, to be exact, as I have argued elsewhere, the dialectic between the symmetry between *noesis* and *noema* and the asymmetry where the "*noesis* envelops the *noema.*" This dialectic reflects Husserl's description of the transcendental ego as simultaneously self-contained and absolute in that it "no longer has a horizon that could lead beyond the sphere of his transcendental being and thus relativize him,"[36] and relational in that "it is solely in relation to intentional objectivities."[37] Ultimately, Nishida distinguishes between three different relationships between *noesis* and *noema:* the static but symmetric opposition in the *phenomenal world;* the asymmetric precedence of the *noesis* over the *noema* in the *lived world;* the dialectic of the symmetric and the asymmetric relationships characteristic of the *world of intelligibility,* which I call the *actual world.* The *actual world* displays a non-dualism of *noesis* and *noema* and defies both the binary structure characteristic of the *phenomenal* (and for that matter, the *abstract*) *world,* and the logic of *lived positionality* characteristic of the *lived world.*

The Actual World

The search for self-awareness finally discloses the *actual world* to the non-dualistic phenomenologist. Nishida argues that in the *world of self-awareness,* where the "*noesis* envelops the *noema,*" self-awareness, paradoxically, eludes the self. Self-awareness, Nishida argues, in different contexts necessitates the co-existence if not the self-identity of opposites such as *noesis* and *noema,* affirmation and negation, self and other. The former non-duality addresses the paradoxical character of self-reflexivity where "the self sees itself"; the latter two non-dualities thematize the psychological paradox, which I have elaborated elsewhere, that, in order to be affirmed by an other, I first must accept her/his independent existence which, in turn, objectifies and negates me. In Nishida's language, "the 'I' exists as an 'I' in that it recognizes the Thou as Thou"[38]—more drastically, that "without a Thou there is no 'I.'"[39] Either case, however, necessitates a *non-relative contradictory* identity of some kind or a "non-relative other inside."[40] In short, Nishida argues that paradoxes such as *affirmation-qua-negation* ((Jap.: *kotei soku hitei*), *non-relative negation* (Jap.: *zettai hitei*), and the *non-relative contradictory self-identity* (Jap.: *zettai mujunteki jiko dōitsu*) of *noesis* and *noema* constitute the logical *sine qua non* of self-awareness. I believe that these kinds of expressions have two fundamental implications: the transformation of the self and a non-dual structure.

Both Dōgen and Nishida are concerned with self-awareness as the *non-contradictory self-identity* of *noesis* and *noema*, and existence *qua being-in-itself* and consciousness *qua being-for-itself*. They describe the *actual world* in non-positional terminology. In a famous passage of his "Shōbōgenzō Genjōkōan," Dōgen identifies self-awareness *qua* "studying the self" as "forgetting the self" and as "realizing myriad *dharmas*." Dōgen describes this transformation as a transition from a self-centered attitude of "applying oneself to the *dharmas*" to the decentered attitude "when *dharmas* approach the self."[41] Nishida expresses this transformation more drastically when he observes that "[t]o truly see itself, the self must have lost self-consciousness"[42] and "[t]o die to oneself is to negate one's desire. But to die to one's desire is to live in the true self."[43] Elsewhere, he explains that "[t]he more the self advances the more it encounters working without a working subject."[44] This transformation of the *willing self* described as "forgetting the self" and as "[t]o die to oneself" displays three basic characteristics: transpersonalization, transindividualization, and decentralization. It is important to note the difference between transpersonalization and depersonalization and between transindividualization and deindividualization. I choose the term "transpersonalization" to distinguish this transition from "I" to "who"[45] from a process of depersonalization from "I" to "It." The self-aware self does not lose his/her personality and becomes purely impersonal, but rather expands the horizon of the person, which *qua* person necessitates a non-duality of personal and impersonal elements. My very somatic existence combines personal and impersonal aspects: While my body expresses my personality and my feelings, etc., it is made of impersonal elements such as cells. By the same token, the self-aware self does not lose, as I have argued elsewhere, his/her individuality but expands his/her horizon to include non-individual elements. Again, while my getting up in the morning cannot be described as peculiarly individual, the way I get up can; in other words, my getting up is simultaneously individual-yet-non-individual.[46] Self-awareness, in this sense, transcends selfhood, individuality, and subjectivity; at the bottom of the experiential "I" one can find, as already anticipated by the phenomenologies of Sartre and Merleau-Ponty, universality, worldliness, preconscious existence, and intersubjectivity. In the process of this transformation the *phenomenal world,* which centers around the *noetic* polarity of the individual and personal *cogito,* makes way for the *actual world* where no particular center is privileged. In this world, individuality and personality have lost their privileged roles as well. The *actual world* constitutes neither the world of objects constructed by the *cogito* nor the *lived world* inhabited by an ever-expanding self, but rather manifests itself non-thetically and pre-reflectively independent of a particular ego-polarity; it is neither the being that is *present-at-hand* (*Vorhandensein*) as a phenomenal object nor the *being-along-side* (*Miteinandersein*) within the *lived world.* In this sense, Heidegger's "being-in-the-world" becomes a being-(the)-world, not in the sense of expanding the subject to engulf everything else, but rather in the sense of dissolving the subject and thus de-centralizing the world.

This non-positional modality of self-awareness can be illustrated, as Merleau-Ponty does, with the example of a musical performance, during which the self-conscious awareness of myself as an agent retreats and thus discloses the selfless activity of playing piano. Rather than being an act of the musician, the music plays itself through the presence of the musician; in the words of Merleau-Ponty, the performer "feels himself and others feel him to be at the service of the sonata; the sonata sings through him or cries out so suddenly that he must 'dash on his bow' to follow it."[47] The very event of playing music is devoid of any projecting intentionality. By the same token, pre-reflective awareness is devoid of any *noematic* content[48] and beyond objectification. However, that does not mean that self-awareness is devoid of any content. Non-positional awareness does not comprise an unconscious but an "unself-conscious" awareness,[49] that is, an awareness devoid of thetic positionality. At the same time, the music performed is neither individual nor personal but an individual and personal expression (Jap.: *hyōgen*) of the transindividual and transpersonal beautiful (Jap.: *bi*). The performance, then, is at once individual-yet-non-individual and personal-yet-non-personal.

The key to the *actual world* lies in Nishida's conception of *zettai, non-relative,* and his conception of the *non-relative contradictory self-identity.* While it is usually translated as "absolute," I prefer the term "*non-relative*" since it indicates that the "*actual world*" clearly transcends all dichotomies including the correlativity between the dualism of the *phenomenal world* and the monism of the *lived world*; it transcends even the relativity between the absolute and the relative. In his "The Logic of Topos and the Religious World View" ("Bashoteki Ronri to Shūkyōteki Sekaikan"), Nishida conceives of the *non-relative* as that which "opposes nothing," "negates itself within itself" in an act of "non-relative negation,"[50] and, as self-negation (Jap.: *jiko hitei*), "transforms itself into the relative."[51] His arguments in favor of the "*non-relative*" are rather straightforward. Because "the non-relative, which opposes the relative is not the non-relative,"[52] a juxtaposition of relative and *non-rela-*

tive is untenable; in other words, the *non-relative* faces nothing(ness). However, a mere negation of the relativity does not constitute the *non-relative* but, analogous to the monism of the *lived world*, a oneness that either falls into a solipsism of subjectivity or implies, if not posits, the dichotomy of the *phenomenal world* as its own opposite. Consequently, it comprises the *contradictory identity* which transforms itself in an internal act of negation into its own opposite, the relativity between the dichotomy of the *phenomenal world* and the oneness of the *lived world*.

Rejecting both the logic of externality characteristic of the *phenomenal world*, which posits the self vis-à-vis the world of objects, and the logic of internality characteristic of the *lived world*, which contains the inhabited world within the intentionality of the *lived body*, Nishida seeks a logic which avoids the fallacies of externalism and internalism and which can theorize that which negates the self inside in an act of *affirmation-qua-negation*. Nishida calls this principle of self-awareness *non-relative nothingness*. So defined, the *non-relative* neither appears in the *phenomenal world* nor is engaged in the *lived world;* neither does it constitute something (or everything for that matter) in addition to the *phenomenal* and the *lived world*. For Nishida, it is the transcendental ground of the correlativity between the duality of the *phenomenal world* and the oneness of the *lived world*, which simultaneously transcends and grounds this relativity. In other words, the transcendental ground *qua* the *non-relative* is simultaneously identical with and different from the correlativity between the *phenomenal* world and the *lived world*. While the relative transcendental ego *qua* the *lived body* simultaneously transcends, as well as grounds the *mutual opposition* between *cogito* and *cogitatum,* the *non-relative* transcendental non-ego simultaneously transcends and grounds the *existential* ambiguity between the *phenomenal* and the *lived world*. However, contrary to the *lived world*, which posits the *phenomenal world* as an other, the *actual world expresses* itself in the correlatively of *phenomenal* and *lived world non-positionally qua* its own self-negation. So defined, the transcendental is simultaneously self-contained and absolute in that it, to paraphrase Husserl's words words, is without a horizon, by means of which it implicitly points beyond itself, and relational in so far as it is constituted in relation to and, subsequently, dependent on its "intentional objectivities." Transcending the relativity of *phenomenal* and *lived world*, the transcendental non-ego differs from the *somatic cogito;* positing itself *qua* the *lived world* vis-à-vis the *phenomenal world*, the transcendental is identical with the *somatic cogito*.

While expressions such as Nishida's *non-relative contradictory self-identi-ty*" and "the world where subjectivity and objectivity unite" (Jap.: *shukyakuō-titsuteki sekai*) are, due to their paradoxical character, rather uninformative, I believe that these formulas imply that the *actual world qua non-relative contradictory self-identity* determines itself in the dialectic between the *lived world* and the *phenomenal world*. In a dialectic reminiscent of Hegel's definition of identity and difference, Nishida seems to define the *phenomenal world* as the opposition between the *phenomenal world* and the *lived world* and the *lived world* as the unity of the *lived world* and the *phenomenal world*. It is pivotal to read Nishida's dialectic of the *noematic* and the *noetic* determination of the *actual world* on two levels: From the perspective of the static and embodied-yet-alienated *cogito*, self and world, *noesis* and *noema* are existentially separated and subsequently alienated from each other; the self of the *lived world*, on the other hand, constitutes the unity of subject and object, self and world. The *phenomenal world* thus signifies the static encounter of self and world, while the *lived world* signifies the active engagement between self and world. This dichotomy between the *phenomenal world*, which is characterized as dualistic, static, temporally linear, and phenomenal, and the *lived world*, which is characterized as monistic, dynamic, atemporally circular, and transcendental, is illustrated by Dōgen's distinction between the "people outside the mountains" and "inside the mountains." While Dōgen's allegory of the "people outside the mountains" symbolizes the *phenomenal world*, where the *cogito* encounters its givenness as that which limits and determines its own subjectivity, the image of "people inside the mountains" serves as a freeze frame of the *lived world*, where the self creatively engages the allegedly external world. *"Cogito"* and *"willing self"* do not describe two different agents but one agent viewed from two different standpoints. The self characteristic of the *lived world* is different from the *phenomenal world* (it is nothing in relationship to the *phenomenal world*) and therefore conceives of itself as that which statically opposes the world as disembodied subject. This conception, however, constitutes an abstraction of the *lived* self. The "real" self, which actively interacts with the world, is bestowed with affectivity and somaticity and, subsequently, is intimately linked with the world. When I pick up my guitar, the very act of picking up my guitar escapes the binary structure of this world insofar as its actional unity transcends the dichotomization and external negation characteristic of the *phenomenal world*. However, my activity of picking up the guitar is only effectively real or relevant insofar as it *expresses* itself as the transformation of the "previous state" within the *phenomenal world*—the guitar is now in my hands. This transformed situation can now be known and objectified, while the unity of my action cannot. It is this abyss brought about by a *unifying activity* that ruptures the correlative structure of the *phenomenal world*.

Notes Towards Transcendental Relativism

Although Kasulis and Nagatomo have argued that the three-liners characteristic of Buddhist non-dualism outline the epistemic transformation from the self-conscious *cogito* to selfless self-awareness, I believe that a second interpretation of these riddles that supports a transcendental relativism is possible. Such a transcendental relativism is born of the insight that the ground of human experience simultaneously resides within and without the *phenomenal world*. I have already mentioned the paradoxes evoked by phenomenological descriptions of the transcendental ego in particular, and the relationship between the phenomenal and the transcendental in general. Faced with these contradictions, Merleau-Ponty decided not to privilege the standpoint of either existential or transcendental phenomenology, but struggled to develop a phenomenology that does not succumb to the fallacies of empiricism and transcendental idealism by reducing the world to either the phenomena of our experience or transcendental essences, respectively. Such a non-dualistic phenomenology takes as its starting point the phenomenological standpoint where "I am of the world" and, simultaneously, where "I am not it."[53] Subsequently, the phenomenological standpoint and, for that matter, the standpoint of every philosophy, simultaneously implies "infinite distance" and "absolute proximity," "negation" and "identification."[54] In the introduction to his *Phenomenology of Perception,* Merleau-Ponty urges the necessity of such a non-dualistic phenomenology when he observed that "[i]t is true, as Marx says, that history does not walk on its head, but it is also true that it does not think with its feet. Or one should say rather it is neither its 'head' not (sic) its 'feet' that we have to worry about, but its body."[55] In his *The Visible and Invisible* he takes this project one step further to formulate a phenomenology "beyond dualism and monism, because dualism has been pushed so far that the opposites, no longer in competition, are at rest the one against the other, coextensive with one another."[56] Such a non-dualistic phenomenology must be grounded in the paradox—even Sartre remarks that the principle of non-contradiction "presides over the relations of being with what it is not."[57] Transcendental relativism in general is supported by paradoxes that the philosopher encounters in the search for self-awareness *qua* non-duality of existence and essence, personal identity *qua* non-duality of identity and difference,[58] the epistemic foundations of which necessitate a non-duality of fact and essence as well as a non-duality of subjectivity and objectivity. In the literature outside of the philosophical discourse this *actual world* has been indicated by, as Steven Laycock points out, Kurt Goedel's Incompleteness Theorem and Werner Heisenberg's Uncertainty Relation. Wargo argues similarly that any epistemological theory that attempts to theorize the ground of knowledge, be it Kant's *First Critique,* Bertrand Russell's theory of type, or, as I have demonstrated earlier, transcendental phenomenology, has to confront the paradox and the realm I have called the *actual world.*

Buddhist non-dualism addresses the paradox lying at the bottom of the ground of experience *qua* transcendental non-ego by extending the dual conception of the transcendental ego *qua cogito* and *qua* transcendental ego to a threefold conception of selfhood, consisting of the *cogito,* the transcendental ego *qua* the *lived body,* and the transcendental non-ego *qua* the dialectic of the *cogito* and the transcendental ego. As we have seen, Mohanty himself points towards Advaita Vedānta's dialectic of identity and difference to sort out the "baffling enigma" of "the relation between the empirical . . . and the transcendental" and concludes that "[t]he Platonic two-world theory dies hard, and once they are separated, every attempt to put them together is destined to fail."[59] It is for this reason that Buddhist non-dualism conceived of the third layer, the *actual* world. The monism of the *lived world* implies either a solipsism of *my world* or what John Searle calls a "conceptual dualism" between the phenomenal and the *lived* world. Only a second order of transcendental *qua* transcendental non-ego can provide the standpoint of "no standpoint." Since the second order transcendental ground does not possess the unilateral positionality of the *somatic cogito* and, by virtue of transcending the perspectivalism of the *cogito*, transcends selfhood, it is more adequately called, as Buddhist non-dualism has maintained for the last two millennia, "transcendental non-ego," *anāman*. Thus defined, "the transcendental ego is anti-monistic, (in that) it respects pluralism and is tolerant of diversities."[60] This transcendental non-ego is not different from the empirical and the transcendental self but it comprises their very dialectic.

Postulating such a dialectic between empirical and transcendental egos, transcendental relativism gives us a coherent theory why, as Mohanty notes, the empirical and the transcendental ego do not constitute two different entities but rather reveal two different standpoints and, as Michael Hammond, Jane Howarth, and Russell Keat argue, "transcendental and existential phenomenology can be seen as two different versions of the same kind of philosophical activity."[61] To cite Kasulis's summary of Nāgārjuna's position, "any assertion (or position for that matter) or distinction only highlights one aspect of a situation and, in so doing, casts into shadows an equally important, though incompatible, aspect."[62] While human experience entails both the *phenomenal* and the *lived world* (and transcendental constitution theory and essentialism for that matter), the perspectival standpoint of the reflective philosopher only captures one of these dimensions and obscures the other. When the phenomenologist highlights the *phenomenal world*, s/he discovers the correlativity of *cogito* and *cogitatum* and, subsequently, the existential plight of the *being-for*-itself as well as the relativity of the *cogitatum* which is constituted *for-the-self*. However, if the phenomenologist highlights the *lived world*, s/he discloses the transcendental reality of the *somatic cogito qua* transcendental ego. This logic can be also applied to the dialectic of fact and essence, the mind-body problem, the controversies between positivism and idealism, as Nishida does in his *An Inquiry into the Good* ("Zen no Kenkyū"), to the debate between philosophical externalism and internalism, and other philosophical controversies that center on the external-internal dichotomy such as the problem of personal identity. From the standpoint of the *phenomenal world*, personal identity can be described as a causal continuity of events, as does Derek Parfit, while the transcendental perspective would define personal identity either in terms of the *noetic* act or its reification *qua* the Leibnizian *monad*.

Finally, non-dualistic phenomenology allows the philosopher to theorize a transcendental foundation without committing to absolutism, and to accept the perspectival and historicist predicament of human experience and knowledge without having to concede the self-defeat inherent in the projects of radical relativism and historicism. Having accepted the constitutive nature of my consciousness, I cannot but recognize the perspectival nature of my experience and knowledge. At the same time, the very notion of relativism and perspectivalism presupposes, albeit implicitly, a transcendental ground. As Husserl noted in his *Cartesian Meditations,* the very assumption of collective knowledge, that is, that my ideas are communicable, presumes a transcendental intersubjectivity. Given this paradoxical predicament of human knowledge, phenomenology at once is a "never-ending process, an open system"[63] and reveals idealities "in the very act in which [they are] grasped."[64] To paraphrase Mohanty's evaluation of Husserl, phenomenology thus defined is "a moving to and fro between" existential and transcendental phenomenology or, in regard to essences, "transcendental 'empiriography' and an *eidetics* of transcendental life."[65] The key to this transcendental relativism is the elusive nature of the ground of human experience that Merleau-Ponty and Nishida call "the invisible" and "nothingness" respectively. Given our perspectival nature, the very ground of our constitutive acts, which lets us step back and imagine possibilities and conceive of worlds and realities beyond *our world,* is elusive in that "it retreats in the measure that we approach."[66] Buddhist non-dualism thus reaffirms the phenomenological project of the tragic philosopher who "is haunted by the gulf that separates philosophic reflection and unreflective experience, a gulf that he seeks to bridge not by speculative constructions but by intermediate phenomena, though never quite completely."[67]

Notes

1. This essay is based on my research for and excerpts from my forthcoming book, *Beyond Personal Identity* (Richmond, Surrey: Curzon Press, 2000).
2. Mohanty, *Phenomenology,* 67.
3. Mohanty, *Transcendental Phenomenology,* 139.
4. The phenomenological movement is best defined by Herbert Spiegelberg, *The Phenomenological Movement: A Historical Introduction* (The Hague: Nijhoff, 1960).
5. Husserl, *Cartesian Meditations,* 20.
6. Thomas A. Kochumuttom, *A Buddhist Doctrine of Experience: A New Translation and Interpretation of the Works of Vasubandhu the Yogācārin* (Delhi: Motilal Barnasidass), 3-5.

7. Mohanty, *Phenomenology*, 92.

8. Jean-Paul Sartre, *The Transcendence of the Ego*, trans. Forrest Williams and Robert Kirkpatrick (New York: Hill and Wang, 1990), 93.

9. Mohanty, *Transcendental Phenomenology*, 144.

10. Ibid., 139.

11. Ibid., 153.

12. Dōgen Kigen, *Shōbōgenzō*, ed. K. Tamaki (Tokyo: Daizō Shuppan Kabushiki Kaisha), vol. 1 (1993-94), 95.

13. While the terminology of *nirvāṇa* and *saṃsāra* lends itself to a metaphysical interpretation, at least Mahāyāna thinkers (with the possible exception of Pure Land Buddhists) have been quite adamant and consistent in conceiving of them as epistemic attitudes rather than ontological realms.

14. Dōgen Kigen, *Shōbōgenzō* 1 (1993-94), 95.

15. Ibid., 94.

16. Tamaki Kōshirō, ed. and trans., *Gendai Goyaku Shōbōgenzō* 1 (Tokyo: Daizō Shuppan Kabushiki Kaisha), 94.

17. Nishitani Keiji, *Shōbōgenzō Kōwa* 3: *Genjōkōan, Busshō I* (Tokyo: Kabushiki Kaiwa Chikuma Shōbō, 1989), 32.

18. Ibid., 35.

19. Wargo argues that Nishida's mature theory of knowledge attempts not only to explain the relationship between knower and known but also to address what Wargo calls the "completeness problem," that is, the question "How can we have knowledge of the foundation of knowledge?"

20. Neal Donner and Daniel B. Stevenson, *The Great Calming and Contemplation: A Study and Annotated Translation of the First Chapter of Chih-i's Moho-Chih-Kuan* (Honolulu: University of Hawaii Press, 1993), 124-26.

21. Nishida developed his epistmological theory of the three universals in his essay "The World of Intelligibility" ("Eichiteki Sekai"). In his later works such as *The Fundamental Problem of Philosophy* (*Tetsugaku no Kompon Mondai*), he shifted his focus toward the issues of intersubjectivity and the historical self. Nevertheless, I believe that, despite this shift in focus and terminology, his work exhibits a clear consistency as far as his conceptual schema is concerned.

22. Dōgen Kigen, *Shōbōgenzō* 1 (1993-94), 407.

23. Ibid., 407.

24. The literal translation of "*jiko o hakobite*" is "to carry the self."

25. Dōgen Kigen, *Shōbōgenzō* 1 (1993-94), 94.

26. Nagatoma Shigenori, *Attunement through the Body* (Albany: State University of New York Press, 1992), 103.

27. Nishida Kitarō, *Nishida Kitarō Zenshū* 6 (Tokyo: Iwanami Shoten, 1988), 293.

28. Ibid., 5, 158.

29. While present-day commentators on Dōgen, such as Kasulis and Nagatomo, generally interpret the *lived world* as the epistemological reorientation of everyday awareness, I propose to follow Nishida and interpret the *lived world* additionally as the world of activity that juxtaposes the static dichotomy of self and world characteristic of the *phenomenal world*.

30. In his *Mind as Mirror and the Mirroring of the Mind* (Albany: State University of New York Press, 1994), Laycock argues that Merleau-Ponty's phenomenology, which shows quite a few similarities with Nishida's account of

the *lived world*, displays a monistic world view.

31. Nishida Kitarō, *Nishida Kitarō Zenshū* 9, 176.

32. Nagatomo Shigenori, *Attunement through the Body*, 99.

33. In his *Attunement through the Body*, Nagatomo employs Husserl's notion of sedimentation and Merleau-Ponty's notion of habitualization in order to stratify a theory of attunement to conceive of the process by means of which the dualism between, in the language of Ichikawa, "subject-body" and "object-body" is overcome.

34. Ibid., 232-43.

35. See note 33.

36. Husserl, *Cartesian Meditations*, 73.

37. Ibid., 65.

38. Nishida Kitarō, *Nishida Kitarō Zenshū*, 7, 85.

39. Ibid., 7, 86.

40. Ibid., 6, 387.

41. Dōgen Kigen, *Shōbōgenzō*, 1, 94.

42. Nishida Kitarō, *Nishida Kitarō Zenshū*, 5, 356.

43. Ibid., 6, 291.

44. Ibid., 3, 362.

45. Nagatomo Shigenori, *Attunement through the Body*, 96-102.

46. This notion of human existence has also been elaborated by Thich Nhat Hanh, and reverberates C. G. Jung's concept of individuality.

47. Maurice Merleau-Ponty, *The Visible and the Invisible*, trans. Alphonso Lingis (Evanston, Ill.: Northwestern University Press, 1968), 151.

48. Thomas Kasulis, *Zen Action/Zen Person* (Honolulu: University of Hawaii Press, 1981), 75.

49. Nagatomo Shigenori, *Attunement through the Body*, 230.

50. Nishida Kitarō, *Nishida Kitarō Zenshū*, 11, 397.

51. Ibid., 398.

52. Ibid., 396.

53. Merleau-Ponty, *The Visible and the Invisible*, 127.

54. Ibid., 127.

55. Merleau-Ponty, *Phenomenology of Perception*, trans. C. Smith, xix.

56. Merleau-Ponty, *The Visible and the Invisible*, 54-5.

57. Jean Paul Sartre, *Being and Nothingness*, trans. H. E. Barnes (New York: Washington Square Press, 1956), 124.

58. In my forthcoming *Beyond Personal Identity*, I have argued that Nishida and Dōgen's conception of personal non-duality is simultaneously commonsense and beyond the grasp of mainstream philosophical discourse.

59. Mohanty, *Phenomenology*, 92-93.

60. Mohanty, *Transcendental Phenomenology*, 143.

61. Michael Hammond, Jane Howarth, and Russell Keat, *Understanding Phenomenology* (Oxford: Basil Blackwell, 1991) 261.

62. Thomas Kasulis, *Zen Action/Zen Person*, 22.

63. Mohanty, *Transcendental Phenomenology*, 18.

64. Mohanty, *Phenomenology*, 71.

65. Ibid., 92.

66. Merleau-Ponty, *The Visible and the Invisible*, 150.

67. Mohanty, *Transcendental Phenomenology*, 18.

Chapter 8

Heidegger and Transcendental Philosophy

David Carr

One of the many philosophical concerns I share with J. N. Mohanty is that of working out the idea of transcendental philosophy. Kant inaugurated the idea in his first *Critique,* and it was then taken up by J. G. Fichte. Its most important twentieth-century proponent was Edmund Husserl, who claimed to incorporate the best insights of Kant (and Fichte to a lesser extent) and to recast transcendental philosophy as transcendental phenomenology. Like Kant, Husserl claimed to be launching a new philosophical project that went beyond the particular findings presented in his own work, and could be taken up and continued by others. It is perhaps inevitable that Husserl's project suffered the same fate as Kant's: his ideas were taken up by thinkers too strong and too original to consider themselves merely as followers continuing the work of a founding father. As we all know, philosophy is not exempt from the Oedipal pattern Freud saw so clearly.

Of course, the same pattern may be exemplified in the relation between Kant and Husserl. While Husserl praises Kant highly for initiating transcendental philosophy,[1] he is also severe in his criticisms. Intent on working out his own ideas, he may be more inclined to emphasize his differences from Kant than to stress their similarities. It is also important to remember that many of Husserl's formulations emerged from a polemic with the neo-Kantians. Anyone attempting to compare their work should perhaps beware of accepting uncritically Husserl's version of Kant and of their respective ideas of transcendental philosophy. Considerations such as these lead some of us to seek out those underlying themes that constitute transcendental philosophy as a unified project. In a sense, this is to take both philosophers at their word that it is a project that exists beyond the work of individual thinkers, important as they are.

There are other reasons for undertaking this task. As the work of Kant and Husserl was taken up and transformed by their successors, it was also reinterpreted to the point of misrepresentation—or so it seems to some of us. This could certainly be said of the German Idealist version of Kant, including that of Fichte, and of most of the thinkers who took up the idea of phenomenology while rejecting its transcendental interpretation. Here I am thinking primarily of the early Heidegger, and of the French phenomenologists Sartre, Merleau-Ponty, and Ricoeur. These thinkers made their own way by emphasizing their differences from Husserl and subjecting many of his ideas to a critique. Chief among these, of course, was the very idea of transcendental philosophy itself. For many of even his most sympathetic successors, one of Husserl's biggest mistakes (perhaps second only to the close connection with Descartes as emphasized in *Ideas I* and *Cartesian Meditations*) is his identification of phenomenology with the transcendental tradition. But what they say about that tradition, even as embodied in Husserl's work, seems to bear little relation to the essentials of transcendental philosophy.

Perhaps the broadest, most negative, and at the same time most influential portrait of transcendental philosophy is that presented by Heidegger, not so much in his early work as in the later writings, when he leaves even phenomenology behind. Heidegger's sweeping portrait of modern philosophy as a whole, from Descartes through Nietzsche to Husserl, lies behind the conception of a "post-modernity" advocated by such French philosophers as Foucault and Lyotard. Embedded in this portrait of modernity is an account of transcendental philosophy as perhaps the summation of a modernity that needs to be surpassed.

It is my view that Heidegger presents us with a caricature of transcendental philosophy that overlooks what is truly distinctive about it, that blurs the lines which separate it from other aspects of the modern tradition, and that fails to recognize the manner in which transcendental philosophy itself incorporates a trenchant critique of the modern tradition from which it springs. In this paper I want to take up various aspects of Heidegger's interpretation of transcendental philosophy and show where they miss the mark. The conception of transcendental philosophy I defend here is essentially the one I share with J. N. Mohanty, and which owes much to my reading of his work on this subject, even where our emphasis is sometimes different.[2]

It is important to emphasize that in the following critique of Heidegger's reading of Kant and Husserl, I shall not be appealing merely to historical accuracy. While I think that Heidegger ignores many things that Kant and Husserl explicitly say, my discussion situates itself at the level of broader issues. Heidegger's attack is openly and admittedly a strong interpretation, and I am countering it with one of my own.

There are four elements of Heidegger's characterization of transcendental philosophy to which I want to respond. Heidegger makes the following claims:

1. Transcendental philosophy is simply a version of metaphysics. As he puts it in "berwindung der Metaphysik," transcendental philosophy is "die neuzeitlich Gestalt der Ontologie."[3] All metaphysics asks after the being of

beings; modern philosophy, of which transcendental philosophy is the extreme form, characterizes the being of beings as subjectivity. Subject replaces substance as the central term, and transcendental philosophy is the metaphysics of the subject.

2. Transcendental philosophy is representationalism. The being of beings, including that of the subject, since in self-consciousness it represents itself, is reduced to a representation for the subject. "Seiendheit besagt jetzt Vorgestelltheit des vor-stellenden Subjekts."[4]

3. It follows that transcendental idealism is just another version of idealism, a stage on the way to Hegel's absolute idealism. The world as a whole is essentially reduced to a representation or world-picture. Heidegger characterizes modernity, as in the title of one of his essays, as "Die Zeit des Weltbildes," the age of the world-picture, and transcendental philosophy plays a key role in this age.

4. Central to modern philosophy as a whole is the concept of method. From Descartes' method, through deductive, mathematical methods, to scientific or experimental methods, it is this concept that connects metaphysics to modern science and ultimately to its culmination in technology. "Das Ende der Philosophie zeigt sich als der Triumph der steuerbaren Einrichtung einer wissenschaftlich-technischen Welt."[5] The concept of method is central to transcendental philosophy as well, notably in Husserl's phenomenological reduction.

I will now discuss these four topics in turn.

Metaphysics, Epistemology, and Critique

Is transcendental philosophy, as suggested by Heidegger, to be understood as a metaphysics of the subject? The fact is that for both Kant and Husserl, transcendental philosophy is not to be understood as metaphysics at all. In a way, for both thinkers metaphysics is certainly *at issue*, but precisely for this reason it is not the rubric under which they classify their own work. Kant is explicitly addressing the question of whether metaphysics, as conceived and practiced by his predecessors and contemporaries, is possible at all as a science. What he proposes is a *critique* of metaphysics, a project that is prepared for by a critique of mathematics and natural science. These disciplines claim in different ways to have knowledge of the world; Kant's task is not to provide support for their claims, or to add to them, or to replace them with claims of his own, but to inquire into how they are possible. (See A12/B26).[6] Husserl's phenomenology, likewise, does not consist of knowledge-claims about the world, whether scientific or metaphysical. By "bracketing" these claims, he turns his attention from the world and its objects to the experiences in which they are given. Like Kant, he emphasizes the "how" question: the "'how' of manners of givenness." (CR 165f.)

Both thinkers thus conceive of themselves not as producing knowledge about reality or the world, but as *reflecting* on such knowledge; not as saying things about the world but as describing our experience of the world. In their own view they are neither adding to scientific knowledge nor contributing to a specifically philosophical theory of the world that might be called metaphysics. If neither philosopher thinks that he is engaged in metaphysics at all, then *a fortiori* neither is proposing what he thinks of as a metaphysics of the subject, whether as a metaphysical theory based on the subject or as a metaphysical theory about the subject. In Kant's case, of course, a metaphysics of the subject (in the form of "rational psychology") comes explicitly under his critical gaze, and his distinction between the empirical and the transcendental subject is directly related to this critique. The same can be said of Husserl, especially with reference to what he calls the "paradox of human subjectivity."(CR 178)

Kant and Husserl, in seeing themselves not as contributing to knowledge about the world but as reflecting critically on such knowledge, take up the modern reflective tradition inaugurated by Descartes and continued by the British Empiricists. According to this tradition, epistemology, in the sense of a critical reflection on knowledge, must come before metaphysics. This was the early modern conception of the order of inquiry or of proper philosophical *priorities*. Descartes believed that the critical question—whether knowledge is possible at all—could be settled, and philosophy could move on to metaphysical questions. For the Empiricists, too, this was the proper order of inquiry, even if their arguments led to the conclusion, finally drawn by Hume, that the assurances about knowledge sought by Descartes could not be found.

Kant and Husserl are both impressed, but not convinced, by Hume's skeptical conclusions. In response, they make a crucial break with this traditional modern conception of philosophical procedure. For them the critical reflection on knowledge is not a prelude to a revived and reassured metaphysics in the old style, that is, in the sense of a science of the world that at once builds upon, goes beyond, and complements the existing sciences. Transcendental philosophy as critical reflection becomes an end in itself rather than a prelude to something else, and its relation to "positive" knowledge of the world is very different from that envisaged by the early moderns. Even though the term "metaphysics" reappears in a positive sense in both thinkers,[7] it is seen not as a subject matter apart from transcendental philosophy but as a subordinate part of it. For Kant and Husserl, it is fair to say, genuine knowledge about the world, insofar as this is possible, and within its own limits, is to be found in the sciences. For Husserl, though not for Kant, this includes the social, psychological, and humanistic disciplines as well as the natural sciences. Husserl also believes that we have a prescientific familiarity, a kind of knowledge by acquaintance, with the world. But there is no further body of knowledge, as in the traditional conception of metaphysics, which goes beyond the sciences, makes up for their deficiencies, and somehow incorporates their results into a grand theory of the whole. The only thing apart from our experiential and scientific knowledge of the world is our critical reflection on it, that is, transcendental philosophy itself, which lies, as Kant suggests,[8] not *beyond* scientific knowledge but on *this side* of it.

The idea that critical reflection is distinct from metaphysics and can be practiced independently of it, is simply not acknowledged by Heidegger. We are not asserting, of course, that Heidegger is unaware of this crucial distinction in Kant and Husserl, or has simply overlooked their claim that they are not doing metaphysics at all. He simply, flatly denies the distinction: "'Theory of knowledge,' or what goes by that name, is in essence metaphysics and ontology founded on truth conceived as the certainty of the securing representation."[9]

It must be said, of course, that Heidegger is not the first to challenge this classically modern distinction. He has been preceded most famously by Hegel, notably in the introduction to the *Phänomenologie des Geistes.* Hegel tries to undermine the distinction by asking why the critical reflection on claims to knowledge does not itself count as knowledge. If metaphysics is knowledge of the whole, why is knowledge about knowledge not itself knowledge of part of the whole and thus part of metaphysics? His overall strategy is to point to the many assumptions that underlie any such reflection, assumptions that are arguably themselves metaphysical assumptions.

Hegel's argument is brilliant, though it has hardly commanded universal assent. But it is at least an argument, an internal critique of the whole modern notion of the priority of epistemology over metaphysics. Heidegger, by contrast, offers no argument for his claim that all modern philosophers, Kant and Husserl included, are "really" doing metaphysics, whatever they may say or think they are doing. It is true that Heidegger devotes a whole essay to a detailed paragraph-by-paragraph analysis to Hegel's introduction to the *Phänomenologie.*[10] But this essay can hardly be read as an endorsement or adoption by Heidegger of Hegel's argument. Indeed Heidegger's purpose there seems consistent with his treatment of other modern philosophers: he wants to demonstrate that Hegel's thought is yet another manifestation of the modern metaphysics of the subject. His approach is like Hegel's in emphasizing unspoken metaphysical assumptions; but the assumptions he finds in Hegel's text are not those Hegel would recognize, but the same ones he finds everywhere else: the interpretation of the being of beings as subjectivity.

We shall return later to the idea that the critique of metaphysics itself harbors metaphysical assumptions. For the moment we can point out that it is *Heidegger's* assumption, for which he nowhere gives an argument, that anyone attempting a critique of knowledge, prior to and independently of metaphysics, is actually, but unknowingly, giving expression to a metaphysics. Is this true of Kant and Husserl, contrary to what they think? Should we simply accept Heidegger's view because he states it? No, but we should treat Kant's and Husserl's conception of non-metaphysical transcendental philosophy with the same caution. Charitably, we should treat Heidegger's claim about the relation of

transcendental philosophy to metaphysics as a *hypothesis,* supposedly confirmed in his interpretations of the philosophers he treats. Even if we are not
convinced by his interpretations, his hypothesis is one worth considering. But
equally worthy of attention is the assumption, or hypothesis, at the heart of
transcendental philosophy, that metaphysics can be "bracketed" and subjected to
a reflective critique.

Our own procedure here will be to favor *that* hypothesis, and seek *its*
confirmation in our own interpretations of transcendental philosophy. It is an
aspect of the tradition inaugurated by Kant and continued by Husserl that has
been all too quickly dismissed by Heidegger and his followers, and it needs to
be reinstated as a key to the proper understanding of that tradition. In the
following sections we shall be taking seriously this hypothesis. After a lengthier
exposition of the transcendental project, we will take up the question of whether
it can be sustained in a manner that survives Heidegger's critique.

The Critique of Representationalism

For Heidegger, as we have seen, modern philosophy is characterized by the
shift of the traditional notion of substance to the knowing subject. This subject
exists not through properties or predicates in the traditional sense but through
representations—pictures of objects or a picture of the world as a whole. Heidegger assimilates both Kant and Husserl to this modern tradition, overlooking
or ignoring the fact that the critique of the notion of representation is the very
core of their whole project.

It is certainly true, as Heidegger says, that the notion of representation is
central to the modern tradition and the key to its many problems. He is also right
that it results at least in part from considering the mind according to the traditional notion of substance. Also known as the "way of ideas," according to
which the mind is directly related only to its own thoughts, the notion of representation closes the mind off from the rest of the world and raises the question
of whether knowledge and experience are even possible, and more radically, the
question of how they should be defined. Once the problem of our relation to the
world is set up in this way, it is almost inevitable that the only possible out-
comes are skepticism or idealism. Either the gap between ideas and the "external
world" can never be bridged at all, or the external world is simply *reduced to*
ideas or representations (as in Leibniz and Berkeley) and itself becomes a property of mind. The latter solution, in which a metaphysical thesis comes to the
rescue of an epistemological problem, is the one that interests Heidegger. And it
is of this that he accuses both Kant and Husserl in their role as metaphysicians,
but in doing so he misunderstands them completely.

While the term *Vorstellung,* which corresponds roughly to the English
and French versions of *idea* in early modern philosophy, is central to Kant's

theory of knowledge, Kant's approach to it is new. The problem is that *Vorstellungen* are determinations of the subject or the mind; if the mind relates only to its own determinations, no knowledge is possible, for knowledge must be of objects, that is, must be about the world. Agreeing with Hume that neither reason alone nor sense experience (in the empiricist sense) could ever guarantee the connection between ideas and things, Kant concluded that the connection must be *a priori*: his answer is precisely the transcendental unity of apperception, conceived as the *objective* unity of self-consciousness (B139) relating the "I think" through representations to objects. It is not to be derived from experience, but is a condition of the possibility of experience, that the "I think" accompany all my representations and in doing so relate them to objects. The role of the transcendental unity of apperception is not only to unify the manifold of experiences in the subject *a priori,* but equally *a priori,* to also unify them in an object. In other words, the *I think* is transitive or intentional.

It is important to understand Kant's use of the terms *"a priori"* and "transcendental" when he applies them to the "I think," the unity of apperception, and the relation of representations to an object. He is saying that these constitute the very essence of experience, and that philosophically we cannot expect to derive them from anything simpler or more basic. Kant's starting point is that "we are in possession" of certain cognitions, which means that we *have* experience, in his full sense of that term. This starting point is as much the key to his role in modern philosophy as the notion of the "Copernican Revolution." Indeed, it is another way of looking at it. It is Kant's response to Descartes' starting point and the Humean skepticism to which it ultimately leads. Instead of starting with the encapsulated mind and then asking how we get out of it to the world, we must begin with a notion of mind which is already (that is, *a priori*) outside of itself and in the world.

For Kant the unity of apperception is the "supreme principle of all employment of the understanding." (B136) Thus he places it even above the categories. His argument for the unity of apperception is similar to that for the categories, but it must come first. His argument for causality, for example, is that it cannot be derived from experience, but without it experience would not be possible. Hence it must be considered *a priori* and transcendental, a condition of the possibility of experience. But causal relations are relations among objects, not representations. Hence the objective (that is, intentional) character of experience establishes in general the realm to which the categories apply. Objectivity alone, of course, is not enough, so certain features of the objective realm, like causal interaction and regularity, must be considered *a priori* as well. But without the objective aspect of the unity of apperception, there would be nothing—that is, no world of objects—to which the categories could apply.

As for Husserl, he is not a representationalist: the impetus for his entire development can be found in his *Logical Investigations,* an early attack on the notion of mental representation. This is what we may call the "realist" element in his early work, and is of a piece with his attack on psychologism—that is, on the attempt to collapse the object of consciousness into consciousness or to confuse the two. Like Kant, he places the objective relation—intentionality—in first place, recognizing that it is essential to experience and that it cannot be derived from anything more primitive.

Husserl's starting point is in this respect the same as Kant's, but he expresses it in a different way. Husserl does not present an argument based on the inadequacy of mental representations to secure the objective relation, but rather shows that the idea of such representation cannot be backed up by a phenomenological description. In *Ideas I* he devotes a whole section (ID1 43) to what he calls the "fundamental error" of believing that perception "does not reach the physical thing itself" but only a picture of it, or perhaps a sign or symbol for it. We understand perfectly well what it is to see a picture (say a photograph of my house), which "stands in" for something else and genuinely re-presents it, and how that differs from seeing "in person" or "in the flesh" (*leibhaftig*) the thing it represents. Here the very concept of a representation presupposes the idea of direct seeing, indeed doubly so, since a) the depicted object is something that *could* be seen directly, and b) the picture itself *is* seen directly, in contrast to the thing it depicts. In spite of being "transcendent," in the sense of belonging to "reality" as distinct from consciousness, the object of perception (cf ID1, § 42) is present, directly given to the perceiver as itself.

For Husserl it is not just the object of perception but "reality" as a whole, indeed the *world*, which transcends consciousness. But consciousness is not somehow cut off from this transcendence; on the contrary, it is *as* transcendent that object and world are directly given to consciousness. This is possible because consciousness is nothing that *could* be cut off from the world: as intentionality it is *nothing but* this relation to the world. For Husserl, the fact that consciousness thus *transcends* itself is what gives transcendental philosophy its name. Kant does not give us a similar account of his choice of the term, nor does he use the term "transcendent" in quite the way that Husserl does. But it is clear that he begins with, and never doubts, the assumption that we *have* experience of the objective world, and that he sees his own task as that of showing how this is possible.

For both thinkers, then, the starting point is that the world is *both* objective *and* given. The historical importance of this starting point cannot be emphasized too much. For pre-Kantian modern philosophers, and even for some post-Kantians, these two features exclude one another: what is objective cannot be given; what is given is subjective and cannot be objective. Kant and Husserl take for granted *that,* and undertake to show *how,* the two go together.

In Husserl's phenomenology of perception, the perceived is given only one-sidedly or perspectivally, subject to the general conditions of perception. This one-sidedness is not a hindrance to the givenness of things; it is not an "appearance" or "representation" standing *between* us and the objects. On the contrary, it is our very mode of access to them. For Kant too, objects are given to us subject to the conditions of both sensibility and the understanding—space, time, and the categories. This is just the "how" of their givenness. The over-arching condition, as we have seen, is the transcendental unity of apperception. But this principle precisely describes the essential character of consciousness itself as conscious of the world. It simply says that if the world is to be given, we must be conscious of it. Kant's search for the conditions of the possibility of experience is first of all the attempt to state *what* experience is, that is, to lay bare its basic structure, or, as he puts it, the *form* of thinking (*die Form des Denkens*, A93/B126). We can now see how close this is to the Husserlian project of phenomenological description as the description of the *essence* of consciousness, of objectivity, of world.

Thus we must stress the givenness of the objective world, in both thinkers, in order to counter the charge that their position is a representationalist one. But it is also important, in our interpretation of the transcendental tradition, to stress the world's transcendence (in Husserl's sense) or objectivity (in Kant's sense). This feature of the tradition is often underplayed, since it seems to run counter to the original insight that got the whole thing going. Kant's great innovation, after all, is the idea that the mind, instead of passively mirroring an independent and self-sufficient reality, is active and productive. Kant describes it as "prescribing laws to nature, and even of making nature possible." (B159f). Husserl's term is constitution, and both thinkers describe consciousness as synthesis.

But constitution is not creation; synthesis does not manufacture the world. As Kant says, the understanding "does not produce its object as far as its *existence* is concerned." (A92/B125) For Kant this means that our intellect is finite. It is often thought that the mark of this finitude is the role played by sense in his theory. Indeed, Kant speaks of sensation as the raw material that is shaped and fashioned by the understanding (A1). The early Husserl, too, employs the notion of hyletic data brought to life by an animating intention. But if this were the only sense of finitude, they would indeed come close to the blasphemous "humanism" that seems to be the true source of Heidegger's critique: as if human reason replaced God in all but the creation of prime matter.

In fact, the metaphor of matter formed by the mind is very misleading in both thinkers. The unformed matter of sensation is not, for either of these philosophers, the genuine mark of human finitude or the sense of the world's transcendence. If in transcendental philosophy the mind does not create the world, it is not because some kernel of uncreated, pregiven stuff is required for the mix. It is because what the mind genuinely does produce is not existence but meaning. And the primary meaning it generates is that of the objectivity or transcendence of the world. The attempt to absorb that transcendence *into* subjectivity, in the manner of Leibnitz or Berkeley, or even of Fichte and Hegel, would be for Kant and Husserl to confuse meaning with being. Furthermore, the meaning generated by subjectivity is itself finite in the sense that it does not exhaust all the possibilities of being.

Transcendental Idealism

Both Kant and Husserl characterize their position as transcendental idealism, and both are concerned with distinguishing this position from realism *and* idealism in the usual sense. Realism and idealism are both metaphysical theories about reality and its relation to the mind. The danger here is to think that transcendental idealism is some third metaphysical position, perhaps somehow combining the other two. Both Kant and Husserl have often been considered in this way, even by their most sympathetic commentators. Kant is often characterized as affirming *both* the reality of the mind-independent world (things in themselves) and the merely mental character of the objects of our experience (appearances). Husserl, who rejects Kant's notion of the thing-in-itself (see CM156), is more often characterized simply as an idealist who "reduces" the real world to mental phenomena, and this in spite of the fact that he apparently wants to hold a direct-realist theory of perception. As metaphysicians, Kant and Husserl do not come off very well. Transcendental idealism, considered as a metaphysical theory, seems not to be very coherent.

But a great deal of sense can be made of transcendental idealism if it is taken not as a metaphysical alternative to or mixture of realism and idealism, but as a critical reflection on experience, science, *and* metaphysics, a reflection on the form or essence of experience situated at a different level from metaphysical concerns. Henry Allison points out that Kant once spoke of "formal" as opposed to "material" idealism (B 519n.), and wishes he had stuck to this terminology. For Allison, Kant reflects on the "limits and conditions of human knowledge," that is, on the *form* of consciousness, "not on the contents of consciousness or the nature of *an sich* reality."[11]

This formulation permits us to see more clearly the affinity between Kant's transcendental idealism and Husserl's, not only as a search for the essence or structure of experience, but also as a reflection that *brackets* the existence of the objects of experience. Both thinkers could be said to be concerned with the objects of experience, but from a particular point of view; not straightforwardly or directly, not as they are "in themselves," but as they appear, with respect to the conditions and characteristics of their appearance. Husserl's "bracketing" procedure has its origin in a distinction he makes in the *Logical Investigations* between *"the object as it is intended (der Gegenstand, so wie er intendiert ist)* and simply the *object which* is intended (*und schlecthin der Gegenstand, welcher* intendiert ist)" (LI 578, modified translation). Phenomenology is concerned with objects, but only with respect to how they are intended and under what conditions they appear. Anything about the object that lies outside these considerations, whatever it may be beyond the way it is intended, is simply placed out of consideration or bracketed. The "object as" of the *Logical Investigations* becomes the *"noema"* of *Ideas I* and the *cogitatum qua cogitatum* of the *Cartesian Meditations*. To bracket the object which, the object *"schlechthin"* or "in itself," is not to deny it or to doubt it is there, it is just to turn our attention away from it and toward its manners of givenness. If Husserl had seen Kant's thing-in-itself not as some mysterious separate entity, posited metaphysically behind appearances (the standard caricature), but simply as the bracketed object-which, he would not have criticized it as he did.

To sum up, Kant's thing-in-itself, and Husserl's bracketed object and world, are just the straightforwardly, naively taken-for-granted reality of our pre-reflective experience, that we must turn away from if we are to reflect critically on our experience. Kant's appearances and Husserl's *noemata* or *cogitata qua cogitata*, are simply those very same objects considered from a critical-reflective point of view—that is, with respect to how they are intended and under what conditions they appear.[12]

Emphasizing the role of critical reflection in these distinctions, as well as the point of view that goes with it, permits us to conceive of transcendental idealism, indeed transcendental philosophy, not as a set of claims or theses but as a procedure or "research program," in today's parlance. For Kant the key word is *critique*: "this enquiry," he says in introducing his major work and justifying its title, ". . . should be entitled not a doctrine but only a transcendental critique." (A12/B26) Husserl says that transcendental idealism "*is* nothing more than a consequentially executed self-explication," a "*sense-explication*" achieved *by actual work.*" (CM 86) Paul Ricoeur, describing Husserl's procedure, speaks of a "methodological rather than a doctrinal idealism."[13] In other words, Husserl proposes only that we *consider* the world exclusively as phenomenon, purely as sense for us, rather than *asserting* that it is nothing *but* phenomenon, nothing but sense. For him this proposal is formulated in the idea of the phenomenological *epoché* and reduction.

Husserl's proposal is that the philosopher *suspend* the "natural attitude" and take up the phenomenological attitude instead. It is in the natural attitude that the ontological status of the world is asserted or believed in; it is in the sciences of the natural attitude that questions of "what there is" are decided. The natural attitude consists of ontological assumptions about the world ("in itself") and experiences and judgments (both scientific and everyday) in which those assumptions are filled in or made concrete. As we have been insisting, the purpose of phenomenological description (or transcendental critique) is not to deny those assumptions, or to question those experiences or judgments, but merely to understand them. The phenomenological attitude does not replace the natural attitude, but only brackets it to gain a better understanding. Consequently, there is a sense in which it never leaves the natural attitude behind, but constantly returns to it in the "zig-zag" pattern Husserl often refers to.

A passage from the *Crisis* will clarify what we mean. What Husserl calls the "mathematization of nature," which is the key to the success of science since Galileo, is actually a *method,* "designed for the purpose of progressively improving, *in infinitum* . . . , those rough predictions which are the only ones originally possible within the sphere of . . . the life-world." (CR 51f.) The method is to treat the natural world *as* a purely mathematical realm by considering only those features of it that are susceptible to precise mathematical measurement. The philosophers, however, have converted this methodological procedure into an ontological thesis: they "take for *true being* what is actually a *method.*" (CR 51) The result is an ontological thesis: To be is to be mathematically measurable.

Something similar occurs if phenomenological investigation (or transcendental critique) is converted into straightforward idealism. The methodological injunction to treat the world purely in terms of its sense, or the conditions of its appearance, is converted into the claim that it is *nothing but* its sense or its appearance. This would be precisely to "take for *true being* what is actually a method," to convert a procedure into an ontological thesis that by no means follows from it.

To insist that transcendental philosophy is *method* and not *metaphysics,* however, forces us to consider critically the notion of method itself, and to face up to some of Heidegger's critical remarks on this concept.[14]

Method, Metaphysics, and Transcendental Philosophy

The combination of subjectivity and method, it will be recalled, is for Heidegger one of the key features of modern philosophy as a whole, beginning with Descartes. Cartesian method, mathematical-deductive method, scientific or experimental method—all are so many expressions, according to Heidegger, of the relation of *mastery* and *control* between subject and world. The crucial, central role of method in modern philosophy and science demonstrates for Heidegger that the concept of the subject, beginning with Descartes, is intimately tied to the notion of "enframing" the world through technological domination.

This would hold true of Husserl and Kant only if the point of their method was really to "reduce" the world to appearances. But we know that this is not what transcendental idealism means in Kant: the idea of the thing-in-itself prohibits us from thinking that there is nothing to the world but what can be captured in our scientific categories. And it should be clear that this is not what "reduction" means in Husserl. In fact, the term was poorly chosen. What the reduction does is reveal the meaning-aspect of the world that we naively take for granted. This aspect of Heidegger's criticism will apply to Husserl and Kant only if he succeeds, as he tries so hard to do, in including them in the historical sweep of *idealism* that begins with Descartes, culminates in Hegel, and then is articulated as will to power by Nietzsche. If our interpretation is correct, the two transcendental philosophers must be regarded not as part of this historical development, but as a counter-current struggling against it.

As we have seen, they do this not by opting for *realism* but by trying to overcome this tired opposition and move beyond such metaphysical disputes. Of this Heidegger should approve. One of the genuine merits of Heidegger's account of the history of modern philosophy was his tying idealism and technology together, arguing in effect that there is little to choose between modern idealism and realism. The latter, after all, at least as "scientific realism," has conceived of *reality* as precisely that realm of measurable entities and relations that is susceptible to our prediction and control. In other words, realism is reductionist, its "reality" a correlate of human projection and power. This is a genuine phenomenological insight, and one that has been pursued by such thinkers as Michel Foucault,[15] which comes not from worrying whether reality is really "out there" or not, but from reflecting on the sense it has in our scientific practices. Likewise, Husserl and Kant must be seen not as endorsing or denying a scientific conception of the word, but as trying to understand its meaning, and as devising a philosophical method that will allow that meaning to emerge.

Another way of talking about the methodological character of transcendental reflection is to say that its purpose is not to establish claims about the world, but to arrive at a certain point of view on the world, a new way of looking at it. Husserl opposes the natural *attitude* to the phenomenological, and the word he uses, *Einstellung,* could also be translated "standpoint," or "point of view." As Husserl often says, (see ID1, § 61), phenomenology does not deny or even doubt the world, much less forsake it to go off somewhere else. Indeed it deals with the very same world that has occupied us all along, in the natural attitude; it just looks at it from a very special point of view, that is, with respect to its manners of givenness. The purpose of the method—*epoché,* reduction, etc.—is just to establish or attain that point of view.

However, there is another, more subtle problem with the concept of method that is sometimes evident in Heidegger's criticism, though not explicitly so. What we are attributing to Husserl and Kant as the genuine sense of transcendental philosophy is the idea of a philosophical method that is metaphysically neutral.[16] Any such method may nevertheless be suspected or accused of harboring metaphysical presuppositions. Heidegger's approach to most of the modern philosophers he writes about is to claim that they are giving expression to a "metaphysische Grundstellung"[17] in spite of themselves, that their epistemology or other inquiries make sense only because of the metaphysical position they tacitly hold. This approach, though never very explicit as an argumentative strategy in Heidegger, is something very close to the concept of internal or immanent critique. This, it will be recalled, was the strategy employed by Hegel in his critique of the whole epistemological approach of his modern predecessors. This strategy is also used explicitly against Husserl by

Jacques Derrida. "Do not phenomenological necessity, the rigor and subtlety of Husserl's analysis, nonetheless conceal a metaphysical presupposition?" This is the question with which he begins his *Speech and Phenomena*, whose purpose is to provide an affirmative answer.[18]

Heidegger and Derrida both seem to suggest that such presuppositions are inevitable, that we cannot avoid being part of the metaphysics of our age. The same point could be made in a quite formal way: Can any method really stand on its own, without theoretical commitments or underpinnings? What, exactly, is a method? Simply put, it is a set of prescriptions for getting from A to B, from some starting point to some destination. Do not these prescriptions depend on the *theoretical* claim that A and B are really related in a certain way?

It is an interesting irony that, among those who answer this question in the affirmative, we find Edmund Husserl himself. Of course, he makes the point with reference not to phenomenology but to logic. The first conception of logic he addresses in the "Prolegomena to Pure Logic" is the one that treats it strictly as a normative discipline or technique (*Kunstlehre*)—that is, as a method—for how to think correctly. Husserl argues at length that logic or any discipline so conceived cannot stand alone. "Every normative discipline," he writes, "demands that we know certain non-normative truths . . ." (LI 88) In this case, these truths will be embodied in pure logic conceived as an eidetic discipline. Does it not follow that phenomenology, conceived as a method, *must* have metaphysical assumptions?

This point may not apply, however, to a method whose purpose is to reflect critically on the very metaphysical presuppositions that are at issue. To be sure, any such critique may *in fact* operate under just the sort of hidden assumptions that Heidegger and Derrida have in mind, and anyone is free to try to root them out, just as Heidegger and Derrida have claimed to do. But to assert that any critique must always, in principle, make and be unaware of such presuppositions is something else. For one thing, it would apply to, and thus presumably call into question, Heidegger's and Derrida's critiques as well. But the larger point to be made is that the critical enterprise is a *self*-critical undertaking constantly reflecting on its own presuppositions with a view to bracketing and understanding them. It is a never-ending process of critical self-reflection *that is not designed to come to a stopping place with the assertion of some metaphysical theory*. This is no doubt what Husserl meant by calling himself a perpetual beginner in philosophy.

This is what we meant by saying that metaphysics was certainly *at issue* in transcendental philosophy, though it is not itself metaphysics. It is in the deepest sense a critique of metaphysics for both Kant and Husserl. Kant made the point that by this he did *not* mean a critique of books and systems. (B27) He meant instead a critique of those deeply held beliefs toward which reason itself inclines us in its demand for ultimate rational satisfaction. Likewise, Husserl discovers and unearths those profound and fundamental, but taken-for-granted and unreflected, convictions (*Urglaube*) that make up the natural attitude—the ultimate metaphysics. Both thinkers realize that traditional philosophy—metaphysics—arises out of the structure of human experience. But their approach to it is not to contribute further to it but to reflect critically on its origins.

Conclusion

In this essay I have tried to counter the main lines of Heidegger's misleading portrayal of transcendental philosophy. I have attempted to arrive at a unified version of the transcendental tradition that combines the best insights of Kant and Husserl. As presented here, transcendental philosophy is anything but a representational theory, and transcendental idealism is not a metaphysical thesis. Its focus is intentionality or the transcendental unity of apperception—that is, the relation of experience to the transcendent or objective world. It does not take up this relation in order to affirm or deny it, to reduce it to something else or to derive it from something else. It simply asks how it is possible or how it works. Its purpose is to describe the basic structures of experience, and for this purpose it has devised a method. Transcendental philosophy consists in the perpetual and renewed application of this method to all levels of our experience, and to the world of objects, persons, and other entities and relations that our experience reveals.[19]

Notes

1. See Edmund Husserl, "Kant und die Idee der Transzendentalphilosophie" in *Erste Philosophie* vol. 1, ed. R. Boehm, Husserliana 7, (The Hague: M. Nijhoff, 1956), 230ff.

2. See Mohanty, *The Possibility of Transcendental Philosophy* and *Transcendental Phenomenology*. See also my "Mohanty on Transcendental Philosophy," 1-11, and Mohanty's response, 269-71, in *Phenomenology: East and West*.

3. Martin Heidegger, *Vorträge und Aufsätze* (Pfulingen: Neske, 1959), 74

4. Martin Heidegger, *Nietzsche,* vol. 2 (Pfulingen: Neske, 1989), 169.

5. Martin Heidegger, "Das Ende der Philosophie und die Aufgabe des Denkens" in *Zur Sache des Denkens* (Tübingen: Max Niemeyer Verlag, 1969), 65.

6. I am following the usual practice of referring to the pages of the Academy Edition of the *Critique of Pure Reason.* I use the Kemp Smith translation (London: McMillan, 1963). References to Husserl use the following abbreviations: CM= *Cartesian Meditations: An Introduction to Phenomenology,* trans. D. Cairns (The Hague: M. Nijhoff, 1963); CR= *The Crisis*

of European Sciences and Transcendental Phenomenology: An Introduction to Phenomenological Philosophy, ttrans. D. Carr (Evanston, Ill.: Northwestern University Press, 1970); ID= *Ideas Pertaining to a Pure Phenomenology and to a Phenomenological Philosophy*, First Book, trans. F. Kersten (The Hague: M. Nijhoff, 1983); LI= *Logical Investigations*, trans. J. N. Findlay (New York: Humanities Press, 1970).

7. See Kant's *Grundlegung zur Metaphysik der Sitten* (Hamburg: F. Meiner Verlag, 1957), 4, and CM 156.

8. Immanuel Kant, *Prolegomena to Any Future Metaphysics*, trans. P. Carus, J. W. Ellington (Indianapolis: Hackett, 1977), 113n.

9. Heidegger, *Vorträge und Aufsätze*, 75.

10. Martin Heidegger, "Hegels Begriff der Erfahrung" in *Holzwege* (Frankfurt: V. Klostermann, 1957) Two volumes of the Heidegger *Gesamtausgabe* (Frankfurt/Main: V. Klostermann) are devoted to Hegel: Vol. 32, *Hegels Phänomenologie des Geistes*, ed. I. Görland, 1980, and Vol. 68, *Hegel*, ed. I. Schüßler, 1993.

11. Henry Allison, *Kant's Transcendental Idealism* (New Haven: Yale University Press, 1983), 26

12. This is essentially the view put forward by John Drummond in *Husserlian Intentionality and Non-Foundational Realism* (Dordrecht: Kluwer, 1990).

13. Paul Ricoeur, *Husserl* (Evanston, Ill.: Northwestern University Press, 1957), 36.

14. See G. Funke, *Phänomenologie: Metaphysik oder Methode?* (Bonn: Bouvier, 1979).

15. See also Thomas Nagel, *The View from Nowhere* (New York: Oxford University Press, 1986), 9, 26.

16. See Mohanty, *Transcendental Phenomenology*, 160: Among the distinctive features of his conception of transcendental phenomenology are "a notion of *criticism* . . . (and) a certain *neutrality* as between metaphysical realism and metaphysical idealism."

17. Heidegger, *Holzwege*, 91.

18. Jacques Derrida, *Speech and Phenomena*, trans. D. Allison (Evanston, Ill: Northwestern University Press, 1973), 4.

19. For a further exposition of these views see my book *The Paradox of Subjectivity: The Self in the Transcendental Tradition* (New York: Oxford University Press, 1999). This paper is an adaptation of parts of chapter four of that work.

Chapter 9

Transcendental Transitions

Rudolf A. Makkreel

In his essay "Transcendental Philosophy and Life-World," J. N. Mohanty distinguishes between two forms of transcendental philosophy: the Kantian and the Husserlian. The former, to cite Mohanty's own words, "investigates the *a priori* conditions of the possibility of a given body of *truths* . . . such as Euclidean geometry and Newtonian physics"; the latter, which is "not committed to any such privileged body of truths" inquires into "the constitutive conditions and origin of any such theory regarded as a *meaning*-structure (its truth-claim suspended)."[1] This contrast is used to support the important claim that the transcendental need not be *a priori* as Kant thought.

Mohanty makes some other significant distinctions between these two forms of transcendental philosophy that are also intended to argue for the inferiority of the Kantian position. The main function of this essay will be to explore various ways of considering Kant's transcendental project that can restore some of its promise. By tracing Kant's own development as he moves from the first, or A, edition of the *Critique of Pure Reason* to the second edition of 1787 and beyond, it becomes possible to discern points of transition within Kantian transcendental philosophy and to see more similarities with the contemporary phenomenological-hermeneutical project of exposing constitutive meaning-structures.

From Pre-existing Forms to Precedence Relations

In examining the transcendental as a mode of constituting objects as we know them, Mohanty focuses on the Kantian categories as forms of consciousness and contrasts this to a wider conception of subjectivity available in Husserlian philosophy. Here, to cite Mohanty again, "the constituting subjectivity is concrete, sensuous-hyletic and also intentionally meaning-bestowing, corporeal and historically developing, anonymously constituting and reflectively discovering its operations."[2] From this we get the impression that we should leave behind the Kantian approach as hopelessly limited by a narrow mode of subjectivity, a perspective based on pure consciousness, and a priori formalism. Now there is no doubt that Kant at times encourages this kind of stereotype about his transcendental position and that Husserl is much more successful in approximating the rich conception of the transcendental that Mohanty wants to develop. Nor do I want to deny that Husserl's conception of transcendental phenomenology has made tremendous strides in keeping the idea of the transcendental alive and relevant. Nevertheless, I want to indicate that there are moments of insight into the transcendental found in Kant's writings that are just as important to preserve and that fall outside the stereotypes that have "grounded" the debate in the dual sense of founding it and of causing it to founder.

Since Kant often approaches the transcendental-empirical distinction in terms of the contrast between form and content, he allows himself to speak of the transcendental conditions of experience as a priori forms of consciousness that pre-exist the content of sense. This is especially the case in the first edition of the *Critique of Pure Reason*, where Kant sometimes lapses into a psychological idealism. All this makes it possible to conceive of Kant's transcendental conditions as abstract and fixed forms that are hopelessly removed from any understanding of historical change. The challenge for subsequent Kantians such as Cassirer has been to bridge that gap. To do this it becomes necessary to focus on other tendencies in Kant's transcendental approach so that we can replace speculations of transcendental psychology about pre-existing forms of consciousness with logical reflections about formal relations. While Kant will never give up the claim that transcendental conditions are a priori, I will argue that the meaning of this term shifts enough in Kant's work that it can shed the archaic character that Mohanty assigns it. When Mohanty defines the transcendental as a mode of constituting subjectivity that need not be a priori, I assume that he means to negate the idea of fixed, pre-existing forms of consciousness. However, even Husserlian transcendental constitutive conditions must assert some mode of precedence over what they constitute. Absolute pre-existence is replaced with relative precedence. If it can be shown that Kant's later reflections about the a priori also abandon the idea of fixed forms that merit absolute priority, then the precedence being claimed by Kantians and Husserlians need not be all that different.

Objective Transcendental Meaning Relations

Kant allows us to think of the transcendental not merely in terms of constitutive forms of consciousness that make explanative claims about the origin of our knowledge, but also as a mode of logical analysis that is less speculative. If we analyze our knowledge of the objects of the world as a mode of judgment, then we can suspend synthetic claims about transcendental psychology to replace constituting acts of mind with constitutive logical conditions. Kant gives us both the logical and psychological modes of the transcendental in the A edition of the *Critique of Pure Reason*, but in the B edition he moves more clearly away from transcendental psychology to replace constituting acts of mind with constitutive logical conditions.

Kant distinguishes transcendental logic from general logic in that it relates representations not merely to each other, but to some object transcending consciousness. Kant's analytic-synthetic distinction is proposed as a general logical claim that merely makes a determination about how representations are related to each other in consciousness. If a predicate B is already contained within the representation associated with a subject-term A it is considered analytic, if not, synthetic. But if a synthetic predicate at the same time opens up some aspect about what it *means* for something to be an object of experience, then it can also be considered a transcendental category. A category is thus a predicate that is synthetic, applies *a priori* to objects, and is constitutive of their *meaning*. Such a constitutive concept acquires its meaning from being a representation (*Vorstellung*) that is at the same time a schematic presentation. (*Darstellung*) of an object. Representations as part of consciousness are temporal and will disappear unless they can be related to something that transcends this flux of consciousness. The category of substance is one such concept to which representations can be related. When we apply this category, we regard at least some of the successive representations in consciousness as attributes of something that underlies and unites them.

Kant claims that this transcendental logical relation is not purely conceptual or mental, and that apart from an imagined relation to some object transcending consciousness, the synthetic principles of the conceptual understanding "are entirely impossible."[3] It is such an imagined object that is able to "exhibit (*darthun*) the objective reality"[4] of a concept of the understanding. The chapter on the schematism explains that the categories of the understanding are only bare unities of representations until they are schematized by the imagination. Schemata mediate between intellect and sense by imaginatively transforming the rules involved in categories into temporally ordered sequences of operations. The categories thus "acquire their [objective] meaning from sensibility, which realizes the understanding in the very process of restricting it."[5]

What this shows is that Kant does not regard his transcendental principles as a set of truths apart from their being applied to empirical experience. It is only by such application that truths can be arrived at.[6] Although Kant regards his transcendental principles as *a priori* formal conditions for establishing empirical truths about the world, Mohanty's distinction between Kant's privileged body of truths and Husserl's meaning-structures is not borne out. Kant's transcendental principles are not pre-existing truths and are valid only to the extent that they schematically project or delimit what it means to be an object of experience.

The Transcendental *A Priori* and Its Relation to the Empirical

The fact that the transcendental only makes sense in relation to the empirical givens of experience does not then divide Kant from Husserl. To be sure, Husserlian phenomenology goes further in accepting at least one other mode of interdependence. The technique of the *epoché* allows us to start with factual claims and move to the transcendental level– that is, we can suspend empirical truth-claims and transform them into their meaning-assumptions. If the transcendental is arrived at through such an *epoché* or suspension of natural judgments, then it would seem that it could not be considered a *priori* in Kant's sense of "independent" of experience. But the independence from experience claimed by Kant is compatible with a temporal dependence on it. Thus Kant writes in the introduction to the *Critique of Pure Reason* that "although all our cognition commences *with* experience, yet it does not on that account all arise *from* experience" (B1). Temporal psychological dependence does not entail logical dependence. Beyond this, Kant distinguishes between a relative independence of "this or that experience" (B2) and genuine a *priori* cognitions that "occur *absolutely* independently of all experience" (B3). And here in turn we find Kant distinguishing between "pure" a *priori* cognitions that abstract from all empirical content and those a *priori* cognitions such as the "proposition 'Every alteration has its cause,' " which is "not pure, since alteration is a concept that can be drawn only from experience" (B3). Pure a *priori* cognitions would seem to be logical truths such as A=A that need make no reference to experience in any sense. The not so pure a *priori* cognition offered as an example by Kant turns out to be the transcendental principle of causality. Its meaning makes reference to experience, but its truth is independent of it. Transcendental cognition is thus for Kant absolutely = logically independent of all experience, despite being both psychologically dependent on experience in terms of genesis and unintelligible without reference to experience in at least general terms. Whereas the pure logical a *priori* abstracts from all empirical content, the transcendental a *priori* does "not abstract from all content of cognition" (A55/B80). This allows us to say that the transcendental a *priori* abstracts from particular empirical intuitive content, but not from what is intuitable as such. The transcendental a *priori* is unintelligible apart from the schematic imagination referred to above.

We can summarize as follows: The transcendental a *priori* cannot be known apart from the real as we experience it. The proper way to conceive the transcendental a *priori* for Kant is to consider it as not dependent on experience for its justification, but as dependent on it for its psychological discovery = perception. Moreover, we can only apperceive the transcendental *a priori* in conjunction with possible experience, but once apperceived it is independent of all subsequent experience. Its apperception is not dependent on further confirmation through perception. It is not some inductive truth that could be falsified by future experience. It is in this sense that we can characterize Kant's *a priori* as independent of the empirical, yet intimately tied to it.

From the Synoptic Order of the Given to Synthetic Order

The criticism has often been leveled that because Kant considers transcendental conditions as purely formal, he makes the transcendental subject the sole source of the form of experience or knowledge. This seems to assume that what is given in experience is a "chaotic disarray of sensations,"[7] to cite Mohanty. Now Kant may speak at times as if the mind imposes *a priori* forms on raw data provided by the senses. But the situation is more complicated than that even in the first edition of the *Critique of Pure Reason*.

That Kant never contemplated a situation in which we confront isolated or chaotic sense impressions becomes clear if we look at the opening of the so-called subjective part of the A Deduction of the Categories in the *Critique of Pure Reason*. Kant writes: "If every individual representation were entirely foreign to the other, if it were isolated and separated from it, then there would never arise anything like cognition, which is a whole of compared and connected representations. If therefore I ascribe a synopsis to sense, because it contains a manifold in its intuition, a synthesis must always correspond to this. . . ." (A97). Kant hereby grants that the content of sense is given to us in synoptic patterns. But these patterns are purely spatial. The reason that we need to synthesize or actively connect the impressions that we receive synoptically, is that qua mental representations these impressions have been appropriated temporally. It is to the extent that these representations are considered as part of the inner flow of consciousness that they become subject to temporal dispersion. To counteract such possible temporal dispersion we need three modes of synthesis: a synthesis of apprehension to hold together what is given and to represent the manifold of sense *as* a manifold; a synthesis of reproduction to be able to bring back a preceding representation as consciousness moves forward to new representations in the time sequence; and finally, a synthesis of recognition whereby a reproduced representation can be identified as being the same as what was represented before.[8]

Kant describes these three syntheses as transcendental acts even though they deal with empirical manifolds. What is given as synoptically ordered is assented to synthetically as a manifold and then acted on by the other two syntheses to be able to distinguish distinct parts within the manifold. That which is reproduced is held onto as our attention shifts and then is assigned a distinct identity by the synthesis of recognition.

The identity produced by the synthesis of recognition is conceived formally and Kant ends the objective part of the A Deduction with the problematic claim that "the way in which the manifold of sensible representation (intuition) belongs to a consciousness precedes all cognition of the object, as its intellectual form, and itself constitutes an *a priori* formal cognition of all objects in general, insofar as they are thought (categories)" (A129f). This claim and the positing of a distinct "transcendental object = x" are eliminated from the B Deduction because they stand in danger of reducing transcendental idealism to a psychological idealism where objects are "merely in us" (A129). In the B Deduction it is made explicit that the understanding cannot generate its own objects. The knowledge of the understanding is now defined as consisting "in the determinate relation of given representations to an object" (B137). Consequently, "the synthetic unity of consciousness" is now considered "an objective condition of all cognition, . . . under which every intuition must stand *in order to become an object for me*" (B138). No longer is Kant willing to speak of a special transcendental object merely in us—transcendental knowledge relates directly to empirical objects. Or, as Kant puts it, "no *a priori* cognition is possible for us except solely of objects of possible experience" (B166).

It is important to note that Kant calls the transcendental unity of apperception not subjective but objective. A subjective unity is a determination of inner sense and therefore merely psychological or mental. The transcendental unity of apperception is objective, not in being a special object that can be known by itself, but as the condition for knowing any phenomenal object outside the mind. This could be said to constitute a logical formulation of the phenomenological principle of the intentionality of consciousness.

Three Kinds of *A Priori* Forms in Kant

In the rest of this essay I will attempt to explicate how Kant conceives the relation between form and content in experience. And as we begin to move beyond the confines of the *Critique of Pure Reason,* we will also find subtle modifications in Kant's conception of form, and with it of the transcendental and the *a priori.* All this will make his views more reconcilable with the phenomenological standpoint.

In an appendix to the Transcendental Analytic entitled "On the Amphiboly of Concepts of Reflection," Kant moves beyond the general concepts of the understanding that are constitutive of experience—the so-called twelve transcendental categories—to other general concepts that are necessary to reflect on these conditions of experience. Among these concepts are those of identity and difference, inner and outer, matter and form—concepts that Kant had been using throughout both the Transcendental Aesthetic and Transcendental Analytic. Concepts of reflection serve to define what distinguishes the two sources of our experience—sensibility and understanding. They also allow us to relate all other concepts back to one or the other source. From this perspective, the Subjective Deduction, with its three transcendental syntheses productive of the "identity" of a representation, really belongs to the subjective, reflective consideration of transcendental conditions rather than to their objective, constitutive consideration.

It is in the discussion of concepts of reflection that Kant clarifies in what sense form can precede content. He agrees that for a "pure understanding" that could directly know things-in-themselves, matter would be prior to form. But since concepts of the human understanding are not "related to objects immediately" (A267/B323), and require the cooperation of the senses, categories must be mediated by the forms of intuition to be applicable to objects. Whereas from the perspective of the intellect, matter as the determinable must precede form as its determination, from the perspective of intuition, form "(as a subjective constitution of sensibility) precedes all matter (the sensations), . . . space and time precede all appearances and all *data* of appearances, and instead first make the latter possible" (A267/B323). The form that precedes content here is indeterminate, that is, that of space and time in general as the parameters of all experience. The determinate form that empirical knowledge aims at can only be generated by the work of the understanding on intuition.

Whereas in the A Deduction Kant had spoken of the temporal succession of representations as a kind of given of inner sense, in the B Deduction he claims that the awareness of succession presupposes "motion as an action of the subject" (B155), which although it need not involve physical movement, does require at least an imaginative reference to space (see B154). This transition in Kant's transcendental thinking means that Kant can no longer merely appeal to an indeterminately pre-given temporal form. Accordingly, he now writes: "The understanding therefore does not *find* some sort of combination of the manifold [that is, the pattern of temporal succession] already in inner sense, but *produces* it, by *affecting* inner sense" (B155). The form of temporal succession is neither found *a priori* in inner sense, nor is it found *a priori* in the understanding. A determinate *a priori* pattern of temporal succession is produced by the joint "motion" of the understanding and sense and turns out to be spatio-temporal.

It seems that Kant's initial reliance on indeterminate *a priori* forms is to a large extent a product of having divided the *Critique of Pure Reason* into separate expositional parts: specifically, the Transcendental Aesthetic and the Transcendental Analytic. But the conclusions of the Aesthetic and the Analytic do not make sense without each other. The reworkings in the second edition indicate a transcendental transition to the joint production by sense and understanding of more determinate *a priori* forms.

Further transcendental transitions can be ascertained by moving to Kant's *Critique of Judgment*. There the status of the transcendental is transformed by the fact that aesthetic judgments are singular. When I say, "this rose is beautiful," I am not making any claim about all roses. However, the judgment is *a priori* in that I expect all other human beings to be able to agree with me. By contrast to the pleasantness of the taste of foods about which I do not expect universal agreement, the pure, disinterested pleasure involved in apprehending the form of a rose I do expect to be, in principle, shareable with all. Now the *a priori* claim about form being made here is not demonstrable, and to that extent, I can never be certain that I have chosen correctly in declaring a particular flower or a specific work of art to be more than pleasant or pretty. Since there is a social dimension to this disinterested pleasure, it is possible that I might want to revise my aesthetic choice in light of the taste of others. Aesthetic judgments could also be called "presumptive," since Kant characterizes the inferences of reflective judgment as "logical *presumptions.*"9 The presumption here is that the disinterested pleasure is a function of a harmony among my cognitive faculties (the understanding and the imagination) which is a necessary condition for knowledge in general. Because I am implicitly appealing to a general harmony that is also necessary for all human knowers to have knowledge, I have reason to presume that the harmonious pleasure can be universally shared. However, I cannot really be sure that any pleasure I feel is the product solely of such a harmony. Therefore, the transcendental status of the aesthetic judgment must cope with a reduced sense of the *a priori*. This *a priori* of reflective judgment is not predictive and certain, but merely presumptive. It can at best express the hope for universal agreement.

Elsewhere I have tried to argue that the transcendental *a priori* conditions appealed to in the *Critique of Pure Reason* are foundational whereas those that are appealed to in the *Critique of Judgment* are orientational.10 In the *Critique of Pure Reason* the knower is described minimally as a finite, rational being with a transcendental ego that has the capacity to unify what is given to it by inner and outer sense. Only when it comes to the givens of the senses do the possible peculiarities of the human body even become relevant. Otherwise, the categories and the general forms of space and time are conceived as applicable to any finite, rational being whether this be an earthbound human being, a Martian, or even a more angelic being. So conceived, the knowing ego is basically disembodied and unlocated. It could be said to represent the view from nowhere.

The situation is different in the *Critique of Judgment*. There the aesthetic judge is placed into a human community and the universality presumed is valid merely "for us (human beings in general)."11 Sometimes Kant also distinguishes the *Allgemeingultigkeit* (universal validity) expected of theoretical, epistemic claims from the *Gemeingultigkeit* (common validity) of aesthetic claims. The reason for this is that aesthetic claims are felt and ultimately presuppose a *sensus communis* whereby feelings can be communicated. We are in no position to impute aesthetic pleasure to other finite, rational beings such as angels and Martians who might have a different psychic makeup. The *sensus communis* is thus *a priori* in a more limited sense of projecting a shared or communal sense, equated by Kant with the power to judge, which "in reflecting takes account (*a priori*) in our thought of everyone else's way of representing" (C3 §40, 160; Ak 5, 293). Kant also describes it as a "broadened way of thinking" (C3 §40, 161; Ak 5, 293) by transferring ourselves to the standpoint of other humans to reflect on our own mode of judgment. What this broadened way of thinking does is to orient us within the human community. Just as perceptual orientation places us in the midst of the world so that we can locate ourselves relative to all four quadrants of the world, so communal orientation helps us to contextualize our own mode of representing and judging the world.

In his essay "What Is Orientation in Thought," Kant appeals to orientation to empower us to move around purposively in the world. As Kant writes: "To orientate oneself . . . means to use a given world region (*Weltgegend*)—and we divide the horizon into four of these—in order to find the others. . . . If I see the sun in the sky and know that it is now midday, I know how to find south, west, north and east. For this purpose, however, I must necessarily be able to feel a difference *concerning* my own subject (*an meinem eigenen Subject*), namely, that between my right and left hands."[12] The capacity to discriminate between different regions is correlated with a subjective capacity to distinguish between the left and right sides of my own body. Kant considers this bodily oriented feeling "*a priori*,"[13] and it refers not just "*within* my own subject" as the standard translation leads us to believe, but to those parts of my embodied self, namely my hands, that can point beyond me. This orientational feeling allows me to locate and direct myself in the world of nature. Here *a priori* does not mean pre-given, but is projective. It is formal, but not in the usual abstract sense, for it allows me to place myself concretely through my body and its specific relation to the sun above it.

I propose that aesthetic judgments as reflective have an analogous orientational function by locating individual judgments in relation to the human world at large. Reflective judgments are comparative judgments and allow us to "put ourselves in the position of everyone else, merely by abstracting from the limitations that may happen to attach to our own judging; and this in turn we accomplish by leaving out as much as possible whatever is matter, that is, sensation, in the representational state and by paying attention solely to the formal features . . ." (C3, §40, 160; Ak5, 294). Kant is still interested in form, but note that he does not say that all matter will be excluded. This is because aesthetic or reflective form is not the same sense of form that was used in the *Critique of Pure Reason*. The *a priori* forms of space and time were said to precede the matter of sense, but when Kant speaks of aesthetic form he makes it clear that he is reverting to the traditional Aristotelian sense of form as specifying some difference in the genus of matter.[14] The aesthetic form of the flower is not some indeterminate abstract form (such as spatiality) that precedes natural perception, nor is it some more determinate form *produced* by the understanding and sense (such as the time-line of our experiences). Instead, it is a specific form that is *found* in a singular experience. To appreciate the flower, I must discern its formal arrangement within the matter of my perception. Here Kant comes closest to the phenomenological art of discerning formal structures within concrete, empirical experience.

To the extent that the aesthetic form of a flower is found, it could be said to be *a posteriori,* but if it arouses the pure formal harmony of the cognitive faculties involved in disinterested aesthetic pleasure, it can be considered to be *a priori.* Just as Kant calls the necessity of the aesthetic judgment "exemplary," we can say that such an aesthetic form is *a priori* in an exemplary way—it stands as a model for the human community. But what is exemplary is not unconditional—it can in principle be replaced by another model.

This loosening up of the *a priori* is never fully acknowledged by Kant, but it follows from his own explication of the subjective necessity of aesthetic judgments in §§19-22 of the *Critique of Judgment.* Whereas the objective necessity of epistemic judgments is unconditional, the subjective necessity of aesthetic judgments is conditioned on there being a *sensus communis,* which Kant goes on to acknowledge is a presumption that may be either constitutive or regulative. If it is the former, then taste is "an original and natural ability"; if the latter, then "only an ability yet to be acquired and [therefore] artificial" (C3, §22, 90). Being unable to decide this issue, Kant is forced to strip the *a priori* of taste of its certainty. The judgment of taste involves the *a priori* expectation that everyone ought to assent to it, yet as Kant goes on to say, we "could count on that assent, only if we could always be sure that the instance had been subsumed correctly under a [common] basis" (C3, §19, 86). The presumptive expectation of the *a priori* claim of taste incorporates a degree of uncertainty and has no predictive force.

A very different and indirect acknowledgment that what is considered to be *a priori* may need to be revised is found in the *Anthropology from a Pragmatic Point of View* when Kant criticizes number mysticism. The Ptolemaic system, according to which "there are supposed to be seven planets, seven notes in the scale, seven simple colors in the rainbow, and seven metals," is charged with inventing a kind of "would-be *a priori.*"[15] A number that may define a certain region of reality is made exemplary for others in an unwarranted fashion. Here Kant seems to warn that too much reliance on *a priori* rules can impede scientific progress.

Kant's implicit warning not to expand the extent to which the *a priori* should be relied on, can be used to remind us that the purpose of a transcendental critique is to set the limits of possible knowledge. But if critical philosophy is characterized by the constant awareness of the limits within which we know, it may also be possible to apply limits to the *a priori* conditions that we bring to the process of knowing. This would mean that we must continually ask ourselves whether we can reduce the number of transcendental conditions that we rely on.

Conclusions and Suggestions

Let me conclude by reiterating the following six claims as the results of these reflections on Kant's transcendental philosophy.

1. Transcendental principles are not pre-existing truths and are valid only to the extent that they schematically project what it means to be an object of experience.

2. The transcendental a priori defended in the Critique of Pure Reason can be apperceived only in conjunction with experience, but once recognized it is independent of all subsequent experience.

3. The synthetic order imposed on sense by the mind merely transposes a synoptically ordered, spatial manifold into a temporal sequence that can be apprehended as a manifold.

4. Kant becomes increasingly aware that the transcendental unity of apperception is objective, not in being a special object that can be known in itself, but as the condition for knowing any phenomenal object outside the mind.

5. There are at least three kinds of a priori form operative in Kant's overall philosophy: a) the indeterminate forms such as spatiality that precede matter in that they are the presupposed receptacles for receiving sense impressions; b) the more determinate forms produced by the cooperation of the understanding and sense; and c) the specific forms discerned in aesthetic apprehension.

6. The greatest transition in Kant's transcendental approach occurs through the introduction of the last sense of form. From the perspective of reflective judgment, a priori form is not predictive, but presumptive. It is preliminary not in a foundational way, but as exemplary for orientational and evaluative purposes.

If we consider Kant's reflections about the transcendental a priori conditions of thought in this expanded way, his philosophy can be made more directly relevant to current intellectual problems in both the natural and human sciences. Instead of being pegged as a dated philosophical correlate of Newtonian science, Kant's transcendental approach can be applied to still unresolved issues concerning the intelligibility of our current interpretive paradigms. It is ironic that Kant's most recognized contributions to transcendental thought, namely, the conditions of the determinant judgments of the natural sciences as laid out in the first Critique of Pure Reason, are precisely the ones that are most dated. His inquiries into the conditions of reflective judgment are actually more relevant to the current situation. They need to be expanded beyond Kant's own aesthetic and teleological applications and generalized to all domains where human values and cognitive considerations intersect.

To return to the contrast between Kantian and Husserlian transcendental philosophy that inaugurated this essay, I think that the main difference can be located in terms of how the second of the concluding claims is interpreted. Kant and Husserl both conjoin the transcendental and the empirical. But whereas Kant correlated the transcendental conditions of the determinant judgments of the natural sciences primarily with *possible* experience, a phenomenologist must do so with *actual* experience. Once this transition is made, then no transcendental condition can be immune to change, for as we discern the richness of experience more fully, we will also have to adjust the conditions of its intelligibility. Here Dilthey can be said to stand at the real point of transition between Kantian and Husserlian philosophy. In an early draft of Book Four of his *Introduction to the Human Sciences,* he shows his Kantian colors by directing his attention to the "conditions of consciousness" that introduce a "deductive element" into our "constructions of the real world."[16] However, Dilthey also proceeds to distance himself from Kant by claiming that "the real conditions of consciousness and its presuppositions, as I grasp them, constitute a living historical process, a development; they have a history, and the course of this history involves their adaption to the ever more exact, inductively known manifold of sense-contents."[17]

There is a sense in which Kant is right to insist that transcendental conditions, once recognized, cannot be falsified by more experience. That which makes experience possible in the first place cannot be refuted by the further details of that experience. However, as the scope and depth of our experience is expanded with human development—something not really considered by Kant—its conditions or presuppositions may need to be revised.

Moreover, if, as suggested earlier, critical philosophy fosters an awareness of the limits of the epistemic claims made by our experience, reflection on this could also indicate that the presuppositions that we bring to our experience may also need to be delimited. For Dilthey, this suggests the possibility that, over time, certain transcendental conditions of experience can be disposed of. This makes for a bolder narrative of transcendental transitions than we have found in Kant, namely, a history which involves "the introduction, modification, and elimination of . . . presuppositions."[18] From this perspective transcendental conditions would become crutches that can eventually be dispensed with, and transcendental transitions would be more than modifications within the *a priori* conditions that make meaning possible. Transcendental logic would become a self-limiting inquiry into limit conditions.

Notes

1. J. N. Mohanty, "Transcendental Philosophy and Life-World," in Tom Rockmore and Vladimir Zeman (eds.), *Transcendental Philosophy and Everyday Experience*, (Atlantic Highlands, New Jersey: Humanities Press, 1997), 33-42.

2. Mohanty, "Transcendental Philosophy and Life-World," 35.

3. Immanuel Kant, *Critique of Pure Reason*, trans. and eds. Paul Guyer and Allen W. Wood (Cambridge: Cambridge University Press, 1998), A157/B196; *Kants gesammelte Schriften*, herausgegeben von der Preussischen Akademie der Wissenschaften zu Berlin, 29 vols. (Berlin: Walter de Gruyter, 1902-83) (hereafter Ak), 3, 139.

4. Here and in the next citation, I have used the Kemp Smith translation; all other citations will be from the Guyer-Wood translation. Immanuel Kant, *Critique of Pure Reason*, trans. Norman Kemp Smith (New York: St. Martin's Press, 1965), A157/B196; Ak 3, 145.

5. Kant, *Critique of Pure Reason*, A147/B187.

6. In the A Deduction Kant speaks of "an a priori formal cognition of all objects in general" (A129f.) preceding empirical cognition, but this is not repeated in the B Deduction.

7. Mohanty, "Transcendental Philosophy and Life-World," 56.

8. For a more detailed discussion of these three syntheses and their significance see Rudolf A. Makkreel, *Imagination and Interpretation in Kant: The Hermeneutical Import of the 'Critique of Judgment'* (Chicago: University of Chicago Press, 1990), 20-9.

9. Immanuel Kant, *Lectures on Logic*, trans. and ed. J. Michael Young (Cambridge: Cambridge University Press, 1992), 627.

10. Immanuel Kant, *Critique of Judgment*, trans. Werner Pluhar (Indianapolis: Bobbs-Merrill, 1987), (hereafter C3), §90, 355; Ak 5, 462.

12. Immanuel Kant, "What Is Orientation in Thinking," in Hans Reiss (ed.) *Political Writings*, (Cambridge: Cambridge University Press, 1991), 238; Ak 8, 134. Translation has been revised.

13. Kant, "What Is Orientation in Thinking," 239.

14. See Makkreel, *Imagination and Interpretation in Kant*, 19n.

15. Immanuel Kant, *Anthropology from a Pragmatic Point of View*, trans. Mary J. Gregor (The Hague: Martinus Nijhoff, 1974), 67.

16. Wilhelm Dilthey, *Introduction to the Human Sciences*, vol. 1 in Rudolf A. Makkreel and Frithjof Rodi (eds.), *Selected Works*, (Princeton: Princeton University Press, 1989), 500.

17. Dilthey, *Introduction to the Human Sciences*, 500-01.

18. Dilthey, *Introduction to Human Sciences*, 500.

Chapter 10

How is Transcendental Philosophy— of Mind and World—Possible?

David Woodruff Smith

How is transcendental philosophy possible? How is transcendental phenomenology possible? How is transcendental philosophy of mind possible? How is a transcendental approach to mind-and-world philosophically tenable in light of what we know today about the physical structure of the world and its influence on our own consciousness in brain process? And what about the influence of history and culture on our experience and theorizing?

J. N. Mohanty has pursued transcendental philosophy for decades, working through and beyond Husserl's results. Let us carry on the pursuit.

The standpoint here is a perspective on phenomenology framed by three papers, presented by Mohanty, Robert Sokolowski, and the present author in a symposium titled "Varieties of Phenomenology" at the Twentieth World Congress of Philosophy, held in Boston in August of 1998. I propose to extract certain issues from the conversation on that occasion, to frame anew the problematic of transcendental philosophy, and to invite Professor Mohanty's reflections on those issues.

What Is Meant by "Transcendental"?

The *Oxford English Dictionary* crisply defines "transcendental" as a variation of "transcendent." The latter originally meant whatever transcends or goes beyond something (as in value). In philosophy, however, "transcendent" was defined by the Scholastics to mean whatever transcends the Aristotelian categories of substance, quality, quantity, etc., and "transcendent" or "transcendental" was thus applied to universal properties such as being and unity, which do not appear on Aristotle's list of categories but belong to any instance of anything on the list. Kant later took over these terms within his own system, turning from properties of things to concepts through which we understand things. For Kant, "transcendent" applies to metaphysical things-in-themselves or *noumena,* which transcend Kant's categories of the understanding, the conceptual categories that define things-as-they-appear or *phenomena.* Kant applies "transcendental" then, by contrast, to presuppositions of knowledge, to conditions of the possibility of knowledge, especially to conditions on the applicability of concepts such as those of substance, quality, quantity, etc. Accordingly, Kant defines "transcendental philosophy" as philosophy that studies such synthetic *a priori* conditions of the possibility of knowledge. "Transcendental" has come thus to mean, in extension, the sort of philosophy practiced by Kant, in which we dig back into the "conditions of the possibility" of our knowledge.

Husserl did not feature the term "transcendental" in his earlier works. Husserl wrote in a realist, broadly Aristotelian vein in his well-known *Logical Investigations,* but he later wove Kantian idioms into his system in *Ideas,* where he promoted "transcendental phenomenology" and "transcendental idealism." Whether tilting toward Aristotelian or Kantian motifs or a synthesis thereof, Husserl broke new ground in his theory of intentionality. Indeed, Mohanty, Sokolowski, and I agree that, after Husserl's work, *intentionality* is the heart of the transcendental. The question is how to articulate what is "transcendental" in a philosophy that gives pride of place to intentionality. Broadly, Husserl terms "transcendent" the objects of our intentionalities, while he calls "transcendental" the structure that makes intentionality work. That structure consists in content or sense, dubbed *noema,* and its processing in acts of consciousness, called *noeses.* (These cognate Greek terms play off Aristotle's own idioms of psychic activity.)

It is customary, then, to define transcendental philosophy by abstraction from the philosophical systems of first Kant and later Husserl. We assume, for present purposes, that Husserl made significant advances over Kant, specifically in the details of his analysis of intentionality. There is something in intentionality, in other words, that begets a "transcendental" conception of philosophy.

Views of the Transcendental

When Mohanty gathered essays into a book titled *The Possibility of Transcendental Philosophy* (1985), he took transcendental philosophy to be based à la Husserl on transcendental phenomenology defined as "reflection upon consciousness in its object-constituting role," that is, in intentionality, a type of reflection that begins by "delineating the structure of a *noema.*"[1] This project he takes to be an evolution of Kant's project of seeking conditions of the possibility of knowledge or, using Husserl's term, "intentionality."

More recently, in his World Congress presentation on transcendental phenomenology,[2] Mohanty focused on twenty theses about intentionality. Some theses characterize intentionality, familiarly, as an act directed toward an object through a sense or meaning. Less familiarly, theses characterize the subject-side of an act, distinguishing between I-intentionalities, we-intentionalities, and anonymous-intentionalities. Here lie the forms of individual and collective intentionality and the oft-neglected form of intentionality that is without any obvious subject either individual or collective. (Anonymous intentionalities, I believe, include those ideas we share with no sense of their origin, for instance, that the sun always rises.) A final group of theses elaborate Mohanty's specific conception of transcendental philosophy: intentionality constitutes the world; the world constitutes intentionality; the truly transcendental principle is consciousness-of-the-world; and the empirical *is* the transcendental. For Mohanty, then, transcendental philosophy begins with the structure of intentionality, in which both consciousness and world are intertwined and mutually "constituted."

This is not to say, and I believe denies, that the world is reduced to or built up from contents of consciousness, as in classical idealism. This view precludes the recently fashionable project of naturalizing intentionality by reducing it to properties of physical systems such as the functional properties of neural processes in the brain, as in recent functionalism or other variations on classical materialism. This view also precludes the trendy suggestions that all the world is but a construct of forms of life or discourse or cultural history—a cultural or textual idealism loosely associated with structuralism, poststructuralism, deconstruction, postmodernism, and cultural studies.

Sokolowski presented a somewhat different view of transcendental philosophy in his World Congress essay "Trancscendental Phenomenology":

> Transcendental phenomenology is the mind's self-discovery in the presence of intelligible objects. It describes what it means for us to be datives of manifestation or agents of truth and responsibility, what it is to move into the "space of reasons." It analyzes various forms of intentionality, . . . I differentiate the phenomenological sense of "transcendental" from its scholastic and Kantian senses. . . . [3]

For Sokolowski, then, in consciousness, in different forms of intentionality, the mind discovers both objects (the world) and itself—and, I would stress, the *intentional relation* of consciousness to its objects. So, again, the structure of intentionality launches not only transcendental phenomenology but also the ramifications of a transcendental philosophy that interrogates reason, truth, responsibility, value, and so on. In earlier works Sokolowski has stressed the special attitude of transcendental reflection as the methodological key to transcendental phenomenology. For Sokolowski, this attitude is part of what distinguishes the phenomenological sense of "transcendental" from the

Scholastic and the Kantian senses. But what I want to stress here in Sokolowski's view is the evolution of concepts of the transcendental, from the Scholastic to the Kantian to the Husserlian to the conceptions here focused on intentionality. For I want to move on to a still different sense of "transcendental," a sense that I believe, nonetheless, follows in a lineage of philosophical senses of the "transcendental."

In my own World Congress essay "Ontological Phenomenology" (1998), I did not lobby for "transcendental" phenomenology or a transcendental philosophy grounded thereon. Rather, I outlined an "ontological" phenomenology, where intentionality—admittedly the paradigm "transcendental" structure—takes its place in a formal ontological structure I dubbed *three-phase* ontology. That approach would seem quite at odds with the "transcendental" bracketing of ontological questions. However, I want to press that ontological perspective toward a conception of transcendental philosophy—a conception that is more appropriate to the twenty-first century than strictly Kantian or Husserlian approaches. In this gesture I mean to join in the spirit in which Professor Mohanty has read both Husserl and ancient Indian philosophy and so meditated on the possibility of transcendental philosophy. I mean also to join in the spirit in which Professor Sokolowski wrote of moving beyond Scholastic and Kantian conceptions of the "transcendental" into Husserlian conceptions. The following conception, however, would move beyond the prior ones, perhaps in ways divergent from past "transcendentalists."

From Husserlian Formal Ontology to *Three-Phase* Ontology

I should like to propose a conception of transcendental philosophy that grows out of an account of the interdependence of phenomenology and ontology. That account began with Husserl's conception of formal ontology and then moved to a special *three-phase* ontology.

In "Mind and Body," I reconstructed a version of Husserl's systematic ontology, beginning with his distinction between formal and material ontology.[4] The roots of this distinction are discernible in logical theory, in the distinction between form and content of linguistic expressions. However, the distinction here is between "formal" and "material" essences of entities in the world, and this ontological distinction, full-blown, originated with Husserl. Thus, *formal ontology* posits formal categories, whereas *material ontology* posits material categories to which the formal categories apply. Specifically, Husserl posits the *formal categories* of Individual, Essence (including Species, Property, and Relation), State of Affairs—and Number, Set, Order, Part, Dependence, etc. (Some details are debatable.) Husserl also posits three *material categories*: Nature, Culture (*Geist*, "Spirit"), and Consciousness. These three categories he calls "regions"; these are the highest material genera of things in the world, and the formal categories apply to entities within each region. (Under Nature, for instance, there are natural individuals, relations, and states of affairs.) So we may organize Husserl's categorial ontology with the following architecture:

MATERIAL CATEGORIES

FORMAL   Nature   Culture   Consciousness
CATEGORIES
Individual
Relation
State of Affairs

In "Ontological Phenomenology," I outlined a different type of categorial scheme called *three-phase* ontology.[5] According to this scheme, every entity in the world has a nature that divides fundamentally into three formal aspects or *phases*: form, appearance, and substrate. Thus:

1. The *form* of an entity is how or what it is: the kinds, properties, relations, that make it what it is.

2. The *appearance* of an entity is how it is known or apprehended: how it is "intended" as thus-and-so in appropriate acts of consciousness.

3. The *substrate* of a thing is how it originates: how it comes to be, where it comes from, its history or genetic origin if temporal, its composition or material origin if material, its phylogenetic origin if biological, its cultural origin if a cultural artifact—its ecological origin in a wide sense.

We may situate three formal phases of an entity in the following architecture:

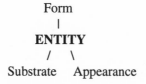

Form
|
ENTITY
/   \
Substrate   Appearance

I should stress two guiding principles. First, this three-phase structure is itself formal, part of the formal essence of an entity—it is a higher-order formal structure. There is thus a recursion on "form," as the overall *form* of an entity includes its material and formal essences in Husserl's sense, and this formal three-phase structure is part of its form or formal essence. Second, intentionality is tied into this formal structure, since the appearance of an entity consists in the patterns of intentionality through which it may be *intended* (by appropriate minds if such minds exist). This scheme of ontology is thus *phenomenological*, recognizing both intentionality itself and patterns of intentionality appropriate to any entity. Moreover, a phenomenology coordinated with this scheme is *ontological,* recognizing categories of things in the world.

Behind this scheme is the assumption, I would stress, that intentionality has its own irreducible form, namely, the *form of directedness,* schematized as follows:

subject—act-of-consciousness—sense —> object

It is not clear in Husserl's writings whether this structure is that of a relation, i.e., intentionality is "relation-like," but is it properly a *relation?* I believe intentionality is not a relation (under the formal categories) but rather a unique *form* that should be recognized as such in a fully developed formal ontology. (Intentionality has its own "logic," or formal ontology, as distinguished from the logic of sentences about intentional acts of perception, etc.) Thus, whatever material categories we recognize, and whatever lower-level formal categories we recognize, we should also recognize, first, the form of intentionality itself and, second, the formal structure of three phases in the "essence" of any entity.

In another context I would stress the different kinds of analysis or explanation an entity deserves: its role in intentionality (phenomenology), its place in the world-order (formal and material ontology), and its material substrate (natural and cultural sciences). Here, however, I want to turn to the question of "transcendental" philosophy, assuming this higher-order three-phase structure.

A Recursive Ontological-Phenomenological Approach to Mind and World

Husserl's errant pupil Martin Heidegger got one thing right in *Being and Time*: In our everyday intentional experience (*Dasein's* modes of *verhalten,* by another name) we have a circumspective awareness of the being and modes-of-being of things, including, saliently, ourselves (*Dasein*) and our experiences-of-things (*verhalten,* or relating-to). When we later reflect on the nature of things, in the ongoing enterprise of philosophy or science in the widest sense, we thematize the structure and being of things in general and our intentionalities in particular.

Many centuries have produced certain key results in our reflection on mind and world (recognizing Husserl's pivotal role in articulating intentionality):

1. There are many kinds of things and events in the world, including ourselves and our experiences and actions.

2. Consciousness resides in our experiences and actions.

3. Each act of consciousness—perceiving, imagining, thinking, willing

cum acting—is enacted by a subject (that may be individually, collectively, or "anonymously" dispersed in past cultural formations—let us focus as usual on the individual subject).

4. Each act of consciousness is intentional, that is, directed toward something, its object (that may be an enduring thing, a passing event, or even an act of consciousness, and that may or may not be actual).

5. Each act of consciousness is directed toward its object through a particular sense or meaning (that may be shaped by language, perception, historical inheritance, and more).

6. The structure of intentionality is thus the formation:

subject—act-of-consciousness—sense—>object

Bearing in mind this sketch of the form of intentionality, we can lay the ground for a new conception of transcendental philosophy.

Our approach to an overall philosophy of mind-and-world should be seen as *recursive*. We can begin philosophical reflection by characterizing basic structures of the world. Aristotle began this task by listing ten categories, and we would continue by revising our scheme of categories as we proceed. As we fill in the details, we will turn ultimately to the structure of consciousness. Then we will find that consciousness is intentional, and its intentionality deserves its own categorial analysis. In order to accommodate consciousness in our basic ontology, we will expand our repertoire from ontology *per se* to phenomenology, from what we say there is to how we find we experience what is.

Alternatively, we can begin philosophical reflection by characterizing our basic experience of the world. Husserl began this task by unfolding the structure of intentionality, and we would continue by revising our account of intentionality as we proceed. As we fill in the details of our account of acts of consciousness and the objects in the world that they "intend," we will turn ultimately to a scheme of basic categories of things in the world. What kinds of objects of consciousness do we find, and how would we organize this array of things in the world, including ourselves and our intentional experiences and actions? In order to fit our account of intentionality itself into a wider account of the variety of things in the world, we will expand our repertoire from phenomenology *per se* to ontology in general.

Whether we begin with our experience and expand our horizons to the basic categories of the world, or whether we begin with a survey of basic categories and narrow our horizons to our own acts of consciousness, we will go back over the same ground, especially as we continually revise our overall world-view to accommodate our overall range-of-experience. In this way, our philosophical reflection on the nature of mind-and-world is recursive, moving from either consciousness to world and back over this route again, or moving from world to consciousness and back over this route again.

In a picture, the path of philosophy of mind-and-world proceeds as follows:

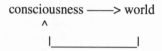

In our consciousness-of-the-world, we find the world as we experience it. And in our reflection on the nature of the world, we find our consciousness-of-the-world. We continue to refine our overall account of mind-and-world or world-and-mind. The structure of intentionality is pivotal to this practice and to its results.

The vexed issue of foundationalism now looks terribly simplistic. We do not simply begin with consciousness and work out to the world, nor do we simply begin with the world, with ontological categories, and work into language and consciousness. The path to knowledge of mind and world is more complicated: it is recursive, traversing relations between mind and world, seeking further understanding, further confirmation of the emerging world-view.

In this approach to philosophy we had better find (a) our best ontology, especially our best categorial and formal picture of the world. Furthermore, we had better find (b) our best scientific picture of the world, of the material substrate of things, including our consciousness-of-the-world. But we had also better find (c) our best phenomenological picture of consciousness-of-the-world, including our intentionalities and the intentional presentations of things (what Husserl called "*noemata*").

These pictures of mind and world find their place in the *three-phase* ontology I sketched: under Form, Substrate, and Appearance respectively. *Three-phase* ontology expands our horizons from appearance in consciousness to form and substrate. This scheme applies to any entity in the world, from trees and bees to quarks and quasars—to our own acts of consciousness. The three-phase structure of any entity emerges in our formal analysis of entities only after considerable reflection, after recursing and abstracting on the different aspects of various kinds of entities and of acts-of-consciousness. Indeed, it emerges only after reflection on higher-order forms that organize the kind of categories that Aristotle began with.

If we could see so broadly at the beginning of philosophical reflection, we could lay out the three-phase structure as axiomatic and proceed from there to the intricacies of ontological and phenomenological structure and their relation to the physical and cultural substrate. However, this pattern of abstraction is not apparent in our everyday activities—as Heidegger's phenomenology indicates, on the heels of traditionalists like Hume and Kant. But neither is phenomenological structure apparent in our everyday activites—it took many centuries of reflection for the phenomenological and thus the transcendental to emerge with clarity, whether in the European or Asian traditions.

Transcendental Philosophy

Transcendental philosophy, I submit, consists in the practice of philosophy through a recursive process of moving between consciousness and world and back. Its aim is an expansion of our overall *understanding* in the widest sense of *things* in the widest sense. (This is a paraphrase of Wilfrid Sellars's definition of philosophy—Sellars had read his Husserl and emulated Kant while admiring natural science. One could also say, "To the things themselves!")

The structure that defines the course of philosophy, over which it "recurs" or has "recourse," is simply the structure of intentionality. Thus, the transcendental way gives pride of place to intentionality, both in method and in results.

We experience the world in intentionality, and know both the world and our consciousness therein. We abstract and analyze phenomenological structures of our own acts of consciousness just as we abstract and analyze ontological structures of many kinds of things we find in the world—including *inter alia* our consciousness and our selves (the subjects of our consciousness, both individual and collective). In the special sciences we abstract and analyze "material" structures of various kinds of things we observe, infer, and engage. We continue to articulate, refine, revise, and theorize. In this way we produce our conception of the world including ourselves and our consciousness. Some features of the world are phenomenal, others are formal; some are material, others are substrative. And all take their place in the three phases of the diverse entities about which we philosophize.

When Husserl spoke interchangeably of "pure" or "transcendental" phenomenology, he meant the study of "pure" or "transcendental" consciousness, from the lived first-person point of view. Given his categorial scheme, what is "pure" and so "transcendental" in phenomenology is its *abstraction* of the features of consciousness from those of nature and culture: that is, the abstraction of moments (dependent parts) of Consciousness from concrete acts, thus leaving aside or bracketing their moments of Nature and Culture. And intentionality is the crucial *form* that phenomenology abstracts from consciousness. (See my "Pure Logic, Ontology, and Phenomenology."[6])

Transcendental philosophy is usually put at odds with both naturalism and historicism, which stress the ties of our experience to the physical-biological and the historical-cultural respectively. Yet the natural and cultural sciences are vitally important in our full understanding of mind and world, as we trace out in empirical detail the physical, biological, and cultural substrate of our experience and the world around us. Husserl's ontology *cum* phenomenology begins to sort out just how these aspects of mind and world are *interdependent*. The details of dependence are unsettled in Husserl (as he tilts toward idealism in *Ideas*), but dependence itself has emerged as a formal ontological category (in the Third of the *Logical Investigations* and again in *Ideas*). *Three-phase* ontology would put these things in their place, integrating phenomenology, ontology, and natural science, by charting the interdependence of appearance, form, and substrate.

Three-phase ontology is thus a higher-order ontology that aims to put in their "formal" place the results of phenomenology along with those of formal ontology and of natural and cultural science. Phenomenology is already transcendental in that it focuses directly on intentionality. But *three-phase* ontology remains transcendental in that it defines the place of intentionality in the formal structure of things and does so by recursive analysis of mind and world.

If you will, what makes a philosophy *transcendental* is its remembrance of its own place in the world—which is the practice of intentionality in understanding the order of things, including intentionality. *Three-phase* ontology is thus a transcendental philosophy.

How Is Transcendental Philosophy Possible Today?

The short answer: Follow the path of philosophy prescribed above.

Notes

1. Mohanty, *The Possibility of Transcendental Philosophy.*
2. _____, "[Untitled: principles of phenomenology]." *Proceedings of the Twentieth World Congress of Philosophy* (Bowling Green, Ohio: The Philosophy Documentation Center, 1999-2000), forthcoming.
3. Robert Sokolowski, "Transcendental Phenomenology," *Proceedings of the Twentieth World Congress of Philosophy* (Bowling Green, Ohio: The Philosophy Documentation Center, 1999-2000), forthcoming.
4. David Woodruff Smith, "Mind and Body," in Barry Smith and David Woodruff Smith (eds.), *The Cambridge Companion to Husserl,* (Cambridge and New York: Cambridge University Press, 1995), 323-93.
5. _____, "Ontological Phenomenology." *Proceedings of the Twentieth World Congress of Philosophy* (Bowling Green, Ohio: The Philosophy Documentation Center, 1999-2000), forthcoming.

6. _____, "'Pure Logic, Ontology, and Phenomenology,'" *Revue internationale de philosophie*, forthcoming.

Chapter 11

Utter Unreflectiveness

Lester Embree

Jiten Mohanty and I sat together on the plane from New Delhi to New York after the conference on "Phenomenology and Indian Philosophy" in January 1988. At the meeting he had had a conversation with a friend about whether or not one can be conscious of something without any awareness of time and he asked me what I thought. Immediately and without thought, I suggested that one might focus exclusively on an ideal object and while doing so be oblivious of anything temporal. Jiten smiled in his characteristic way and we went on to discuss other matters.

It has been awhile, but I wish to take this opportunity to follow-up on that suggestion, but this time with some thought or, more precisely, phenomeno-logical reflection. I will begin with some clarification of the concept of attitude and then describe how one can be aware of something without being aware of time. I could have drawn on the doctrine of marginal consciousness developed by our shared friend, Aron Gurwitsch, if I had felt need for the support of an authority, but have chosen not to do that.

The following is not an exercise in philology but in phenomenology. That means that my account can be examined by others or even by myself at a later time by reflectively and either seriously or fictively observing cases from conscious life of the sorts mentioned and then *eideating*. When matters are evidenced to be as I describe them, my account will be confirmed, and when my account is mistaken or incomplete, the reader is encouraged to correct or complete it phenomenologically.

1

Many phenomenologists would say that what one first finds upon reflect-ion are processes or even acts of sensuous perceiving. I suspect, however, that this is a product of the naturalism that plagues philosophy in our time. For those whose outlook has not been naturalized through study of engineering, naturalistic science, and certain types of philosophy, what one first finds upon reflection are attitudes and these are first of all characterized by their positional components. Ask an American male undergraduate about his attitude toward professional football and typically he replies that he likes it. This is not a passing feeling but an abiding attitude.

Further inquiry and reflection readily discloses that such a student has encountered the playing of that game chiefly representationally through watching television and also that it is a social observation of players and thus, in just these two respects, it is already not an act of sensuous perceiving. But, again, the first thing he probably remarks upon is the positive affective component of liking. Correlatively, he would probably also say, "Professional football is good."

Affective attitudes can be sorted in various ways. For example, they can be sorted according to the temporality of the object. Thus far in the football example, the temporality is vague, that is, it is indeterminate whether games in the present, past, future, or at all such times are referred to. Upon reflection, however, it is clear that football games, when they occur, do occur in time. One can fondly remember this or that past game or, less determinately, just how football was so much more wonderfully played at some earlier time.

Nostalgia, regret, guilt, shame, and pride are easily illustrated retrospective affective attitudes. Attitudes toward the future include hope, fear, and anxiety. And besides prospective as well as retrospective attitudes there are attitudes toward present objects. Ask the student while he is watching a game and he may well reply that he likes what he is seeing.

There are other positional attitudes toward objects in time. Those of the practical or volitional sort can be negative in being directed at efforts to destroy, prevent, diminish, etc. or positive in being directed at efforts to create, preserve, enhance, etc. Interestingly, however, there are no practical attitudes directly intentive to present or past objects, although one can be indirectly positively intentive to them in willing their preservation or restoration.

If one has been exposed to lots of naturalistic science and recent philosophy, one probably tends not only to be naturalistic but also intellectualistic in orientation. This signifies that concerns with the affective and conative components of attitudes tend to be disregarded for the sake of thinking, believing, and evidencing. Having paid respect to the affective and conative attitudes, more intellectual attitudes can now be turned to.

2

On the level of common sense thinking, thinking in the cultural as well as the formal and naturalistic disciplines, and even most of philosophy, there are preoccupations with what to call a matter, what to say about it, whether to believe in it or not, and how to justify such believing through evidencing. When this cognitive attitude prevails, one can still find feeling and striving in the background.

Most generally, there are two sorts of objects. There are the real or, better, the temporal objects. For transcendental phenomenologists, these include conscious life in its non-worldly status as well as houses, automobiles, bubble gum, etc. Then there are ideal objects. Normal adult humans are latently familiar with various sorts of them.

Patent familiarity with ideal objects is often produced in introductory logic courses. There one can become adept at recognizing the logical forms that particular judgments and the theories built up from them have. One can also become adept, whether it is accepted or not in the school of the theory of logic one's instructor subscribes to, at recognizing the universal or eidetic forms words or states of affairs exemplify.

Or to consider a little arithmetic, the number names "one, two, three" are expressive of concepts, indeed formal concepts. When what is enumerated is not specified verbally, they can be reexpressed with symbols, and they can be combined such that there is $1+2=3$, $3-2=1$, etc. Moreover, one can become clearly and distinctly aware of the formal universals of oneness or unity, twoness or duplicity, and threeness or triplicity that are instantiated by the formal concepts expressed by "one, two, three" or habitually bestowed upon matters in the process of counting them.

3

One more distinction between attitudes needs to be mentioned. When the student is asked about professional football, he may reflect. It is not improbable that he merely answer on the basis of habit, or indeed, because of what others have said or what he has long been expected to say. But he might also turn to his attitude and observe and analyze it, however briefly and superficially, and thus produce, with the justification of a modicum of evidencing, the statement "I like it" or the correlative equivalent statement "It is good."

Intellectuals, especially in the humanities and some schools of thought in the social sciences, reflect fairly habitually and may not appreciate how a naturalistic scientist does not. An astronomer, for example, does not regularly fret over how stars appear to and are posited by him, or are perceived with or without instruments by which he is aware of them. Then there are the belief characteristics constituted in *doxic* components of his conscious life, the states of stellar affairs constituted in his thinking, and how some objects may be tacitly good or bad or at least handsome, plain, or ugly.

Besides such unreflectiveness in a science, there is unreflectiveness in everyday life. While driving, one can of course reflect on how the road presents itself correlative to one's encountering of it, especially if one is bored while driving (and influenced by phenomenology!), but that is unusual. What is usual is to ignore or overlook not only the encountering and its components but also the object as it is encountered. Then there is simply the road and other cars in one's focus. What is evidenced when one reflects is an utterly unreflective attitude.

4

Can one be aware of something with no sense of time, no awareness of objects as located in time, as present, past, or future, or as going on in time whether staying the same or changing? For the present writer, this is difficult to do. He is too habituated to reflecting. But he does recognize that his tendency to reflect is unusually strong and also habitual. And he is nevertheless confident that he could train himself or be trained by others to be utterly unreflective on purpose and, in addition, to be so in a special attitude that is directed exclusively toward ideal objects, such as 1+2=3, which are not temporal. This possibility is clear.

PART 3

Understanding and
Knowing from the Indian Perspective

Chapter 12

Is Understanding Teachable?

Arindam Chakrabarti

I do not know, I am not aware of any way to teach this. It is other than what is known and other than what is unknown. That is what I have heard from those previous teachers who have explained it to us.

—*Kenopaniṣad*, 1/3-4.

The grammar of the word "knows" is evidently closely related to that of "can," "is able to." But also closely related to that of "understands"(Mastery of a technique)

—Wittegenstein, *Philosophical Investigations*,150.

1

Comparative philosophy, across times and across traditions, is a risky business. The meanings, for example, of Sanskrit epistemic and cognitive words are tantalizingly similar to, yet very hard to map onto, the meanings of English epistemic and cognitive words. We are tempted (and philologically licensed) to translate *"jñāna"* as "knowledge," but Nyāya *Sūtra's* first use of the term *"jñāna"* is in the phrase *"mithyā-jñāna"* whereas "false knowledge" would be a howler. Doubt is a kind of *jñāna*, but it is surely not knowledge. Getting wiser, we try to reserve *"pramā"* for knowledge but then we face deep trouble about the justification-condition, the lack of which in the standard Indian account of *pramā*[1] even a strong Nyāya causal reliabilism seems unable to remedy. Moreover, remembering can be knowledge but never *pramā* according to most schools of thought (the Jaina being one exception).

Working for decades at the unsung but challenging frontier between Western and Indian phenomenologies of knowledge, Mohanty has not only grappled with these terminological issues but has always recognized that these issues are not merely terminological. On the English side, along with many others, he has tried to place the concept of knowledge within the nexus of the concepts of consciousness, awareness, believing, understanding, and thinking. On the Sanskrit side, along with some others, he has tried to place "*jñāna*," within the nexus of words like "*cit*," "*buddhi*," "*bodha*," "*pramā*," etc. But unlike most other comparative philosophers who have either forged ahead with facile, tentative translations of, say, "*artha*" with "meaning," or given up hope of finding any counterpart, say, of "*pramāṇa*" in English, Mohanty has neither been rash nor pessimistic. Wherever needed he has crafted newer concepts like that of "quasi-sinn"[2] to accommodate the overlap between the Fregean idea of a word's mode-of-presentation of an object and the Nyāya notion of reason for application of a word to an object. He has also given small but radical twists to such standard traditional (in this case, Advaita Vedānta) tenets as: "Every entity is an object of witness-consciousness, either as known or as unknown" by replacing the "either or" with an "and," thereby coming up with the fascinating thesis that partial unknowing is a *cognitive* relation that an awareness bears with its object. What has come to be known is not only something that was hitherto unknown, it is, to use K. C. Bhattacharyya's language, known and felt as partly unknown.

But maddening problems arise even for Mohanty when he wittingly tries to mix traditions and asks: Is thinking a kind of *anubhava* or *smṛti* or *kalpanā*? Is *understanding bodha,* or *pramā,* or *jñāna*? Yet without raising these trans-traditional questions, it is not possible for us honestly and deeply to grasp even intra-traditionally, the relationship between *jñāna* and *bodha,* or between *cit* and *pramā.* Simply rehearsing the traditional definitions (are even *lakṣaṇas* definitions?) or translating them literally into vernacular or English would not satisfy those of us who have been seduced by both Wittgenstein's deed-centered description of language and Kumārila's force-centered imperativist theory of sentence-comprehension; we shall keep itching to ask: "Is the twin-propulsion (the propulsion in the words and the propulsion in the command-receiver) theory of Mīmāṃsā a kind of *use*-theory of sentence-meaning?"

One of these maddening difficulties that Mohanty has lived with for a long time is the question whether the classical Indian epistemologists of language had, or felt the need to have, any rich concept of grasping a thought or a proposition without accepting it as true.[3] This question arises out of any attempt at a modern reinterpretation of the Nyāya-Buddhist-Mīmāṃsā-Vaiśeṣika controversies centering knowledge from verbal testimony, and is closely related to the more basic question whether the Indian philosophers had a concept of thinking and thinkable thoughts or propositions at all. The central issue is best stated in the form of the following conundrum:

1. Correct understanding of someone's uttered sentence (*śābdabodha*) is a kind of knowing.

2. A falsehood or a false sentence can be correctly understood, with or without belief.

3. A falsehood cannot be *known,* because knowledge is by definition true.

Mohanty has often tried to get out of the resulting inconsistency by rejecting the first assumption: Understanding is *not* knowledge proper but a degenerate variety of knowing.[4] But he would then have to give up his own equation of understanding with *śābdabodha,* because according to the Naiyā-yikas, to have a veridical *śābdabodha* from someone's true sentence is to have full knowledge and not any degenerate, beliefless, variant, or cognitive state. Although Nyāya would not admit that "I eat chairs" can generate *śābdabodha* in someone who is convinced that chairs are inedible, and although Wittgen-stein[5] does say that we can *understand* such a sentence, that is not reason enough to argue that Nyāya *śābdabodha* is not the same as Wittgenstein's understanding and that all that was just a terminological confusion! Perhaps we have a genuine disagreement between Nyāya and Western analytic philosophy here. Nyāya has no difficulty assigning a deliberately contrary-to-knowledge, wish-induced, cognitive state (*āhārya jñāna*) to the kind of "comprehension" we have of something we regard as patently false or impossible. But Nyāya would not call something "understanding" or *bodha* unless it has a real possibility of turning into knowledge and is therefore credible. I have often wondered whether Nyāya would simply not reject the second proposition and get out of the jam. What is recognized to be false is not fit for understanding—if understanding is the same as *śābdhabodha.*

For many reasons I now think it is not a good idea to give up either statement 1 or 2 in the conundrum. In proposing, instead, to drop or qualify 3, I openly go against Mohanty who comments: "let me take it as uncontroversial (1) that we *do* understand false sentences but (2) do not have knowledge upon hearing and understanding such a sentence."[6] When I understand, even believe someone's statement that Indira Gandhi was Mahatma Gandhi's niece (which is a falsehood) I do understand and to the extent have knowledge in so far as I have correctly interpreted the speaker's utterance, though it is not a piece of knowledge about Indira Gandhi. I have gathered knowledge about the meaning of an utterance and its falsity can be detected only in the backdrop of a whole lot of true beliefs. I know correctly who Indira Gandhi was and who Mahatma Gandhi was and what it is for someone to be someone else's niece, etc. And thus although my resulting belief turns out to be false, like all cognitive contents, the content of that false belief is made out of bits of correctly cognized or *known* objects and properties and relations. So in a sense, we could say that a falsehood, too, can be known, albeit in its bits and, after all, what is beliefless understanding except knowing the bits correctly and also knowing how they were to be connected had the entire content been believed? What is known when we cognize erroneously are bits of the same reality that would have been known, *in the right order,* if we had been cognizing veridically. So, the way out of the conundrum is through rejecting the third premise of the conundrum.

The underlying issues here are not all clarified by the quick "solution" above. A lot more light needs to be thrown on the questions: What kind of knowledge is understanding? What are its objects or knowables? And I propose, in this paper, to throw an oblique beam of illumination on these questions by raising the closely connected issue of teachability of understanding, thus linking back to Mohanty's critical interest in the Indian theories of knowledge from the experts' utterance. Knowledge (except controversial first personal indexical qualia facts) is transmissible. If understanding is knowledge then it should be possible to bring somebody to understand something by teaching. But is linguistic understanding or, for that matter, understanding of any sort—at all teachable? The question, at first, may sound unexciting. In order to make the pendulous movement of philosophical doubt behind it palpable, let me dramatize two opposite points of view between which the argument swings.

2

Whether she learns from reason, from experience, or from inspiration, the ideal learner in the West gathers knowledge all by herself. Plato says in a famous passage of the *Theaetetus* that there may be teachers who can persuade someone else to accept a truth, but no one can plant knowledge in the head of someone else because to cause me to believe, even believe truly, is not to bring me to understand, and without understanding there is no real knowledge. There is only one person who can bring me to understand something, viz., myself. Centuries later, John Locke—whose theory of knowledge is deeply antithetical to Plato's—also compares received learning with borrowed wealth, admonishes that the floating of other men's opinions in our brains makes us not one jot the more knowing, and concludes that men must think and know for themselves. Thus, both Rationalists and Empiricists seem to deny the obvious phenomenon of transmission of understanding or knowledge through teaching. In contrast, the classical Indian knowledge-seeker, whether he wishes to learn music, dance, architecture, grammar, logic, theology, philosophy, or astronomy invariably turns to a teacher, a tradition, a chain of masters-and-disciples. Whether it is something as trivial as learning the meaning of a word or something as momentous as knowing who I am or how to live wisely, freely, blissfully through work or wisdom or both—one is required to submit to a teacher. "How much can one really understand by following one's own reasoning? The learning of those who have not sat at the feet of earlier scholars . . . does not attain complete definiteness," says Bhartṛhari in his seminal work "Of Sentences and Words." Torn between such opposite paradigms of knowledge-gathering, between autonomy and authority, we start to see the point of our initial question:

Is there any education in understanding except self-education?

3

But what is this understanding that is supposed to be so unteachable? One obvious answer is this: *Understanding is knowledge of meaning.* Standing somewhere between the grandeur of wisdom and the triviality of informational knowledge, understanding—a much wider and less well-defined notion than simply the grasp of the meaning of a linguistic expression—could be characterized as a deep, connected, and re-applicable knowledge of the reason, cause, principle, or mode of functioning of something. Besides a remark or a joke, we can be said to understand a mathematical proof, a scientific or philosophical theory, a person, a society, a work of art, a kind of music, and a whole lot of other things. Anything which fits into a structure and admits of explanation or interpretation can be said to be understood.

In this paper I concentrate primarily on linguistic understanding because first of all, the truism *to understand S is to know what S means* suggests to me that if one could determine the exact variety of knowing—of which knowing the meaning of a bit of speech is—one would get a very important clue to the nature of other sorts of understanding as well. Second, the grasp of a concept crucial for any kind of justified belief or structured thought can best be handled theoretically in terms of our understanding of a word, especially a predicate. Third, one of the classical forms of philosophical enquiry has been to ask for the exact meaning of a word like "real," "true," "good," "cause," "free," "just," "know," or even the word "meaning" itself. It seems that understanding of such key words constitutes the central core of philosophical knowledge, if there is such a thing as philosophical knowledge. Fourth, if Bhartṛhari or Quine is to be trusted, all knowledge is in a deep sense linguistic. To give a quick metaphysical argument: Linguistic communication opens up other people's minds for us, and the very concept of an objective outer world that gives content to the notion of belief, truth, and justification is the concept of a public world available as a target of reference and description equally to other people; thus, cracking the mystery of understanding speech would be indirectly cracking the mystery of all knowledge claiming objectivity. In a narrowed-down form the question is this: "Can one person teach another person what a certain expression means?" Once again the question sounds trivial. The answer, it seems obvious, should be, "yes!" Strangely enough, through a rather complicated process of reasoning, St. Augustine in his early dialogue "De Magistro" (The Teacher) answers the question with a clear "no." Echoing but not quite repeating Plato's recollection theory of learning, Augustine argued that no teacher ever teaches us anything. Taking knowledge of the meanings of words as his chief example, he tries to prove in the first part of his dialogue that nothing can be taught without signs.

In the second part he argues that nothing can be taught with signs. So nothing can be taught. If "learning" means picking up genuine knowledge from the instruction offered by other people then none of us ever learn anything from others. An obvious difficulty at this point would be this: don't we learn something—if nothing more than this startling truth that teachers teach us nothing—from Augustine's own writings? Is not the dialogue in "The Teacher" operationally self-defeating? Augustine anticipates this objection and responds: If at the end of reading the dialogue the reader's understanding comes to agree with Augustine that is because the inner light within the heart of the reader has seen the point of each step of the argument on its own. Augustine did not teach the reader the truth of the conclusion, the reader's own reason had taught itself.

4

The structure of the argument in "De Magistro," as far as I can extract and reformulate it in contemporary idiom, is as follows:

DM1.   If the meaning of a word could be taught at all, it could be taught either by ostension/exhibition or by words.

DM2.   Through ostension/exhibition meaning cannot be taught because ostensive definitions could always be misinterpreted. Besides, many important words have meanings which cannot be exhibited or pointed at. For example, try exhibiting the meaning of the word "cousin" by gestures or point your finger towards the meaning of "not."

DM3.   We cannot be made to know anything by words we do not already know by first hand experience.

Therefore, the meaning of a word cannot be taught at all.

The second premise of this argument, DM2, anticipates an extremely subtle and crucial point about the inadequacy of ostensive definitions, a much more well-worked-out version of which we find in Wittgenstein's *Philosophical Investigations* (27-64). Although we do try to convey what is meant by a proper name like "Jesus," a color adjective like "red," a common word like "rabbit," or a mental-state-word like "pain— all by pointing at things like a picture of Jesus, an arbitrary sample of a red surface, an instance of the rabbit-kind, or a physical manifestation of the state of pain—such a gesture runs the risk of misfire, ambiguity, indeterminacy, and wild misinterpretation in each of these cases.

The most contentious premise, however, is the third one, DM3, since it denies the possibility of conveying any knowledge through words, and especially denies that the meaning of a word could be explained and thereby imparted to another person through verbal means. A sub-argument for this premise could be reconstructed from Augustine's text (and indeed could be traced back to ancient sceptical sources). This sub-argument runs as follows:

A. When words are uttered, either the hearer knows their meaning already or he does not.

B. If he already knows their meaning then the words do not give him any knowledge.

C. If he does not know the meaning (of all or some) of the words then the words only generate a sensation of noise—which is not even knowledge of words as words of a language.

Therefore, in either case, when words are uttered nothing new is known by the hearer.

Thus, understanding of a word being un-teachable either verbally or non-verbally, remains un-teachable, period.

Now it is one thing for us teachers to feel utterly baffled from time to time by the difficulties of explaining some concepts to students, but quite another thing to concede the nihilistic conclusion that no linguistic understanding is, in principle, conveyable through instruction. The conclusion of the Augustinian argument must be false. Yet the argument and the sub-argument look formally valid. Therefore something must have gone wrong in the premises.

I propose to question the very first premise (DM1) that claims there could only be two ways of teaching meanings, by verbal explanation or by ostension/exhibition. There can be a way of teaching by exemplifying the use of an expression that is neither of these two ways. This is how most of us learn our first language. Parents and people around us do not try to point or exhibit or enact the meaning of a verb like "walk" or "sit," neither do they start explaining in other words what walking or sitting means. They just use the word in the right context and let us watch them use it. Augustine anticipates this way of resisting his first premise because he himself gives the example of a bird-catcher. Suppose someone ignorant of how birds are trapped followed the bird-catcher step by step and inquired what could be the purpose of the man's equipment. Suppose the bird-catcher, seeing him all attention, and eager to display his skill, got ready his twigs, tubes and hawk and caught a bird, would he not teach the spectator what he wanted to know by the action itself and without any signs?

Apart from the weak protest that even this way of teaching is open to the same incompleteness and indeterminacy as teaching by ostension/exhibition, Augustine more or less agrees that knowledge of language can be imparted, given enough intelligence in the learner, through this method of demonstrating the use of words rather than demonstrating what is meant by them. But perhaps that would not count as teaching in the strict sense because first, it is totally passive—the bird-catcher is only letting the learner watch him do it—and second, it relies so heavily on the learner's capacity to figure it out on his own.

A lot of weight is attached to this notion of passive teaching in Classical Indian theories of learning. Taken to an extreme it leads to such metaphorical expressions as: "the tree has taught me tolerance," "The earth has taught me forgiveness," etc. An eager Ekalavya could learn the art of archery by just watching Droṇa train the princes and later by just imagining that the statue of Droṇa was teaching him. He learned from Droṇa but Droṇa obviously did not teach him. The problem with this third way of teaching and its extension is this: it is surely the most common way of learning a practice but from the fact that A learned from B it does not follow that B taught A. The converse failure of entailment is witnessed by all of us teachers quite often: From the fact that B taught A, it does not follow that A learned from B. I shall, therefore, try to attack the anti-teaching argument more directly at a different step, assuming that the first premise is correct and there is no third way of explicit teaching of meaning.

The real sophistry of Augustine's argument lies in the third premise that tries to prove that with words no new knowledge, no new understanding can be effected. To start with, this is proved on the basis of a simple trick with the plural "words," which could mean either single words taken distributively or a sentence as a string of words. Suppose I tell my daughter: "Cats eat rats." She knows what each of those words means, so by uttering those words I have not given her any new lexical knowledge. But she does not know that cats eat rats, the fact meant by the entire sentence and hence, in a loose sense, by those words. Thus, although I did not teach her what each of those words mean, her knowledge of a new fact about feline diet is something I as a teacher can claim the credit for. On the contrary, if she does not know Hindi and I had taught her what "barph saphed hoti hai" means, I may not have taught her that snow is white, which she already knew, without it also being true that I taught her nothing. Changing the example to an explanation of meaning like "A teetotaler is a person who abstains from alcoholic drink," we can easily see how a new knowledge of meaning can be transmitted through old words already understood by the learner.

But Augustine's complaint against teaching by words is much deeper than the sophistry exposed above. It springs from the Platonic distrust of testimony as a source of knowledge. Even sentences of the Bible, Augustine says, do not give us knowledge but only useful true belief as long as he can just take them as trusted words of an authority. Until my daughter herself sees a cat eating a rat, her belief in the content of my words would not become knowledge. By the same logic, an elder man's testimony to the effect that the words W has the same meaning M can at best give the learner of a language a true belief that W means M but in order to understand W the learner has to see what W means in actual use by her own light and work it out from the situation and the neighboring words.

As a general epistemological thesis, I think, this distrust of testimony is quite wrong-headed. I have argued for the irreducible respectability of knowledge from words elsewhere. Without engaging in the debate here, let me say just this: If the autonomous knower sticks rigidly to her principle "know it yourself" then she cannot make use of any public language even to preserve or classify information for her own future use, let alone for posterity. One can consolidate and deepen one's knowledge of semantic value by noticing further connections in usage, but for the primitive connections between noises and what they stand for in a certain language, it is foolish to ask for any more justification than the speakers of that language tell us that those noises stand for those sort of things. Since the only possible languages are public languages, the person distrustful of others' teachings about meaning is left with no language whatsoever. It is impossible to participate in any human social transaction without implicitly accepting native speakers of a language as habitual true-believers and truth-tellers. Even experiencing the world would be severely impoverished if I cannot claim that a certain flower is a rhododendron because that is what I was told it was called.

The basic fallacy in the Augustinian argument could be revealed in a simpler way as stemming from an equivocation with "teaching." Notice the following two uses of the verb "to teach": in the sentence "The *Gītā* teaches us that the soul does not die" and in the sentence "P. K. Sen taught me logic." It is clear that we can substitute the former use of the verb "teach" with "tell." "The *Gītā* tells us that the soul does not die" is perfectly fine. But we cannot do that for the second use. "P. K. Sen told me logic" does not make sense. Conversely, we can rewrite the second sentence as "P. K. Sen taught me how to solve logical problems" but there can be no "teaches-how-to" equivalent of the first statement. When somebody tells me that something is the case he usually does not give me any recipe for future creative use. If P. K. Sen told me for each formal proof of a theorem that this is the exact sequence of steps and I could merely repeat them faithfully he would not have, thereby, taught me logic. Teaching logic is thus not just teaching that or telling, it is *teaching how* or training. Now we can safely formulate the following principle about rules in general and meaning-rules in particular: 1) A has successfully taught B a rule only if, after being taught, B can figure out the results of a particular application of it in a fresh case on his own. 2) If B has figured out something on his own then no one, not even A, has taught him that. From these two premises it seems to follow that 3) if A has taught B how to apply a rule then A has not taught B that in a particular untaught case the rule yields such-and-such specific results.

If we ignore the distinctions between teaching-how and teaching-that, we could state this conclusion with misleading brevity: "If A has taught B then A has not taught B," which may look like proving that for all A and all B, A never teaches B, as long as A and B are distinct persons.

5

Of course, my rebuttal of one particular argument against the possibility of teaching does not conclusively establish that understanding can be taught. But positive possibility-proofs are as hard to come by as positive existence-proofs. All I can do to make my positive case stronger is to spend a little more time on the exact nature of understanding or knowing what a word or sentence means, and thereby get clearer as to what is done when such knowledge is imparted. I have implied just now that understanding may be conveyable by teaching how rather than teaching that. A tourist guide can teach an American tourist that in Hindi "*main videshi hun*" means that I am a foreigner. But just gathering that information will not give the tourist understanding of even that sentence. Someone who teaches him how the words in that sentence could be combined in other ways with other words, and how the structure-dependent properties of that sentence affects what other sentences logically follow from that sentence, etc., so that the foreigner can use or follow the use of hitherto unheard sentences consisting of heard and learned words—begins to teach him the language.

Now teaching how presumably imparts knowing-how. But is the understanding that I pick up from such a training in a language just a skill or is it mastery of a practice? Of the two classical modes of knowledge, knowing-how and knowing-that—practical skill and propositional awareness—which one fits the nature of understanding better?

Michael Dummett has argued that the practical-versus-theoretical dichotomy turns out to be spurious when applied to a speaker's knowledge of a language. Let me try to rehearse in my own way some of his arguments to prove that grasp of meaning is neither exclusively theoretical nor exclusively practical knowledge.

Since the meaning of a declarative sentence is a proposition, knowing the meaning of such a sentence, one could expect, would be just knowing a proposition. But the matter is not that simple. Take the false sentence "Clinton is bald." We all understand it perfectly well. What proposition does it express? Presumably, the proposition *that Clinton is bald.* When we know its meaning, that is, understand it, we do know *that* proposition, don't we? To know that proposition is to know that Clinton is bald, which none of us do because we neither believe it nor is it true. Trying to defend the claim that understanding is propositional knowledge, we could point out that to understand that sentence is to know that the sentence "Clinton is bald" in English means that Clinton is bald; to understand the Sanskrit sentence "*Gaṅgā nīlā*" is to know *that the sentence "Gaṅgā nīlā" in Sanskrit means that the Ganges is blue,* which is not to know that the Ganges is blue but still to know *a proposition.* The problem with this response is that it fails to preserve the important identity between the sentence-meaning and what is known when a sentence is understood. For that "*Gaṅgā nīlā*" *means that the Ganges is blue* is not the meaning of that Sanskrit sentence. The meaning of a sentence does not include the sentence once again. There is a threat of a vicious regress lurking there.

Shall we therefore drop the idea of knowledge of what a word or sentence means in the sense of awareness altogether and reduce the speaker's or competent hearer's understanding of a sentence-meaning to a mere ability or competence—like knowing how to ride a bicycle? Apart from the fact that our understanding of an individual sentence as a consequence of our mastery over the language to which it belongs is often episodic, it can happen in a flash and then can also elude us—and none of this is possible with mere knowing how. Even our mastery over the basic vocabulary, in spite of being dispositional, is more cognitive and has a deeper inner side to it than externally detectable skills. Of course, we no longer believe in a psychologistic Lockean code-conception of meaning where to understand a word is to call up an idea associated with it and to speak is to translate one's private mentalese into English, Hindi, or Japanese. Our mastery over concepts that serve as the meanings that words contribute to sentences must be manifestable in overt linguistic or non-linguistic practice. But to be manifestable in practice is not to be reducible to practice. A perfect parroting of swimming or cooking would be swimming or cooking, but a perfect parroting of speaking French will not be speaking French. If understanding Sanskrit was merely an ability to utter some sounds and react physically and appropriately to the utterance of some sounds, then one can know what it is to speak Sanskrit without knowing Sanskrit, just as one knows what it is to swim even if one does not know how to swim. But one cannot do so. It takes nothing short of knowledge of Sanskrit to enable someone to know what it is to speak Sanskrit. Therefore understanding is not just knowing-how.

Dummett's own suggestion is that it is a unique third kind of knowledge, namely *knowing-what*. The mistake of the argument examined a couple of paragraphs earlier was that it treated "what the sentence means," in the example "the speaker knows what the sentence 'Clinton is bald' means," as a noun-phrase standing for the object of understanding-knowledge. Dummett seems to think that knowing what the sentence means cannot be broken up in that manner: it is not knowledge of what-the-sentence-means but unanalyzeably knowledge of *what-the-sentence-means*. The nature of this peculiar *knowing-what* is still very unclear to me, but it seems highly plausible that this is the sort of knowledge—neither *techne* nor *episteme* but a bit of both—that *we* try to generate in our philosophy students when we are trying to teach them, say, the difference between cause and reason, or the meaning of Hume's sentence "Whatever is may not be," or the meaning of a multiply quantified sentence like "some tourists go to all museums in some cities" without necessarily agreeing with it. If a student memorizes all that I have told her and all that she has read in the history of philosophy but cannot use the distinctions in new cases that I or the book did not discuss; if she cannot tell, on her own, how the fallacy of *svarūpāsiddhi* (or the mark's absence in the subject of proof) happens in cases other than the hill, smoke, and fire—then my teaching has failed. Now, there is a part of this teaching that remains unsaid, just as there is a part of conveying the sense of a word that remains unspoken. The teacher of philosophy can teach best by actually doing philosophical loud-thinking in class and letting the students watch her do so. This need not be passive teaching in so far as the teacher's choice of the style, topic, emphasis areas, and doubts raised and positions refuted would be actively geared to the pupil's specific needs. But this teaching-how to handle proofs, refutation, concepts, and distinctions would at best give the student something like a knowledge of rules. But one cannot and should not supply further instructions as to how in each case to apply these rules. This should be left to the judgment of the student. Kant calls this judgment the faculty of application of rules and remarks:

"Though understanding is capable of being instructed and of being equipped with rules, judgment is a peculiar talent which can be practised only and cannot be taught. . . . It is the specific quality of so-called mother-wit and its lack no school can make good." (*Critique of Pure Reason*, B172) This mother-wit, I claim, is what Bhartṛhari called "*pratibhā*," which comes in the form of a generative transformative capacity for rule-following as well as in the form of the flash of synoptic understanding. It is partly innate, and partly emerges out of proper training and what I like to call knowledge by contagion through being with a competent teacher. Even the mother-wit needs a nudge now and then and a skillful teacher follows no particular set of rules to decide how best to give these nudges. Philosophical understanding is an emergent symbiotic effect of my teaching-how, the pupil's mother-wit, our joint belonging to a self-changing continuous tradition of thought, and the student's submissive-subversive immersion in that tradition.

Notes

1. J. N. Mohanty, *Reason and Tradition in Indian Thought* (Oxford: Oxford University Press, 1992), 33. Mohanty tries to narrow down the sense of *jñāna* to a state of consciousness that claims to be true of its object. But that seems to exclude forms of awareness like doubt or wondering what something is that are included as varieties of *jñāna* in Nyāya and Vaiśeṣika thought. The concept of the latter kind of awareness called "*anadhyavasāya*" in Praśasta-pāda's early Vaiśeṣika work, if developed, could go a long way towards filling up the lacuna of a clear category of *thinking* as a cognitive act in Indian philosophy that has been remarked on by Mohanty.
2. RTIT, 83-9.
3. RTIT, 83, 250-55.
4. RTIT, 32.
5. Wittgenstein, *The Blue Book* (Oxford: Blackwell, 1958), 21.
6. RTIT, 254.

Chapter 13

J. N. Mohanty's Critique of Word as a Means of Knowing and "Authorless Tradition"

Purushottama Bilimoria

Introduction: *Maṅgalaṃ Gurave*

In his versatile treatment of important themes, issues, and problems in Indian philosophy, Professor J. N. Mohanty has not flinched from making intelligent reflections on the somewhat controversial and difficult view about an avenue toward possible new knowledge. Embraced nonchalantly by a good number of classical Indian philosophers, or ruefully agonized over and rejected by others, this theory had since fallen by the wayside and attracted little or no serious intellectual attention among contemporary Indian thinkers. I am referring here to the belief in (the) word or language as a means of true cognition (*śabdapramā-ṇa*), or put another way, that there is a variety of cognition that is indefeasibly and irreducibly word-generated (*śābdajanya*). In classical Indian philosophy this view had attained doctrinal status. While interest in modern times persisted for its linguistic ramifications as well as some perfunctory implications for comparative philosophy, no one thought it held out any significant epistemological promises.[1] But I did, and so I travelled to the United States in 1981 to seek out Mohanty, whose writings on phenomenology and (a little later) Indian philosophy had long before become part of my own philosophical formation. Under my arm was a manuscript on *śabdapramāṇa* (with the subtitle of, "Word as Valid Means of Knowing") that I desperately wanted him to read.[2] He was on his way to India, so this first encounter was extremely brief. However, the manuscript was read afterward and I arrived at his home in Norman, Oklahoma, in the wintry-chill of November 1983 minus my mislaid baggage. In the context of this hospitality, we began a long, drawn out, mild-mannered *vivāda* (among various topics) on the problem of *śabda* (word) and its place among the pramāṇas (means of knowing). The dialogue has meandered its way through countless conversations and meetings, alongside some of his esteemed colleagues in Indian philosophy and phenomenology in different continents. For example, during the gathering in Calcutta for his 1986 presidential address to the Indian Philosophical Congress on this very topic, there was a further exchange on current thinking. Another significant occasion was a symposium on śabdapramāṇa in 1987 in Oxford (in response to a sudden surge of interest on this problematic among a handful of Indian but also Western thinkers). Mohanty presented what would be his major paper on the theory of śabda-pramāṇa—which has haunted and preoccupied me since. Walking along with him by the river Isis the next morning, I learned about some further aspects of Nyāya objections to the Mīmāṃsā position (which I had addressed in the symposium) that I had not understood before, and am still trying to come to terms with. Questions I had remaining from those and other conversations have continued to be discussed in correspondence with Mohanty (for example, while writing the introductory biographical sketch to an anthology of his early essays)[3] and over numerous breakfasts, lunches, and joyful car rides with him in many cities around the world including Melbourne, where he was duly honored by admiring Australasian phenomenologists and analytical philosophers alike. One section of this present essay stems from a paper I delivered in his presence at the SACP International Philosophy Conference organized in his honor by Professor Bina Gupta in Bhubaneswar, India, January, 1999.[4] This homage to a sterling thinker in our midst does not refrain from critical exchanges that have been part of the aforementioned dialogue or "A conversation of mā-navas (mankind)."[5]

The Verdict on the Word as a Means of Knowing

I will now turn directly to Mohanty's views on śabdapramāṇa that appear in several places in his voluminous writings, but are most systematically addressed in two places: the aforementioned paper at the Oxford symposium and his "Foreword" to my book entitled Śabdapramāṇa: Word and Knowledge (1998),[6] which together have been reworked into a chapter in his book on Reason and Tradition in Indian Thought (1992).[7] In a nutshell, he argues as follows: As an indicative sentence śabda can be said to have a semantical competency (yogyatā) to generate linguistic understanding, but it would not eo ipso yield knowledge about perceptible, much less imperceptible objects, without the corroborative aid of perception or inference. In short, śabda is not an independent pramāṇa. When taken beyond its logical limits, śabda (most notably in the form of scriptural utterances, śruti, injunctive sentences or moral imperatives, or testimony imbibed from hearing and interpreting verbal instructions spoken by morally and intellectually competent speakers) can be said to generate belief (even in strongest sense of *belief*). These beliefs can be, for example, about supersensible things, of God, and more significantly about normative values (oughts and noughts), but they cannot lay claim to *knowledge qua facts*. The supplemental thesis of *śruti* as *apauruṣeya*, that is, authorless canons contain revealed truths, is simply muddled.

Staying with the genealogy for a while, now and then Mohanty would return to reconsider the *śabdapramāṇa* doctrine and attempt to see it in more sanguine light. But he could not countenance certain weaknesses in the thesis he had first noted some twenty years back.[8] The debate on *śabdapramāṇa* in the wider community of Indian philosophers, perhaps as a consequence of this strong rebuke, has also remained somewhat muffled. However, around the early-to-mid-1980s, there was a marked change in his attitude as more substantive work on the Mīmāṃsā and Gaṅgeśa's (navya-Nyāya) theory of language emerged, and he himself began to ponder on the relation between modernity and tradition in the wake of widespread doubts, no less in Western philosophical quarters, on the lingering remnants of positivism and ordinary language philosophy. This was reinforced by a more sympathetic note towards the idea of tradition and interpretation that reverberated in Gadamer's work, largely in the ambiguous shadows of Hegel and Heidegger, and J. L. Mehta's acknowledged comparative work on these masters.[9] Thus, coming to the Indian tradition—just to give two instances—in an article on "Remarks on the *Pramāṇa* Theory" turning to the comparative reflection on *śabdapramāṇa*, he would, with characteristic sanguinity, suggest that it is here that "the true foundation and deeper roots of the Hindu tradition lie." He continues in the same tone:

> The mere recognition of *śabda* as a means of knowing is itself a novel feature of the Indian epistemologies. The Western epistemologies recognize one or more of the following sorts of knowledge: perception, reasoning, introspection, and memory. Many, in more recent philosophy, have come to emphasize the decisive role that language plays in shaping our knowledge. But to the best of my knowledge, no one recognizes language—or verbal utterance—as by itself a means of generating knowledge about the world. And yet how much do we know simply by hearing others, by reading books, etc.? Not to speak of the religious and moral beliefs we derive from perusal of the scriptures. The Indian epistemologies consequently not only recognize *śabda* (that is, hearing the utterances of a competent speaker) as a means of knowing, but as the decisive source of our cognitions about all those matters that transcend the limits of possible sensory experience.[10]

Of course, in the past there have been Western philosophers who have taken seriously the idea of "testimony" as a valid source of knowledge, and its episte-

mological worth is being rediscovered, but this need not detain us presently.[11]
In *Reason and Tradition,* Mohanty makes the following argument:

> (T)he theory of language (*śabda*) as a means of true cogni-
> tion (*pramāṇa*), indeed as the one mode of knowing which
> can override all others, needs to be looked at afresh. It is here
> that tradition and modernity come headlong into conflict.
> Even if it is true that the life-world does not fully determine
> the philosophical problems, it nevertheless appears that for a
> people whose faith in the infallibility of the scriptures is con-
> siderably weakened . . . *śabdapramāṇa* cannot any longer
> provide the theoretical basis for a satisfactory philosophy. But
> that is not to reject language (*śabda*) altogether as a means of
> true cognition (*pramāṇa*). What is necessary is to re-examine
> the priorities and relative strengths and weaknesses. . . . But
> one also needs to recall the distinction between understanding
> a sentence *p* and knowing that *p*, the different ways in
> which language is central to cognitive enterprise and to nor-
> mal and religious life, and the problems connected with the
> notions of a text and its interpretations. The methodological
> insights would, I believe, rehabilitate the tradition's self-un-
> derstanding, without returning to the naive use of *śabda-
> pramāṇa* to which a return is just impossible.[12]

Without doubt this is a powerful and decisive pronouncement on *śabdapramāṇa* after the Buddhist philosophers had ravaged the doctrine centuries back, and
its effect has not worn thin in the years since. Younger scholars who came to
this field from a background in both Western and Indian philosophies, took up
(or had pre-empted) this caveat as a challenge and set about re-considering the
theory. First, by returning to the texts to find and present a clear and faithful
articulation of just what the theory involved; second, by analyzing the doctrine
with reference to cognate theories in other systems and philosophies; and third,
by offering a philosophical defense that harbored neither a sectarian commitment nor a prejudgment about the matter in question. I, for one, have continued
to question the strict adherence to certain binaries in modern thinking, as are
repeatedly rehearsed in the contemporary Indian squabble over the claims in
regard to *śabdapramāna.* Distinctions such as "sense/reference," "objective/-
subjective," "knowledge/truth," "fact/value," and "understanding/knowing,"
appear to me to be in some ways strained, on a par with the analytical-synthetic
distinction which Quine has skillfully overturned. They may even be a trifle
arbitrary given that they gain their force and hence particularity within the
history of the (Western) analytical framework, but have now come under severe
attack in the works of such recent philosophers as Davidson, Putnam, Dummett, MacIntyre, and Rorty, to name just a few.[13] The larger disputes within the
halls of Western analytical philosophy need not detain us here, however, as the
resources within the Indian philosophical tradition and phenomenology broadly

conceived might suffice. (Mohanty is quite cognizant of these disputes; besides, he had already separated the "life-world" of "tradition" from the strident essentialism of "orthodoxy," and his reference-point for hermeneutic phenomenology or "text and interpretation" crossed over from Husserl, Gadamer, and Foucault to Mīmāṃsā and Bhārtṛharian hermeneutics.[14] What I argue for is that the distinction between "understanding p" and "knowing p" on which Mohanty's counterargument seemed to be based is not as menacing as it first appears—especially from a phenomenological and transcendental philosophical perspective—and therefore the resistance offered to the thesis needs to be softened even further.

In general, Western philosophers who have been drawn to reconsider the plausible claim about the validity of evidence from testimony do not concern themselves with the linguistic elements that have been a mainstay of Indian philosophies since antiquity. That is, concerns with the logico-grammatical analysis of the sentence, sentence-meaning and its understanding that might or might not be involved in gathering, sifting, and reviewing the wherewithal for the generated *jñāna* or cognition. Their concern instead has been purely with the epistemological question, namely, with *beliefs* and belief conditions, and what it would mean to, as it were, "take on board," whether on the basis of good reason(s), or with warranted epistemic justification, or sufficient evidential support, or simply on the basis of its non-causal coherence with other-known and true beliefs, etc., whatever it is that a competent speaker says or *shows* through their utterance. Doubtless, there is a plethora of theses and problems associated with each such move. But if one can get around Gettier's problem that a person could have wrong reasons (or no good reason) for believing a true proposition p, implying that a person has justified true belief of p but lacks knowledge of the truth of p, then a theory of non-inferential justification derived from evidential support and reliability of testimony may well be the way to go. (I shall return to this later.) Consider also that *speech-acts* (locutionary, illocutionary, perlocutionary utterances), which also tend to lead one to form certain beliefs (for example, that the deal clinched with the handshake will be honored, etc.), would appear to circumvent ordinary linguistic analysis, as J. L. Austin and John Searle have drawn to our attention. More anecdotally, while writing the entry on "Testimony in Indian Philosophy" for *The Routledge Encyclopedia of Philosophy*, I discussed the Indian theory with Bernard Williams in Berkeley. Williams seemed thoroughly puzzled when I attempted to explain that at least according to the Nyāya-Mīmāṃsā (via Mohanty's margins notes on that draft), what is grasped from hearing an utterance (that is, the sentential meaning) is more than the structure of the cognitive state constructed from the grasped words: that *vākyārtha* is literally the "object out there" *(viṣayatā)*, a compound object whose components are the component word-meanings, and that this has bearing on what is "known" in such an understanding *qua* reference. *This is all very interesting, but what do the linguistic features*—he wondered—*have really to do with the more pressing epistemological claim, if anything, that would seem to be at issue here and in need of analysis?Belief, statement, reasons.*[15] Perhaps, in a way, Mohanty is also right when he notes that the conditions of linguistic understanding (for example, expectancy, competence, semantic fitness, contiguity and intention)—need not be the same as the conditions that, when satisfied, deliver what amounts to "knowing," that is, unassailable knowledge in the auditor about a state of affairs. In other words, is there any logical connection between the two parts of the theory—the semantic-phenomenological and the epistemic—in the same way that, for instance, Kant asked about the causal link between thinking (or understanding) and knowing? But on the other hand, inasmuch as this side of the equation is presented as the antecedent to the truth of the cognitive state (*pramā*), Indian philosophers throughout have spent an inordinate amount of time worrying about the kind of theory of meaning (naming, reference over sense, relational holism) that is involved in linguistically generated understanding (*śābdajanya; śābdabodha*). It would appear the latter is not sufficient, perhaps not even necessary, for establishing the claim to the autonomous character of this *pramāṇa*. A thesis that is considered to be peripheral to the larger theory does not stand in need of refutation, or its alternative a defense, but that is what appears to have been happening, or there is ambivalence about it (and I, too, have been no less guilty of this overdetermination).[16] On the other hand, Indian philosophers have been committed to the view that the epistemic content of the word-derived cognition is more primitive (originary) than presupposed by the otherwise persuasive categories of belief or propositions. That has also been Mohanty's point.

Hence I intend, in the rest of the essay, to revisit the treatment of *śabdapramāṇa* in Mohanty's work, for the traditional defense of *śabda* as a plausible means of knowledge stands or falls on whether a convincing set of responses have been forthcoming to Mohanty's catalogue of objections calling into question this doctrine. Since this is a large debate, I shall focus only on its salient features for the purposes of this critique.

Meaning, Sense, and Reference

Let us begin with meaning, which is implied in the phenomenology of understanding, and which is entailed by a theory of *śābdabodha* or grasping "sentential meaning." What is grasped when an utterance is heard? Most Indian philosophers have suggested a combination of theses, beginning with isolated word-meanings (*padārtha*) to very complex interrelation of word-meanings and even "holism" of impartite propositional meaning. Keeping to the modest theory for the time being, let us that say word-meanings are coalesced in a syntactical relation in fulfilling certain linguistic conditions and conventions that help generate comprehension of the sentential meaning (supplemented with the principle that the whole is greater than the sum of the parts). But what do these meanings denote or signify? What is their content? Here one might be tempted to say, of course, "sense": what is given in *thought* or proposition and is of a more general kind than implied in rigid designation or simple naming or a mode through which *reference* is made to the extralinguistic world. However, Mohanty argues that neither the Naiyāyikas nor the Mīmāṃsakas (exegetical scholastic) schools "had anything like the Fregean concept of sense as contradistinguished from reference." In other words, the concept of *"padārtha"* does not include what Frege calls "mode of presentation" or "that which determines reference." It is the referent itself. In the Fregean language, one grasps the referent, but not the sense. Understanding a sentence, then, entails grasping the entity or complex relational entity it denotes. Strictly speaking, neither *darśanas* is concerned with what one can call "understanding the meaning of an expression." One is rather concerned with how hearing a sentence, under appropriate conditions (for example, when the speaker is honest and reliable and known to be so), serves as means of acquiring valid knowledge, that is, as a *pramāṇa*. When these appropriate conditions are fulfilled, understanding amounts to knowing, that is, grasping, not the sense, but rather the ontological structure that obtains."[17] There is a direct correspondence of the oblique cognitive structure with the objective (ontological) structure. However, Mohanty has expressed concerns about a theory of linguistic meaning (*śābdabodha)* that only makes reference to the relational (ontological) structure (namely, a white cow out there) and does not involve an account of the eidetic structure in the cognitive state where the hearing is (being) processed. But we should note that Mohanty's reading of Indian theory of meaning is informed by his own leanings toward a modified referential theory of language,[18] that is, expressions contain an intention or idea that is directed towards the extralinguistic world. "Intentionality" (the "idea" or *eidos* that is responsible for pointing to an object and interpreting the subjective content presented to consciousness), which is so germane to phenomenology, wears rather thin in the Indian theory as it becomes a transparent, diluted, erased vehicle of reference. He shares with Frege the view that if expressions are to have truth-value, this would be better determined by some state of affairs in the world—like predicative expressions with singular terms. Frege's further ambivalence over the difficulty with unsaturated entities as referents and the uneasiness of the relation between particulars and universals that he could not resolve need to be borne in mind, for this informs his formulation of "sense" as much as the imperative to retain the unity of sentence meaning. Prabhākara in India had similar concerns about the difficulty of grasping unsaturated objects outside until it, as it were, owned up to a meaning, attached itself to a universal or genus (*ākṛti*), and related itself to other (saturated) objects; in short, unless it passed through a propositional attitude. An austere theory of reference, it would follow, which does not pay heed to the context-sensitivity of the reference, could not succeed in the task; otherwise the object would not find its designated relation with other objects. Nevertheless, Mohanty finds support for his austere reading of the Indian theory in K. C. Bhattacharyya's adage: a word refers "*directly* to the thing, expresses the thing, *touches* it in a sense." The sentence at once refers to an objective relation, through which it obtains objective reference.[19] But this too suffers from being reified on a physicalist model of sense-object contact (*indriyasannikarṣa*) an axiomatic requirement for sensory cognition in Nyāya that is translated into a referential requirement for linguistic grasping. The problem of interpretation within experience of "the given" (epistemic or linguistic) is eliminated in Nyāya because its preeminent project is to "fit" ordinary experience to an already determined catalogue of ontic categories (*padārtha*), "the *is*" (ontological, even metaphysical). It has been pointed out variously in later work in the tradition that a single word certainly needs an object as its reference (even unique reference needs an object, as do names as simple designators); but sentences or ordered whole utterances—*anupūrvivācya*—need have no objects (nor objective relations) as their reference in the extralinguistic world.

To press the same point in another way, if the general theory of the structure of consciousness admits to the possibilities of idealities (*ēidos, tēlos, oūsia*), modes of presentation (*aletheia*) and self reflexivity (beyond indexicals like "I," "that," in the encounter with "facts" in the life-world), why is this denied to experience constituted by verbal "things" (*śabda, pada, vākya*) flooding in as it were from the outside? Such possibilities, literature appears to suggest, did not escape the Indian philosophical tradition broadly sketched. Zilberman has poignantly shown that a thousand years of Indian reflection on the problem of meaning has produced a diverse and competing array of theories that veer toward the deontic or apodictic modality of subjective significations (conceptual contentive) and not always towards the representational mirroring or unmediated direct reference (of the outside world). Without this, the interpretive task of hermeneutic phenomenology, ritual-axiological (scriptural) exegesis, and transcendentiality of syntagms (*apūrvavācaka*) would never have gotten off the ground and been successfully applied to ordinary language (*laukika*) discourse. When it comes to conventional communicative discourse, Mohanty's reading of Indian philosophy betrays the impression that the entire tradition was burdened with a quasi-Russellian theory of reference which, however, is not sufficient for the theory of understanding entailed by the thesis that takes *śābdabodha* to be, by definition, true, all because something like a Fregean sense is missing. When Bhartṛhari formulated his pregnant *varṇa-sphoṭa,* saturated meaning-syllable; when the commentators on Patañjali's *Yogasūtras* levitated "meanings" out of words; when Gaṅgeśa and his commentators insisted on the primacy of "*intended* meanings" in consolidating sentential meaning and when the Mīmāṃsakas were heaven-bent on getting across an understanding related to *bhāvana* of *vidhi* (desire-incentive effort from imperitival sentences) under this restricted reading, they were probably all still thinking of connecting expressions with the empirically given world. Even the revised relational content-structure that answers to a general *concept* in understanding in later Vedānta theories of ordinary language instructions, fell short of working up a cogent thesis of "sense" (even in the soft Fregean terms, not to speak of the Platonistic *eidos*).[20] In Bhaṭṭa Mīmāṃsā, "word" and "meaning" are inextricably related (*autpattikatva* of *śabda-artha-sambandha*) and they are together timeless (*kūṭasthanitya*) and therefore *prior* to the world of objects, which also does not exhaust their reach or expanse. Pārthasārathi Miśra reinscribed this relation for ordinary discourse in terms of the *pratyāyya-pratyayaka* (or *samjña-samjñin*) that is, unsaturated "own-meaning" and saturated designation, which it shares with all naming signs. And while this relation is severable and open to reconfiguration by prevailing conventions, its function is not reducible to mere denotation or to reference.[21] *Samjña* is itself nuanced towards "understanding." It would appear to be closer to and a precursor of (if not imported into) the Saussurean thesis of the *signé*, namely, the signifier-signified (*Sr-r-Sd*) relation, wherein the signified may loop-back to another signifier, or forward to a transcendental signified (*Tsd*), which may again be another *Tsr*. The link-chain of signifiers has no semantic closure; if mathematical, logical, and legal propositions can function without reference to the subject's intentionality, then even the Husserlian *Sinn* is not of much use. Likewise, according to the Mīmāṃsakas, who are the legalistic mind in the tradition, Vedas are sacred words, *mantras* and *saṃhitas* (songs), that reinscribe themselves, rekindle their middle voice, and manifest their hidden meanings, either in the act of sacrifice or in the transgressive *apūrva* (deferred traces). This is how the Vedas as *language speak*. Their empirical sources have been buried in historical amnesia; so why cannot the Mīmāṃsā take *Vaidikavacanam* (notably as *vidhi, noyoga, atideśaka*) or mandatory injunctions as paradigmatic of such imperative propositions, and yet remain *artha-centric* in contradistinction to the Nyāya's *padartho*—or naive ontologo-centricism.

Nevertheless, Mohanty remains suspicious of the strains of *psychologism* that come with such suggestions as canvassed above. He urged that without such a thesis that underwrites *thought*—in the Fregean sense with de-emphasis on semantic-syntactic in place of the logical and epistemic structure of knowing—an adequate theory of understanding would never be forthcoming. Hence, by injecting a quasi-*Sinn* or needed soft theory of sense (for which he invokes Frege and Husserl, not Saussure or Derrida), Mohanty has been able to lend support to the erstwhile theory of *śabdabodha* that better succeeds in delivering understanding via the *prakārata* (qualifier) related to the qualificand and grasped in the semantic structure of the sentence (hence, "I get it, that is a white cow," or, "You want me to feel happy"). That is a welcome move; the work of ontological reference via *meaning* (*śabdabodha*) stands complete.

The Logical Problem

However, the ontological "buck" as it were, stops there: with an eye on Kant's epistemological strictures, the further construal that one therefore *knows* that there is a white cow out there remains to be questioned. To understand S is not necessarily to know S. One response to this challenge has been to collapse the requirement of understanding itself with the requirement of knowing, so that truth is, more or less, made a condition of sentence-understanding. The argument is that, a sentence "*a is F*" is characterized by fitness *(yogyatā)* (which we had earlier noted as one of the four semantic-phenomenological conditions of sentential understanding) only if *a* is *F*. "Idleness is green," "He is sprinking fire with martians" cannot generate any understanding (stalemated *yogyatā)* since they are each false *(apramā)*.[22] But this evidently makes *yogyatā* do the job of truth, which has only made the problem vicious; in any case the argument is fallacious. As Mohanty has retorted, to know S falsely is not necessarily to fail to understand S. If all understanding were simply true—that is, yeilded *pramā*—then a false *śābdabodha* would be a contradiction in terms. In an intuitively clear sense, one understands a false sentence, so that hearing a false sentence being uttered by a speaker taken to be competent generates in the auditor the awareness that this could not be true.[23] It can only be understanding of the "meaning" (in some sense of the term) of the sentence. So this strategy will not work.

There is another possible strategy that I wish to suggest. There is a theory of linguistic understanding that is not constrained by either of the two difficulties just pointed out, that is, reduction to "direct object-relation" meaning requirement or collapsing knowing with understanding. The suggestion is that (a) meaning and reference not be collapsed, as they are not in later Mīmāṃsā-Vedānta theories of meaning, especially in Pārthasārathi Miśra and *Jaimininyā-yamālāvistara;* (b) the signification (that is, propositional understanding) of a sentence be kept independent of the question of truth or falsity; and (c) a claim to knowledge on the basis of this understanding would require knowing what would be true *if* it were true. Strawson's more general epistemic formulation is instructive and can be enlisted to support the modified *prāmāṇya* requirement: "To understand a sentence is to know what thought it expresses or is capable, in given contextual circumstances, of expressing; and to know this is to know what we would be believing if we took the thought to be *true.*"[24] And *mutatis mutandis,* if we took the thought to be *false.* Both false or, better, "mock" understanding and "false cognition" are distinct possibilities within this analysis; neither amounts to significant knowledge, but that is not the whole issue here. We "know" a lot of things about and in relation to the world, some of which are true, some of dubious value, and some plainly boring.

A supplemental strategy invokes the condition of *āptabhāva,* that is, reliability—to strengthen the belief in the truth of the transmitted propositional understanding. One formulation of it embeds a principle that requires more than a mere absence of evidence against the reliability of the speaker: it requires that one have evidence in favor of it. Thus: If B hears and understands A utters p with all appearance of sincerely speaking from knowledge, and if B has no other evidence for or against p, B is justified in believing that p *if and only if* B has evidence for A's reliability (at least in matters pertaining to p). To further strengthen this formulation, I would add *yogyatā* and *sāmarthya* (pragmatic viability or outcome) as corroborative requirements that will pick out those expressions that are not likely to deliver meaningful understanding, and those that will fail to be empirically workable. The latter is not intended to reduce the criterion of reliability to pragmatism, but to relate the claim p to some real events in the world and lead to some satisfactory result; conversely, its absence would be a cause for doubt. Here we have combined reliability with fallibility and workability, as the triune marks of *guṇa* of a verbally-transmissible belief. Admittedly, inductive inference has been sneaked into the argument. Ironically, in Nyāya also, truth is never self-evidentially given, as it relies on a number of conditions that are built into their criteria of true cognition for its truth and tenacity.[25]

This leaves one last question raised in Mohanty's critique: how *sui generis* is the object of *śabdabodha*? That is, does it or does it not need the demonstrative backing by perception and inference? Put another way, if the same S is known by one of the other *pramāṇas* then what is the prerogative being claimed by *śabda?* It may still depend (for its initial knowledge) on these other more mundane modes of acquaintance with the world. Or conversely, if this same object is not accessible in these other ways, then how will one ever be certain about its veracity? To unpack this conundrum we are once again returned to the sense-reference distinction via the locution of another binary, namely, *de re* and *de dicto* knowledge. The argument goes as follows: "[O]ne needs to be able to distinguish between a proposition and the thing to which the proposition obtains, and one does not have the latter distinction unless one has also a prior distinction of some sort between sense and reference. The Indian philosophers do not have this last distinction, and so cannot distinguish between *de re* and *de dicto* knowledge. All knowledge is *de re*."[26] This is explained with the help of an example, as when a competent speaker utters "A horse is running." Upon hearing this I am supposed to know a *res,* a thing being in a state of action, but which thing? Whatever epistemological strategy one uses, there is no gainsaying that what is known here is parasitical upon perception and inference, and is not an independent function. That is the case with *laukika śabda* or ordinary words where these refer to perceptible words; where we are referred to (alleged) supersensible objects, there is likely a function of an extension of inference in the manner of transcendental deduction (*arthāpatti*). Likewise, in the case of the broader appeal to commonplace testimony—the mass of information and knowledge we are said to derive from hearsay, from reading books and newspapers, or (nowadays) "surfing the Internet"—we are said to know "only inasmuch as the possibility of perceptual confirmation or inferential backing is taken for granted."

To sum up this quiddity: in the case of indicative sentences about perceptible objects, the mere hearing of competently spoken utterances can be said to yield knowledge "only on the presumption of verifiability by either perception or inference. *Śabda*, then, in this domain, is not an independent *pramāṇa*. In the case of supersensible realities—such as God, or soul—I will defend a similar thesis: *śabda* can generate belief, very strong belief as a matter of fact, but not claim to know unless and until some other *pramāṇa* is brought in support, either inference or some mode of supersensible perception if permissible."[27] Curiously, the latter is elevated as a *bona fide* episteme (in the Foucauldian sense) under *yogaja-pratyakṣa*, the power of supersensible, or, in Heideggerian terms, the transcendentalized sensuousness, in Middle Nyāya. There is nothing that can escape the beyond-sights of *yogipratyakṣa*, literally, "mystico-empiricism": neither universals or absence, not even God; eternal time (which is collapsed into the divine substance by thirteen century C.E.); the otherwise invisible traces of good and bad actions (*adṛṣṭa*); *karmas* and souls of alterity, or other creatures; and even the normally unpredictable future, the omega-point, infinity, and other inconceivable enigmas. How deep does a critique like Mohanty's cut into such speculative epistemology that violates both Ockham's razor and Hume's constraint that impacts on early Naiyāyika-razor?

Validity of the Vedic Texts Revisited

Regarding the traditional claims about the authority of the Vedas qua *śruti* *prāmāṇya* and its alleged authorlessness *(apauruṣeyatva)*, Mohanty has tended to be swift in his disavowal of such a possibility. For this particular mode of "knowledge" does not, *prima facie* at least, square up with his understanding of the general theory of *pramāṇa* as a theory of rationality; if anything, the doctrine of *śruti* appears to dispense with reason altogether in the interest of the "wisdom" of tradition, the testimony of the elders (whoever they might be), the "heard word" passed on from time immemorial, and so on. Indeed, the logicality and rationality of the Navya-Nyāya analysis of cognition seemed to find little echo in this doctrine to which, however, a number of Naiyāyikas remained committed (although during the Middle Nyāya period the prerogative in this area had reached an unprecedent height). Any thinking person should find this a rather odd and puzzling situation, or simply an anomaly that had to be set aside. And yet it is recognized that reflections on *śruti* in the hands of the "metaphysicians of culture" (for example, in the *Upaniṣads,* the *Artha-śāstras* and *Dharma-śāstras, bhāṣyas,* and indeed in the Mīmāṃsakas construction of *nyāya* used for reasoning through scriptures), gave the tradition the philosophical virtues of inspiration, dialogue, jurisprudence or legal reasoning, *vādavivāda*, hermeneutic, empathy, critical tolerance, and pluralism of voices.

But there is another more significant role that testimony of received "wisdom" can be said to play in the shaping of a tradition: namely, in its contribution to the moral discourse and what one ought to do or not do, echoing here Kantian distinction between "is" [descriptive] and "ought" [imperative] statements, and how one interprets these imperatives in different times and epochs as history moves on.[28] In short, Mohanty grants *śabda qua śruti-prāmāṇya* its ethical and interpretive worth, despite its epistemological "soft-peddling," and because of it, or its otherwise *aesthetically* superior claims. Is there just the "is/ought" divide to worry about, at the neglect of the aesthetic, the sublime, the virtues, the narrative and mythological?

But there is a flaw even in the modest concession, as it stands in violation of Hume's admonition that "ought" cannot be derived from "is." For the so-called supersensibles (other world qualias) and moral situations from which "ought" or imperatival understandings are derived are themselves, in one theory at least, "reals," or part of "what is" and what are *known* to be so (*atitva, sattā, nitya, prameya*), and unabashedly brought under *padārthas* in the move to transcendentalize Gautama's naive realism, most visibly among philosophers of the Middle Nyāya period and onwards.[29] How the universe *is* determines how one is to *act*. But to know *how* the universe is, or ought *to be,* requires one to heed to the originary or founding vision of the *ṛsis,* who, so the theory goes, "heard" it via a chain of successions from the Demiurge (*Headgod*), and who in turn has mimesis of the conventions (*saṃketās,* of word-meaning relations of *vācya*) promulgated in the previous cosmic-generation and *dharma*-calculi (*adṛṣṭa*) of its inhabitants, and their cyclically *infinitum.* "Ought" does not stand detached from the world of beings—as the sublime does (in Kant at least). Hence, either the theory of *śabdapramāṇa* is all-encompassing or it stands deconstructed. *Ought* cannot flirt with *is;* either it swallows it or is devoured by it, as Hume and Voltaire in their own ways reminded us; and as Middle Nyāya—as it were—*did* it.

Appeal of Tradition: Word as a Means of Knowing and Hermeneutic Phenomenology

There is nonetheless another construal of *śabda* as *śruti* in Mohanty's treatment that I wish to touch upon before closing. Interestingly, he renders *śruti* as "eminent texts of the tradition," and *apauruṣeya* as the self-effacing delimitation of the horizon within which the Hindu tradition understands itself, and within which Hindus understand themselves. To elucidate this unorthodox interpretation, he invokes Hegel's notions of *Sittlichkeit* and *Moralität* and

draws on Gadamer's thinking on "tradition" as the medium of cultural transmission of values, mores, customs, techniques, and actions as well as its own
self-understanding up to that historical moment. And so the discovery of the
meaning of a tradition is never finished; it is, as Gadamer and Levinas would
say, an infinite process in the totality of self-and-*other* discovery. Thus to claim
any degree of finality for the authority of *sruti* that orthodoxy would seem to
want must be deemed to have a misguided understanding of what tradition is.[30]

As a student of Husserl, with a sympathetic ear to Heidegger's thoughts,
and a close friend of J. L. Mehta (who introduced Heidegger to the English-
reading world) and the Bhattacharyyas in Calcutta, Mohanty has always
cherished an openness to hermeneutics (or hermeneutic phenomenology)—the
art of interpretation and understanding of texts—that grew out of Christian
scholasticism and refined in European critical thought through Schleiermacher,
Dilthey, to Heidegger, Gadamer, and Ricoeur. Thus the question is taken up in
the context of Mehta's predicament of applying Heideggerian hermeneutics to
the texts of the Indian tradition—the *Vedas*, the *Upaniṣads* and the Epics—
while remaining deeply committed to the authenticity of the Indian philosophical
and spiritual tradition, and without doing "cultural violence" in the attempt to
retrieve one's own tradition.[31]

Mohanty clarifies that in the wake of Heidegger's strong thesis, all tasks of
understanding are recognized to be historically situated, that is, "understanding
cannot be presuppositionless, it has to be rather, as Gadamer maintains, *from
within* a tradition, and as belonging to the 'effective historical consciousness'
(*Wirkunggeschichte*) of the text."[32] Although the teleological historicity of
Hegelian hermeneutics may not be the precise imperative here, what stands at
the beginning—the originary moment—of any tradition of thought is what also
chalks out its trajectory, and it is to that founding insight on the distant horizon
that we reach back in order to seek new possibilities of interpretation and
thinking (*Denken; vicāra,*). Therein lie the horizons of self-understanding of a
people and its culture. Some, including Mehta, Mohanty notes—a contrasting
parallel to Heidegger's uncovering of the *being* of Being in its originary Greek
roots—took the concepts of *ātman* and *the brahman* as being poised at the
helm of Indian thought.[33] But the worrying question for Mohanty remains:
whether anything of real worth can be retrieved from one's tradition? "Can we
retrieve from those texts an ontological—not epistemological or logical—
process of self-understanding that is also a self-interpretation?" And he answers
this himself, with a slight demur: "It is here, and not in the much used (and
abused) 'mystic experience,' that the real essence of the thesis of '*śabdapramāṇa*' lies. I find here a[n] [r]approachment (*sic*) between Mehta's reading
of the Indian tradition and mine, coming from two different perspectives,
though both wedded, in some sense, to phenomenological openness to the
truth." However, despite the juxtaposition of the discourse of hermeneutics with
that of *śabdapramāṇa* in this generous tribute to his friend, in his more analyti-

cal mood, as we have seen, Mohanty severs the very ontological connection he pleads for. He draws a fine logico-epistemological line between *śabda* understood as ordinary word of natural language and *śabda* understood in the wider sense of "textuality" of authority and traces of "tradition," and indeed as "*vāc*" (the preeminent Brahmanical texts). At base is the suspicion that a simple return to the founding insights may not be sufficient if these do not also permit themselves to be "interpreted in a radically new manner" (*pace* Foucault). *Sruti* being an inexhaustible reservoir of richness, this possibility is there; however, all such interpretations also founder on account of arising "from *our* present perspective."[34] Nietzsche's perspectivism and nineteenth-century psychologism becomes a bugbear for an aspired objectivism in philosophical understanding. Even more ominous are the signs that this may get us back to the situation of "the Europeanization [of the Earth]," nihilism, technology, loss of sacred and "end" of philosophy.[35] A veritable "hermeneutic circle" indeed that would engulf both the West and the East. There would be a foreclosure of the goal of the "unity of rational thinking."

One may nonetheless worry about the imported categories in this appraisal of the *Indian* tradition that echo the Orientalist-Hegelian progressive (Aryanized) myth of the "national spirit" imposed upon an unsuspecting "despotic" Asiatic people (and other non-European cultures). Equally, the Gadamerian thesis on "tradition" has yet to satisfactorily answer a major objection raised by Habermas, Adorno, and Foucault, in respect to the elements of ideology or the systematic distortion of cultural transmission and communication by countervailing nondemocratic forces. Ricoeur's sound compromise requires that the hermeneutic process involve an internal critique even as one is attempting to understand and communicate the understanding. The rise of a strident Hindu fundamentalism and its usurption of "the Bhāratiya [Indian] tradition" might ring a warning bell for us well.

To be sure, Mohanty would agree with Ricoeur in arguing that the way to handle the issue of tradition is not to reduce it univocally to a set of antiquated and anachronistic beliefs, or to blindly regurgitate its apparently receding spirituality, or to suppress it with an iron hand, but rather to enter it, empathetically, interact with it and in this dialectic allow a fresh understanding to emerge. Indeed, the distance—*difference*—that time and history (diachronic and synchronic) creates between a thinker or interpreter and the tradition provides an idle setting for the hermeneutic reflection to happen. For one can then, in retrospect, take into account the totality of past interpretations, and therefore more easily contextualize the tradition *qua* its representative ("eminent") texts to the present set of conditions and circumstances. And this connects nicely with the spirit of the "authorless texts" that he had earlier dismissed as being simply "muddled." Who could put it better than this "physician of culture"?

The concept of *apauruṣeyatva* (or the property of not having a human author), then, is—as I understand it—the concept of the primacy and autonomy of the eminent text over the subjective intentions of the author. It is also the concept of the role the eminent texts such as the *sruti* play in delimiting the horizon within which our tradition has understood itself and, within the tradition, we have understood ourselves. *The more we need to know the author to understand or interpret a text, the less fundamental it is. The less we need to know the author in order to understand or interpret a text, the more foundational it is.*[36]

Concluding Reflections

We have just analyzed three aspects of the problem Mohanty has raised in connection with the doctrine of *śabdapramāṇa*. His major contention has been that a Fregean theory of sense has been absent in Indian semantics, that Indian semantical theories are basically referential. For this reason a theory of understanding distinguished from knowing is absent in the tradition and the two cannot be collapsed into some opaque thesis of "verbal knowing." He has been unrepentant about this conviction, although he has been prepared to recognize a theory of sense in Indian semantic that is closer to Husserl's understanding of *Sinn* than it is to the Fregean *Sinn* (hence Quasi-*Sinn*). In short, he rejects that the sense-reference distinction as we have it in Frege is to be found in Indian philosophy, for the simple reason that the Fregean *Sinn* belongs to a different ontological dimension and is to be distinguished from particular concrete or abstract objects of reference, as well as from internal structures of cognitive episodes. What is grasped, all pretensions aside, is closer to Husserlian *sense* than it is Fregean *reference,* which therefore wedges an unbridgeable hiatus between a phenomenology of understanding (which is a strength of *śabda* as linguistic grasping) and logico-epistemological status of what is grasped in *knowing.* To the former domain belongs the function of the hermeneutic of *interpreting* linguistic discourse; to the latter the function of empirically scrutinizing and verifying the claims so unleashed. (That is the preserve of *pramāṇa,* to which *śabda* for reasons already outlined, cannot have a *sui generis* claim). The testimony of tradition, with qualifications, may broaden the horizon of self-understanding in respect of the former, but it delivers rather little in respect of the latter claim. Numerous scholars have since produced remarkable studies in response to these charges. This dialogically-inspired essay has attempted to push the frontiers a step further, but this cannot be the last *word* on the controversy. When all is *said, shown, and done,* the credit for stimulating, nay, for provoking modern interest in the Indian and comparative analysis on this doctrine, rests with none other than Mohanty.

Notes

1. When I first started to survey the literature on *śabdapramāṇa* in journals and annals of Indian philosophy in the mid-1970s, I found at most two solid references: a full chapter in D. M. Datta's *Six Ways of Knowing* (Calcutta: University of Calcutta, 1972) and Swami Satprakashananda's *Methods of Knowledge—according to Advaita Vedānta* (Calcutta: Advaita Ashram, 1974), both leaning toward Vedānta. Nothing as yet on the Nyāya counterpart, except for Sibajiban Bhattacharyya's highly technical Gadādharan work on *śābdabodha*. There were of course a large number of papers on every aspect of philosophy of language that drew extensively from literature and theorization relating to *śabdapramāṇa* (in the major *darśanas*), but hardly any connections were being made to the logical and epistemological challenges presented by this doctrine. Standard works on Indian Philosophy by Max Muller, S. N. Dasgupta, Jadunath Sinha, S. Radhakrishnan, M. Hirayanna, Ninian Smart, etc., included expository segments in rather apologetic or overly idealistic-salvational tones. In other words, the twin-shadows of Logical Positivism and Ordinary Language Philosophy being pursued fervently in the West since the 1920s, along with remnants of Hegelian idealism, orientalism, and fascination with Buddhist *nirvāṇa*, all but effaced the epistemological location of *śabda* as a *pramāṇa* in Indian philosophical culture. From Malkani to Bhattacharyyas to Hacker the pattern seemed to be the same, or there were expositions of the more mystical kind when Bhartṛhari's *Sphoṭa* ("flashpoint understanding") was what took their fancy (for example, with Gopinath Kaviraj and T. R. V. Murti). This is not an insignificant point when we bear in mind that Professor Mohanty studied philosophy and mathematics in India in the 1940s and 1950s, and his exposure to Indian thought—as indeed also to Western thought—occurred in this ambiance, although he had moved on to phenomenology, being inspired by Rash Vihari Das to read Boyce Gibson's translation of Husserl's *Ideen* in 1949. Thus one of his very early essays, "Husserl's Phenomenology and Indian Idealism," appeared in 1951. I have also discussed these early developments in my introductory essay "A Fusion of Disparate Horizons" in P. Bilimoria (ed.), *J. N. Mohanty: Essays in Indian Philosophy Traditional and Modern* (Delhi/New York: Oxford University Press, 1993, 1995), ix-xxxii. Hereafter cited as EIP.

2. Although the manuscript had been read initially by Professor Karl Potter in Seattle and Professor Bimal Matilal in Oxford, the latter felt that in view of the strong phenomenological component in the analysis canvassed therein it would be best if Professor Mohanty cast his critical eye over it.

3. See note 1 above.

4. See the Editor's introduction.

5. A play on Rorty's now famous, albeit gender-wise incorrect, adage, it also echoes the title given to Mohanty's review of B. K. Matilal's *Perception* (Oxford: Oxford University Press, 1986) in the *Times Literary Supplement,* 10 October, 1986; and on Sanskrit cognate of "Mankind" in its etymological form of "not rather [*ma*] new [*nava*]," or the Nietzschean howler "man does not even exist," or that he *should* try again.

6. Purushottama Bilimoria, *Śabdapramāṇa: Word and Knowledge: A Doctrine in the Mīmāṃsā-Nyāya Philosophy* (*with reference to Advaita*

Vedāntaparibhāṣā *"Agama"*): *Towards a Framework for Śruti-Prāmāṇaya* (Dordrecht/Boston/London: Kluwer Academic Publishers, 1988), vii-xii. Hereafter this work will be cited as WKP.

7. J. N. Mohanty, *Reason and Tradition in Indian Thought: An Essay on the Nature of Indian Philosophical Thinking* (Oxford: Oxford University Press, 1992: hereafter RTIT), 249-59; also the chapter, "Phenomenology and Indian Philosophy: The Concept of Rationality," in EIP, 258-73.

8. The first reference I have come across is a very short 1977 version of the paper on "Indian Philosophy: Between Tradition and Modernity" *Bharata Manisha*, II, 1977, 5-12, but it was lacking sufficient coverage of the inviolable authority of *śabda*. It underwent radical revisions until its final appearance in RTIT, see note 12 below.

9. See *Transcendental Phenomenology*, We return to this discussion later and in notes 31-35 below.

10. RTIT, 231-2.

11. Montague took it seriously; Russell entertained the idea, connecting it with reliability noting its uses in law but denied it was epistemically autonomous; Hume earlier had simply relegated the notion of reliability to sheer credulity with no justification, and this prejudice continued through Russell and Ayer. It was Reid and Wittgenstein who made modern philosophy rethink this reductionist approach. Also see essays in *Knowing from Words: Western and Indian Philosophical Analysis of Understanding and Testimony*, B K Matilal and A Chakrabarti (eds.), Synthese Library, vol. 239 (Dordrecht: Kluwer Academic Publishers, 1994). The volume includes essays by Peter Strawson, Ernst Sosa, John McDowell, Michael Dummett, Michael Welbourne, A. J. C. Coady, etc.

12. RTIT, 23. This much-revised version (cf. Note 8 above) appeared in 1982 (shortly after my initial visit to Norman, Oklahoma, the sympathetic tone) as "Indian Philosophy Between Tradition and Modernity," in Rama Rao Pappu and R. Puligandla (eds.) *Indian Philosophy: Past and Present* (Delhi: Motilal Banarsidas, 1982), 33-52. See also Mohanty's "The Concept of Rationality" EIP, 258-73 and his "Language and Reality" in *Phenomenology and Ontology* (The Hague: Nijhoff, 1970).

13. Much of the current upheavals and debates I am referring to have been summarized and articulated with Richard Rorty's own responses in his *Truth and Progress Philosophical Papers* (Cambridge: Cambridge University Press, 1998). Mohanty discusses Rorty more generally in RTIT, 285-7, rejecting his philosophical relativism.

14. RTIT, 11 and notes 5, 16, 85 on Mīmāmsā and Grammarian theories of meaning, and 288-9, on Mehta and Heidegger and other unworkable binaries.

15. Based on personal conversations that took place in 1995 during my visit to Northern California.

16. See my work WKP.

17. RTIT, 78-9.

18. J. N. Mohanty "On Reference" in Harald Delius & Günther Patzig (eds.) *Argumentationem, Festschrift fur Josef Konig* (Göttingen: Vandenhoeck & Ruprecht, 1964), 159-69; "Remarks on the Content Theory," *Visva Bharati Journal of Philosophy* 2, 1965, 38-42. Mark Siderits has the right approach, I think, when he locates a Fregean type of "sense" in the Prābhākaran theory but then uses Buddhist critique to regale against it for its ontological

excesses, as with most Indian theories of meaning. See Siderits, *Indian Philosophy of Language Studies in Selected Issues* (Dordrecht: Kluwer, 1991), ch. 3.

19. K. C. Bhattacharyya, in *Studies in Philosophy* (Calcutta: Progressive Publishers), vol. I, 83.

20. See "*Śabdabodha*" in my WKP.

21. I have dealt with a number of these approaches and issues in a number of papers, most significantly in "Liberating Language: Pārthasārathi Miśra on the Sentence and Its Meaning," in *Indian and Beyond Aspects of Literature, Ritual and Thought Essays in Honour of Frits Staal,* Dick van der Meij (ed.) (London/New York: Kegan Paul International 1997), 27-49; "On the Idea of Authorless Revelation (*apauruṣeya*), in Roy Perrett (ed.), *Indian Philosophy of Religion* (Dordrecht: Kluwer Academic Publishers, 1989), 143-66; "Authorless Voice: Tradition and Authority in the Mīmāṃsā: Reflections in Cross-cultural Hermeneutics," *Nagoya Studies in Indian Culture and Buddhism: Saṃbhāṣā,* 16, 1995, 137-60; and "Hindu Doubts About God: Towards a Mīmāṃsā Deconstruction," in *International Philosophical Quarterly* 30, 4, 1990, 482-99; and WKP.

22. The argument was made by Arindam Chakrabarti, drawing on *Siddhāntamuktāvalī,* in his paper "Understanding Falsehoods: A Note on the Nyāya concept of *Yogyatā,*" (*The Journal of the Asiatic Society* 27, 1986, 10-20), addressed by Professor Mohanty in his foreword to WKP and reproduced in RTIT (note 7 above). (My apologies for my initial misspelling of Chakrabarti's name that finds its way into the RTIT chapter.)

23. Mohanty's foreword to WKP.

24. I have discussed this is my paper, "Evidence in Testimony and Tradition," *Journal of the Indian Council of Philosophical Research* 9, no. 1, (1991), 73-84; I draw handsomely on recent epistemological tinkering with evidence in testimony, especially by Leslie Stevenson, "The Epistemology of Testimony," paper presented at the Australasian Association of Philosophy Conference, 1990.

25. See J. N. Mohanty, "*Prāmāṇya* and Workability: Response to Potter," *Journal of Indian Philosophy* 12, no. 4 (Dec. 1984), 43-7.

26. RTIT, 251.

27. RTIT, 253.

28. EIP, 269.

29. I have developed a thesis about this intervention in my paper "Transcendental Categories in Search of an Epistemology—The Trouble Ontology of Middle Nyāya Realism." An earlier version of this paper was presented at the American Academy of Religion (Philosophy of Religion and Hinduism Sections) November, 1998, and at the SACP International Conference in Bhubaneshwar, January, 1999.

30. Discussed in his foreword to WKP.

31. Introduction to J. L. Mehta's *Philosophy and Religion Essays in Interpretation* (Delhi: ICPR and Motilal Banarsidass, 1990), vi-vii.

32. Ibid.

33. Ibid. See also William Jackson, *J. L. Mehta on Heidegger, Hermenutics and Indian Tradition* (Leiden: E. J. Brill, 1993)

34. Ibid., ix.

35. Ibid., x, but for a more sympathetic note to Mehta's pleas to the inadequacy of objectifying, representational thought, and the extremes of

subjectivism and objectivism, see RTIT, 289-90.
    36. RTIT, 259.

Chapter 14

Nyāya Realism, Buddhist Critique

Mark Siderits

Professor Mohanty has always maintained that Nyāya is epistemologically realist—that on the Nyāya account of veridical cognition (*pramā*), the object of veridical cognition (*prameya*) is mind-independent, or independent of the means of veridical cognition (*pramāṇa*) whereby it is apprehended. Buddhists, of course, criticized Nyāya realism in a variety of ways, and Mohanty has helped us appreciate the power of the Nyāya response to these criticisms. Recently new questions have been raised about Nyāya's commitment to realism. Here, too, Mohanty has ably represented the Nyāya defense. I shall not be questioning the claim that Nyāya is realist. But there may be more than one way to deny epistemological realism, and it is possible that Nyāya responses are effective against only certain sorts of critiques of realism. It is also possible that modern interpreters of the classical Indian debate over realism have paid insufficient attention to important ways in which it differs from the seemingly similar debate in modern European philosophy—despite Mohanty's warnings.

I propose to examine some facets of the Nyāya-Buddhist exchange with these questions in mind. I shall begin by distinguishing among three senses of "realist," one metaphysical and two epistemological. I shall then investigate Mohanty's recent attempt to distinguish Nyāya epistemological realism from the idealisms of Berkeley and Yogācāra. I do so in order to raise the question whether we—Mohanty included—have been sufficiently careful to distinguish between the modern idealist problematic and the classical Indian. Finally, I shall have something to say about the confrontation between Nyāya realism and Madhyamaka anti-realism. There, too, I shall raise the question whether elements of the modern problematic have not illegitimately colored our understanding of that debate. But in this case my principal target will be my own past work on the subject. I would add that while I shall disagree with some of Mohanty's views in what follows, I do so with the intent of honoring the importance of his work.

In veridical cognition, there is congruence or conformity between the cognition and its object. The basic intuition behind epistemological realism is that there is an essential asymmetry in this relation, in that the veridicality of the cognition is determined by how the object is. This means that the object of cognition must be mind-independent. There are, though, a number of possible ways in which something might be said to be mind-independent. The first is by being something the existence of which is independent of mind and mental states, by being the sort of thing that could exist in a world devoid of all mentality. Since classical Indian philosophers did not posit a "third world" of abstract objects, we can say more positively that for the Indian tradition, something is mind-independent in this first sense just in case it is physical. Since the view that there are physical objects is ordinarily construed as a metaphysical thesis, to hold that there are mind-independent objects in this sense is not to make an epistemological claim.

A second way in which something might be said to be mind-independent is by having a nature that is unaffected by its relation to cognition. This counts as a variety of mind-independence because cognition is here understood as a preeminently mental event or activity. About something that is mind-independent in this way it always makes sense to ask if a cognition accurately reflects the way that it is independent of its being cognized. The veridicality of a veridical cognition taking it as object will depend on the cognition's correctly representing the way that entity is apart from its being cognized. On one understanding of so-called secondary properties such as phenomenal color, this sort of mind-independence is exactly what they lack: there is no such thing as the way that a color is apart from its being cognized. It is a hallmark claim of epistemological realism that truth can outrun justification. If things are mind-independent in this second sense, then it is possible that there are aspects of an object that no veridical cognition (of a less than omniscient cognizer) can fully capture. For instance, it might be that objects have properties that can never be adequately represented in our cognition by any sense modality.

A third way in which something might be said to be mind-independent is by having a nature that is not affected by its relation to the mental activity of conceptualization. If things are mind-independent in this sense, then it is once again possible that there are aspects of an object that can never be adequately represented in the cognitions of finite cognizers—that no matter how veridical, our cognitions shall always somehow fall short. But here the inadequacy would stem not from such things as limitations on our sense faculties; it would have to do instead with the concepts that we employ in grasping the nature of the object. For instance, it might be that even our best efforts at understanding the object will inevitably involve the use of concepts that distort its nature in some way, or that are simply incapable of adequately capturing some aspect of its nature.

The distinction between the second and third senses of mind-independence requires that we be able to distinguish between ways in which the nature of the object might be affected by its relation to the act of cognizing, and ways in which its nature might be affected by the employment of concepts in its apprehension. And it might be claimed that since there is no cognizing an object without the use of concepts, there is no way to prise apart these two elements. That is, it might be claimed that this distinction is compromised by its involvement with the so-called myth of the given. Both Nyāya and the Yogācāra-Sautrāntika school of Buddhism would, however, dispute the claim that there is no such thing as non-conceptual cognition. Indeed, Nyāya would insist that the possibility of so-called *savikalpaka* perception, where the object is represented within a propositional structure, requires that there be a prior non-conceptual grasping of the elements that fall within the structure. (This is justified by the principle that one cannot apprehend a relationship without prior apprehension of the relata.) Moreover, they would assert that in *savikalpaka* perception itself we can still distinguish between the object's relation to cognition and its relation to the concepts that express that propositional structure. For, they would claim, even where we have reason to believe that those concepts are adequate to the task of representing objects of this sort, it still makes sense to ask whether the nature of the object is affected by its relation to cognition. For instance, the cognition of hairs on the moon (had by someone with ophthalmic disorder) might be represented as: {(hair inhered in by hairiness) related through contact with [(moon inhered in by moonness) qualified by (white inhered in by whiteness)]}. Since the structure of this cognition is properly regimented in terms of the *padārthas,* the categories that Nyāya claims represent the ultimate structure of reality, the cognition cannot be deemed faulty on grounds of conceptual adequacy. The contact relation, however, does not have the nature of relating moon and hair apart from this cognition.

Corresponding to these three senses of mind-independence, we may formulate the following three kinds of realism:

Realism$_1$: the view that there exist entities that are independent of mind and mental states; in the classical Indian context this is equivalent to the view that physical objects exist.

Realism$_2$: the view that the nature of the object of cognition is independent of its being apprehended by a cognition.

Realism$_3$: the view that the nature of the object of cognition is independent of the concepts employed in its apperception.

Realism$_1$ is a metaphysical thesis, while realism$_2$ and realism$_3$ are distinct kinds of epistemological realism. The denial of realism$_1$ is the metaphysical thesis of idealism, according to which there exist only minds and/or mental states. This view was held by Berkeley and by the Yogācāra school of Buddhism. As it happens, Berkeley and at least most Yogācārins also denied realism$_2$. Berkeley does so when he challenges the proponent of realism$_1$ to say just what the unperceived object is like. If we cannot, then given the verifica-

tionist account of meaning that he champions, Berkeley takes it to follow that
the object can have no nature apart from its being cognized (that is, "perceived"
in Berkeley's terminology). The Yogācāra-Sautrāntika doctrine of *svasam-
vedanā*, to the effect that the object of cognition is none other than the form
(*ākāra*) that is immanent to cognition, is likewise tantamount to the denial of
realism$_2$. Or at least this is so when this doctrine is conjoined with the Yogācāra
thesis of impressions-only (*vijñapti-mātratā*). (Sautrāntikas took the form that
is immanent to cognition to be a representation of the external object.) In this
case there can be no such thing as the nature of the object apart from its being
cognized.

But the denial of realism$_2$ does not follow from the denial of realism$_1$. For
one might deny that there are physical objects, yet still maintain that the object of
cognition, while mental in nature, is independent of cognition. This would
require thinking of cognition as itself formless (*nirākāra*), as does Nyāya. But
there is a long tradition within Buddhist Abhidharma of seeing consciousness
(that is, *vijñāna skandha*) in just this way, as something that merely illuminates
the object without taking up its content into the consciousness itself. Append to
this the idea that the object of cognition is mental in nature (in Abhidharma
terminology, is a *nāma dharma*), and it becomes possible to deny realism$_1$
while affirming realism$_2$. One can deny that there is anything existing outside
minds or mental streams, yet still affirm that the truth about an object might
outrun what is disclosed in our cognition.[1]

Daya Krishna recently raised the question whether Nyāya is properly
thought of as realist, given its view that all existents are cognizable.[2] He had in
mind Berkeley's famous dictum, "To be is to be perceived" (*esse est percipi*),
when he raised this question. Given the apparent similarity between "*esse est
percipi*" and "*astitva jñeyatvam*," he wondered whether the Nyāya position is
not better classified as a form of idealism akin to Berkeley's. In his response in
defense of Nyāya as a form of realism, Mohanty[3] set out to show how the
Nyāya claim about cognizability differs from Berkeley's dictum. I propose that
we look at that response in some detail. In it, Mohanty displays his characteristic sensitivity to important but frequently overlooked differences between the
Indian and modern European traditions. But while he comes close to making the
point we just saw concerning the separability of the denial of realism$_1$ from that
of realism$_2$, in the end he appears to miss it. I believe there may be an important
lesson to be learned from this.

Mohanty's strategy is to seek to show that Nyāya means something quite
different by its "all existents are cognizable" than what Berkeley intended by his
"to be is to be perceived." First he points to Nyāya extensionalism, in particular
to the fact that Nyāya does not countenance such alethic modalities as necessity.
Berkeley clearly thought he had demonstrated a conceptual necessity in his
dictum, so that to assert existence just is to assert that something is perceived by
some perceiver. Nyāya instead merely claims that "existent" and "cognizable"

happen to be coextensive. Since Nyāya is innocent of the notion of necessity, this is not to be thought of as a conceptual truth. Second, Mohanty points to the difference between Berkeley's "perception" and Nyāya's "cognition." Berkeley clearly had in mind a kind of direct, unmediated grasping by the conscious subject of something that is immediately present to it. It is called "perception" precisely to suggest the sense of concrete immediacy that is ordinarily (but according to the empiricist mistakenly) attributed to sensory experience of external objects. Nyāya means something far broader by "cognition": a cognitive state yielding reliable information about its object. This may be relatively unmediated, as with sense-perception (though for Nyāya the object of sense-perception is typically external to the perceiver). Or it may be mediated by such processes as inference, speech production, and comprehension. To say that an object is cognizable is just to say that it can be apprehended by some such reliable process or other. Third, Mohanty points to the fact that Nyāya gives a causal account of cognition. Since the object is itself among the causes of a reliable cognition, it must be in some important sense independent of cognition. Hence Nyāya is realist.

At this point, however, Mohanty concedes that much the same things may be said of the Yogācāra account of cognition, and so he proceeds to point to the difference between Nyāya and Yogācāra over cognition's being formless (*nirākāra*) or having form (*sākāra*) as decisive. What this overlooks is the possibility that a Yogācārin might agree with the Naiyāyika that cognition is itself formless, that the form it apprehends is wholly within the object that is the cause of the cognition, all the while maintaining that the object is mental in nature. Mainstream Yogācāra did not hold this position, but it is a tenable view nonetheless. It is possible to deny realism$_1$ while maintaining realism$_2$. The Nyāya doctrines and arguments that Mohanty describes establish realism$_2$, but not realism$_1$.

Of course Nyāya is realist$_1$ as well. What is worth exploring is not this question but why it is that we might overlook the difference between realism$_1$ and realism$_2$, and suppose that an argument for the latter establishes the former as well. Here Mohanty's list of ways that the Nyāya cognizability thesis differs from Berkeley's dictum is instructive. Where Berkeley sees necessity, Nyāya sees just coextensionality; where Berkeley requires immediate presence of the object, Nyāya does not; and Nyāya understands veridical cognition in terms of the notion of a reliable causal process, whereas Berkeley presumably does not. The third point suggests the contrast between epistemological internalism and externalism. On the internalist view, knowledge requires that the subject *have justification* in a way that is accessible to the subject, so that the subject can show justification. Hence internalism is characterized by the KK thesis: in order to know, one must know that one knows. The externalist view is rather that knowledge requires just that the subject *be justified.* Externalist accounts of knowledge are typically couched in terms of a set of causal conditions the

fulfillment of which results in the subject being justified. The Nyāya understanding of veridical cognition suggests an externalist approach. Berkeley, by
contrast, would want to add the internalist constraint that the knower have
access to the conditions that justify their claim to knowledge.

This in turn throws light on the second contrast. Following Descartes, in-
ternalists have tended to classify ways of cognizing in terms of relative degrees
of certainty, with those that are more secure generally understood as apprehending an object that is in some sense closer to the cognizer. It thus makes
sense that for Berkeley, cognition should paradigmatically involve an object that
is mental in nature and immediately present to consciousness, since it is
tempting to suppose that only then can the cognizer be assured that the object is
as it is represented. And this in turn throws light on the first contrast. The
conceptual necessity Berkeley sees in his dictum derives from his verificationism: to be is necessarily to be perceived just because we cannot know what it
would be like for something to exist unperceived. And this verificationism
crucially involves internalist assumptions. What we can know of sensory
experience are presumably just ideas, since only these are directly accessible to
the experiencing subject. But to understand the realist$_1$ hypothesis that sensory
experience derives from physical objects we must be able to specify what such
objects would be like. And this we cannot do, given that something that is
immanent to consciousness can never be like something that is utterly distinct in
nature from consciousness. Once we accept the internalist picture of knowledge,
realism$_1$ and realism$_2$ will both fail, and *sākāravada*—the doctrine that the form
of the object is immanent to cognition—will follow as an inevitable consequence.

The suggestion, then, is that it is internalist and verificationist presuppositions that make it appear as if realism$_1$ and realism$_2$ must stand or fall together,
and so make us miss the possibility that one might consistently affirm realism$_2$
while denying realism$_1$. There is little if anything that turns directly on this
point. We already know that the metaphysical views of Yogācāra must be
carefully distinguished from those of Berkeley. That a *nirākāravadin* formulation of the Yogācāra thesis of impressions-only should be possible simply
means that other arguments are necessary if Nyāya is to properly distance itself
from Yogācāra as well as from Berkeley. What should interest us here is that
the internalist framework of modern European philosophy should so easily
come to color our reading of the Indian tradition, when the latter is decidedly
externalist in orientation. Might something similar occur when it comes to
investigating whether Nyāya is realist$_3$? I shall claim that it can and has, in at
least two episodes. The culprit in the first is Roy Perrett, in the second it is me;
but Mohanty figures in both.

Perrett claims that the Nyāya thesis that everything that exists is nameable
and knowable commits Nyāya to a kind of idealism, namely, what in my
scheme would be called anti-realism$_3$.[4] For, he points out, it follows from the
claim that everything is nameable and knowable that everything is conceivable.

And he quotes Nagel's characterization of a relevant form of idealism: "The idealism to which this [realism] is opposed holds that what there is is what we can think about or conceive of, or what we or our descendants could come to think about or conceive of." The argument appears air-tight. According to Nyāya, everything that exists is conceivable—indeed, conceivable just in terms of the set of Vaiśeṣika categories. Does this not make Nyāya guilty of just that "philosophical narcissism" that Mark Johnston complains of in current Dummettiananti-realism?[5] Is this not tantamount to the claim that the world must be cut to patterns congenial to our mode of conceptualization?

That it is not may be seen by considering once again Mohanty's point about Nyāya extensionalism. What Nyāya would claim is just that "existent" and "conceptualizable in accordance with the Vaiśeṣika categories" are coextensional. While we may be inclined to read necessity into this claim, Nyāya would not, indeed could not. Moreover, having seen necessity here, we may be wont to account for it by attributing to Nyāya an implicit verificationist presupposition. And the sort of strong verificationism that would be required is indeed incompatible with realism$_3$. But this attribution would be a mistake, for here we would once again be reading internalism into an externalist tradition. Nyāya claims that all reals may be subsumed under one or another of the categories. This may be true. And it may be possible for us to know that this is true. But if it is true, this is not for the reason that the nature of the object of cognition necessarily conforms to the categories we employ in its apperception. Whatever else Nyāya may be guilty of, it is not guilty of philosophical narcissism.

The sort of anti-realism involved in the denial of realism$_3$ is not unknown in the Indian tradition. When the Madhyamaka school of Buddhism claims that all things are empty (that is, niḥsvabhāva), this may be understood as the claim that there are no existents having natures independent of modes of conceptualization arising out of conventional human practices. Within the Buddhist tradition this is tantamount to the claim that there is no such thing as the ultimate truth. Buddhist scholasticism (Abhidharma) distinguished between conventional truth and ultimate truth, the former consisting of useful but not fully accurate descriptions of the world, the latter consisting of completely accurate descriptions of the world that are too prolix to be useful in most contexts. The inaccuracies involved in conventional truths stem from the fact that they use terms that are mere convenient designations, terms that may falsely suggest, for example, that what is in fact a mere assemblage of parts is instead a single whole existing over and above the parts. (The notion of a conceptual fiction was originally applied just to cases of mereological supervenience, but later came to be applied to any case where the application of a concept may be thought to introduce falsification.) The upshot of such use is a conventional ontology of conceptual fictions—conventionally existent entities having distinctive natures only relative to our employment of the relevant convenient designations. The ultimate ontology, by contrast, consists of entities whose natures are wholly independent of all concepts reflecting human institutions and practices.[6] To say that all things are empty is to say that there are no such ultimately real entities, and thus that there can be no ultimate truths. It would then follow that realism$_3$ is globally false, that the nature of what exists is never independent of the conceptual resources used in apprehending the world.

In both the *Nyāya Sūtra* and the Madhyamaka text *Vigrahavyāvartanī* we find the record of an early debate between Nyāya and Madhyamaka over the issue of realism$_3$. From the Nyāya side there is the charge that the Mādhyamika cannot prove that all things are empty without employing some reliable means of cognition (*pramāṇa*) or other; but if all things are empty then any purported reliable means of cognition would be devoid of the nature of a *pramāṇa*, and thus incapable of proving that all things are empty. Hence it cannot be established that all things are empty. From the Madhyamaka side there is the charge that the Naiyāyika cannot prove that any particular cognitive process is a reliable means of cognition without reliance on facts concerning the nature of the object of cognition; and these can only be ascertained through the employment of some reliable means of cognition. Hence due to mutual dependence between means of cognition and objects of cognition, it cannot be established that certain cognitive processes bear the nature of *pramāṇas*.

We may call the Madhyamaka critique of Nyāya methodology the mutual dependence objection. And we may call the Nyāya critique of Madhyamaka procedure the self-stultification objection, since it claims that the truth of the doctrine of emptiness would rule out the possibility of its establishment. Now the mutual dependence objection is given as a *purvapakṣa* in the *Nyāya Sūtra;* but it is also found in the Madhyamaka text *Vigrahavyāvartanī,* where Nāgārjuna uses it as part of his response to the Nyāya self-stultification objection. Given its occurrence in this context, it is unclear whether Nāgārjuna thinks of the mutual dependence objection as no more than a reply to the objection—one that is merely meant to show that if all things are empty, then there could be no means of reliable cognition in the realist$_3$ sense, so that it is unreasonable to demand that such instruments be used in establishing emptiness. It is instead possible to see the mutual dependence objection as aimed somewhat higher: as meant to show that serious reflection on our epistemic situation actually vindicates the doctrine of emptiness. Is the mutual dependence objection intended to serve as itself a positive argument for emptiness, or is it meant merely as part of a reply to an objection? I am going to claim that it must be seen in the latter way. But to see why, we should first investigate the former alternative.

The mutual dependence argument—that is, the mutual dependence objection understood as a positive argument for the doctrine that all things are empty—would begin with the point that we cannot determine which cognitive processes are reliable unless we already possess reliable information concerning the object of cognition, and that such information can only be forthcoming through the employment of reliable means of cognition. Mohanty takes the argument to be meant to show that epistemology and ontology are inseparably linked, and he appears to see this as a genuine threat to Nyāya realism.[7] Why might this be? One way of understanding the claim of mutual dependence is that it brings out the fact that we must use what might be called a method of reflective equilibrium in order to arrive at an adequate account of the reliable means of cognition: utilizing beliefs about the nature of the object to formulate and test hypotheses concerning means of cognition, using these in turn to further refine our beliefs concerning the nature of the object, and so on until we reach a state of relative equilibrium. Why should it be thought that such a procedure cannot yield genuine knowledge as to which are the reliable means of cognition? And why should this be taken as establishing that all things are empty?

I once answered these questions in the following way.[8] Suppose that through the use of this method, we arrive at an account of the reliable means of cognition, the employment of which then yields a substantive account of the nature of the object. Given the nature of the method of reflective equilibrium, it is in principle impossible to rule out the hypothesis that we might be equally justified in accepting some different account of the reliable means of cognition, and some different set of beliefs about the nature of the object. And the reliability of a cognitive process consists in its being true to the nature of its object. Since we cannot say whether the set of cognitive processes actually arrived at through the method of reflective equilibrium is true to the nature of the object, it follows that it is in principle impossible to know which are the reliable means of cognition through the use of such a procedure. And, it may be added, the method of reflective equilibrium represents the only feasible strategy for discovering the reliable means of cognition. Thus the Nyāya project is unfeasible; the very idea of a reliable means of cognition makes no sense. Indeed, the very distinction between epistemology and ontology collapses, and realism$_3$ turns out to likewise be meaningless.

It should be obvious that this argument has internalist and verificationist presuppositions. Only an internalist would suppose we must answer all possible skeptical challenges. Only a verificationist would take underdetermination to show that something cannot be meaningfully asserted. And regardless of what we think of internalism and verificationism, it should be equally clear that a Mādhyamika could not employ these contentious doctrines in an argument for the claim that all things are empty. While it is false that Madhyamaka can consistently use only *reductio* (that is, *prasaṅga*) arguments, it is certainly true that Madhyamaka cannot employ assumptions that the opponent does not share. And Nyāya is clearly externalist in its epistemological orientation. Moreover, Nyāya extensionalism means that it must also reject verificationism. Indeed, there is good reason to believe that no party to the classical Indian debate over the reliable means of cognition could have accepted internalism and verificationism.

Notice, too, just how readily the Naiyāyika can respond to such an argument. The strategy of the reply at *Nyāya Sūtra* II.16 is not (as Mohanty seems to suggest) to invoke the doctrine of *pramāṇa saṃplava*, the doctrine that an object may be cognized by more than one means of cognition. It is rather to point out that a given entity or event may function on one occasion as a means of cognition, and on another occasion as an object of cognition. Of course, this response would be utterly beside the point coming from an internalist: such "evidence" could have no justificatory value given that it is generated entirely within the charmed circle of accepted epistemic practices and pre-theoretical intuitions about the world. For the externalist, on the other hand, this is the obvious line to take. It is, first of all, consistent with the overall approach externalists take toward investigation of the means of knowledge, which is seen as no different in kind from the investigation of any other object. It is, moreover, an effective response, given this approach. For the externalist, the method of reflective equilibrium is precisely what should recommend itself as the preferred approach to epistemology. If the same methods, when applied to the object and to the methods whereby we acquire beliefs about the object, yield mutually consistent results, that counts as evidence for there being a greater likelihood that our methods are reliable. So Nyāya has a response to this argument that is both obvious and effective. Since Madhyamaka is not known for giving arguments that are readily refuted, this should make us wonder whether the mutual dependence argument is the best interpretation of the texts.

There is yet another reason to question the above argument. Suppose that internalism and verificationism were generally accepted among classical Indian epistemologists. Then the mutual dependence argument might appear to work as a proof of anti-realism$_3$—which should make us suspicious. From their practice it seems that Mādhyamikas thought of the establishment of emptiness as something that must proceed in a piecemeal fashion, involving a variety of different arguments designed to address a variety of distinct metaphysical theses. That the mutual dependence argument might seem, at least to an internalist, like a kind of master argument for emptiness runs counter to this spirit. And the self-stultification objection gives us reason to deny that there could be such a thing as a Madhyamaka master argument. For imagine that anti-realism$_3$ is true. Then any means of cognition employed in a purported master argument will be reliable only relative to some mode of conceptualization arising out of a contingent set of human practices. There can be no *a priori* guarantee that it will function as an effective means of proof under different circumstances; and there is good reason to suspect that it will not. The best that the champion of emptiness can hope for is that for each epistemic context there be some procedure that is treated as reliable for that set of human institutions, and that functions within that context to undermine acceptance of realism$_3$. If all things were indeed empty, there could be no final proof of this fact.

What then is the point of the mutual dependence objection? I would now describe it as no more than one part of Nāgārjuna's response to the self-stultification objection. That is, it is not itself designed to discredit the Nyāya project of seeking to determine the reliable means of cognition. Instead, it is meant to show why it is reasonable for those who deny realism3 not to follow the Nyāya procedure of first establishing the reliable means of cognition and then using them to establish emptiness. In *Vigrahavyāvartanī*, Nāgārjuna begins his reply to the self-stultification objection by agreeing that if he had a thesis (*pratijñā*) he would need to follow the Nyāya procedure, but then he denies that he has a thesis. By a "thesis" I take him to mean a statement with realist3 truth-conditions. Having said that he has no such statement to defend, he then proceeds to try to discredit various possible ways of establishing the reliable means of cognition, coming eventually to the mutual dependence objection. I take this section as a whole to be predicated on the assumption that we already have reason to reject the notion of realist3 truth-conditions. What it is meant to show is that given that assumption, there could be no certification of a means of cognition as ascertaining realist3 truth-conditions, and thus that there would be no point in first trying to determine which are the reliable means of cognition. The establishment of the doctrine of emptiness must proceed along some other route.

This is not to say that Madhyamaka has no critique of the Nyāya project, however. While the mutual dependence objection does not serve as an argument against the very possibility of there being reliable means of cognition in the realist3 sense, there is a Madhyamaka argument that can be used to cast doubt on the Nyāya view that certain belief-forming processes are intrinsically reliable. This is the argument of the first chapter of *Mūlamadhyamakakārikā*, Nāgārjuna's examination of causation. What this argument is meant to establish is that causation is itself thoroughly intentional in nature—that the causal connection between entities or events is as much the result of our mode of conceptualization as it is of the relata themselves. If this is so, then no cognitive process can bear intrinsically the nature of being a reliable means of cognition. For to say of some cognitive process that it is a reliable means of cognition is to say that it serves as a causal conduit whereby the nature of the object determines the content of the cognition. So if causation is a conceptual fiction, then something's being a reliable means of cognition must likewise be conceptually constructed. Something can be a reliable means of knowledge in the Nyāya sense only within the context of some set of institutionalized human practices.

Nāgārjuna does not make this argument in *Vigrahavyāvartanī*, which is given over exclusively to replying to objections. Nor does he apply his critique of causation to the case of Nyāya in *Mūlamadhyamakakārikā*, where the arguments are aimed entirely at Ābhidharmikas. There is, however, discussion of just such an argument in both *Nyāya Sutra* II.8-11 and in chapter 5 of Āryadeva's *Śataśāstra*. This is the argument to the effect that something cannot be a reliable means of cognition in any of the three times. What we can see in this argument is the application of Nāgārjuna's critique of causation to the case of a means of reliable cognition considered as the cause of veridical cognition.

Central to the critique of causation in chapter 1 of *Mūlamadhyamakakārikā* was the claim that the causes and conditions cannot be said to be productive of the effect before the effect is produced, after the effect has been produced, or while the effect is undergoing production. In the first case the causes and conditions have not yet produced anything, so they cannot be said to be productive. In the second case, the effect having already been produced, a second production would be superfluous. And the third case is ruled out by the fact that for something that bears its own intrinsic nature, there can be no such thing as a process of undergoing production; only something composed of parts could be said to come into existence over time, and wholes are mere conceptual fictions. Consequently, causation cannot be construed as a realist₃ relation. As *Bhāva-viveka* puts it, causation necessarily incorporates an element of expectancy (*ākāṅkṣa*). Now where, as in an externalist epistemology, the means of cognition are thought of as the causes of veridical cognition, this analysis will apply directly to them. It cannot be ultimately true that something is productive of a veridical cognition either before or after such a state has arisen, and there can be no time during which such a state undergoes production. We can make sense of the notion of a reliable means of cognition only by abandoning the idea that things have natures that are independent of the mode of conceptualization that arises from a way of life.

I shall not seek to take the debate beyond this point, though I am sure that Nyāya has interesting things to say in response to the above argument. My chief aim here has been just to try to get clearer about the terrain on which the Indian debate over epistemological realism has been conducted. A chief attraction of Nyāya for many of us today is its uncompromising espousal of a thorough-going realism. It will come as no shock to be told that this realism involves a rejection of the internalist legacy of Descartes. What is worth noting is that Buddhist critiques of Nyāya realism were mounted from a shared externalist terrain. The current movement toward naturalizing epistemology and semantics is widely seen as promising a final vindication of realism. Given this movement's reliance on causal accounts of knowledge and reference, questions concerning the realist₃ credentials of causation may yet need to be answered before victory can be proclaimed.⁹

Notes

1. For a discussion of the *nirākāravada* tendency within Yogācāra see Kajiyama Yuichi, "Controversy between the *sākāra-* and *nirākāra-vādins* of the Yogācāra School—Some Materials," *Indogaku Bukkyogaku Kenkyū* 14, no. 1 (1965), 26-37.
2. Daya Krishna, "Is Nyāya Realist or Idealist?" *Journal of Indian*

Council of Philosophical Research 12, no.1 (1994), 161-3.

3. "Is Nyāya Realism or Idealism?" *Journal of Indian Council of Philosophical Research* 13, no.1 (1995), 167-9.

4. Roy Perrett, "Is Whatever Exists Knowable and Nameable?" *Philosophy East and West* 50, no. 2, forthcoming.

5. Mark Johnston, "Verificationism as Philosophical Narcissism," in James E. Tomberlin (ed.), *Philosophical Perspectives* 7: *Language and Logic* (Atascadero, CA, Ridgeview Publishing Co., 1993), 307-30.

6. For most Ābhidharmikas this meant all concepts save those that specify kinds of *dharmas* and the relations into which they can enter. For the Yogācāra-Sautrāntika tradition, however, this meant all kind-concepts. The idea behind this radical nominalism was that all aggregation involves an intrinsically falsifying accommodation to human interests; terms that collect together the members of a kind represent no more than what is convenient for humans.

7. In RTIT, 234.

8. See my paper, "Nāgārjuna as Anti-Realist," in *Journal of Indian Philosophy,* 16 (1988), 311-25.

9. Putnam has long argued that a realist construal of the naturalizing project is inevitably compromised by the fact that causation is ineliminably intentional. See, for example, *Realism and Reason* (Cambridge: Cambridge University Press, 1983), 211-21. For an interesting application of this point to the interpretation of Wittgenstein, see Gordon Bearn, *Waking to Wonder* (Albany: SUNY Press, 1987), 191.

PART 4

The Possibility of
a Global Philosophy: Some Reflections

Chapter 15

The Advance of Indian Philosophy in the Works of J. N. Mohanty

Stephen Phillips

A goal, or dream, shared by specialists in classical Indian philosophies is for classical reflection to influence contemporary philosophic endeavors; that the thought of Nāgārjuna, Vācaspati, Gaṅgeśa, et alia, become as universally available and as commonly drawn upon as that of Aristotle and Descartes, at least when the issues that occupied the great classical minds are addressed. Recently, however, the work of Jitendranath Mohanty has made me worry that the ideal may be flawed, that the advance of Indian philosophy may lie elsewhere than in providing resources for the discipline, the current and future philosophic discipline, globally conceived. Formerly, I viewed Mohanty's work as guided by the dream, or, indeed, as itself a paradigm of drawing on classical philosophies, a pattern to be many times duplicated by philosophers who would eventually be educated, as a matter of course, in the wealth of Indian as well as Western thought. Doubtless, the cognoscenti could see that Mohanty's understanding of Indian traditions informs even those explorations of his—in phenomenology and elsewhere—where he does not mention anything Indian. And the professor has often explicitly brought the philosophy of the Indian schools to bear on contemporary concerns. Of course, Mohanty is much too much one of us, too much himself a specialist in classical Indian systems, for the rest of us to feel very satisfied in his example. Anyone who has produced the groundbreaking work he has,[1] and who is expert in several schools and debates across schools, could be expected to bring that learning to whatever he takes up. The real dream is that non-specialists, philosophers who know no Sanskrit, be taught by Indian traditions and influenced by them in informing their views.

When I say that Mohanty has suggested to me that this ideal is flawed, I do not mean to refer to any frustration dreamers may encounter in looking for signs of fruition. Before searching in journals and elsewhere for this paper, I was, it turns out, wishfully thinking that it could be reported that: in epistemology, one now finds the Nyāya reliabilism; in philosophy of language, the Mīmāṃsaka understanding of verbs; in aesthetics, the classical theory of suggestiveness or of *rasa;* in ontology, Vaiśeṣika views of natural kinds; in philosophy of religion, classical defenses of mystical experience; in ethics, the Jaina argument for non-injury, and so on. I had hoped that these Indian approaches were becoming, if not common currency in these fields, pretty familiar. Research has disappointed me, even though one could hope that I have not been diligent enough. However, in epistemology, where my search has been fairly thorough, and where, because of the classical prominence of the *pramāṇa* issue—the issue of "justifiers" or "instruments of right cognition (perception, inference, and so on)—no American who is prominent in the field seems to be aware of classical Indian theories."[2] And I have yet to find an epistemology textbook, even an anthology, that includes or indeed mentions an Indian author or view. In ontology, I have found only a single stray reference.[3] In philosophy of religion—an area where, because of the accomplishments of religious studies scholars and other factors, one would especially expect awareness of at least the general, most intellectual dimensions of Eastern religions—fine philosophers make crude mistakes about the terrain of Indian theology and speculative spiritual theory.[4]

What's the difficulty? Why haven't we specialists been more successful in educating our philosophy peers? Now, it is possible to read Mohanty as suggesting, by his own example, a strategy to help us do better, an example and strategy that do not challenge the dream. So let me first say a few words about how we specialists, on this interpretation of him, might, following Mohanty's example, work more effectively. Then I'll turn to the rejection of the dream by Mohanty.

Mohanty's work suggests that we specialists need to think more about topics and less about schools and individual thinkers. We expect too much if we expect, for example, a non-specialist philosopher of language to dig through a presentation of Kumārila, or of the vital points of Mīmāṃsaka as a whole, or of the development of so seemingly specific a topic as the Mīmāṃsaka understanding of the role of verbs in sentence meaning, to mine what we may rightly see as rich veins of philosophy. For, so long as the presentation is couched in historical terms, with lots of names spelled in diacritics, etc., the presentation will be too hard to understand. Mohanty, in contrast, especially in his recent book, *Reason and Tradition in Indian Thought,*[5] as well as in tens of articles, talks of views and arguments, not schools or people, using such indistinct phrases as "the Indian philosophers" and "the Indian theory of" whatever he is concerned with. Mohanty draws from interschool debates without regard for niceties of attribution, and flushes out positions for their intrinsic interest apart from historical setting. At the heart of philosophy are, after all, issues, views, and arguments, not persons. We specialists need to think more, to think *along with* the classical texts, to be more critical, evaluative, and less detailed in our expositions, as well as original on the issues that the classical texts engage—at least this is what Mohanty's example would seem to advise, assuming the dream.

But Mohanty, I have recently surmised, rejects, or at least does not endorse, the dream. He has a different vision. In *Reason and Tradition in Indian Thought,* the philosopher does, to be sure, mount a globalist rebuttal of a cultural relativism that has as its most visible spokesperson Richard Rorty. Mohanty counters Rorty's thesis by alluding to earlier parts of the book: it is simply obvious that, despite lack of historical influence, classical Indian thinkers and Western philosophers of almost every period "have been doing the same or similar things—if not always or in all respects, certainly sometimes and in some respects."[6] Mohanty asks if the same relativism is to hold with respect to the Indian grammarian tradition, such that *vyākaraṇa* would not be grammar, as, so Rorty implies, *ānvīkṣikī* is not philosophy. It is embarrassingly obvious to us specialists that Rorty and company are wrong, that his position reveals an ignorance of non-Western philosophy. Mohanty writes, "It is indeed sickening to find philosophers argue a thesis about a field about which they know next to nothing—and so inevitably using arguments that follow *a priori* from their methodological premises, expecting that no empirical evidence could show them wrong."[7] All who promote the ideal of a future global philosophic discipline, where classical Indian systems are integrated into both undergraduate and graduate education, would doubtless see Mohanty doing yeoman's work in such refutation of Rorty, that is, see Mohanty preparing the way of the future by clearing away such willful ignorance. However, I repeat, Mohanty does not endorse the ideal; he rejects it, albeit subtly, and in favor of a distinct dream.

The rejection is deeply and intimately tied up with the advance of Indian philosophy in the work of J. N. Mohanty, my unwittingly fortunate title. The flaw in the dream, Mohanty implies, is its displacement of Indian traditions, inevitable dismemberment of Indian systems for recombination in largely discontinuous theories, and the death of Indian philosophy in the enrichment of a global discipline. Mohanty's vision is, instead, the revitalization of Indian philosophy through continued work that accepts many uniquely classical Indian assumptions and much of an interlocking scheme of categories while making improvements and refinements. A careful reading of Mohanty's work in Indian philosophy shows that he brings his Western learning to the improvement of Indian systems, or, since he is very radical in his willingness to disassemble planks of traditional worldviews for contemporary use, for the making of new *darśana*-s—nothing is sacrosanct—let us say that he brings his Western learning to the advance of the whole of Indian philosophy. Mohanty advances Indian philosophy by showing how a needed distinction is implicit in some comment or other of a classical author (a time-honored procedure), or by undermining a view by elucidating its motivations in terms of rival Indian positions, by re-interpreting classical commitments, and in other ways that preserve broad lines of continuity. Throughout the history of philosophy, whether Eastern or Western, prior philosophic efforts live on through the evaluative responses of later generations, and Mohanty's selectivity as well as his enlivening and critical advocacy have brought Indian philosophy to bear not just on contemporary philosophic concerns, but given it a life of its own. Western thought can inform modern Indian philosophy; providing resources is a two-way street.

What about the English medium that Mohanty and philosophy professionals in India today use? Is not the predominance of English a sign that philosophy in India belongs to a global discipline? Is not Indian philosophy, as practiced in the classical civilization, inextricably tied to the Sanskrit language? Mohanty has worried out loud about these and similar questions. In an essay entitled, "The Future of Indian Philosophy,"[8] he calls for Indian philosophers to recognize the enormous change in what he calls the life-world from classical times, change that includes replacement of Sanskrit with English as the medium of Indian philosophic discourse. This is hardly a call for abandoning Sanskrit studies, but rather a frank admission of the modern reality within Indian universities. It is in Indian colleges and universities, Mohanty assumes, that Indian philosophy, namely, philosophy broadly continuous with classical thought, will be rooted and prosper. Today in India, there are, to be sure, pundits who, speaking and writing in Sanskrit, continue classical traditions in unbroken lines. But Mohanty is not sanguine about the prospects of further continuance, apparently because he sees that young people with the intelligence and ability to assume those mantels are going to the universities to become professors, or into professions that promise still greater financial rewards. Thus it is in the universities where the successors of the classical philosophies will, if anywhere, thrive.

The real possibility for this is connected with, in Mohanty's view, thought's ability to transcend culture, or, as he puts it, the life-world. Indian philosophy does not necessarily depend on Sanskrit nor on any life contingency, but is comprised of issues, views, and arguments that typically are not tied to a cultural space. And this, I may say, seems clearly right with the *pramāṇa* discussions, as well as with much in ontology and philosophy of language. We might well wonder, however, whether ethics and classical Indian religious or spiritual views are not irredeemably tied to cultural assumptions. Of course, this is much too large a topic for a proper airing here. Still, I should like to point out that Mohanty finds a way of engaging, for example, even the Mīmāṃsaka thesis of the ethical authority of *śabda*—usually rendered in the pertinent context as the moral authority of "scripture," but which Mohanty interprets as "hearing moral precepts," a cognitive act he defends as the proper means to ethical knowledge.[9] The Mīmāṃsaka thesis, like many other classical ideas, gets transformed in Mohanty's hands. But he manages at the same time to achieve broad lines of continuity and thus to advance Indian philosophy.

It is difficult to find the right tone for assessing a vision, and at the risk of sounding offensive, let me offer a few words of criticism. There seems to me to be little merit in continuity for its own sake, that is, in aiming at continuity with classical thought. Education, learning what the classical philosophers have held and why, seems the extent of our duty. Perhaps it all depends on where, very literally, one is sitting—in New York or Chennai—for instance. But if philosophy transcends culture, then philosophers should be prepared to make sharp breaks with cultural determinations of the past. Furthermore, I am thoroughly confident that much in classical Indian philosophy would repay every modern effort of scholarship and reflection and that broad lines of continuity will naturally evolve. I am less confident, however, that this is true regarding traditional ethical and spiritual views.

On the other hand, it may be in these areas where Mohanty's vision should hold sway. Regarding ethical and spiritual views, conservatism may be good in itself, and perhaps continuity should be consciously sought. In favor of this, a couple of considerations´ may be adduced without, hopefully, conceding too much to the cultural relativists (who sometimes make similar points). First, it may be impossible to present a non-question-begging argument to establish ethical or spiritual positions, though if certain classical views are assumed, a significant, self-supporting case could be constructed. Second, Indian civilization flows in deep-hewn channels of ethical and spiritual positions, so deep, perhaps, as to rule out, as a practical matter, any major shift. Thus, in these areas, philosophers would have, from a practical point of view, a duty to address beliefs and practices closer to home. But where is home? For some, this has no obvious answer.

Notes

1. Mohanty, *Gaṅgeśa Theory of Truth* (New Delhi: Motilal Banarsidass, 1966), which is a translation and interpretation of *Gaṅgeśa* and the New Logic, helped renew interest in this important area of Indian thought, and set a high standard for philosophic scholarship.

2. Authors, some of whose works I have checked, include John Pollock, Alvin Goldman, Laurence BonJour, Fred Dretske, Gilbert Harmon, and Keith Lehrer.

3. By David Armstrong, to a paper by Kisor Chakrabarti on the Nyāya Theory of Universals: David M. Armstrong, *Nominalism and Realism* (Cambridge: Cambridge University Press, 1978), 109.

4. Such an otherwise stellar light as William Alston, for example, in addressing the very problem of religious pluralism, identifies Judaism, Christianity, and Islam as the only theistic religions, and treats Hinduism as though it totally lacked a theistic strand: *Perceiving God* (Ithaca: Cornell University Press, 1992).

5. See RTIT.
6. RTIT, 287.
7. RTIT, 288.
8. Published in Purushottama Bilimoria (ed.), *Essays on Indian Philosophy, Traditional and Modern* (Delhi: Oxford University Press, 1993).
9. RTIT, 257.

Chapter 16

Rationality and Tradition(s)

Eliot Deutsch

I have frequently remarked that the finest tribute that one can offer a philosopher, I believe, is not so much to talk *about* his or her work—valuable as this exercise might be in its own terms—but to think *with* him; to extend, as far as one can, what one finds valuable in his work within the framework of one's own self-appointed tasks. I am deeply honored to have the opportunity to "think with" my esteemed colleague and dear friend Jiten Mohanty on this occasion of our recognizing his great achievements as a creative thinker and as an exemplary person. Mohanty has been notable not only as a first-rate scholar of, and contributor to, both Indian analytic philosophy and to Husserlian phenomenology, but as one who has brought Indian and Western thought together in ways that, while allowing the different traditions to maintain their own unique integrity, have enabled them to challenge and learn from each other and thereby to become mutually enhanced and enriched.

One of Mohanty's special philosophical concerns is the nature of rationality. Although he has not written on this subject at great length,[1] it has been an issue of enduring interest to him, as I know from numerous discussions with him—and this is the "thinking with" theme that I want to explore here briefly in the context of cross-cultural philosophical engagement.

1

It can readily be shown that various cultural traditions often display fundamentally different epistemic positions and attitudes regarding the nature of truth, requirements of formal reasoning, what counts as evidence, and so on.[2] A general principle of rationality, it would seem, would call for any tradition to be open to alteration in its structures of thought and basic beliefs in the light both of its own experience as it develops (sometimes radically) new ways of thinking and as it engages other traditions.

Alasdair MacIntyre has shown quite effectively, I think, although drawing an unhappy conclusion, how a rationality embedded in a tradition needs, through engagements with other traditions, to recognize the possibility of its own inadequacies.

> Rationality understood within some particular tradition with its own specific conceptual scheme and problematic, as it always has been and will be, nonetheless requires *qua* rationality a recognition that the rational inadequacies of that tradition from its own point of view—and every tradition must from the point of view of its own problematic view itself as to some degree inadequate—may at any time prove to be such that perhaps only the resources provided by some alien tradition . . . will enable us to identify and to understand the limitations of our own tradition.[3]

And thus: "rationality requires a readiness on our part to accept, and indeed to welcome, a possible future defeat of the forms of theory and practice in which it has up till now been taken to be embodied within our tradition."[4]

David L. Hall and Roger T. Ames have pointed out in the context of Mac-Intyre's interest in possible comparisons between Aristotle and Confucius that

> It needs to be noticed that MacIntyre's examples of cultural incommensurability continue to be largely drawn from scientific models. Despite the fact that MacIntyre is well aware that the Confucian moral vision depends little on what we would take to be theoretical or conceptual claims, he still insists that the comparison [between Aristotle and Confucius] be pursued if at all at this level because the ultimate goal of such comparison is to determine the truth or falsity of claims made.[5]

In short, MacIntyre's comparative enterprise regarding rationalities seems to rely, if not exclusively then certainly predominately, upon " forms of theory and practice" taken as conceptual claims at the expense of those rationalities that see theory and practice as fundamentally inseparable.

How, then, one might well ask, ought the cross-cultural or "comparative" philosophical project in general be carried out? To begin with, it would seem obvious enough that before one can engage another tradition in such a way as to appreciate its distinctive achievements and acknowledge its—and one's own tradition's—shortcomings, one must first come to some kind of sound understanding of it, an understanding that, it seems to me, must be essentially hermeneutical in character. We inevitably bring our own "prejudices" or predispositions to interpret and judge what is initially alien to us, as these are informed by our cultural and personal experience and then, through letting as far as we can the other tradition speak to us in its own terms, develop a negotiating process, as it were, between our prejudgmental forms and patterns and the content and conceptual structures of that tradition. We aim then to alter our prejudices in the light of that negotiation or encounter.[6]

The cross-cultural hermeneutic engagement, though, does not demand that, in Clifford Geertz's terms, we "go native." Rather, we seek, and sometimes attain, understanding of another tradition in terms of what we share and what we find distinctive—for better or worse—in it, but always within the altered background framework of the integrity of our own philosophical being.

Richard Rorty, in what one might call his "sophistical" pragmatism, with its unabashed ethnocentrism, based at least in part on his fear that without it we might "lose any capacity for moral indignation," will have none of this. Rorty allows that the pragmatist "can only say, with Hegel, that truth and justice lie in the direction marked by the successive stages of European thought." This means, he says, "that the pragmatist cannot answer the question 'What is so special about Europe?' save by saying 'Do you have anything better non-European to suggest which meets *our* European interests better.'"[7] Rorty continues this rather bizarre argument further in his "On Ethnocentrism: A Reply to Clifford Geertz" when, in social-political terms, he states:

> You cannot have an old-timely *Gemeinschaft* unless every-one pretty much agrees on who counts as a decent human being and who does not. But you can have a civil society of the bourgeois democratic sort. All you need is the ability to control your feelings when people who strike you as irredeemably different show up.[8]

But a great deal more is needed for an "old-timely *Gemeinschaft*" let alone a genuine "civil society of the bourgeois democratic sort," not the least of which is the willingness to learn from others who might appear initially to be "irre-deemably different" from ourselves and to acknowledge the possibility that they might have uncovered sources of knowledge and value different from our own that may provide new ways for attaining self-understanding and the wisdom to create a just civil society. It is a strange "pragmatist" indeed who would close off in advance this possibility.

A genuine pluralist approach, then, would want to rule out the meaning-fulness of a radical incommensurability obtaining between various traditions if for no other reason in virtue of the very recognition by one tradition of the existence of the other tradition. Anything totally alien could not, in the first place, be recognizable as being different from us as there would, by definition, be nothing that could be identifiable as being the same.[9] In this context, J. N. Mohanty's question seems relevant: "Could it be," he asks, "that there are *other* worlds, *other* modes of thinking . . . which are yet accessible to us, not because we are all the same, but because (i) we can transcend our own 'worlds', (ii) our 'worlds' howsoever different nevertheless have overlapping contents, and (iii) a common identical world is in the process of being constituted by such overlapping contents and by the reflective process of trying to make sense of each other."[10]

I am not sure about the last of Mohanty's three points; in fact, I think he is probably wrong there and we can have all the creative encounter we want without seeking a "common identical world," for this seeking leads all too often to the demand for a *replacement* of one tradition by another rather than to their mutual enrichment. Alasdair MacIntyre favors just such a replacement as a way out of both relativism and pluralism, and indeed out of a certain kind of absolutism, when he allows that

> When two large-scale intellectual traditions confront one another, a central feature of the problem of deciding between their claims is characteristically that there is no neutral way of characterizing either the subject matter about which they give rival accounts or the standards by which these claims are to be evaluated. Each standpoint has its own account of truth and knowledge, its own mode of characterizing the relevant subject matter [*"relativism"*]. And the attempt to discover a neutral, independent set of standards or mode of characterizing data which is *both* such as must be acceptable to all rational persons *and* is sufficient to determine the truth on the matter about which the two traditions are at variance has generally, and perhaps universally, proved to be a search for a chimera [*"absolutism"*].[11]

MacIntyre then concludes that "The multiplicity of traditions does not afford a multiplicity of perspectives among which we can move [*"pluralism"*], but *a multiplicity of antagonistic commitments, between which only conflict, rational or nonrational, is possible*" [italics mine].[12]

Surely, however, there are other possibilities of *critical* engagement between traditions, of rational ways of cross-cultural evaluation. As Stephen Toulmin notes: "Certainly—on the face of it—'rational enterprises' do exist, within which the ideas of different epochs and cultures can be quite properly described as more or less 'well-established', 'adequate', 'discriminating', 'true', or 'rationally based'; and can be described in these terms, without merely rationalizing a parochial preference for our current standards."[13]

It remains to show how this is possible.

2

In the context of explicating his notion of virtue as "a state of character concerned with choice, lying in a mean, that is, the mean relative to us, this being determined by a rational principle, and by that principle by which the man of practical wisdom could determine it," Aristotle allows that ". . . not every action nor every passion admits of a mean; for some have names that already imply badness, for example, spite, shamelessness, envy, and in the case of actions adultery, theft, murder. . . . It is not possible, then, ever to be right with regard to them; one must always be wrong."[14]

Following Aristotle's lead, in the context of moral judgment it can, I believe, be convincingly argued that we have "exclusionary principles" at work which deny admittance, as it were, into the arena of positive moral value of certain kinds of behavior in virtue of their being utterly violative of the core values of personhood and freedom.[15] The torture, the humiliation, of another person are destitute of intrinsic moral value (albeit in some exceptional circumstances one might be strongly inclined to justify them prudentially) and hence cannot be accorded the possibility of having inherent moral worth. And so with certain epistemic practices: there are those that by their very nature could not possibly be truth-knowledge producing and are thus void of cognitive value. Exclusionary epistemic principles set the boundaries between the rational and the irrational and, like Aristotle's rejection of certain moral practices, they do function *universally*.

Take the law of non-contradiction. Positivists were at one time convinced that the law was not about the way things are in the world (the law as such was not capable of empirical verification), rather it functioned somewhat like a rule of etiquette, it *regulated* a kind of pre-existent cognitive behavior (the application of words/sentences/statements to facts or states of affairs) but did not necessarily *constitute* rational thought as such. But quite clearly the law of non-contradiction is—or at least strongly appears to be—foundational for rationality insofar as any rational practice must abide by it.[16] If self-contradiction were not prohibited, there would be no way to distinguish the true from the false by any criteria whatsoever.

However, as Kant astutely observed, the law of non-contradiction, while functioning as a "universal and completely sufficient principle of all analytic knowledge," provides only a negative criterion for synthetic knowledge: a synthetic statement that contradicts itself cannot be true (or false)[17]—or, as we want to put it, cannot at the outset enter the domain of the true or false. The principle of non-contradiction, or any other of the "laws of logic," however, can tell us nothing regarding what statements are true or false. It functions like the skeletal structure of a building that requires to be filled-out with walls, windows, doors, and the rest in order for the building to become livable—and livable in many different ways. With respect to any particular epistemic practice (nomic explanation, instrumental determination, justification of actions) one needs always to understand those general principles of thought or action whose violation would preclude the possibility of fulfilling the intentionality of that particular rational undertaking. One would be irrational epistemically if one claimed to be playing a truth/falsity-conducive game but was dwelling cognitively in the realm of the exclusionary.[18]

Although it might sound somewhat disquieting to speak of irrational explanations or beliefs as being incapable of being true or false rather than being simply false, this way of speaking has the added advantage of enabling one to see truth and falsity across a continuum within the rational. For a belief to be false (or lack truth to whatever degree) it must be formed in such a way as to be capable, at least in principle, of being true. Exclusionary principles that preclude ways of thinking and acting from entering the arena of the true and false altogether, must thus also allow us to distinguish them from various rules that regulate particular rational practices, the violation of which would only lead to falsehood or inadequacy.

Exclusionary principles, as indicated, are those which, if adhered to, preclude the possibility of certain ways of thinking from entering the arena of the credible. They are of two kinds: the "foundational" and the "operational." *Foundational* exclusionary principles are those which, if adhered to, would not allow a person to even get started in any rational practice whatsoever (for example, again, the rejection of the law of non-contradiction, or perhaps of any accepted "law of logic"). As we have noted, although laws of logic are not by themselves productive of substantive knowledge, their rejection would simply and effectively shut one off from the possibility of attaining truth or knowledge and therefore from the domain of the rational. *Operational* exclusionary principles, on the other hand, consist of those conditions that demarcate rational practices, and which, while taken to be universal at any one time, are in principle subject to historical revision under changing circumstances. Foundational exclusionary principles are invariant—we can not imagine epistemic situations in which they would not be effective; operational exclusionary principles are historically variant, for any set of which we can imagine situations where some of the principles could be subtracted from the set while others could be added.[19]

For example, for us today any set of operational exclusionary principles would surely include the demand for coherence, falsifiability, and shareability. A belief must in principle be part of a web of belief that is otherwise sustainable as a background corpus of knowledge so that the belief coheres with that structure and is not asserted in a manner that radically deviates from it. One would be irrational if one were to affirm—rather than simply suspend judgment regarding—a belief that was utterly incompatible with everything else one felt justified to believe. Rationality calls always for at least the possibility of there being a systematic order in experience.

A belief must also be framed in such a way that it is always potentially subject to revision and defeat. It must in short be fallible. Although one might rightly hold to the initial validity of one's perceptions/conceptions, they must always be acknowledged to be, in principle, subject to being false at that very time and be open to revision in the light of future experience. By this exclusionary principle we would regard as epistemically irrational X's holding a belief Y when, for whatever psychological factors, X is compelled to hold Y and would accept nothing to count against it. Avoiding the so-called "genetic fallacy," we would have to allow that Y might be true, but that X nevertheless is in no position to justify Y and in this instance would not be thinking rationally in affirming it.[20]

We also hold today that a belief and the reasons given for it must be shareable and such that they could, in principle, be convincing to another belief-practitioner. One would not be playing the belief-affirming game if one claimed that one's belief could not, in principle, be communicated to another or seen by him to be justifiable. In short, although one may reason to oneself, as it were, about the validity of one's beliefs, for a belief to be rational it must be inherently inter-subjective in character.

These operational principles, while universally binding for us at this time, are nevertheless susceptible to alteration and elimination under very different epistemic situations. It is conceivable (albeit barely), for instance, that falsifiability might be dispensable in some possible world because the state of knowledge in that world was so complete that all beliefs held there were incorrigible.

In the meantime, in this actual world, criticizing or evaluating beliefs (of one's own and those of others) is a two-stage affair: first, examining the belief and reasons allegedly supporting it in terms of seeing if the belief enters the arena of the rational by way of its crossing over the exclusionary boundary by not violating its foundational and operational principles; second, on the positive side, determining, on the basis of various positive criteria adhered to by a given community of practitioners, the degree to which a claim is warranted. The first stage or test determines whether a belief has the possibility of being true (or adequate or right) in terms of its not violating the conditions that are accepted as defining the practice as rational; the second determines the degree of truth, adequacy, or rightness of the belief in terms of its fulfilling the set of conditions that are accepted by the appropriate community as necessary for truth attainment within the context of various general criteria.

This appeal to the epistemic standards of communities of practitioners in justifying various substantive beliefs is not, of course, to be construed as telling the whole story of justification, for there clearly are "givens" of our experienced world which must be taken into account in any claim to justified belief. There is, in other words, a conventional dimension or element in all justificatory rationality, but it does not bear the entire weight of what is called for in justification. We need always to show that there is some strong connection between the positive criteria we employ in our practices of justifying belief and the belief being "true."

It must again be stressed, however, that while telling us that there are necessary conditions for the attainment of knowledge, exclusionary principles do not provide us as such with (formulaic) sufficient ones. Exclusionary principles, in their universality, are essentially negative in import. They tell us more about what we cannot do than about what we should positively do in attaining truth and knowledge. A kind of pernicious absolutism arises when, ignoring "styles of reasoning" and the positive criteria for various belief-producing practices, one transforms an exclusionary principle into a single, positive program—of action, of thinking, of political organization—where a one, correct pattern of behavior and a one right way of thinking gets announced that has a presumed enduring, universal reach. I believe exclusionary principles, when properly understood, provide a basis for acknowledging the possibility (and indeed desirability) of a plurality of right ways of acting and thinking.[21] They make possible, and indeed call for, a creative bringing forth of diverse rational expressions.

On the "negative" exclusionary side, then, agreement might not always be attained cross-culturally as to the appropriate content of operational exclusionary principles (although once a certain practice is in place experience strongly suggests that general agreement is usually reached here), but, even acknowledging possible cultural differences regarding operational exclusionary principles, that does not mean that one is disentitled to hold rigorously to those grounded in one's own tradition. Good reasons for the necessity of those operational exclusionary principles (in terms of showing how if they were violated the intentionality of the given rational practice could not be fulfilled) would, of course, have to be provided. And with foundational exclusionary principles, as we have seen, any notion of rationality compels their acceptance. If one were to deny this situation in favor of a thoroughgoing radical relativism one would, in the end, have to deny any universal validity whatsoever to the exercises of reason, which would be a self-defeating denial if ever there was one. Failures in a philosophical tradition—our own or others—to enter into the positive domain of rationality in virtue of failures to cross exclusionary boundaries is certainly a basis for justified rational criticism.

On the "positive" side, once exclusionary boundaries are passed and various procedures for discovery and justification enter the court of possible true/false, adequate/inadequate, right/wrong judgment according to the historically-changeable criteria set by communities of inquirers, the pluralist is strongly inclined to look primarily toward the possibility that alternative procedures within different cultural perspectives are indeed genuinely "alternative," that is, potentially offering new and valuable insights and sources of knowledge, rather than their being only objects of negative criticism. This does not rule out, however, the pluralist's ability to recognize inadequacies in the other's rational practices and show how one's own way of thinking and acting might be better than the other's way; for it is the case that where universality obtains on the exclusionary side, various positive *aims* or general *purposes* will emerge and will, while always open to revision in the light of future experience, set ideal standards of rightness for specific practices. As Toulmin also notes:

> A collective human enterprise takes the form of a rationally developing "discipline", in those cases where men's shared commitment to a sufficiently agreed set of ideals leads to the development of an isolable and self-defining repertory of procedures; and where those procedures are open to further modification, as to deal with problems arising from the incomplete fulfillment of those disciplinary ideals.[22]

This does not mean, though, that one must determine what is indispensable within the positive criteria of a given rational practice for it to move towards the fulfillment of its ideals, for such determination always runs the unnecessary risk of taking what is required for one "style of reasoning" to be the norm for all other styles.[23]

The relativist's argument, then, that because any justification for a particular model of rationality can only be given in terms and by criteria already presupposed or given in that model, it is impossible to judge in any proper way between it and another model, that "truth," in short, can only be determined according to the norms of "our" culture, and can be set aside when exclusionary principles are brought into the picture and an understanding is had of how different ensuing models may each attain, or fail to attain, a rightness appropriate to them.

Genuine criticism may also be directed to the basic moral values that centrally inform a culture's rationality or "style of reasoning." Once again, on the exclusionary side, one is certainly entitled to challenge another culture's actual moral practices and ideals (indeed it might be argued that one is morally obliged to do so) when they appear to be violative of the very possibility of human flourishing in virtue of their betraying the primary values of human dignity and freedom (with the understanding, of course, that our own cultural practices and ideals are open to the same criticism from others).

And on the positive side, the very training in cross-cultural sensitivity necessary for understanding can yield a heightened awareness of the ways in which other societies as well as one's own do fulfill (and also oftentimes fail to realize) the possibilities those moral values afford for human flourishing. Moral imagination comes strongly into play here, for one is called upon to see what it would mean to live and think in the light of those values and the rational goods that might thereby be attained.

On the "positive" side, then, one can, I should think, learn to live happily and not begrudgingly with a genuine plurality of traditions with their respective models of rationalities and worlds and an ongoing creative engagement between them. Just as we do not have—and assuredly do not want to have—a single conception, say, of art which would result in all works of art being the same, so with our portraits of the world, our conceptions and beliefs, our values, we do not have—and many of us would not want to have—a "common identical world" which comes about either from our simply "trying to make sense of one another" or from an antagonistic conflict between contending traditions where, at the end of the battle, we would be required to "transfer our allegiance to that hitherto alien tradition."[24] On the contrary, and I suspect that Jiten Mohanty would strongly support this conclusion, we might have—and rejoice in having—many forms and ways of achieving philosophical insight and understanding which, through cross-cultural encounter, allow for and promote the creative alteration and enrichment of our own way.

Notes

1. See Mohanty's RTIT and "Phenomenology and Indian Philosophy: The Concept of Rationality," in *Philosophy and Phenomenology*, D. P. Chattopadhya, et. al. (eds.) (Albany: State University of New York Press, 1992).

2. See, for example, A. S. Cua, "Reason and Principle in Chinese Philosophy," Arindam Chakrabarti, "Rationality in Indian Philosophy," David Bastow, "Rationality in Buddhist Thought," and Majid Fakhry, "Rationality in Islamic Philosophy," in Eliot Deutsch and Ron Bontekoe (eds.), *A Companion to World Philosophies* (Oxford: Blackwell Publishers, 1997).

3. Alasdair MacIntyre, "Relativism, Power, and Philosophy," in Michael Krausz (ed.), *Relativism, Interpretation and Confrontation* (Nortre Dame: University of Nortre Dame Press, 1990), 201-202; originally published in *Proceedings and Addresses of the American Philosophical Association*, 1985, 5-22.

4. Ibid., 201-2.

5. David L. Hall and Roger T. Ames, *Thinking from the Han* (Albany: State University of New York Press, 1998), xii-xiii.

6. It has also become something of a commonplace now in comparative studies to note that one approaches another culture not only from within the general "prejudices" of one's own cultural background, but quite specifically from where one currently stands philosophically within that background. For example, it is quite apparent that German Indologists of the last century, such as Paul Deussen, read Indian thought through the lens of Idealistic metaphysics, and that in our own times Western readings of Asian traditions have often been highly "analytic" in character. And also from East to West: one has only to read several texts of the Kyoto School of Japan to see how their interpretations of Western thought were highly colored by various Buddhist values and concepts that deeply informed the thinkers of that school, such as Nishida and Nishitani. Every generation, it seems, writes anew the history of its own culture and inescapably that of others relative to the fashions and interests of its times.

7. Richard Rorty, *The Consequences of Pragmatism* (Minneapolis: University of Minnesota Press, 1982), 173.

8. Richard Rorty, *Objectivity, Relativism, and Truth,* Philosophical Papers, Vol. 1 (Cambridge: Cambridge University Press, 1991), 209.

9. Interpreting what another culture's expressed beliefs regarding themselves and the world mean is obviously necessary before we can entertain their truth and value, and some degree of presumed commensurability between those

articulated beliefs and our own is in turn obviously necessary for that interpreting to take place.

10. J. N. Mohanty, "Phenomenology and Indian Philosophy: The Concept of Rationality," 9.

11. Alasdair MacIntyre, *Whose Justice? Which Rationality?* (Notre Dame: University of Notre Dame Press, 1988), 166.

12. Ibid., 368.

13. Stephen Toulmin, *Human Understanding*, Vol. 1 (Oxford: Clarendon Press, 1972), 85.

14. *Nicomachean Ethics*, II, 6, 9-14, trans. W. D. Ross, in *The Basic Works of Aristotle*, (ed.) Richard McKeon (New York: Random House, 1941). 15.

Cf. my *Creative Being: The Crafting of Person and World* (Honolulu: University of Hawaii Press, 1992), chapter 11, "A Creative Morality."

16. A possible exception to this is certain theoretical-epistemic practices in quantum mechanics, but even here this seems to have more to do with indeterminacy or with the principle of excluded middle than with non-contradiction as such. (See, for example, Willard Van Orman Quine, "Two Dogmas of Empiricism," in *From a Logical Point of View* [Cambridge, Mass: Harvard University Press, 1953], 44-6).

17. Kant writes: "The universal, though merely negative, condition of all our judgments in general . . . is that they be not self-contradictory; for if self-contradictory, these judgments are in themselves, even without reference to the object, null and void. . . ."

"The *principle of contradiction* must therefore be recognized as being the universal and completely sufficient *principle of all analytic knowledge;* but beyond the sphere of analytic knowledge it has, as a *sufficient* criterion of truth, no authority and no field of application. . . . [I]n regard to the truth of this [synthetic] kind of knowledge we can never look to the above principle for any positive information, though, of course, since it is inviolable, we must always be careful to conform to it." *Critique of Pure Reason*, trans. by Norman Kemp Smith (London: Macmillan, 1929), A151,152.

18. Exclusionary principles may, if one prefers somewhat more positive-sounding rule-language, be said to be *rules of admissibility* for entrance into the domain of the rational. To refer, however, to the law of non-contradiction as an exclusionary principle, the violation of which . . , rather than as a necessary condition, the fulfillment of which . . , has the advantage of marking off a clear demarcation between the rational and the irrational and, by insisting on their being non-productive by themselves of knowledge and truth, of providing a basis for a plurality of truths on the rational side. Violate the principle and you cannot be an articulate knower, follow it and you may, but not necessarily will, be a participant in the producing of knowledge and truth.

19. This does not mean, however, that we can relativize operational exclusionary principles to local practices as such, for any such rational practice must presuppose those very principles if it can hope to be effective according to its own positive criteria.

20. It might also be argued that, at the other extreme, any clinging to a radical skepticism regarding the possibility of ever having adequate beliefs about anything would be irrational, on the grounds that such an epistemic attitude would run directly contra to that initial presumption of validity we

accord our perceptions/conceptions that is a condition for our sanity. If every time one observed something and judged it to have such and such properties and one simultaneously withheld one's assent to that judgment, one couldn't even begin to negotiate one's way in the world. One would be frozen and imprisoned in a contradiction of one's own making. This is not to say, though, that one is disentitled to withhold one's assent to some candidate for belief, for this withholding is not a matter of epistemic skepticism but a realization that at the present time one doesn't have sufficient information to render a proper (justified) judgment. This epistemic attitude presupposes the possibility that one could have or acquire the necessary information.

21. The advent of non-Euclidean geometries, for example, nicely shows how exclusionary principles of the most general nature, such as, once again, the law of non-contradiction, do not necessitate a single system (of geometry or of logic itself) but can tolerate, indeed promote, diverse systems with their own specific rules and primitive axioms.

22. Stephen Toulmin, *Human Understanding*, 359.

23. In matters of social philosophy this becomes especially apparent. To secure agreement on the need for human rights, for example, all too often translates into the demand that any proper conception of human rights must conform to *our* way of understanding what they are and mean; the tendency, that is, to absolutize what is thought to be indispensable for their achievement.

24. Alasdair MacIntyre, "Relativism, Power, and Philosophy," 202.

Chapter 17

My Philosophical Position Today/Response to My Critics

J. N. Mohanty

Philosophical conversation is successful if it leads to a monologue, and out of such monologue one emerges again into a dialogue. So has been at least this philosopher's experience with thinking. The friends who have contributed to this volume have for long been participants in philosophical conversation and their participations have made me converse with myself. To construe their questionings as criticism that need replies is to trivialize their contributions; even more trivializing would be the response that the critics did not quite understand the points I was making in my writings. However, instead of simply replying, I will first let my response take the form of an admission, a statement, a confession, of the philosophical positions I hold now in the light of the criticisms of my friends, leaving it to them, if they so wish, to reexamine their original comments. I value their comments too much to claim that my "replies" could just make them evaporate. To the contrary, no philosophical argument, or no philosophical point made, ever totally disappears; it has numberless lives, and reappears in many guises. In the end, all philosophical arguments are fragile, and yet argue one must. So, after this statement, I will briefly formulate what my responses to the criticisms made and questions raised would be in view of the statements given of my position.

Husserl and I

My friends associate me with Husserl. I am regarded by many as a Husserl scholar. I think of myself as a philosopher who has found Husserl's thought inspiring, helping me to forge my path amidst competing theoretical positions. I have also found his person, his commitment to rigorous thinking, and courageously standing up against those who wanted to control thought with their ideologies, equally inspiring. My experience as a Husserl scholar, attempting exegesis of Husserl texts, has taught me how to read and interpret texts with utmost care (and I should add, charity) and, in his special case, to match his sentences with my own inner experience of things. As those who have carefully read my writings would know, I have not simply expounded, or even interpreted, Husserl. I have freely expressed my disagreement with him, suggested modifications of his theses, and sometimes introduced new ideas. As I have said at one place, reading Husserl has not led me to be confined to the limits of his thinking, but has rather set me free to pursue my own path in thinking.

But before I read Husserl, I had already been introduced to Kant's first *Critique,* and read Vaihinger's Commentary on it with Rash Vihary Das in Calcutta. Since then, I have not overcome the temptation to indulge in Kant exegesis, and as those who have taken my Kant courses know, I have indulged in the niceties of Kant interpretation with utmost delight. I must have read the *Critique* some twenty times over, and every time I have experienced the sheer surprise at encountering texts whose significance I was discovering anew.

What is common to Husserl and Kant is transcendental philosophy, and my interest came to be focused upon this kind of philosophy—both on what is common to the two, and what separates them.

Indian Philosophy as the Permanent Background

It is quite possible that Indian philosophy had already brought me to the vicinity of Husserlian thinking. This has been pointed out to me more recently by Bina Gupta, the editor of this volume, and also by Joe Margolis. I did not quite realize this up until Bina Gupta insisted upon such a possibility. Many in India think of me as a scholar in Navya-Nyāya because of the book I wrote on Gaṇgeśa. Only a few know that before I studied Navya-Nyāya, I was a student of Vedānta. The two schools of thought taught me two quite different things. Vedānta provided an understanding of the nature of subjectivity as "pure consciousness," and even if it stands in sharp contrast to Husserl's intentionality thesis, nevertheless the idea of consciousness as that which, though itself non-worldly, makes the world manifest, found a resonance in certain strands of Husserl's thought. The idea of *epoché* did not seem strange to me. To the contrary, it seemed as if I was familiar with it all along. Navya-Nyāya, with its super-rigorous analytic distinctions and highly sophisticated cognitive logic, had prepared me for Husserl's *Logical Investigations.* The two interests merged nicely. Husserl's phenomenology and Indian philosophy formed the permanent background of my thinking.

As in the case of Husserl, so also in the case of Indian philosophy: I did not choose to be a mere expounder. I wanted to be an interpreter, sometimes suggesting radical, and more often not so radical, changes. In this I was inspired by the great innovators of the past, especially by the great Raghunātha Śiromaṇi. As contrasted with those who recognized only the so-called "spiritual" side of Indian thought, I was impressed by the logical, discursive aspect. As against those who would see only the analytic work done by Indian philosophers, I could not but emphasize their important phenomenological findings. Altogether, I believe, I am striving towards a total understanding of Indian thought, and always hope I have been able to further it a few significant steps ahead.

Four Dogmas to be Overcome

It would help my readers to appreciate the nature of my thinking, if I formulate precisely the need I have felt to overcome what I may call four dogmas. I will call them: (1) the dogma of "exclusive oppositions"; (2) the dogma of the "privacy of the mental"; (3) the dogma of the irreducibly public availability of language; and (4) the dogma of "one-level philosophical truth." In a sense, (2) and (3) are examples of (1), but they are separately stated here in view of the central role they play in contemporary Western thought.

Let me begin with the last one. Philosophical thinking has not only a linear development (in history, and also in the thinker's own inner mental life), but is bound to have many different levels. What holds good at one level may not hold good at another, while it may still continue to hold good at the former level. It would be unacceptable to say that the truths at level one, after one moves on to level two, are cancelled even for the superseded level. Realism with regard to external objects holds good at the level of pre-reflective perceptual experience, and it continues to have that validity for that level even after, at a higher level, it is shown (if it can be) that the perceived object is a construct. Coming to an issue that is directly relevant to my present purpose, admitting essences at one level of discourse is not superseded, at that level, by interpreting those essences as but meanings.

The multi-leveled character of philosophical discourse is connected with dogma (1). If you are an essentialist, it is held you cannot also be a historicist, if you believe in process you cannot also admit invariant features. If you admit the primacy of language (for philosophical purposes), you cannot have the primacy of consciousness. In one of my early books, I had—fresh from Werner Heisenberg's seminar in Göttingen—formulated for phenomenology the principle of complementarity: Just as particle theory and wave theory give complementary descriptions of the micro constituents of matter, so I proposed the realistic theory—that we perceive material objects, determine essence, and apprehend ideal entities such as numbers; and the constitution theory—that all such objects are constituted in appropriate intentional acts, are complementary descriptions, not opposed theories between which a philosopher must choose. This principle of complementarity I would still defend. Only after you admit ideal entities can you set the task for their "origin" in history, language, or consciousness. For a nominalist, there is no such problem.

Just a quick word or two regarding dogmas (2) and (3). It is almost uncritically taken for granted that the mental is the private and the bodily is public. This contrast is maintained by reducing the mental paradigmatically to toothaches and pains and raw feelings, while the large domain of thoughts and theories is just left out. Likewise, there are bodily sensations and feelings which are private. The bodily, we have learned from phenomenology, may also be intentional, while the mental may be non-intentional. If the mental is taken to be psychological and private, that is because of a certain interpretation of the mental, not because of how the mental is in itself. Under a different interpretation, the intentional act, having a meaning or *noema* of its own, and thereby conferring meaning upon its object, becomes, or rather is revealed as always having been "transcendental." What it is in itself is an unanswerable metaphysical question. The same sort of remarks regarding language would illustrate dogma (3) by showing how language may be treated in a naturalistic framework and in a phenomenological framework.

To return to dogma (4), we have learned from Hegel's *Phenomenology* that truth does not lie only in the conclusion arrived at, but also in the path traversed. The multi-leveled character of philosophical discourse precisely substantiates this Hegelian insight.

Experience

The words "experience" and "empirical" have been much abused in philosophy. Kant himself used "experience" in many different senses. When he says all knowledge begins with experience, he means by "experience" sensations. But he also held that experience is the ordered connection of perceptions. By "possible experience" he meant one systematic structure of interconnected perceptions connected by the Analogies of Experience. Later in the nineteenth century, two German words came to stand for what was simply called experience: *"Erlebnis"* and *"Erfahrung,"* the former signifying "experience as lived through" and the latter what is simply experience of something or other. The use of *"Erlebnis"* by Dilthey and Husserl was already a leveling off of a more original use, for example, by Goethe, where *"Erlebnis"* stood for a momentous experience as when the poet saw the Strassburger Cathedral.

I have resisted using "experience" in the narrowed down, thin, and emptied sense of sense-impressions, and have preferred the thick and rich sense in which it has many levels and dimensions. Even in ordinary usage one speaks of "life-experience," "moral experience," "poetic experience and religious experience." Since the rise of modern hermeneutic thinking there is a suspicion against all such usages of "experience," I believe, on the ground that one generally has in mind the thought of a completely unmediated, immediate feeling and forgets the interpretive, textual, background of tradition that is involved. Granted that the latter is true, the right consequence is not to deny any legitimate use of "experience," but to expand such use to include the hermeneutic element (as does even the talk of "perception"). When Hegel called his 1807 *Phenomenology* the "Science of the experience of consciousness," however misguided the use of "experience" may seem to be, I am now satisfied that Hegel had a point: experience is consciousness' engagement with itself and its world, it is multi-leveled, multi-dimensional, and historical. Taken in this sense, consciousness' recognition of itself as transcendental—brought about through history and through *epoché*—and of its world, initially presented as always having-been-there, as "constituted," is also experience, and thus may be said to be empirical. The more you restrict and empty the sense of "experience," the more is the gap between the empirical and the transcendental. The more you liberalize the sense of "experience" and give it richer, even historical meaning, the less is that gap. Our goal, as Hegel's was, is the elimination of that gap.

Reason

The old question, still surviving in Kant, if knowledge arises from experience or from reason, is no more relevant today. The idea of reason as a faculty, indeed the faculty psychology as a whole, is unnecessary, just as the derivation of "Reason" from a cosmic, or transcendent, Logos—though interesting from the point of view of *Ideengeschichte*—has no philosophical merit, though carrying lots of philosophical baggage, today. Indian philosophy never asked this question, and did not easily divide into empiricism and rationalism.

However, the Kantian doctrine that all conceptual thinking aims at the goal of presenting its object in intuition is rehabilitated in phenomenology through the thesis that all intentional acts aim at fulfillment, but not all that is intended can be presented intuitively. Hence the distinction between the merely symbolic, empty, and significative intention and the authentically fulfilled intention. Thus every intentional act that is not intuitive is conceptual. It has a correlative *noema*, which is either a concept or a proposition. Intuition, however, presents its object, not simpliciter, but always as such and such that is, under a description. Knowledge in the true sense is a synthesis of identity between the way the object was intended and the way it is presented in the fulfilling experience.

Reason is manifested in human cognitive experience in three ways: first, in the way very different *noemata* hang together to lend a certain unity to experience; second, in the way the *noemata* tend to be fulfilled in experience, thereby generating an authentically certified belief as to the way things are; and finally, in the ceaseless movement towards totalization. The first is what Kant called "possible experience," the third is a Kantian Idea of Reason, the second is sought to be captured in "the empricist's Verifiability thesis."

I will illustrate the role of reason in experience in two ways. First, consider perception of an external object, which is typically an example of empirical cognition. The object at any time is being perceived from a certain perspective, so that only a profile is presented. But in the very conception of an object it is pre-delineated that there are other profiles, an infinite number of such from as many perspectives, so that the unity of the object is the unity of an infinite totality, a sort of Kantian Idea. Thus Reason is involved in organizing even the simplest perceptual experience.

The other example I will here give is the way a multiplicity of *noemata* signify one and the same object. The example will help us to deal with the relativism which maintains that there are radically different worlds. The *noemata,* if they do indeed refer to the same object, will have overlapping contents (as in the picture of intersecting spheres) through which, even where different worlds (cultures, traditions, rationalities, etc.) are concerned, communication could be established.

Reason, so understood, is not an oppressive power imposed *ab extra,* but rather operates in the interstices of experience, rendering experience expressible, shareable, and communicable.

A *Priori,* Essences, and Necessities

The *a priori,* then, is within the structure of the empirical. If numbers are *a priori,* and if there are two apples, there is an *a priori* right in the world. It need not be in the mind. What then is known *a priori* is not known without any experience, but is recognized in the midst of experience. Universality and necessity are still marks of the *a priori.* But, first of all, many of the necessary (and so *a priori*) truths are only conditionally necessary, as are the mathematical truths whose necessity hangs upon the axioms, definitions, and the systems concerned. Essential truths such as what is colored must be extended and are hypothetical in nature: "If something is colored, it must be extended." But it is not necessary that something is colored. Essences are essences in as much as the world is structured in a certain way. The Cartesian *cogito* is necessary as amounting to: *If* I am thinking, then I must exist. But it is entirely contingent that I am thinking or even that I exist.

To those who deny any essential truth whatsoever, I offer an entire set of examples:

Formal essences: A=A

A is greater than B entails B is lesser than A
If A is greater than B and if B is greater than C, then
A is greater than C.

Material essences:

All mental acts are intentional
Dasein (that is, human existence) is being towards death
Orange is intermediate between red and yellow

The formal essences are true of any possible world. The material essences are true of the world as we find it, and there may also be some possible worlds in which they are not true. Is there any non-formal essence which is true in every possible world? I will return to this question a little later.

Truth

I agree with Kant that the nominal explication of "truth" is agreement with object. But that says nothing about a general and sufficient criterion of truth. Kant goes on to say that this is impossible to give, but he proceeds to give one that is "conformity to possible experience." Note that here "possible experience" has to be understood in the Kantian sense. It does not mean experience that is possible in the logical sense, but rather one interconnected whole of experiences connected by the Analogies of experience. Upon proper explanation it turns out to be the Kantian equivalent of "world." How to determine what is compatible with possible experience? Or, how to determine that what seems now to be so compatible will not be rejected by the ongoing process of experience? It seems to me, at this point of my thinking, that as long as a belief is not thrown out by experience, that is, not yet proved to be false, it is to be regarded as true. This is the only empirically verifiable definition of "truth." "True" = "what is not yet known to be false." This is the Vedāntic definition of truth in terms of *abādhitatva*.

Now, will it apply to the so-called essential truths? An essential structure, which is an ontological structure, is, by definition, not dependent on my cognition of it. No cognition or belief in what is purportedly essential is immune to possible defeasibility. If the claim that p is essential is defeated, then it shows that p is not an essence, it was only taken to be so.

Time and History

In many different ways, at many different levels, time and history enter into human cognition. After making these clearer, I will turn to the ontological position of time and history. I will not lay too much emphasis on the seemingly obvious fact that all knowing occurs in time and in a historical situation. If "knowledge" is taken in an episodic sense, it surely occurs in time. Even in a non-episodic sense, knowledge is historically conditioned. But the content of knowledge that is a propositional thought is not, in that manner, a temporal and historical entity. On the contrary, it makes sense to claim that a proposition is neither temporal nor historical, not in the sense that it is outside of time but rather in the sense that temporal and historical predicates cannot be meaningfully affirmed or denied of it.

As a matter of fact, I am not impressed by the large metaphysical thesis that everything is in time. What is "everything"? Numbers are not in time. Propositions are not either. Physical laws, in which time may function as a variable, are not themselves temporal objects. Neither is everything that is in time constantly changing. One mode of being in time is to endure, or to be permanent. Kant rightly said that only the permanent changes. The perishing particular, the Buddhist's *svalakṣaṇa*, does not change. It dies, while another is born.

Not everything is historical. History pertains to the human existence and the human world. History is always "history of Ø," where "Ø" stands for what may be called an ideal entity (such as "science," "music," "philosophy"). Human consciousness is both temporal and historical: *qua* empirical, it is in time and in history; *qua* transcendental, it is the source of temporality, while human existence is the source of historicity. Without consciousness, there is no time. If we posit time even in the absence of consciousness, such positing requires consciousness and we imagine what things would be in its absence, such imagining being a mode of consciousness.

The Transcendental and the Empirical

A conscious experience is an empirical event, process, or state (depending upon which ontological category one prefers) insofar as one locates it in the spatio-temporal order, gives it a causal explanation, and ascribes it to a bodily organism. The same conscious experience is an existential phenomenon, inasmuch as it is a mode of being-in-the-world, an intentionality of a *Dasein,* a way of dealing with the situation in which the *Dasein* finds itself. Identically the same conscious experience—with its *noetic-noematic* structure, and as constituting an ego as its point of origin and the world as its horizon within which its object acquires its meaning and place—is also transcendental.

Thus the empirical is also the existential and the transcendental. This identity is "enigmatic." It would not do to say that if all three are the same, only the empirical exists while the other two are its philosophical interpretations. For various reasons, I believe the reverse to be true or at least closer to the truth. The "empirical" is defined in terms of the causal order, and this is an interpretation, however powerful, of one's own consciousness as lived through by oneself. The transcendental is the source and the *topos* of all interpretative meanings, including its own interpretation as "transcendental." Such concepts as "causality" involving objective time-order, physical nature involving concepts of material substance, all are constituted—that is, have their phenomenological origin—in the rule-governed structure of consciousness. It is not as though the empirical originates from the transcendental. It is rather that what we mean by "empirical" has its origin in the transcendental.

I reject the two-world theory. Consciousness is, in its innermost nature, transcendental—the same consciousness which interprets itself, under strictly definable conditions as human, as biological and physiological, as bodily, as social, in brief, as empirical. I have fundamental objections to the way the distinction between the empirical and the transcendental is usually drawn, which misleadingly suggests as though the transcendental subjectivity is not the subject's experience of herself. The other member of the pair, that is, the "empirical," also misleadingly suggests that one experiences only oneself as bodily and as a member of the natural and social orders. "Experience," as I have said earlier, is multi-layered. I experience myself as bodily, as an existent *Dasein,* as a part of nature, as subject to external causality, but also—once I bring into effect the *epoché*—as transcendental subjectivity. As transcendental, I am also a cognitive, affective and willing, acting, speaking and moving around, not a mere thinking ego.

I have always held, and still hold, that transcendental subjectivity ("subjectivity" being a broader concept than "consciousness") has a layer of pre-reflective corporeality, and is also linguistic, besides being temporal and historical. All this raises difficult questions regarding its transparence. If it were not transparent, it would not serve as the foundation of all being and knowledge. And yet how could it have this stratum of corporeality without having some opacity within itself? How could it be linguistic, without being surpassed by the diachronicity of language? How could it be temporal, without having, with every living present, a memory of what is gone, and that too without traces of all its forgotten past?

Consciousness and the World

Realism posits the world as outside of consciousness, idealism locates the world within consciousness. Both are wrong inasmuch as consciousness has neither an out-side nor an inside. Consciousness is rather a correlation between the *noetic* acts and noematic meanings. The world is a structure and interconnectedness of such meanings, and is the correlate of consciousness. The two, consciousness and the world, together, in their correlation, constitute transcendental subjectivity.

Classical phenomenology has insisted on the thesis that consciousness *constitutes* the world. Naturalism has insisted on the thesis that the world *produces* consciousness. The latter is a one-sided thesis, and, in order to make sense, must be able to posit the world as prior to and independent of consciousness. But it is not in a position to do so. The opposite thesis of phenomenology is also one side of the truth. Being intentional, consciousness is of the world, so that without this world-*noema*, there is no consciousness. Hence the two complementary propositions:

Consciousness constitutes the world.
The world constitutes* the consciousness.

The asterisk is intended to make the reader think of the change of meaning of "constitution" that has taken place.

The true transcendental foundation is: consciousness-of-the-world. Realism deletes the hyphens and separates the different components of the total structure. But it cannot in fact do so. I want to keep them tied together. Realism describes the naivety of pre-reduction experience. I am describing what is discovered as a result of the *epoché*.

As one proceeds from one level of experience to another, both the nature of consciousness and the nature of world undergo transformations. We learn this from Hegel's *Phenomenology*.

Transparency, Reflexivity, and Foundationalism

Consciousness is not only intentional, but is also reflexive. It is directed toward itself in the very same act that is directed toward an object other than itself.

In Indian philosophy, this phenomenon is called *svaprakāśatva*, which is defined by one writer as "without being an object of knowledge, consciousness is appropriate for such usage as expresses immediate awareness" (*avedyatve sati aparokṣavyavahārayogyatva*). It is not as though this phenomenon is recognized by all philosophers, but I believe this reflexivity is a central feature of consciousness. However, I have also come to recognize that reflexivity is of various degrees. The so-called unconscious intentionalities are intentionalities with a very low degree of self-awareness, such that when such an intentionality is "discovered," the person (who has it) recognizes that she was all along aware of its presence. Discovery (possibly with the help of a psychoanalyst) of an unconscious desire deep within one's psyche is not like discovering a fossil in one's backyard. One lends one's consent to and acknowledges the presence all the while of that desire. Part of the claim of consciousness to be "foundational" on the part of transcendental philosophers is justified with reference to this self-reflexivity. All objects are "manifested," "presented," "given," "thought of" through consciousness, while consciousness also manifests itself.

An extreme formulation of this thesis was given by Sartre. The French philosophers—Merleau-Ponty, first of all—have challenged this Sartrean thesis of the transparency of pre-reflective consciousness. I think this challenge is based upon certain apparent phenomena that are taken to be located within the heart of consciousness. These are, in brief: body, language, time, and history, and I should add (following upon suggestions of some more recent phenomenologists) birth and death. I have argued elsewhere that the three, namely, body, language, and time, may be regarded either as objects of consciousness and so as falling outside of it, or as themselves characterizing subjectivity itself. It is only in the latter case that they could go against the alleged transparency of consciousness. However, I am skeptical about the latter argument. Bodily subjectivity is subjectivity insofar as it is intentional and reflexive, it knows itself for what it is. If I do not find the neural and chemical processes transparent, because they do not belong to the lived body *qua* lived. The lived body or the bodily subjectivity is reflexively aware of its own opacity, its own massiveness, its resistance to thought—which is to say it is self-transparent. I would say the same of language. Language in the sense of Sassure's *la langue* falls outside of consciousness, but as *la parle* is subjective. The speaker is aware of her intention and what she is saying. She may not be a grammarian, a syntactician, or a historian of her language, but they all fall outside of subjectivity, and not knowing them does not go against the alleged transparency of subjectivity. The same holds true of time: the transparency of consciousness is questioned on the ground of the very nature of internal time-consciousness, the phenomenon of the perishing now being replaced by retention of the just-no-more, a retention of that retention, and so on. But how does the phenomenologist discover the alleged temporal structure of consciousness? Precisely, basing on the way this temporality is experienced within. Retention is given both as retention of what is just gone, and also as a now that is just vanishing. If all consciousness is not given as present, that is exactly what it should not be given as. The retention-now-protention structure is reiterated, and this iteration is presented by consciousness as being true of itself. The above arguments, together with the thesis of degrees of reflexivity, preserve the transparence thesis in the form in which it is needed as the ground of the thesis advanced by the opponents of that thesis.

Consciousness has also a history. There is also a consciousness of history. History of consciousness is that process through which consciousness expands, enlarges, and transforms itself while its object, the world, also gets transformed. It is a process of self-interpretation and, correlatively, also interpretation of its world. I have in mind the sort of process that is portrayed by Hegel in his *Phenomenology.* The entire account presupposes two things: consciousness is hermeneutical, that is, interpretive (of itself and its world); it is also characterized by what came to be called, in the phenomenological tradition, historicity. I accept these two theses. But consciousness could be hermeneutical and marked by historicity, yet it would not be able to write, present, and reenact its history if it were not also capable of recollecting and describing the process it has gone through. Some form of transparency thesis is called for. The history is not simply constructed, it is described. Consciousness is a witness to its own becoming.

Philosophy, Science, and *Sinn*

There is a widely shared belief among philosophers in America, to the effect that philosophy is continuous with science. I have never been able to agree with this view, partly because I have never been able to precisely understand the position. If philosophy were continuous with science in the sense in which one would ordinarily understand the idea of continuity, doing philosophy would be a kind of doing science, and if this were true most scientists would recognize that what philosophers do is like what they do. And yet the thesis that philosophy is continuous with science is a position with which most scientists do not agree. What possibly may be meant by the statement is that good philosophy—that is, philosophy that the proponents of that position regard as good philosophy—ought to be so continuous even if most philosophy is not. But even if we consider the philosophies as done by those who hold this view, the philosophies, for example, of such people as Quine, Carnap, Fodor, Dummet, and Dretske, even if these thinkers may think that what they do is continuous with science, no scientists—physicists, neurobiologists, or computer scientists—would agree with their views and regard their philosophies to be scientifically vindicated or would agree that what they are doing is an extension of science.

Philosophy, on my view, is discontinuous with science, just as science is discontinuous with everyday life.

Writers such as Richard Rorty have told us that the age in which philosophy claimed to provide a foundation for the sciences is over. The sciences do not need any foundation, on their view, and certainly not from philosophy. Philosophers in the past attempted to construct three kinds of foundational systems. They either sought after an epistemological theory (rationalism, empiricism, or a Kantian mix), or they were looking for a good theory of scientific method (the demarcation problem, or a Millean sort of inductive logic, or a formalized theory of the syntax and semantics of scientific language), or they set the goal of constructing a metaphysical system integrating the results of the various sciences and developing a satisfactory doctrine of categories (of which Whitehead seems to me to be the best available example). The first two have proved themselves out-of-date. Most importantly, the search for a scientific method has been a search for a chimera, there is no such method. Metaphysical systems would always remain a possibility, but they need to go beyond the natural sciences and to integrate their provisional results with the deliverances of other modes of experience, moral, religious, and aesthetic. The question of their commensurability would still remain open.

Many contemporary philosophers are scientific realists, and many more have wrongly taken scientific realism to entail a sort of physicalism. There are three remarks I would like to make in this connection. First, there is a weaker version of internal realism that follows from the internal deliverance of scientific consciousness. But every mode of consciousness gives a similar realistic account of its objects. Religious belief, by itself, has a realistic story of the objectivity of its object. The scientist, by necessity, is a realist with regard to the domain of its research. But this does not entail an external realism. Second, the naive (and so external) scientific realist has in mind the perfected science and has no place in his conception of science for the historicity of science. Third, even taking science, especially physics, as it is now, its picture of the world is not physicalistic. Our pre-scientific conception of material body—of "hunks" of matter—has no place in the physicist's world of elementary particles. To these three remarks, I may add a fourth. There are two kinds of arguments for scientific realism which are widely regarded as decisive. One, which to my mind is the better of the two, argues from the practical consequences of the results of the sciences, results that are embodied in technological advances and this fact is taken to entail scientific realism. I am not convinced that it does entail realism. It only shows that scientific research is inseparable from practice, and that the web of practice hangs together, carrying no firm implications for ontology. The other argument, impressive by its logical power, is nevertheless weaker in its onto-logical strength: it argues from the semantic theory of the way rigid designators acquire their power to designate the things they do designate to a realistic theory of the essence of the designated entities. I have found the transition from the semantic theory to the theory of essence unconvincing.

For me, scientific theories are complex *noematic* structures which are correlates of scientific consciousness. Their constitution presupposes the consti-tution of highly idealized geometries, theories of time, theories of measurement, and mathematical techniques. In conclusion, they are high-level idealizations of the perceptual world, achievements of historically developing thought, agreed upon by the community of investigators and confirmed by successful—for all practical purpose, accurate—prediction. The picture of "correspondence" to reality does not fit.

If perception undetermines science, the sciences underdetermine philos-ophy.

Underlying the above account of constitution of scientific theories is the concept of *Sinn* which I have found useful in Frege and Husserl. From the semantic point of view this entire account is threatened by a theory of direct reference, such as Russell's or Kripke's, which dispenses with the *Sinn*. For me, the viability of the concept of *Sinn* guarantees the difference of philosophy from the sciences of fact. At the same time, the sciences themselves are *Sinn*—structures, as any science has to be. We humans are condemned to *Sinne*.

My earlier questioning, if there is a concept of *Sinn* in Indian philosophy, was not a simply idle curiosity. It was the result of having been raised in a certain conception of philosophy and the consequent attempt to understand why the Indian thinkers did not quite distinguish between philosophy and the sciences. Now I think that as the philosophers (no matter of which school amongst the Indians) reflected upon their vocation, they came to demarcate a domain of abstract entities they were, by implication, referring to when they were talking about whatever they regarded as real, and thereby positing a domain of what I have elsewhere called quasi-*Sinne*, without hypostatizing them to be entities in the full-blooded Fregean sense.

Advaita Vedānta

How or or where do I stand in relation to Advaita Vedānta? For an Indian philosopher of my generation, it is difficult, if not impossible, to be indifferent to Advaita Vedānta. This applies to me even after three decades of living in the West. A large part of my early education in philosophy was in Advaita Vedānta. My first philosophy teacher in Calcutta was Nalini Kanta Brahma who was an excellent Advaitin, and saw to it that I did not have any doubts about the truth of Advaita. (He once told me if I still had any doubts, after having studied with him, the fault must lie in him as a teacher.) But during the years I was studying with him, I was under the spell of Sri Aurobindo, and shared his critique of Śaṃkara's *Māyāvāda*. I was never convinced—nor am I now—that the world and finite individuals are false appearances. I am still not satisfied that the Advaitin has shown that the world is false. He has a better case if by "false" he meant, as he often means, "to be indescribable either as real or as unreal." I am impressed by the logical structure of the Advaita system, especially by his theory of ignorance as a positive entity whose object (*viṣaya*) and locus (*āśraya*) are the same, that is, pure consciousness; his theory of witness consciousness (*sākṣin*), which directly manifests this positive ignorance; and the different cognitive states (*vṛttijñāna*) and their thesis (as formulated by *Pancapādikāvivaraṇa*) that everything is an object of witness-consciousness either as known or as unknown.

The Advaitins have used their philosophy to support unity of all religions and a spirit of toleration for all points of view. But they surreptitiously want to place Advaita at the pinnacle of all religions, and the spirit of toleration is made to rest on this status of Advaita. It should be obvious that such a move is self-defeating. If any of the Indian *darśanas* has such a spirit of toleration, that should be Jainism. Unity and toleration of all points of view can rest only upon respect for differences and a refusal to accord any one philosophical position the highest status among all.

Identity and Difference

Knowing the other like oneself, finding oneself in others and others in oneself constitute the moral ideal which Vedānta has placed before the Indian mind. But this ideal, despite its nobility, has a fundamental lack. True knowledge of the other, and true respect for the other, is knowledge of, and respect for, the other in the other's uniqueness, that is, *qua* other. Knowing the other like myself, or finding myself in the other *may*—I must emphasise *may*—involve loosing sight of the other's uniqueness, leading to "domination" over the other. I am aware that this likely consequence is contrary to the intentions of the Vedānta, but the Vedāntin should be willing to so expand his concept of identity that the thesis of identity would not end up wiping out differences. Differences, down to the uniqueness of each individual's *svadharma*, need to be respected. The consequences of the post-modern insight for political philosophy are well known. As Gandhi, of all persons, saw most clearly—and so did also Tagore—the idea of "state" should yield priority to "community," to the small community, it needs to be added (contrary to Hegel's glorification of state). Party-oriented democracy is to yield place to the village-centered (in the Western language, community-centered) democracy in which no majority can justifiably oppress a small minority. The Utilitarian "greatest happiness of the greatest number" would have to be replaced by the Kantian respect for each person, freed from the Kantian homogenous notion of rationality. This rehabilitation of Gandhian thinking in the light of the most recent philosophy—confirmed by the decentralized economy of the personal computer and its possibilities for advancing a clean, user-friendly environment, has rekindled my Gandhian enthusiasms of the youth, which provides a satisfying end to the first section of this narrative. That the report consists of a series of theses that are not here argued for could not be avoided, given the nature and limits of this occasion.

Back to the Questions Raised

It is now time that I look back at the points raised by the authors of the essays in this volume. Many of the critics have focused on my essentialism as defended in my 1997 book and on my understanding of transcendental consciousness and its relation to the empirical. In light of the statements made earlier on these topics, let me turn to examine some of these critical questions.

The Empirical and the Transcendental Revisited

When we reduce the question about the relation of the empirical and the transcendental consciousness to the relation between the *jīva* and the *brahman* (in Vedānta), we certainly miss something important and some of the complexities in the former problematic. When one says that the empirical and the transcendental are really identical, one may be meaning that there is an entity that in one context is called the empirical, while in another, transcendental, just as one and the same person is the victor at Jena and also the vanquished at Waterloo. When one says that the two are really different, one may be meaning that there are two entities, different from each other, designated by these expressions. Both ways of articulating their relation are indeed misleading. In order to make a better, less misleading, characterization, let me make a new attempt.

The ambiguities in the use of "empirical" have been hinted at earlier in this essay. In the tradition of Western philosophy, what contrasts with the empirical is not the transcendental but the *a priori*. Botany is an empirical science, pure mathematics is an *a priori* science. Neither is transcendental. The Kantian transcendentals—namely, the categories and the Ideas of Reason, the acts of synthesis and the act of schematism—are conditions of the possibility both of the empirical and of the *a priori* cognitions. But they too are *a priori* and are the subject matter of an *a priori*, but also transcendental knowledge. Empirical and *a priori* first-level cognitions on the one hand, and transcendental (philosophical) cognitions on the other are indeed different cognitions. Having botanical and mathematical cognitions is not *eo ipso* to have transcendental-philosophical cognition. Nor does the Kantian philosopher need to have all the empirical and *a priori* first-level cognitions. Do the two cognitive abilities issue from two different cognitive powers? The idea of "cognitive power" or faculty is too vague to allow any clear decision on this matter. The old and outdated psychology, in terms of which Kant thought, allowed him to speak of different faculties of the mind. By rejecting such language, Hegel spoke only of "thinking" as a developing process. If we can agree that transcendental-philosophical cognition (of the way mind or thought operates making possible natural sciences as well as mathematics) is different from the first-level object-cognition, and that the former exhibits the operations making the latter possible but not thematized in the latter, then we have all the distinction we need without assigning them to separate cognitive powers. So much for the Kantian transcendentality.

Let me now turn to phenomenology. Consider the levels of empirical cognition: seeing a patch of red, perceiving a physical object, listening to a musical performance, and the science of physics. As an *a priori* cognition, consider our old friend, pure mathematics, or perhaps its familiar part, that is, arithmetic. Let us indicate the path that one needs to follow in order to able to unravel the transcendental cognitions which underlie and render these first-level cognitions possible.

Let us hold fast to the seeing the red precisely as it is being seen, but shut out the consideration, the belief, or the theory we may be entertaining as regards what precisely is out there, and how precisely that which is out there is affecting my visual sense-organ and causing me to see what I see. The seeing itself, as it is being experienced, has an internal structure, "seeing-seen," which stands out as invariant. We have, in other words, effected a phenomenological reduction or bracketing of all transcendent beliefs. Also bracketed are all beliefs about what the "I" designates in "I see that patch of red." But even after I do all this— beliefs about me as a biological organism, as a *homo sapiens,* as a social construct, as a philosopher of Indian origin named J.N.M., etc., etc.—it still remains that I am seeing what I am seeing, that the seeing belongs to my continuing process of experiencing, "my" not as though they are my posses- sions, but in the sense that I am what I am by virtue of all these experiences. The unity of (my) mental life, as also of (my) psycho-physical life, is being constituted by all those experiences as so "reduced." At this point, I begin to realize that there are two time-series that underlie "I am seeing that patch of red," and that are being unified, synthesized into various unities that figure in that piece of "reduced" cognition. These three unities are: "that patch of red," "the seeing," and the "I." Transcendental phenomenology has to describe the temporal processes and their syntheses that constitute these unities.

"Perceiving that tree over there": reduction and *epoché* allow one to hold fast to the experience of perceiving and its object, that tree, precisely as it is being perceived. As in the case of seeing the red, here too, there are three unities that get constituted in the inner time experience—the unity of the ego of the perceiver, the immanent unity of the *noetic* act of perceiving, and the tran- scendent unity of the *noema* "that tree over there." The immanent flow of experiences constitutes the ego; the act of perceiving, founded upon the sensing that underlies it, is constituted by having profiles presented from different per- spectives and the passive synthesis of these profiles, fulfillment of the antici- pated continuation of the process of such presentations, and yet never coming to a final closure of these possibilities; likewise in the case with "that tree over there." An accurate description of how these unities and their interrelationships get constituted while the process of constitution recedes to anonymity behind the constituted, is the theme of transcendental phenomenology.

One could exhibit similar processes lying hidden behind the other two empirical cognitions. In each case, one dives deep into the depths of inner time consciousness, and retrieves the step-by-step constitutive accomplishments.

Now we have a rough knowledge of what transcendental phenomenology could bring to light. To return to the question, posed by Margolis, does tran- scendental cognition differ from empirical cognition, and in what sense is the transcendental identical with or different from the empirical ?

Let me suggest an analogy. Water is H_2O. The knowledge of H_2O, as chemistry discovered and handed over to us, is certainly a new knowledge, other than the empirical judgment "This is water." Particle physics and quantum chemistry have further refined our knowledge of the structure of the liquid—

new knowledge, no doubt, and yet the structure is still the structure of water. An analogous relation that holds good between the different layers of cognition is as follows:

1. I perceive that tree over there

2. "I perceive that tree over there"(the quotation marks designate that 1 has been subjected to the *epoché*)

3. The temporal syntheses that constitute the unities "I," "perceiving," and the *noema* "that tree over there"

4. The flux of internal time consciousness in which 3 takes place

Numbers 1 and 2 are clearly the same, excepting that 2 is a "purified" form of 1. Number 3 generates or constitutes 2, the processes described in 3 are still the same as 2 (and 1), in a sense analogous to the sense in which the quantum-chemical unity is H_2O and also is water. Number 4 is the larger process within which a limited phenomenon is described in 3. All three—2, 3 and 4—are "transcendental."

The empirical-transcendental distinction then is not merely logical or conceptual, but is a distinction between different dimensions (and depths)—not horizontal extension of scope, but rather vertical—of cognition. In an extended sense, the transcendental is also experienced; it is not merely a posit, but has to be brought to clarity of givenness, and in that sense, and only in that sense, the transcendental is also experiential cognition.

One still wonders, how can change of my attitude—from naturalistic to the *epoché*—change the subject matter of my thought? True, the tree over there would not undergo a transformation with the *epoché*. But consciousness (of the tree) is transformed with the changed attitude, and only consciousness is transformed therewith. The transcendental constitution is not of my brain states, nor of the tree over there, but of my "perception of the tree" and so of "I" and "the tree over there"—that is of the ego and of the content of that consciousness.

It would be clear from the above that I agree fully with David Carr's critique of Heidegger's criticism of the Husserlian transcendental phenomenology.

Essentialism (Rockmore, Makkreel, and Giorgi)

The essences I admit into my ontology, the invariants which, in my view, pervade and permeate experience and stand out for any scientific thematization of experience, are not *eo ipso* transcendental. They are appropriately to be called "empirical" (note that the three, "*a priori*," "essential," and "transcendental," are not equivalents, even extensionally). Their apprehension and determination presupposes experience. In brief, in order to ward off the suspicion of the Platonist *ante res* thesis, I should say that they are *in res*, à la Aristotle. They too are to be subjected to the *epoché*, they too are in need of a constitution analysis. The phenomenologist needs to be able to show how in the flux of inner time consciousness, essences as invariants come to be given, first as empirical types, then as idealities constituted by acts of idealization exercised upon empirical types. We are first presented with empirical types which, in all their vagueness of boundaries, still "anticipate" the possibility of idealization into strict essences. This is inverting the relation between Kantian concepts and their schemata. Instead of saying that the latter are temporalizations of the former, I would say that in order of constitution the former are idealizations of the latter. We are not concerned with the metaphysical question, which one of the two is ontologically prior. We are concerned with the question of genesis and constitution. The latter question leads us to the dimension of transcendentality.

Concepts and meanings surely are more tractable than essences. They both belong to a different universe of discourse—the epistemological and the semantic. (What I have in mind is the Kantian, not the Hegelian *Begriff*.) This level of discourse cannot be ontologically self-subsistent—it mediates between mind and the world. Leaving these out, the rest cannot simply be flux. Essences find their home in the constituted world.

In a different world, logically possible, essences could very well be different, which shows that the necessity of essential truths is not logical necessity, but rather contingent necessity grounded in the way things are. Oscar Becker had recognized this in Husserl's modal theory a long time ago. However, "formal essences"—the fundamental categories of the empty region of "objects in general"—characterize any possible world. If essences are ontological, not unlike anything else in the world, an essence may be referred to in many different ways, that is, through different *noemata*. Number "2," which is an essence, can be referred to *via* the description "the successor of 1 in the natural number series" or *via* the description "the only even prime number." Meanings are our gateway to essences.

Not all essences are precise, definable essences. Some essences may indeed be vague. Some essences are closer to perception, others to thought. There are feeling-essences such as "anger," which may be presented through different meanings.

Phenomenology and Ontology (David Smith)

The relation between phenomenology and ontology had been adversarial at the beginning. Heidegger posed the question for phenomenology in just such an adversarial manner: "What is the mode of being of intentionality?" suggesting that intentionality is grounded in *Dasein's* being-in-the-world. Husserlians replied that "existence" and "being" are not real predicates of things, but rather thetic predicates of *noemata* and so derive from intentionality, of which, then, "being" cannot be predicated. If a phenomenological ontology is to be possible, then that must be done in some other way, not adversarial but cooperative. Many thinkers have shown the way. But one of the ontologies that lies close to

Husserl's and makes use of Husserl's texts is David Smith's. The phenomeno-logical ontology I was taught in Göttingen (by Hermann Wein) is that of Nicolai Hartmann. In this ontology, there are two spheres of being, the real and the ideal; two moments of being, that (existence) and what (content); the modalities of being (possibility, actuality, and necessity) each of which differs from one sphere to another; and two secondary spheres of being, logic and knowledge. The sphere of real being is stratified into the basic material stratum, the stratum of living beings, the human mind and spirit or *Geist* as exemplified in cultures and societies. The idealities divide into the logical and the mathematical on the one hand, and the (material) essences on the other, the latter again into the theoretical and axiological idealities or values. There are then elaborate doctrines of categories for each sphere, and for inter-sphere relations. David Smith's ontology remains closer to Husserl than Hartmannian ontology. It derives its basic strategies from the ontological concepts Husserl introduces in the first chapter of the *Ideas I*. Smith ascribes to Husserl a sort of neutral monism: the same concrete particular, an experience, or an Ego, falls both under the region of "consciousness" and under the region of "nature," and so exemplifies two essences. This double-aspect ontology is developed in the essay in the present volume into a *three-phase* ontology in which every thing has three phases: a form, an appearance, and a substrate. The last phase belongs to natural science, the first to theory of intentionality, and the second to the cultural sciences. Thus, the resulting ontology synthesizes transcendental phenomenology as theory of intentionality with the natural and the cultural sciences. Many details still need to be worked out. For example, where does the distinction between fact and essence fit in? Where do "meanings" or *noemata* belong? or, values? Neverthe-less, Smith, to my knowledge, formulates the best available phenomenological ontology, and generates one of the best prospects of reconciling natural science with transcendental phenomenology.

Lived Body, Birth, and Death (Schües, Kopf, and Welton)

Schües draws attention to the question of whether the phenomenon of birth (as also of death) can be thematized within transcendental phenomenology. I will focus on this question for a while. There are the following possibilities:

1. That the transcendental ego has no birth and no death, only the empirical ego has
2. That the transcendental ego has both birth and death, and yet it does not and cannot constitute them, they are not for it phenomena
3. That birth and death are constituted phenomena, constituted by and in the life of transcendental subjectivity.

1. This is the way philosophy has classically understood the transcendental

ego. But the transcendental ego of phenomenology is not the classical concept. So let us get rid of the metaphysical idea of soul or *ātman*. Phenomenologically, the transcendental ego may be said to be without birth and death inasmuch as "birth" and "death" cannot be meaningfully predicated of the "I," since "my birth" and "my death" could not have been constituted within my "reduced" phenomenological consciousness. Memory cannot reach back to the past when my life (and my consciousness) began, this beginning as absolute beginning cannot be an event in my consciousness. For if this event was a *now*, it must have had a retentional horizon of "no more," and if my death could be an event in my consciousness, it must have a protentional horizon of "not yet." The flux of consciousness must be represented as both beginningless and endless. But then "my" transcendental ego exceeds, in its extension, "my" empirical ego, and to this excess my experience provides no access, even after the *epoché*. If the transcendental ego is beginningless and endless, and if birth and death are not constituted, not even auto-constituted, phenomena for the transcendental ego, then they are either empirical concepts or metaphysical concepts, but not phenomenologically legitimizable ascriptions to oneself. We understand them emptily, but this understanding will never rise to the level of intuitive clarity.

2. The antithesis of 1, which is the thesis 2, is necessitated by the failure of 1 to make sense. Even when it meets its limits, phenomenology must recognize them as limiting concepts, and must be able to constitute them as what resist constitution. The transcendental ego emptily takes over the empirical ego's concepts of birth and death as constituted in the other's case as *noematic* predicates, and emptily ascribes them to oneself—thereby obliterating the purity of the distinction between the empirical and the transcendental.

3. How can "birth" and "death" be constituted within the transcendentally purified life of an ego? The other's birth and death will be presented as objective phenomena, but what is "my birth" and what is "my death"? According to 1 they will ever remain empty. According to 2 they involve a crossing of the boundary between the empirical and the transcendental, present as limiting concepts for the transcendental ego, and yet they owe their origin to the empirical experience of the other. According to 3, the transcendental ego, in its phenomenological self-experience of its own inner temporality, can follow the "traces" of the just gone phase, and the traces of what was just gone before that phase, and thus may constitute an absolutely new beginning that never had a retentional horizon; likewise with the not-yet, which never will have a protentional horizon.

There are perhaps other possibilities. Grant that the transcendental ego is gendered, that the corporeality, the lived body, which is a transcendental ego's, is marked by gender differences, and then hold that it is only "feminine" transcendental ego who "gives birth," and so constitutes the intuitively filled—and so not empty—sense of an absolutely new beginning, and analogically extend it to her own case. But "death" permits no such constitution. One may simply, in a gender-neutral context, perceive the other as dying, and analogically extend the so constituted concept to one's own case. What then is obvious is that these two concepts cannot be constituted by a solipsistic ego. They are inter-subjectively constituted.

The importance of Schües's problematic is that it is not exhausted by the theme of bodily subjectivity, of the lived and felt body. Birth and death are on the borderline between objective body and the felt-lived body, but in a way that is very different from the way the other ego's body is perceived as what is felt and lived by the other. The corpse is experienced with the sense "what is now only observed, but not felt-lived by any one"; the just born is perceived as one who only lives her body but does not yet perceive it as a Körper.

It is only the Buddhist, of all philosophers known to me, who thematizes "embryonic consciousness" in the link that connects the past life and the present life, and by fusing the natural and the spiritual thought of a phenomenological transition from phase to phase that we do not ordinarily experience, but could possibly experience in a state of yogic deepening and clarity of consciousness.

Both Kopf and Welton make use of the idea of bodily subjectivity. For Kopf, the transcendental ego is nothing other than the lived body, which contrasts with the Cartesian *cogito* which he takes to be the empirical ego. Both are grounded, for him, in the transcendental non-ego, the Buddhist *anātman*. I have some sympathy with this position, inasmuch as the I, the ego—even the transcendentally purified ego—has a constitution, it genetically emerges out of the internal time consciousness, only its genesis is auto-genesis, it constitutes itself, but does not have, unlike in the case of all objects, hetero-constitution. The Buddhist regards the "I" to be constituted out of the flowing *skandhas*. This latter flux is the non-ego, from within which the I arises. I have often spoken of the transcendental ego as arising out of the transcendental subjectivity. Thus, Kopf's idea that the transcendental non-ego is prior to the ego—both transcendental and empirical—in the order of constitution is closer to my thinking than it may appear at first. My concern at the moment is with *identifying* the transcendental ego with the lived body. As I see it, the lived body is an aspect of the transcendental ego. The latter also contains the "reduced" acts of higher order, such as acts of thinking, which cannot be reduced to the bodily intentionality. All the acts of the empirical ego will have their place in the life of the transcendental ego after the *epoché*. The lived body, or the pre-reflective bodily intentionalities will, no doubt, form the primary stratum within the transcendental ego, but the two cannot simply be identified.

Welton finds in the phenomenological concept of body a limit to all those methods and concepts around which Husserl's static phenomenology was structured. For Welton, Husserlian transcendental subjectivity, by its very conception, must be capable of adequate intuitive evidence. Since Husserl claimed that consciousness has an actually given structure, such structure must be available in strict evidence. And yet Welton finds that even on Husserl's own admission such strict evidence, even in the case of transcendental consciousness, is not possible. It is the temporality of consciousness that prevents a total grasp of consciousness. But is not this very temporality, as an essential structure, adequately given? True, not all my consciousness can be presented to me as a now. But why is it supposed that in order to be foundational, it must have to be? What is given, with strict apodicticity, is the structure: retention-now-protention, presentation-representation, the functioning of intentionality within such temporality, and the corporeality that characterizes transcendental subjectivity at its most basic stratum. With so much, and much more, that we can say about transcendental subjectivity, it can function as foundation in spite of the fact that its life is not being grasped in all its *factuality* in toto.

Understanding, Meaning, and Word as a Means of Knowing (Chakrabarti, Bilimoria, and Siderits)

As regards the papers on Indian philosophy, my earlier remarks in the first part of this essay must have made it clear what my responses to the contributions by Deutsch and Phillips are to be. I have to add here then some remarks on the papers by Chakrabarti, Bilimoria, and Siderits.

The core of Chakrabarti's paper is about the kind of knowledge that is yielded by the understanding of a false sentence, and so in fact by the understanding of any sentence, true or false. I argued that understanding the sentence S is P (where the sentence is false) cannot yield knowledge that S is P, for there is no fact that S is P. Chakrabarti wants to maintain that, even on the Nyāya-Russell theory that there is no such thought or meaning that could be grasped, no such proposition that S is P, one may be said to have a knowledge when one understands a false sentence, more particularly, when this understanding is "beliefless." Let us leave out of consideration the question of what belief adds to that understanding. Chakrabarti contends that even in beliefless understanding, and even when the sentence is false, there are some things one knows. These are what he calls "bits of the same reality, which would have been known in the right order, if we had been cognizing veridically." I find in this thesis as presented by Chakrabarti, if I understand it aright, several difficulties: first, to understand "Indira Gandhi was Mahatma Gandhi's niece" (which is a falsehood) presupposes knowing who Indira Gandhi was and who Mahatma Gandhi was and what "being niece" means. Knowing the meaning of a sentence *presupposes* knowing the meanings of the component words, but it is not identical to knowing those bits of entities. The Nyāya position on this matter may be something like this, but then this knowledge of the bits of meanings would be like a *samuhālambana* cognition or a sort of *nirvikalpaka* cognition, but that would be inconsistent with the cognition's having a linguistic expression. So the knowledge must be knowledge of those bits as related in the manner expressed. But that related cognition is, *ex hypothesi*, not true. What then is it about? We are back with the possibility that it is a proposition, a thought, which Nyāya does not countenance.

The "binary opposition" which, Bilimoria suggests, it is time to critique and overcome in the context of Indian philosophy, are sense and reference, facts and values. In the case of literal sentences, I have raised the question if Indian thought has a distinction between sense and reference. Save and except the Buddhist, who denies a referential theory of meaning and upholds an *apoha* theory, the Indian thinkers in general accepted a referential theory. In the case of *śabda pramāṇa*, I favoured the view that the scriptures impart knowledge of ethical truths about what one ought to do, and in that sense, of values, while of facts the scriptures, or *śabda*, are not an independent source of knowledge. But these very questionings presuppose the two binary oppositions to begin with.

Earlier in this essay, I have remarked on the reason why I raised the first question after all. It had to do with drawing a distinction between science and philosophy, a distinction that I accept and that the classical Indian thinkers did not accept. Reflection on their practice, however, led me to posit (or to ascribe to the Indian thinkers the positing of) a domain which I called "quasi-*Sinn*" that serves my purpose well without needing to be reified into the full-fledged Fregean *Sinne*. The alleged binary opposition may be overcome in either of four ways: accept only *Sinn*, deny reference; or accept only reference, deny *Sinn*; or accept an intermediate link in between the two; or accept a third term which synthesizes the two. The first is the Buddhist view, the second the Nyāya view, the third is the Navya-Nyāya position on this matter, which I prefer; the fourth would be a Hegelian sort of position for which I do not know of any parallel in Indian thought.

As regards the fact-value distinction (and the related distinctions between "is and ought" "theory and practice"), Indian thought exhibits the following range of positions. There are those who clearly distinguish between knowing what is the case and doing what is to be done. Śaṃkara famously draws this distinction in his commentary on *Brahmasūtra* 1.1.1. On the other hand, there are those such as the Prābhākaras who hold that a seeming statement of fact is really an invocation to act, or not to act in a certain way, either to achieve a goal or to avoid some undesirable consequence. Likewise, on a certain construal of the Vedānta, existence and bliss being identical, the fact-value distinction is, in the long run, abolished. The Buddhists, in their ontological theory of *dharmas* (or, elements of being), introduce distinctions between elements that are wholesome (*kuśala*) and those that are not (*a-kuśala*). Interpreting the tendency of Indian epistemologists to regard truth as what generates successful practice, Karl Potter suggests that for these thinkers the fact-value distinction does not hold good in the long run. There is also a tendency, less clearly discernible amongst the principal *darśanas*, but more visible in the epics and the *purāṇas*, to ground *dharma* in the nature of the universe. I will not, in this essay, take up a position with regard to these possibilities. What I need to emphasize is that it would be a mistake to correlate the distinction between śabda as a pramāṇa and the other pramāṇas with the distinction generally made between value and fact. The question was not whether śabda cannot generate knowledge of facts or not. The question was if the same facts about which śabda can yield knowledge are not capable of being known by the other means of knowledge. It is this question that led me to assign to śabda a unique domain of possible objects of knowledge, a domain about which the other means of knowledge cannot generate any knowledge. And this I suggested was dharma, which left it an open question whether dharma is not capable of being ontologically grounded, which means if values do not belong to reality or not, or if there are totally value-free facts or not.

Finally, I must acknowledge Siderits's penetrating questions about the way I have often characterized the realism-idealism debate in Indian thought. I have tied Nyāya realism to two premises: the alleged formlessness of cognitions, and the thesis that cognitions are not self-manifesting. From these two positions, I have argued, Nyāya realism logically follows. Yogācāra idealism, on the other hand, takes cognitions to be formed, that is, to have contents and also to be self-manifesting. From both these premises, I have argued, Yogācāra idealism follows.

Now, as against this way of formulating the realism-idealism debate, Siderits advances the possibility—as a matter of fact, the actuality—of a Yogācāra that regards cognitions to be formless (not unlike the Nyāya). Such a variety of Yogācāra may still maintain, within its idealistic framework, that cognitions are caused (that is, as having the fourfold causes or pratyayas, as is well known in the Yogācāra literature). What this supposedly shows is that the thesis of formlessness (nirākāratva) of cognitions, together with the causal genesis of cognitions, does not entail realism.

To this ingenuous objection, I will suggest the following responses to be taken into consideration.

First, it has always seemed to me that there is a theoretical problem in holding that determinate causal conditions produce a cognition that per se has no determinacy built into it. What has determinacy, on the theory suggested by Siderits, is "cognition of O" (where O is a determinate object, and C, the cognition). But since O, ex hypothesi, does not belong to C as its content (if C is formless, nirākāra), the cognition, apart from O, has no form. Such a formless entity could not be generated by determinate causes. This problem arises equally well for Nyāya, as for the version of Yogācāra Siderits refers to.

Second, if the version of Yogācāra that Siderits considers is still idealism, O must belong, in some appropriate sense of "belonging," to C. But it cannot belong to the cognition as its content, for the cognition is formless. How then is O, in what sense, a vijñapti? If the cognition is the entire structure (C-O), then the total entity is not formless. I would like to know what version of idealism we have here.

Third, and this part of my argument for realism is overlooked by Siderits, concerns the other Nyāya premise (which Yogācāra of any sort has to reject): namely, that cognitions are not self-manifesting. Let the cognition be C(O). Since C has no form, the content O must fall outside of C. Since C is not self-manifesting (on the Nyāya theory), the content that initially appears in C that is, O, could not belong to C, and so must be other than C. Yogācāra cannot hold all three: that the C is self-manifesting, that C is formless, and that O belongs to C. If C were self-manifesting, its formlessness would have been manifest and not that C has O as its content. The only way out of this impasse is to invoke the doctrine of *avidyā*, which would account for why C, formless in itself, would nevertheless appear to be having-a-form. But this leads to a different set of problems, some of which the editor, Bina Gupta, has drawn attention to in her introductory remarks.

Future of Indian Philosophy (Phillips)

Indian philosophy, with its stereotypical schools and doctrines fixed through centuries of intra-system and inter-systemic disputes, is not the whole story about this hoary tradition. Contrary to many traditional representations, careful reading of the texts brings to light many loose ends, many ideas nipped in the bud and marginalized by the more powerful forces, despite the tremendous creative energy that went into them. I have therefore tried to revive these lost threads, render alive ideas that were nearly buried, and thereby regenerate the lost creativity.

But what about my "dream" of a world philosophy? (Phillips) More accurately, of a world philosophical conversation? (Deutsch) Let us recall that there is no unimpeded conversation even between different wings of Western philosophy. That conversation has been distorted by the struggle for academic power. The Indian scholars, as a result of centuries of colonial subjugation, have come to look upon Western universities, Western education, and in our case, Western philosophy not as pathways to truth, but as the secure road to power. I have witnessed and taken part in only two instances of genuine conversation where the issue was never East or West, but ideas to be tested and evaluated no matter where they originated. One took place in the sixties around the great philosopher Kalidas Bhattacharyya, the other was initiated on his own—without any knowledge of Western philosophy, but searching for Western philosophical ideas on his own in order to respond to—by Pandit Ananta Kumar Tarkatirtha, also in Calcutta during the sixties. I participated in both conversations over a period of several years. How can I give up the "dream" in that case ?

With regard to Western philosophy, I have noticed a curious difference in this regard between the major camps that is worth mentioning. More analytic philosophers have enthusiastically received ideas from Indian philosophy than have continental philosophers. The analytical philosophers I have in mind are

Strawson, Dummett, and Quine to recall the more well known among them. They have been willing to converse with Indian texts on matters of interest. But continental philosophers, influenced by Husserl and Heidegger, have looked at Indian thought as being radically different from Western philosophy. Their historicistic thinking has led them to think that philosophy in the true sense was a Western project originating with the Greeks and having a history that rules out appropriating so-called Indian philosophy under the same genre. In this matter, my sympathies are with those analytic philosophers, although phenomenology has taught me, not historicism, but a greater sensitivity to phenomena and so a kind of doing philosophy that combines logical analysis with describing phenomena: the Indian philosophers excelled precisely in this combination.

Culture and Philosophy (Deutsch)

There are two conceptions of philosophy. According to one, philosophy is a cultural discipline like literature and painting, but has a truth-claim not unlike the sciences. According to the other, philosophy is a science, either continuous with the natural sciences, or a more rigorous science than the latter. That philosophy is a science had been the belief of philosophers in antiquity, and I must say of the Indian philosophers. In their self-understanding, the history of philosophy was not an essential component of philosophy. You go through history in order to overcome history. The conception of philosophy as a cultural discipline had generally led to an understanding of philosophy as being essentially historical and as reflecting the cultural position of the community at the time. Nineteenth-century Europe brought this conception to the forefront. I must, however, add a third possibility. If philosophy reflects the position of a culture, and if that culture's self-understanding does not include its own historicity, then that philosophy, despite its being intimately rooted in the culture, may never come to perceive itself as being essentially historical.

Philosophy cannot simply be a reflection of the culture in which it is born. It must involve a certain idealization of that culture, such that the philosopher can step back from his cultural milieu and ask critical questions about the basic beliefs and practices of that culture. In being able to do so, the philosopher not only steps back from his own milieu, but establishes the possibility of inter-cultural dialogue. Otherwise, cultural relativism would be the last truth of philosophy.

I have tried to overcome cultural relativism in two ways. In the late seventies and the eighties, I worked with the idea of "overlapping *noemata*" (Husserl) and used the resulting conception of a common core belonging to intersecting spheres of cultures. According to this scheme, even the most radically different worlds may be represented as intersecting spheres, such that any two consecutive circles would have a common area through which communication would be in principle possible. In the nineties, I began to question the representation of a culture as a sphere. It seemed to me impossible to demarcate what is a culture. What we regard as a culture may indeed be a construct out of innumerable different cultures and these last, again, out of still finer differences. Once the putative identity of a culture is dissolved into "systems of differences," "cultural relativism" loses its base, for the relativist cannot tell us what it is to which truth and values are to be relative. The inter-cultural discourse and the universality of philosophy that we seem to have lost, owing to the specter of relativism, is then restored.

About the Contributors

Purushottama Bilimoria is associate professor of philosophy at Deakin University and research fellow in the Department of philosophy at the University of Melbourne in Australia. His major books and writings span theories of testimony and scriptural hermeneutics of South Asia, Hindu classicism, Gandhiana, postcolonial reason and nationalism, emotions East and West, and the Jain art of dying. He is the editor of *Sophia* and serves on the editorial board of a number of academic journals.

David Carr received his Ph.D. from Yale University in 1966 and is Charles Howard Candler professor of philosophy at Emory University. He has published articles on Husserl, phenomenology, and the philosophy of history, and has translated Husserl's *The Crisis of European Sciences.* He is the author of *Phenomenology and the Problem of History* (1974), *Time, Narrative and History* (1986), *Interpreting Husserl* (1987), and *The Paradox of Subjectivity* (1999).

Arindam Chakrabarti is professor of philosophy at the University of Hawaii at Manoa. He is the author of *Denying Existence* and the co-editor of *Knowing from Words.* He has also authored papers on Frege, Kant, Śaṃkara, Udayana and Nyāya-type Realism. He is currently the associate editor of *Philosophy East and West* and is working on a book on moral psychology of the emotions. He is the recipient of a grant from the Infinity Foundation, Princeton, to conduct research on the non-dualistic philosophies of Yogavāśiṣṭha, Bhartṛhari, and Kāshmir Śaivism.

Eliot Deutsch is professor of philosophy and department chair at the University of Hawaii, Honolulu. He is past editor (1967-1987) of the international journal *Philosophy East and West* and a past president of the Society for Asian and Comparative Philosophy. Deutsch received his Ph.D. from Columbia University and has been a visiting professor at the University of Chicago and Harvard and a Visiting Fellow and Life Member at Clare Hall, Cambridge

University. He is the author of fourteen books and over one hundred articles and reviews in professional journals.

Lester Embree (Ph.D., New School for Social Research, 1972) is William F. Dietrich Eminent Scholar in Philosophy at Florida Atlantic University and president of the Center for Advanced Research in Phenomenology, Inc. He has authored, translated, and edited a number of books and articles, chiefly in constitutive phenomenology. His current interests are in the history and philosophy of science (cultural sciences specifically, archaeology in particular), technology, and environmentalism.

Amedeo Giorgi received his Ph.D. in experimental psychology from Fordham University. Not being satisfied with the empirical paradigm in psychology, he searched for another frame of reference for psychology, and found it in Husserlian phenomenology, which he uses for founding psychology as a science. He is the founder of the *Journal of Phenomenological Psychology* and the author of over one hundred articles dealing with phenomenological psychology. He is currently affiliated with Saybrook Graduate School in San Francisco.

Bina Gupta is professor of philosophy and director of the South Asia Language and Area center at the University of Missouri at Columbia. She is the author of *Perceiving in Advaita Vedānta: An Epistemological Analysis* (Bucknell University Press, 1991) and *The Disinterested Witness: A Fragment of Advaita Vedānta Phenomenology* (Northwestern University Press, 1998), and over sixty articles. She is president of the Society for Asian and Comparative Philosophy and a Trustee of the American Institute of Indian Studies. Currently, she is working on a book on consciousness.

Gereon Kopf is assistant professor of history of religion at Luther College. His research explores the non-dual paradigm as formulated in the Buddhist tradition and its philosophical implications in the context of comparative philosophy. He is the author of essays on Dōgen and Nishida and the forthcoming book *Beyond Personal Identity: Dōgen, Nishida, and a Phenomenology of No-Self.*

Rudy Makkreel is the Charles Howard Candler professor of philosophy and department chair at Emory. He is the author of *Dilthey: Philosophy of the Human Studies* (Princeton University Press, 1975, 1992), *Imagination and Interpretation in Kant: The Hermeneutical Import of the Critique of Judgment* (University of Chicago Press, 1990), and co-editor of *Dilthey's Selected Works* (vols. 1, 4, and 5). He is the recipient of grants from the NEH, DAAD, the Alexander von Humboldt Foundation, the Thyssen Stiftung, and the Volkswagen Stiftung.

Joseph Margolis is currently Laura H. Carnell professor of philosophy at Temple University. His most recent book is *What, After All, Is a Work of Art?* (1999).

J. N. Mohanty is professor of philosophy at Temple University and Woodruff professor of philosophy and Asian Studies at Emory University. He is a member of the *Institut International de Philosophie*, Paris and a past president of the Society for Asian and Comparative Philosophy and the Indian Philosophical Congress. He was the recipient of the Humboldt Prize in Philosophy from the German Government in 1993. He is the author or editor of over fifteen books and over two hundred articles and reviews in professional journals.

Günther Patzig is professor emeritus at the University of Göttingen since 1971; he was a professor of philosophy at this institution from 1963-91, He is a member of the Göttingen Academy of Sciences since 1971. He was the recipient of the Niedersachsen Prize for Sciences in 1983. Some of his important works are *Die Aristotelische Syllogistik* (1959), *Sprache Und Logik* (1970), and *Ethik ohne Metaphysik* (1971).

Stephen H. Phillips (Ph.D. 1982, Harvard) is professor of philosophy and Asian Studies at the University of Texas at Austin. He is author of *Aurobindo's Philosophy of Brahman* (1986) and *Classical Indian Metaphysics: Refutations of Realism and the Emergence of "New Logic"* (1995). He is currently working on a four-volume translation of and commentary on Gaṅgeśa's *Tattvacintāmaṇi* (The Jewel of Thought About Epistemology). The first volume, *Epistemology of Perception,* is forthcoming from Oxford.

Tom Rockmore is professor of philosophy at Duquesne University. He has written widely (more than twenty-five books) on many historical and systematic topics, often concerning European philosophy.

Christina Schües holds a Ph.D. in philosophy from the Temple University of Philadelphia. Her dissertation was on the problem of perceptual changes. She has been a student in philosophy, politics, and literature at the University of Hamburg. Currently she is teaching at the University of Hamburg and the University of Lüneburg. Her publications are mostly in the field of phenomenology and political philosophy, and she is now working on a book about the topic of natality and generativity.

Mark Siderits is professor of philosophy at Illinois State University. He works primarily in Indian and Buddhist philosophy, with a special interest in using resources from those traditions to solve problems in analytic metaphysics and philosophy of language. He is currently writing a book on reductionist and anti-realist approaches to the problem of personal identity.

David Smith is professor of philosophy at the University of California at Irvine. He is the author of *The Circle of Acquaintance: Perception, Consciousness and Empathy* (1989) and, with Ronald McIntyre, *Husserl and Intentionality* (1982). He is currently working on a phenomenological ontology with a software research and development company.

Donn Welton, professor of philosophy at the University of New York at Stony Brook, has published two books on Husserl: *The Orgins of Meaning: A Critical Study of the Thresholds of Husserlian Phenomenology* (Nijhoff, 1982), and *The Other Husserl: The Horizons of Trasncendental Phenomenology* (Indiana, 2000). He is currently working on a book on the nature of embodiment entitled *Bodies of Flesh.*